SHELLEY: THE CRITICAL HERITAGE

THE CRITICAL HERITAGE SERIES

GENERAL EDITOR: B. C. SOUTHAM, M.A., B. LITT. (OXON.)
Formerly Department of English, Westfield College, University of London

For a list of books in the series see the back end paper

SHELLEY

THE CRITICAL HERITAGE

Edited by
JAMES E. BARCUS
Professor of English
Houghton College, New York

ROUTLEDGE & KEGAN PAUL: LONDON AND BOSTON

First published in 1975
by Routledge & Kegan Paul Ltd
Broadway House, 68–74 Carter Lane,
London EC4V 5EL and
9 Park Street,
Boston, Mass. 02108, USA
Set in Monotype Bembo
and printed in Great Britain by
Butler & Tanner Ltd, Frome and London

ISBN 0 7100 8148 0

for

WILLIAM S. WARD

who introduced me to
the labors and rewards of
scholarship

General Editor's Preface

The reception given to a writer by his contemporaries and near-contemporaries is evidence of considerable value to the student of literature. On one side we learn a great deal about the state of criticism at large and in particular about the development of critical attitudes towards a single writer; at the same time, through private comments in letters, journals or marginalia, we gain an insight upon the tastes and literary thought of individual readers of the period. Evidence of this kind helps us to understand the writer's historical situation, the nature of his immediate reading-public, and his response to these pressures.

The separate volumes in the *Critical Heritage Series* present a record of this early criticism. Clearly, for many of the highly productive and lengthily reviewed nineteenth- and twentieth-century writers, there exists an enormous body of material; and in these cases the volume editors have made a selection of the most important views, significant for their intrinsic critical worth or for their representative quality—perhaps even registering incomprehension!

For earlier writers, notably pre-eighteenth century, the materials are much scarcer and the historical period has been extended, sometimes far beyond the writer's lifetime in order to show the inception and growth of critical views which were initially slow to appear.

In each volume the documents are headed by an Introduction, discussing the material assembled and relating the early stages of the author's reception to what we have come to identify as the critical tradition. The volumes will make available much material which would otherwise be difficult of access and it is hoped that the modern reader will be thereby helped towards an informed understanding of the ways in which literature has been read and judged.

B.C.S.

Contents

A*   ix

CONTENTS

Prometheus Unbound (1820)

General comment and opinions in 1820 and 1821

'Epipsychidion,' 'Adonais,' 'Hellas,' and general comment from 1822 to 1824

CONTENTS

Posthumous Poems (1824): English and American criticism from
1824 to 1840

Preface

Since the critical reception of any author—even a less controversial one than Shelley—includes not only formal periodical essays and critical notices, but also the letters, journals, and conversations of both the author's friends and his enemies, and of avid and discriminating readers as well as the merely literate, arbitrary standards must be imposed on a volume of this nature. While editorial taste and predilection inevitably shape any selection, every effort has been made to be representative in the selection of responses and to be as comprehensive as space permitted. Two important factors worked in the selection process. First, the early death of Shelley and the subsequent efforts of Mary Shelley and Leigh Hunt, among others, to canonize Shelley a literary saint coupled with a delayed trans-Atlantic reception of Shelley prevented the establishment of a neat closing date near to Shelley's death in 1822. In general, save for American reviewers, few entries written after 1845 were admitted, the year of the first complete American edition of Shelley's poems. The exceptions to these principles were judged significant enough to merit inclusion, either because the notices are intrinsically valuable as criticism, or because they point to a shift in the critics' thinking.

The second factor which no editor of Shelleyean criticism can ignore is the vitality and vigor of the early-nineteenth-century periodical press. In the first quarter of the 1800s, periodicals flourished and wielded an influence unparalleled to that point in English literature. While this fact has been well-documented in scholarly studies, a personal note in 1822 from Bernard Barton, a minor poet with aspirations to literary fame, to Robert Southey speaks volumes: 'The Notice of the *Quarterly Review* is an understood passport to an extensive Circle whose attention I certainly could wish to obtain.' The frequency and vigor with which these powerful periodicals reviewed Shelley's publications, coupled with his relative neglect by literary figures such as Wordsworth and Southey, led to a preponderance of British and American reviews and notices in this edition. Moreover, since Mary Shelley's formal comments are easily obtainable in her editions of Shelley's works and since her diary entries are usually perfunctory, she is not represented in this volume.

In brief, this volume begins with the notices of Shelley's juvenile work and seeks to reprint representative essays, journal entries, conversations, and letters written between 1810 and 1850. Wherever possible the selections are grouped chronologically according to subject, but the numerous exceptions to this principle were dictated by the frequent general surveys of either Shelley's work or his person. No attempt has been made to include Continental reception and reaction.

The editorial devices employed here are standard in this series. The headnotes give complete bibliographical information and reviewer attribution or credit, if known. Footnotes are used sparingly, but the explanatory notes before the selections shed light on little-known figures or personalities significant in nineteenth-century publishing and literary history. The introduction emphasizes the formal reception of Shelley's poems by the established reviewers, leaving the letters, diaries, and journals to speak for themselves. These often personal and uninhibited remarks reveal the fluctuations in Shelley's reputation, the growth of his reputation, and the curious devices by which friends and foes came to admit his genius while appearing to have always done so. A very selective bibliography will assist the student who wishes to pursue the subject in more detail.

Acknowledgments

The giving of thanks, like the giving of praise, is a dangerous enterprise, for the most important is the easiest overlooked. But I wish to mention especially all those scholars and critics listed in the bibliography and mentioned in the introduction. All students and scholars see as far as they do because of the endeavors of other men, and I am grateful to all men on whose shoulders I stand. In addition to the example of William S. Ward, to whom this volume is dedicated, I wish to single out especially the encouragement and enthusiasm of the late William H. Marshall.

Special thanks should also go to the typists and secretaries who worked faithfully to put this volume into the press: Mrs Joanne Pullen, Mrs Diane Stoneberg, and Mrs Dorothy Coddington. I wish also to thank Professors Gordon Stockin and Richard Gould of Houghton College who translated the Greek, Latin, French, and Italian quotations in the text. Moreover, I wish to express my appreciation to the Committee for Faculty Research and Writing Grants of Houghton College for financial assistance for the secretarial costs and duplicating expenses incurred in the preparation of this volume.

Finally, I wish to acknowledge permission received from The Viking Press, Inc. to publish extracts from *The Writings of Margaret Fuller*; from Columbia University Press for excerpts from *New Letters of Robert Southey*; from the Clarendon Press, Oxford, for quotations from *The Letters of Thomas Moore* and *The Collected Letters of Samuel Taylor Coleridge*; from Columbia University Press and the Ralph Waldo Emerson Memorial Association for excerpts from *Letters of Ralph Waldo Emerson*; from Harvard University Press for excerpts from *The Journals of Ralph Waldo Emerson* and a Keats letter in *The Letters of John Keats*; from the University of Nebraska Press for the passage from *The Literary Criticism of James Russell Lowell*; from Humanities Press, for extracts from *Byron: A Self-Portrait*; from B. Franklin for excerpts from *Memoirs of Margaret Fuller Ossoli*; from Cornell University Press for excerpts from *Coleridge the Talker: A Series of Contemporary Descriptions and Comments*; from J. M. Dent & Sons, Ltd for excerpts from *The Complete Works of William Hazlitt*; from

ACKNOWLEDGMENTS

Houghton Mifflin Company, for excerpts from Hawthorne's *Mosses from An Old Manse*; from AMS, to quote from *Robinson on Books and their Writers*; from Macmillan Publishing Co. for extracts from *His Very Self and Voice*; and from Farrar, Straus & Giroux, Inc. for selections from *The Selected Letters of Charles Lamb*.

Introduction

Shelley drowned July 8, 1822, less than a month before his thirtieth birthday. His sudden and tragic death when his maturing genius was just becoming apparent may, however, have helped catapult him from relative obscurity to the front ranks of English literature. In March 1822, John Wilson, writing in answer to the question, 'What is your serious opinion about the present state of literature,' responded:[1]

Why, we live in an age that will be much discussed 'tis over—a very stirring, productive, active age—a generation of commentators will probably succeed—and I, for one, look to furnish them with some tough work. There is a great deal of genius astir, but, after all, not many first-rate works produced. If I were asked to say how many will survive, I could answer in a few syllables. Wordsworth's Ballads will be much talked of a hundred years hence; so will the *Waverly Novels*; so will *Don Juan*, I think, and 'Manfred'; so will *Thalaba*, and *Childe Harold's Pilgrimage*, and the 'Pilgrimage to the Kirk of Shotts,' and 'Christabel.'

John Wilson's amazingly accurate prophecy is marred by the omission of Shelley's major works and those of Keats, although Wilson, in 1819 and again in 1820, had called attention to Shelley's genius.[2] Thanks to the untiring labors of Mary Shelley, Leigh Hunt, and others who kept Shelley's name before the public, Shelley's death became the occasion for an outpouring, on both sides of the Atlantic, of criticism, praise, and censure. Undoubtedly the nature of his death and the determination of his wife and friends contributed to the growth of his reputation, but he was, of course, already infamous for his alleged immorality and atheism. Much of this posthumous criticism, such as that in the American press, attempted to mitigate this censure by demonstrating to the public that his immorality was a higher morality and his atheism a new and more noble form of Christianity.

But the fact remains that during Shelley's brief lifetime and in spite of his prolific outpourings, and although the leading journals and periodicals consistently reviewed his work, except for his close friends and companions the literary world at large took little notice of him. One of the paradoxes that taunts the student of Shelley is the relative silence of his leading contemporaries. Sir Walter Scott, for example, has left no significant comment about Shelley or his work. William

Wordsworth's opinions are fragmentary and inconclusive. Trelawny reported that in 1819 Wordsworth thought nothing of Shelley as a poet. 'A poet who has not produced a good poem before he is twenty-five we may conclude cannot, and never will do so.' When asked about *The Cenci*, he replied, 'Won't do . . .' Trelawny adds that later Wordsworth read more of Shelley's poetry and admitted that Shelley was the greatest master of harmonious verse in our modern literature.[3] Christopher Wordsworth remembered that Wordsworth said, 'Shelley is one of the best *artists* of us all: I mean in workmanship of style,'[4] and Henry Crabb Robinson recollected that Wordsworth placed Shelley above Lord Byron.[5] And Gladstone said that in Wordsworth's opinion Shelley had the greatest native powers in poetry of all the men of this age.[6] But if Wordsworth was unsure about Shelley's poetical abilities, he was adamant in his opposition to Shelley's principles, as recorded by Gladstone, De Vere, and Hartley Coleridge. Perhaps Wordsworth's most quoted comment is recorded by Sara Coleridge: Shelley and Keats 'would ever be favorites with the young, but would not satisfy men of all ages.'[7] In another characteristic Wordsworthian pronouncement, he asserted that 'Shelley's poem on the Lark was full of imagination, but that it did not show the same observation of nature as his poem on the same bird did.'[8]

Coleridge's statements are confined to several references in letters and in a few conversations, although when Miss Coburn has completed the editing of his notebooks, more significant comments may turn up. Except for one famous letter written to Shelley, even Keats has left us few of his insights into Shelley's poetry. Most disappointing of all, of course, are Mary Shelley's letters and journals, for although she repeatedly notes that Shelley has been reading his work aloud or that she and Shelley are copying out a work for publication, she provides no glimpses into her spontaneous and personal reactions to the poetry. She meticulously records when and where she read a poem, but not what she thought about it. In the light of her subsequent commentary and publishing history, this silence is tantalizing. Even Byron who encouraged and supported Shelley, while not always on the best of terms with him, records precious few responses to Shelley's work.

Shelley's lack of reputation, even among his literary contemporaries, probably reflects both the limited number of volumes printed and the method of publication. Later in the century, the first volume of Alfred Tennyson's verse was ignored in part because the country bookseller had not the influence on public taste of a John Murray.

Shelley's first volume, *Original Poetry*, the joint work of Shelley and his sister Elizabeth, was issued by Stockdale, a London publisher and remainder bookseller, who received 1489 copies from the Worthing printer, but probably no more than 100 copies were ever in circulation. *St. Irvyne*, a gothic novel, was published at Shelley's expense and sold badly. Stockdale, the publisher, figured his loss at £300. *The Necessity of Atheism* was published by C. and W. Phillips of Worthing, and all but a few copies were burned. The discoverer of the heresy, the Rev. John Walker, Fellow of New College, kept one, and copies had also been sent to all the bishops and heads of the colleges before the pamphlet had come to the attention of university authorities. But clearly the pamphlet was never widely read.

Of Shelley's more mature works, 250 copies of *Queen Mab* were printed, but probably not more than 70 copies were in circulation during his lifetime. *Alastor* was first printed, again at Shelley's expense, in an edition of 250 copies. John Murray refused to publish it, but it was ultimately published by Carpenter & Son, and Baldwin & Company. As late as 1820 some copies remained. *The Revolt of Islam* appeared first in an edition of 750 copies as *Laon and Cythna*. Although some copies were distributed under the first title, Ollier, the publisher, refused to go on without revision. The poem finally was published with the new title page and after twenty-six pages of text had been cancelled.

Shelley's drama, *The Cenci*, was printed in an edition of 250 copies at Leghorn in 1819 and published by Collier in 1820. *The Cenci* was a success, for it went into a second edition in 1821, the only work which passed into an authorized second edition during Shelley's lifetime. However, *Prometheus Unbound* did not fare as well. Shelley himself thought it would sell no more than 20 copies, and John Gisborne remarked that *Prometheus Unbound* was never intended for more than five or six persons. Ollier, on Shelley's instructions, did send copies to Leigh Hunt, Godwin, Hogg, Peacock, Keats, Thomas Moore, Horace Smith, and Byron. The 100 copies of 'Epipsychidion' were printed to be sold at two shillings, and the author's name was kept a secret. The poem did not arouse much comment. 'Adonais' was printed at Pisa where Shelley could oversee the proofing and printing. As T. J. Wise pointed out, the poem received much more care than any of Shelley's other books. It sold for 3s. 6d., and as late as 1824 a copy could be purchased for the same price.

As the publication figures indicate, Shelley's poems had little chance for wide-spread public success. Printed in relatively small editions, usually at great distance from the author, published by a bookseller who feared, rightfully so, prosecution, and much abused by the leading periodicals and journals, Shelley's poetry clearly had a limited circulation in England and few opportunities to reach a larger audience than those already committed to the author or his principles.

Given the inevitable time lapse between publication in England and critical response in America, Shelley seems to have fared somewhat better among his American near-contemporaries. To be sure, Thoreau apparently ignored him and Emerson questioned whether Shelley was a poet.[9] But Margaret Fuller Ossoli repeatedly sought to interest Emerson in Shelley, and Hawthorne employed the figure of Shelley in two short stories which appeared in *Mosses from an Old Manse* (Nos 99, 100).

In light of the scorn and ire heaped on Shelley in the English press, the sympathy of American periodicals for him, for his poetry, and for his political and social ideas testifies to the vitality and vision of American men of letters. Just as political persuasion influenced English opinion, undoubtedly American critics saw Shelley as a fellow-traveler, a reformer with the spirit of America, and a spokesman for the ideals and aspirations that had already turned the essentially mercenary nature of the revolution of 1776 into a mythic liberation of Prometheus on the national level. Why these critics were not threatened by the popular accounts of Shelley's supposed immorality is a conundrum, but it is interesting to note that most American estimates touch lightly on Shelley's personal life. During his lifetime, Shelley was, however, little recognized in America. Julia Power says that the very first mention of Shelley in any work published in America was in the American edition of Leigh Hunt's *Foliage*, which contained two sonnets on the poet and was dedicated to him.[10] Shelley's work was first noticed in the *Belles-Lettres Repository and Monthly Magazine* for March 1, 1820, but the first American criticism of Shelley was published in the *American Atheneum* for September 1, 1821.[11]

The publisher of Shelley's *Queen Mab* has been indicted by the Society for the suppression of Vice. It is dreadful to think that for the chance for a miserable pecuniary profit, any man would become the active agent to disseminate principles so subversive to the happiness of society.

However, the often favorable reaction of the American press to Shelley was forecast in July 1820 when *The Literary and Scientific Repository* published a selection of excerpts from *The Quarterly Review, Black-*

4

wood's and *The New Monthly* so arranged as to place Shelley in the best light.

This is not to imply, however, that American response was primarily adulation and praise. In all sections of the country, as Shelley's life and work became better known, he stirred controversy, and in the second quarter of the century, leading periodicals in New England, the Middle States, and the South, carried significant and often controversial articles on Shelley. In the North, *The Literary Journal and Weekly Register of Science and the Arts* for January 11, 1834, published an original and appreciative criticism. The *Yale Literary Magazine* (1839–40) also praised him highly. One of the most thorough reviews was written by Orestes Brownson for his *Boston Quarterly Review* (No. 94) for October 1841, but the most exciting notices in the North, if not the best criticism, occurred in the verbal battle between Emerson and Andrews Norton. Since the real issue was orthodoxy versus liberalism, for Andrews Norton Shelley represented the way the new morality was whittling away at the very foundations of true religion. The original article which upset Norton was published in the *Western Messenger* for February 1837, but the controversy grew out of Emerson's now famous Divinity School Address. Nevertheless sides were drawn and Shelley's poetry became the issue. While the controversy produced little significant criticism it does illustrate feelings about Shelley at this period, and the drift of critical thought.

In the Middle States a series of important articles kept Shelley's name before the reading public. Journals of differing quality commented on him, including *Godey's Lady's Book* which published a verse tribute in May of 1831. As early as 1828, the *Philadelphia Monthly Magazine* (No. 81) noted that Shelley was a misunderstood man, but a poet without merit and without any hope of eventual popularity.[12] By 1836, however, the leading Philadelphia magazine, the *American Quarterly Review*, (No. 87) thought Shelley, Wordsworth, and Byron the three greatest poets of the century.[13] In New York a similar division of opinion existed, but critics on the whole were favorable. The *New York Literary Gazette and Phi Beta Kappa Repository* (No. 80) published in 1825–6 the very earliest American criticism devoted entirely to Shelley. While the article begins negatively, on the whole the reviewer applauds Shelley and asserts he was superior to all the poets of his age.[14] Another sympathetic but even more significant critical statement was published by Parke Godwin in *The United States Magazine and Democratic Review* (No. 96) for December 1843. Clearly Godwin's social views coincided with those of Shelley, but he is also an astute critic, especially in his discussions of *Queen Mab* and *Prometheus Unbound*.[15]

Perhaps because literary and intellectual trends seemed to have traveled slowly in the South, Shelley and other Romantics did not receive much attention in southern journals until the 1840s. By the fifth decade of the century the *Southern Literary Messenger* had become as important as northern magazines, and it devoted a considerable number of articles to Shelley. H. T. Tuckerman's article, on the occasion of the publication of Shelley's *Prose Works* in 1840 is representative of an enlightened perspective,[16] but by no means indicates universal acceptance (No. 92), for in December of 1840 'A Friend of Virtue' wrote refuting Tuckerman and attacking Shelley on moral and religious grounds.[17] Throughout the 1840s, however, the *Southern Literary Messenger* published articles, mostly favorable and often written by northerners, praising Shelley and celebrating his genius. Although the American press was anything but niggardly in its attention to Shelley, the fact remains that it was in England that the great and powerful reviews flourished. There an English poet's reputation would be made and it was in the pages of *The Quarterly*, *Blackwood's*, *The Edinburgh*, and *The London* that Shelley sought acceptance.

Juvenalia

Unlike Alexander Pope who saw the wisdom of either destroying his early verse or rewriting it at a later date when maturity had overcome youthful indulgence, Shelley published a volume of verse, *Original Poetry by Victor and Cazire*, two romances, *Zastrozzi* and *St. Irvyne*, and one prose essay, *The Necessity of Atheism*, by the age of twenty. To a twentieth-century reader little in these pieces commends them. Although the more prestigious *Edinburgh Review* and *The Quarterly Review* did not comment on Shelley's early work, the more popular but still respectable journals such as *The British Critic* and *The Critical Review* took up the volumes and reviewed them in some detail.

Given the political unrest and the fear for public morality that characterized the second decade of the nineteenth century, the reviewers' attacks are almost predictable. The anonymous writer for *The Anti-Jacobin Review* (No. 7) raised the battle flag and spoke for other reviewers as well in his comments on *St. Irvyne or the Rosicrucian* (1811). It is the critics' duty 'to mark every deviation from religious and moral principle with strong reprobation; as well as to deter readers from wasting their time in the perusal of unprofitable and vicious productions, as to check silly and licentious writers at an early period of their literary career.' One year earlier the reviewer for *The Critical Review* (No. 5) had cudgeled Shelley on the same grounds for *Zastrozzi: A Romance* (1810). The style and story are so contemptible, he says, that the romance would have passed unnoticed 'had not our indignation been excited by the open and bare-faced immorality and grossness displayed throughout.' The character of Zastrozzi is 'one of the most savage and improbable demons that ever issued from a diseased brain.' Such trash, the reviewer continues, 'is fit only for the inmates of a brothel.'

Notwithstanding the censures for immorality and corruption of public morals, the criticisms are not motivated entirely by political prejudice and puritanical morality. Most of the critics denounce the gothic element recurrent in all three of Shelley's youthful works: the 'Victor and Cazire' volume, *Zastrozzi* and *St. Irvyne*. The writer for *The Literary Panorama* (No. 1) noted that 'modern poets are the most unhappy of men! Their imaginations are perpetually haunted with terrors.' While others bask in the sun, 'these votaries of the Muse of misery see nothing but glooms, and listen to the pealing thunder.' Similarly, although the anonymous reviewer for *The Critical Review* (No. 5) found *Zastrozzi* objectionable primarily on moral grounds, he too concluded that 'not all his "scintillated eyes," his "battling emotions," his "frigorific torpidity of despair," nor his "Lethean torpor" can save Shelley from infamy.'

The British Critic (No. 6) quoted the opening paragraph of *St. Irvyne: or the Rosicrucian* 'believing that some readers will be satisfied and proceed no further.' Those who do will find 'descriptions wilder than are to be found in Radcliffe, and a tale more extravagant than the *St. Leon* of Godwin.' *The Literary Panorama* of February 1811 sarcastically noted the similarities with the gothic horror novels by excerpting sections from *St. Irvyne* under headings such as 'How to Begin a Romance, A.D. 1811' and 'How to End a Romance, A.D. 1811.'[18] In January of 1812 *The Anti-Jacobin Review and Magazine* (No. 7) continued to contrast *Zastrozzi* with Ann Radcliffe's work. The reviewer claims that if the title page had not told him the author was a gentleman, 'a freshman, of course, we should certainly have ascribed it to some "Miss" in her teens; who, having read the beautiful and truly poetic descriptions, in the unrivalled romances of Mrs. Ratcliffe [sic], imagined that to admire the writings of that lady, and to imitate her

INTRODUCTION

style were one and the same thing.' Shelley's youthful interest in the
gothic element persisted throughout his life, and eventually led his
wife Mary to write the classic horror tale, *Frankenstein*.

Although these critics do not agree about the merits of the horror
romance as a genre (the *Anti-Jacobin* reviewer is more sympathetic than
The British Critic), both reviewers agree that Shelley's efforts are inferior to Ann Radcliffe's. Their reasons are similar and still stand today.
'Here we have *description run mad*,' says the *Anti-Jacobin* reviewer, 'every
uncouth epithet, every wild expression, which either the lexicographer
could supply, or the disordered imagination of the romance-writer
suggest, has been pressed into the service of "the Rosicmeian" [sic].'
The same reviewer also censured Shelley's attempts to heighten the
horror by intensifying adjectives describing the action. 'Woe and
terror are heightened by the expressions used to describe them. Heroes
and heroines are not merely distressed and terrified, they are "enanguished" and "enhorred".' Such criticisms are more than a tally of
violations of a debased eighteenth-century critical principle of decorum.
Both here and in the other early reviews the critics speak from a more
objective standard than mere taste and fashion. Their objections are
those of any discerning reader to the youthful and indiscriminate use
of adjectives rather than strong verbs and concrete nouns.

The plots and characterization are also the subject of criticism. The
reviewer for *The Critical Review* (No. 5) noted that characters are
introduced into the narrative of *Zastrozzi* without preparation or moti-
vation, and he lists a series of improbabilities and absurdities. One important exception to this criticism stands out. The reviewer for *The
Gentleman's Magazine and Historical Chronicle* (No. 4) thought *Zastrozzi*
a 'well-told tale of horror:,' and 'so artfully conducted that the reader
cannot easily anticipate the denouement.' He concludes, however, that
the Continental setting is appropriate because the characters and vices
which are useful in the narrative, 'thank God, are not to be found in
this country.'

Several reviewers from this early period object to Shelley's failures
to observe the rules of grammar. The significance of the criticism is
uncertain. Certainly all reviewers at all times find it difficult to distinguish between the ignorance of freshmen and the genius of Faulkner.
The reviewer for *The Anti-Jacobin*, (No. 7), in a remark too reminiscent
of the classroom, comments sarcastically: 'From one who, disdaining
the common forms and modes of language, aims at sublimity both of
thought and expression, a slavish subjection to the vulgar restrictions of

grammar . . . cannot reasonably be extracted.' Still, some of the examples cited by these early reviewers are violations of normal and natural word order and the reviewers feel they lack the fire of genuine poetic expression. Even these apparently cavilling remarks show that the critics had a more balanced and sane judgment of Shelley's early literary output than the casual readers of these reviewers and the repeaters of literary gossip have led us to believe.

Queen Mab

Queen Mab, the first product of Shelley's maturing poetic genius, was written in 1812 and 1813 and privately printed by Shelley in an edition of 250 copies. Since only 70 copies had been disposed of when Richard Carlile bought the remaining stock in December of 1822, circulation of the poem was certainly minimal.[19] The one major contemporary notice of the volume appeared in *The Theological Inquirer or Polemical Magazine* (No. 11) in an article signed F., whom Newman Ivey White tentatively identified as Sir Ronald Crawford Ferguson, a liberal and well-known supporter of all movements toward granting more civil and religious liberty.[20] This notice, in which Shelley was almost certainly involved, carefully avoids giving any clue to the author's identity, but instead quotes profusely from the poem, undoubtedly hoping that the reader of the review would be stimulated to purchase a copy although the reviewer, in a patently absurd story, purports to have purchased his copies on the Continent since it is 'too bold a production to issue from the British press.'

The anonymous reviewer is content to praise the poem in general terms, asserting that the poem is filled with 'sublime descriptions,' 'rapturous gratulation,' and 'fanciful description.' Clearly the author's purpose is to stimulate discussion, and his devices for doing so are time-honored and successful. He apologizes for not proving that the poet is a philosopher of the first rank, but he cannot do so because of 'the boldness of his sentiments, which, in his country, where the freedom of the press is little more than an empty name, it would be hazardous to disseminate.' In a short one-sentence paragraph he calls attention to Shelley's notes to the poem, by asserting that it is not part of his plan to mention 'the copious and elegant notes to the poem.' These notes were, of course, to bear the brunt of the reviewers' attacks a decade later.[21]

In 1821, eight years later, a pirated edition of the poem was printed, to which Shelley objected because he thought the work immature.

9

Probably because the scandal of Shelley's personal life had been aired so publicly, this later edition received a number of critical notices. They are noteworthy, for in spite of the publicity and rumors surrounding Shelley, the critics are almost unanimous in their praise of Shelley's genius. The liberal journal, *The London Magazine and Theatrical Inquisitor* (No. 13) refuses to meddle in either the private scandal or the speculative ideas in the poem. 'If his [Shelley's] opinions are palpably absurd and false, they must fall by their own absurdity and falsehood.' The reviewer believes that Barry Cornwall is more tender and delicate than Shelley, and Keats and Coleridge of more fertile imagination, but he insists that Shelley is a man of genius.

This recognition of Shelley's talent was even extended by *The Literary Gazette and Journal of Belles Lettres* (No. 14), a magazine which consistently attacked Shelley on other points. While the reviewer regrets Shelley's ideas, he insists Shelley's genius is 'doubtless of a high order.' In fact, in the reviewer's judgment, Shelley is not inferior to Southey. At one point he says, 'This is genuine poetry.' This praise of Shelley by the conservative *Literary Gazette* is particularly noteworthy when even the liberal weekly, *The Literary Chronicle and Weekly Review* (No. 16) thought Shelley furnished 'one of the most striking and melancholy instances of the perversion, or rather prostitution of genius, that we ever met with.' Among these notices only *The Monthly Magazine and British Register* (No. 15) took exception. Since the magazine was mildly radical, the reviewer feared that Shelley was being lured into a trap. Even *The Quarterly Review* had been praising his genius as of the highest order. Either the Establishment was laying a plot 'or our Critics are a set of dunces, who cannot distinguish between sublimity and bombast,—between poetry and "prose run mad".'

These reviewers also note a characteristic of Shelley's poetry which all students of Shelley since have commented on: that much of the strength and beauty of his poetry stems from the firmness and fervency of his convictions. Both the disillusioned and disinterested readers and the committed revolutionary have noted this quality in Shelley's writings. The reviewer in *The London Magazine and Theatrical Inquisitor* (No. 13) says,

We apprehend, indeed, that the peculiar charm of Shelley's writing is derived from that complete conviction which he evidently entertains of the justness and importance of all he asserts. This feeling, whether a man's opinions be right or wrong, communicates a force and pointedness to diction, and an interest to composition, which mere labour can never bestow. All Mr. Shelley's thoughts are feelings.

And in an otherwise stern review, *The Literary Chronicle and Weekly Review* (No. 16) reflects that Shelley must have a 'hell in his own conscience, but a man of Mr. Shelley's cultivated mind, cannot but possess strong feelings.'

In the midst of this clear recognition of Shelley's genius and the sincerity of his convictions, nearly all of the reviewers fear that *Queen Mab* undermines the very structure and fabric of all social institutions including marriage, religion, family, and the parliamentary system. *The London Magazine* (No. 13) exhorted Shelley to take up a task truly worthy of his talents, and the reviewer for *The Literary Gazette and Journal of Belles Lettres* (No. 14) so feared Shelley's supernatural origins that like Othello viewing Iago, he expected to see a cloven hoof.

we asked a friend who had seen this individual [Shelley], to describe him to us— as if a cloven foot, or horn, or flames from the mouth, must have marked the external appearance of so bitter an enemy to mankind.

One of the more interesting and more bitter responses to *Queen Mab* is an anonymous volume announced by William Clark in *The Literary Chronicle* as *An Answer to Queen Mab*.[22] In Clark's trial for publishing *Queen Mab*, he cited the pamphlet for his defense, arguing that he had not intended to propagate Shelley's ideas, and in some respects the book may have been written with this purpose in mind. The first chapter takes issue with Shelley's ideas on marriage and the legitimate reasons for dissolving a marriage. The anonymous author (who may be William Johnson Fox) begins with two assumptions: a man will roam if not forcibly held to one spot and, secondly, a woman is inherently weak and unable to take care of herself. 'Men may be often false;—may often forget the vows sworn at the altar, and venture to taste "forbidden fruits:" but to make falsehood a creed, villainy a profession, and injustice a moral duty, is a measure of guilt, for which language has no adequate expression.'[23] He further defines the problem:[24]

Man sighs, vows and betrays:—woman believes, confides, and is undone. The treasure is rifled; and the robber hastes on the high-road of pleasure to make other victims. The institution of marriage *checks*, though it does not eradicate this. It takes care, at least, that part of the female sex shall be, in some degree, protected from the caprice of the *lords* of creation.

Although the author does point out that part of the dilemma arises because the laws obviously favor men, still 'woman can never be raised upon the stage of this bustling world, into an equality with man. . . . Women have no intuitive knowledge to discover the truth of affection, from its dissembled counterfeit. Prone to believe "what seems but fair," how are they to detect the guile that lurks beneath the specious promise of the flatters' tongue!'[25]

In the second chapter the difficulty of Shelley's purported atheism is neatly solved by showing that Shelley has merely substituted Necessity for God. All of the attributes which Alexander Pope attributed to God Shelley attributes to Necessity. Shelley's only error is his assigning attitudes and characteristics to God which are really human aberrations and deviations. Therefore the supposed atheism of Shelley is really a deep and abiding faith under another name.

What stands out in these reviews of Shelley's first poem which promised even better things to come is that these first critics, men who were beset by political, religious, and personal prejudice and who lived in a milieu which expected politics and religion to take precedence over critical taste, found and praised in Shelley's poetry the qualities and virtues which later and perhaps more objective critics have also noticed. Even when motivated by personal preservation, as in William Clark's publication of *A Response to Queen Mab*, there is a willingness to deal with the issues and ideas, although a longer perspective has decided in Shelley's favor rather than the critics'.

Alastor
Shelley wrote *Alastor, or, The Spirit of Solitude, and Other Poems* in 1815. After Shelley had printed 250 copies at his own expense, the volume was published in 1816 by Baldwin, Cradock & Joy and Carpenter & Son. Following upon the rather auspicious earlier reviewers, the notices of this volume are disappointing on several grounds. None of the reviewers pays particular attention to the shorter lyrics although several, including 'Mutability,' are among those most frequently anthologized today. Moreover, with several noticeable exceptions even the comments on *Alastor*, the title poem, reveal little critical taste. Although the conservative *Monthly Review* (No. 20) found 'some beautiful imagery and poetical expressions,' the 'sublime obscurity' of the poems is explained by a poem addressed to Wordsworth which explains 'in what school the author had formed his taste.' The sarcastic reviewer for *The British Critic* (No. 21) complains because he is 'condemned to pore over much profound and prosing stupidity.' He is, therefore, 'not a little delighted with the nonsense

which mounts, which rises, which spurns the earth, and all its dull realities; we love to fly with our author to a silent nook.'

In spite of its conservative bias, *The Eclectic Review* (No. 22) again affirmed Shelley's genius and noted his talent for descriptive poetry. But the reviewer's analysis of the character of *Alastor*, while couched in the language and jargon of the eighteenth century, and reflecting the moralistic biases of a previous age, nevertheless coincides with the darker visions of Romantic poetry as explained by twentieth-century critics like Northrop Frye and Harold Bloom.[26] The reviewer underlines Shelley's interest in the imagination. 'The poem is adapted to show the dangerous, the fatal tendency of that morbid ascendancy of the imagination over the other faculties.' When the imagination achieves this ascendancy the mind is unable to give adequate attention to the 'work-day' life and the discharging of social duties. The poem 'exhibits the utter uselessness of imagination, when wholly undisciplined, and selfishly employed for the mere purposes of intellectual luxury,' without reference to moral ends. The poem has 'glitter without warmth, succession without progress, excitement without purpose and a search which terminates in annihilation.' This unexpected recognition of the crisis precipitated by the inward quest of all Romantic poets from Blake to Yeats strikes a peculiarly modern chord, although one wishes the critic were less blind to the stimuli for such a journey.

Leigh Hunt began his long and loyal defense of Shelley in December 1816 and January 1817 with two brief notices in *The Examiner* (No. 23). Hunt's efforts on Shelley's behalf were to continue long after the poet's death, and in these notices he wisely seeks to give Shelley a sympathetic reading rather than to be an obvious champion. In the December article he discusses Shelley along with Reynolds and Keats as supposed representatives of a new school of poetry, a view which, he says, is wrong. These poets are really the native stream of English poetry, for they have rejected the influence of the French. Their object is 'to restore the same love of Nature, and of *thinking* instead of mere *talking*, which formerly rendered us real poets, and not mere versifying wits, and bead-rollers of couplets.'

Among the reviews of *Alastor*, the most important and most friendly appeared in *Blackwood's Edinburgh Magazine* (No. 24), and may have been written by John Gibson Lockhart. According to a letter Shelley wrote on December 15, 1819 to Charles Ollier from Florence, he was glad 'to see the *Quarterly* cut up, and that by one of their own people.'[27] Shelley, perhaps with false modesty, says the 'praise would have given me more pleasure if it had been less excessive,' and indeed the reviewer does defend Shelley vigorously. The poet has either been 'entirely overlooked, or slightly noticed, or grossly abused.' Although the short poems are vague and obscure and although Shelley is enamoured of dreams of death ('he loves to strike his harp among the tombs'), the poet is 'destined to achieve great things in poetry.' He continues, 'there is the light of poetry even in the darkness of Shelley's imagination.'

The reviewer's finest praise comes as he damns *The Quarterly Review* for its earlier review of *The Revolt of Islam*. Shelley has been 'infamously and stupidly treated in *The Quarterly Review*.' If the prose of *The Quarterly*'s reviewer is compared with Shelley's poetry, one thinks not of 'Satan reproving Sin,' but 'of a dunce rating a man of genius.' Either the *Quarterly* critic is unable to recognize genius or he is a liar. If the first, he ought not to write; if the latter, he is guilty of the very crime of which he accuses Shelley.

In spite of the limited notices and the personal, political, and social biases of the reviewers, to the contemporary ear the reviewers of the *Alastor* volume, while unfair in many respects, reflect a broader spectrum of opinion and a profounder understanding of Shelley's poetry than we might expect. The critics are not totally blind to Shelley's genius, and occasionally, as in *The Eclectic Review* and *Blackwood's Edinburgh Magazine*, their comments point the way that twentieth-century criticism would take.

The Revolt of Islam

The Revolt of Islam, a revision of an earlier poem *Laon and Cythna* which had been written in 1817 while Shelley was living at Great Marlow, appeared in 1818 after Shelley finally agreed to the changes which his publisher Ollier demanded. Although both Shelley and Hunt insisted that only two or three copies of the original poem had been sold, many more than these exist and it was a copy of the original which *The Quarterly Review* saw and reviewed. The poem contains Shelley's views on the state of English society, the necessity for reform, and suggestions for how such a revolution ought to be carried out— unselfishly and bloodlessly—in marked contrast to the French Revolution.

The vehemence of the critical notice which the volume received reflects the close literary and personal ties between Leigh Hunt and Shelley. Since Hunt and his brother John had been imprisoned for slandering the Prince Regent, George IV, the Tory reviews naturally pronounced Shelley guilty by association. Before *The Revolt of Islam* had appeared, *Blackwood's Magazine* (No. 26), in an article on the 'Cockney School,' had attacked Hunt viciously:

His poetry is that of a man who has kept company with kept-mistresses. He talks indelicately like a tea-sipping milliner girl. Some excuse for him might have been, had he been hurried away by imagination or passion. But with him indecency is a disease, and he speaks unclean things from perfect inanition. The very concubine of so impure a wretch as Leigh Hunt would be pitied, but alas! for the wife of such a husband! For him there is no charm in simple seduction; and he gloats over it only when accompanied with adultery and incest.

The fact that Hunt knew Shelley personally and praised him, automatically drew the fire of the conservative reviewers.

The critical exchange between Hunt's *The Examiner* and the conservative reviews centred primarily on Shelley's political and social ideas. Both sides, however, affirmed Shelley's genius again. *Blackwood's* (No. 26) repeated its attack on Hunt and Keats as members of the Cockney School who as poets are 'worthy of sheer and instant contempt.' Unfortunately their views have 'been taken up by one [Shelley], of whom it is far more seriously, and deeply, and lamentably unworthy.' But 'his genius is due its praise.' In spite of his weakness as a philosopher, Shelley, as a poet, 'is strong, nervous, original; well entitled to take his place near to the great creative masters.' In a final thrust, malicious, condescending and ill-tempered, the reviewer says that Shelley is 'a scholar, a gentleman, and a poet; and he must therefore despise from his soul the only eulogies to which he has hitherto been accustomed—paragraphs from *The Examiner* and sonnets from Johnny Keats.' In addition, *The Monthly Review* (No. 27) lamented 'the waste of so much capability of better things.'

About the poetry itself, critical opinion is divided. Leigh Hunt in *The Examiner* praised the deep sentiments of the poem, the grandeur of its imagery, and the sweet and noble versification, 'like the placid playing of a great organ.' Hunt did take exception to the sameness and frequency of sea images and metaphors. The book will not appeal to humanity, he says, because Shelley does not appeal 'through the medium of its [humanity's] common knowledge.' *Blackwood's* (No. 26) is generous in its praise but not uncritical, for 'the author has composed his poem in much haste, and he has inadvertently left many detached parts, both of his story and his allusion, to be made out as the reader best can, from very inadequate data.' The reviewer praises Shelley for 'having poured over his narrative a very rare strength and abundance of poetic imagery and feeling—of having steeped every word in the essence of his inspiration.'

John Taylor Coleridge, in *The Quarterly Review* (No. 28), admitted that the poem is 'not without beautiful passages, that the language is in general free from errors of taste, and the versification smooth and harmonious.' He regrets that Shelley is an 'inspiring imitator' and, in a probable reference to Wordsworth, commiserates with 'another mountain poet' from whom Shelley borrows and to 'whose religious mind it must be a matter . . . of perpetual sorrow to see the philosophy which comes pure and holy from his pen, degraded and perverted.' Only *The Monthly Review* (No. 27) found no redeeming poetic value in *The Revolt of Islam*. According to its reviewer, Shelley's 'command of language is so thoroughly abused as to become a mere snare for loose and unmeaning expression; and his facility of writing, even in Spenser's stanza, leads him into a licentiousness of rhythm and of rhyme that is truly contemptible.' Except for this reviewer, who concludes epigrammatically, 'he [Shelley] goes on rhyming without reason, and reasoning without rhyme,' the other reviewers consistently praise Shelley's genius and his poetic achievement, although they usually find his philosophy either pernicious or valueless or both.

The clash between Shelley's admirers, especially Leigh Hunt, and his adversaries over *The Revolt of Islam* has a familiar ring, not only to those knowledgeable in nineteenth-century literary criticism, but also to all who have listened to both sides in the perennial debates between reformers and defenders of the status quo. *Blackwood's* and *The Quarterly Review* sound the conservative strain. Shelley is naïve, youthful, idealistic. He too easily despairs and is too ready to correct. His solutions are simplistic because his understanding of the issues is facile and simple-minded. Shelley suggests that love, properly employed, will go far toward resolving the social, political, and religious evils of his day. But Coleridge says in *The Quarterly Review*, 'Love is a wide word with many significations, and we are at a loss as to which of them he would have it now bear. We are loath to understand it in its lowest sense, though we believe that as to the issue this would be the correctest mode of interpreting it.' Still Shelley cannot possibly mean it in its highest sense. 'He does not mean that love, which is the fulfilling of the law, and which walks after the commandments, for he would erase the Decalogue and every other code of laws.'

Shelley's adversaries, the conservatives, insist that he has undermined the very fabric of English society, the law, the family, and the Church. Coleridge says, 'As far as in him lay, he has loosened the hold of our protecting laws, and sapped the principles of our venerable polity; he has invaded the purity and chilled the unsuspecting ardour of our fireside intimacies: he has slandered, ridiculed and blasphemed our holy religion.' Coleridge's male chauvinism is revealed in his comments on Shelley's supposed naïveté about the process for effecting change. He attacks the figure of Cythna who 'by her own eloquence rouses all of her own sex to assert their liberty and independence; this perhaps was no difficult task; a female tongue in such a cause may be supposed to have spoken fluently at least, and to have a willing audience.'

Leigh Hunt's defense is worth quoting, for he anticipates the attacks of Shelley's critics before they occur and those of all who are satisfied with the present way of the world. In a passage both eloquent and profound, he says:

They say it is impossible the world should alter; and yet it has often altered. They say it is impossible, at any rate, it should mend; yet people are no longer burnt at the stake . . . But one man,—they say—what can one man do? Let a glorious living person answer,—let Clarkson answer, who sitting down in his youth by a road-side, thought upon the horrors of the Slave Trade, and vowed he would dedicate his life to endeavour at overthrowing it. He was laughed at; he was violently opposed; he was called presumptuous and even irreligious; he was thought out of his senses; he made a noble sacrifice of his own health and strength; and he has *lived* to see the Slave Trade . . . made a Felony.

Hunt's defense in *The Examiner* of 1818 and 1819 is cogent, reasoned, and principled (Nos 25 and 29). He rightly tries to show that Shelley seeks to expose injustice, violence, and selfishness wherever they exist and however disguised. Hunt's argument rests on the premise that, rather than opposing religion and undermining the fabric of society, Shelley is a proponent of a true Christianity, and that he is a genuine follower of Christ, a stalwart defender of the rights and privileges of all men against those who would abridge the rights of the weak and the defenseless. In the October 3, 1819 *Examiner* he says, 'we have no hesitation in saying that the moral spirit of his philosophy approaches infinitely nearer to that Christian benevolence so much preached and so little practised, than any the most orthodox dogmas ever published.'

These differences are not easily resolved. Shelley's unabated idealism, his affirmation of the principle of love, his optimism about man's ability to reform himself stand in sharp contrast to the conservatives' realism, their faith in the system, and their resistance to a change which does not carry with it a guarantee of a better world. The gap between Shelley and his public had grown to a chasm. In spite of Leigh Hunt's masterful defense, the lines were clearly drawn and not until after Shelley's death, when most of his proposals for reform were at least legal realities, would Shelley's reputation be restored.

Rosalind and Helen

In 1818 Shelley completed the title poem for the volume *Rosalind and Helen, with Other Poems* which appeared in 1819. The title poem, begun in 1817, recounts the morbid and sorrowful tales of two women, Rosalind and Helen, disappointed in love, one who married a miser after learning her lover was her brother, and the second the mistress of a now dead 'noble Peer.' The exchange of confidences between Rosalind and Helen provides Shelley with an opportunity to repeat his attacks on the greedy and selfish clergy, the ill effects of superstition and religion, the opportunities the law provides for outwitting innocent women, and the beauties of marriage without benefit of clergy. *Blackwood's* (No. 32) commented: 'God knows there is enough of evil and of guilt in this world, without our seeking to raise up such hideous and unnatural phantasms of wickedness.' In general, the reviewers reiterate their attacks on Shelley's doctrines, adding little new to their earlier arguments. *The Commercial Chronicle*'s attack (No. 31) is typical. 'The poets of this school have the original merit of conceiving that the higher emotions of the heart are to be roused in their highest degree by deformity, physical and moral; they have found out a new source of the sublime—disgust; and with them the more sickening the circumstance, the more exquisite the sensibility.'

Still the reviewers insist that Shelley is a true poet and *Rosalind and Helen*, in the words from *Blackwood's*, 'breathe throughout strong feeling, and strong passion, and strong imagination.' And *The Monthly Review* (No. 33) regretted 'to see so considerable a portion of real genius wasted in merely desultory fires.' Several of the reviewers seek to convince the reader of Shelley's genius by comparing him with other popularly acclaimed poets. Leigh Hunt, always Shelley's defender, compared *Rosalind and Helen* with Wordsworth's 'Peter Bell' (*The Examiner*, May 9, 1819).

The object of Mr. Wordsworth's administrations of melancholy is to make men timid, servile, and (considering his religion) selfish;—that of Mr. Shelley's, to render them fearless, independent, affectionate, infinitely social.... The Poet of the Lakes always carries his egotism and 'saving knowledge' about with him, and unless he has the settlement of the matter, will go in a pet and plant himself by the side of the oldest tyrannies and slaveries;—our Cosmopolite-Poet would evidently die with pleasure to all personal identity, could he but see his fellow-creatures reasonable and happy. . . . But comparisons are never so odious, as when they serve to contrast two spirits who ought to have agreed.

The reviewer in *Blackwood's* (No. 32) thought that not even Byron had written lines superior to those describing the effect of Lionel's death on Helen. He regrets that Shelley has had limited circulation, since his poetry equals that of Barry Cornwall, a truly astounding comparison, for *The Literary Gazette* had included Cornwall in the 'Bread and Milk School' of poetry. Referring back to *The Revolt of Islam*, he says Shelley approaches more nearly to Scott and Byron than any of their contemporaries. Moreover, in this last volume Shelley equals the tenderness and pathos of Wordsworth and Coleridge. Clearly, both Wilson and Hunt sought to enhance Shelley's fortunes and his reputation through associating him with established figures like the much-condemned Byron and the already revered Wordsworth.

Although the reviewers fail to establish or enunciate a standard for criticizing poetry and they are often content with attacking Shelley's views, they recognize Shelley's genius and also his weaknesses. For example, in addition to the title poem, *Rosalind and Helen* contained three of Shelley's best-known poems, 'Ozymandias,' 'Hymn to Intellectual Beauty' and 'Lines Written among the Euganean Hills.' While only the last of these three received notice in the reviews, both *The Examiner* (No. 30) and the generally critical *Monthly Review* (No. 33) praised 'Lines'. Hunt felt that 'parts of the poem are among the grandest if not the deepest that Mr. Shelley has produced, with a stately stepping in measure,' and both journals singled out Shelley's compliment to Lord Byron for praise (lines 167–265), lines which, according to Forman, may have been an afterthought.[28]

On the other hand, John Wilson (*Blackwood's*, No. 32), while anxious to praise Shelley's powers, also noted Shelley had borrowed heavily from Godwin and thus Shelley's 'opinions carry no authority along with them to others. . . . The finer essence of his poetry never penetrates them—the hues of his imagination never clothes [sic] them with attractive beauty. The cold, bald, clumsy, and lifeless parts of this poem are those in which he obtrudes upon us his contemptible and long-expected dogmas.'

The praise for 'Lines Written among the Euganean Hills' and such insights as these by John Wilson show how time has verified the verdict of Shelley's early critics even without the formal statement of literary standards.

The Cenci

The year 1819 was, indeed, Shelley's 'annus mirabilis,' for he suffered much, both personally in the death of his son William, who followed his sister Clara to the grave, and politically in the so-called Manchester massacre, and he also produced his two most important large-scale works, *The Cenci* and *Prometheus Unbound*. Of the two only *The Cenci* was intended for the stage. Although Shelley pointed out, in the introduction, the difficulties inherent in producing the play ('This story of the Cenci is indeed eminently fearful and monstrous: anything like a dry exhibition of it on the stage would be insupportable.'), he hoped that Covent Garden would agree to stage it. In a letter to Peacock (July 1819) Shelley said that the 'principal character Beatrice is precisely fitted for Miss O'Neil, & it might even seem to have been written for her—(God forbid that I shd. see her play it—it wd. tear my nerves to pieces) and in all respects it is fitted only for Covent Garden. The chief male character I confess I should be very unwilling that any one but Kean shd. play—that is impossible, & I must be contented with an inferior actor.'[29]

The play is not, of course, very stageworthy, although Shelley thought it compared favorably with Coleridge's *Remorse* (which is not a very remarkable play either). Again to Peacock (July 1819), Shelley wrote, 'I am strongly inclined . . . that as a composition it is certainly not inferior to any of the modern plays that have been acted, with the exception of *Remorse*.'[30] Both plays were generated by the general enthusiasm and excitement that accompanied the nineteenth-century rediscovery of Shakespeare and other Elizabethan dramatists. The numerous stagings and interpretations of Shakespeare sparked unusual interest in the theatre on the part of other Romantic poets such as Keats (*King Otho*) and even the Victorians. Both Tennyson and Browning tried their hand at the stage, but neither succeeded any better than Coleridge and Shelley.

The reasons for the low estate of nineteenth-century drama are probably legion. The immense size of the newer theatres necessarily led to disaster and limited originality, although the effort of imitating Shakespeare undoubtedly encouraged bombast and pretentious acting. The rebuilt Covent Garden of 1808 seated 3,000 and the new Drury

Lane, built in 1812, held even more. Sir John Vanbrugh, architect of Blenheim Palace, designed the Haymarket, so sacrificing acoustics to grandeur that Colley Cibber damned its 'extraordinary, and superfluous Space' in his 'Apology' (1740). Perhaps even more important for the serious dramatist is the taste of the audience, and in the nineteenth century the mob which preferred splendor, spectacle, and burlesque held sway. In general the best poets avoided the stage altogether except when pressed by men like Charles Macready who hoped that Elizabethan imitations like Browning's *Strafford* (1837) would close the gap between the public and serious theatre.

It was probably inevitable that Shelley would fail as a dramatist, for unlike Keats, he was not even a regular theatre attender. He knew nearly nothing about stagecraft, and it is perhaps a mark of his genius that *The Cenci* is stageable at all. (The play was first performed by the Shelley Society in 1886.) As Shelley himself later realized and wrote to John Gisborne on October 22, 1821, 'You might as well go to a ginshop for a leg of mutton, as expect anything human or earthly from me.'[31] As a drama, *The Cenci* fails on this very point. Even the early reviewers, in addition to their horror about the action itself, noted that the play failed to dramatize real people and real passions, but rather provided an opportunity for two characters to carry on a dialogue of ideas.

Reviewers both sympathetic and hostile to Shelley found the plot line of *The Cenci* objectionable. In 1818 Shelley read the story of Count Cenci, who gloats over the murder of two sons, and who forces incestuous relationships on his daughter Beatrice, and he found the tale a ready vehicle for his customary attacks on the institutionalization of evil in the church and society. Greed supposedly motivates both the Count and the Church, which profits from the Count's indemnities while he lives and which will inherit the family wealth after the execution of Beatrice and her helpers in the murder of her father.

In this post-Freudian age, accustomed to reels of violence, rape, and sordidness, the critical furore over the action is nearly incomprehensible. Although Leigh Hunt called *The Cenci* the 'greatest production of the day' (*The Examiner*, March 19, 1820),[32] most reviewers, like the writer for *The Monthly Magazine* (No. 34), were appalled by this family history 'well adapted to the death-like atmosphere, and unwholesome regions, in which Mr. Shelley's muse delights to tag its wings.' Instead of terror, Shelley only succeeds in inspiring horror and disgust. *The Literary Gazette* (No. 35) was even more offended.

The reviewer begins, 'Of all the abominations which intellectual per-version, and poetical atheism have produced in our times, this tragedy appears to us to be the most abominable.' A fiend must have written the play, he says, 'for the entertainment of devils in hell.' He continues that 'the writer out herods Herod, and outrages possibility in his per-sonation of villainy, by making Count Cenci a character which trans-forms Richard III, an Iago, a Sir Giles Overreach comparatively into angels of light.'

The thought of incest was particularly offensive, too offensive even for some reviewers to name. *The London Magazine* (No. 36) noted that Shelley 'turns from war, rapine, murder, seduction, and infidelity— the vices and calamities with the description of which our common nature and common experience permits the generality of persons to sympathize—to cull some morbid and maniac sin of rare and doubtful occurrence.' *The Monthly Review* (No. 43) could not understand why Shelley chose incest and murder for the modern stage. Such a decision was 'manifest proof of the rudeness and barbarism of a newly-born, or lately-reviewing, literature.' In the same vein, but with more attention or principles of dramatic craftsmanship, *The British Review and London Critical Journal* (No. 45) commented: 'Incestuous rape, murder, the rack, and the scaffold are not the proper materials of the tragic Muse: crimes and punishments are not in themselves dramatic, though the conflict of passions which they occasion, and from which they arise, often is so.'

Several other reviewers also criticized from more clearly enunciated principles. *The Theatrical Inquisitor and Monthly Memoir* (No. 37) drew attention to the low taste of the London theatre audience. Although 'audiences are universally the dupes of feeling and that feeling is too often the wrong one,' the contemporary London stage, he says, suffers from even worse maladies than the tastes of the mob.

The patent puppet-shows of this mighty metropolis are swayed and supplied by individuals who have no emulation but in the race of gain; rash, ignorant, and rapacious, they have rendered the stage a medium of senseless amusement, and if their sordid earnings could be secured by a parricidal sacrifice of the drama itself, we do not scruple to confess our belief that such a detestable sacrifice would be readily effected.

For this reason, the reviewer urges Shelley to give up the stage and devote his talent and energies to something else than the 'loathsome honours of play-house approbation.' A fragmentary philosophy of poetry undergirds the comments of the reviewer in *The New Monthly Magazine and Universal Register* (No. 38) who felt that *The Cenci* story was not only unfit to be told merely as historic truth but even more inappropriate for poetry. Although the imagination is able to soften sorrow and, by its mediating power, to reconcile man to the vicissitudes and brevity of life in this world, it cannot charm away the repulsive and loathsome. Since imagination cannot blend with grief of this magnitude, it only outlines the blackness of *The Cenci* more clearly and fearfully. Beauties may be thrown around such crimes and suffering, but 'as they cannot mingle with their essence they will but increase their horrors, as flowers fantastically braided round a corpse instead of lending their bloom to the cheek, render its lividness more sickening.' This theory of poetry certainly limits the power and influence of poetry, and, some would say, denies poetry its legitimate place as conveyor of man's most essential wisdom about the mysteries of the universe. Few critics today would argue that the imagination is unable to cope with the darkest events in man's individual and communal existence, but, in defense of the critic, few writers since Wordsworth have given thought to finding the 'strength which remains behind' of 'the soothing thoughts that spring out of human suffering' let alone the 'years that bring the philosophic mind.' In the opinion of *The Independent or London Literary and Political Review* (No. 44), 'Improvement and innocent pleasure should be its [poetry's] aim.'

As a play, the critics agree that Shelley's language in *The Cenci* is equal to the best poetry he has written. *The London Magazine and Monthly Critical and Dramatic Review* (No. 36) in a series of truly perceptive comments on the Cockney School, admitted that Shelley has 'more fervid imagination and splendid talents than nine-tenths' of his companions. 'The rich yet delicate imagery that is every where scattered over it, is like the glowing splendour of the setting sun.' *The New Monthly Magazine* (No. 38) praised the diction of the play which is 'scarcely ever overloaded with imagery which the passion does not naturally create.' *The Edinburgh Monthly Review* (No. 39) thought the middle acts contained the best poetry, but the action was too loathsome to quote. In spite of these beauties, the critic felt that Shelley had not 'mastered the very difficult art of English dramatic versification.' Still, that was a trivial matter, for Shelley's 'genius is rich to overflowing in all the nobler requisites for tragic excellence, and were he to choose and manage his themes with ... regard for the just opinion of the world, ... he might easily and triumphantly overtop all that has been written during the last century for the English stage.' *The London Magazine* (No. 40) admired the 'vigorous, clear, manly turn of expression' and asserted that 'his images constitute the very genius of poetry.' In one of the best reviews of the play as a drama, the critic for *The British Review and London Critical Journal* (No. 45) failed to join the general praise of Shelley's poetry. The reviewer insisted that there was nothing really dramatic about *The Cenci*, that versified dialogue is not drama, and that Shelley's language is loose and disjointed; sometimes ambitious, then bald, inelegant, and mosaic. To the twentieth-century reader of these reviews, what stands out is the unanimity of praise for Shelley's poetic powers. In spite of their distaste for the subject matter, nearly all of the critics agree that Shelley has not lost his power to strike the flaming image.

About the characters in the play, there is less unanimity. *The Literary Gazette* (No. 35) thought all the characters reprehensible: 'no good effect can be produced by the delineations of such diabolism . . . whoever may be the author of such a piece, we will assert, that Beelzebub alone is fit to be the prompter.' *The London Magazine and Monthly Critical and Dramatic Review* (No. 36) agreed. 'The characters . . . are of no mortal stamp; they are daemons in human guise, inscrutable in their actions, subtle in their revenge.' Such comments do not, of course, speak to the question of dramatic plausibility, a question which few of the critics take up. *The New Monthly Magazine and Universal Register* (No. 38) however, asserted that the characters with one exception are not only believable, but truly life-like. Shelley 'has at least shown himself capable . . . of endowing human characters with life, sympathy, and passion. With the exception of Cenci, who is half maniac and half fiend, his persons speak and act like creatures of flesh and blood, not like the problems of strange philosophy set in motion by galvanic art.'

The character of Beatrice stands out, of course, and intrigued the critics. As Neville Rogers points out, Shakespeare would have entitled the play, *The Tragical History of Beatrice Cenci.*[33] *The Theatrical Inquisitor* (No. 37) quoted her outbursts following the incestuous encounter with her father as evidence of fine and plausible character portrayal. Leigh Hunt, in *The Indicator* (No. 41) again championed Shelley and praised the character of Beatrice. He attempts, as usual, to explain Shelley's work and, in particular, to answer the critic's objections to Beatrice's refusal to admit her guilt. Beatrice is, according to Hunt, so repulsed by having murdered her father that 'she would almost persuade herself as well as others, that no such thing had actually taken place. . . . It is a lie told, as it were, for the role of nature, to save it the shame of a greater contradiction.'

Throughout these reviews of *The Cenci*, the reviewers grapple with a not very clearly articulated feeling that, in spite of their best efforts to understand and to correct, a revolution in English poetry and thought has occurred. In many ways these reviews repeat the critical attacks and clichés of the previous decade, but there is a growing realization that what had seemed to be an aberration, a perversion, a deliberate and immoral attack on solid English life is in reality a major intellectual event. *The London Magazine and Monthly Critical and Dramatic Review* (No. 36) sounded the alarm. Whereas earlier commentators had encouraged Shelley to model himself after Wordsworth, this reviewer, in his attack on the Cockney School, lumps Wordsworth, Coleridge, and Shelley into one diseased ball.

A few symptoms of this literary malady appeared as early as the year 1795, but it then assumed the guise of simplicity and pathos. It was a poetical Lord Fanny. It wept its pretty self to death by murmuring brooks, and rippling cascades, it heaved delicious sighs over sentimental lambs, and love-lorn sheep, apostrophized donkies in the innocence of primaeval nature; sung tender songs to tender nightingales; went to bed without a candle, that it might gaze on the chubby faces of the stars; discoursed sweet nothings to all who would listen to its nonsense; and displayed (horrendum dictu) the acute profundity of its grief in ponderous folios and spiral duodecimos.

In spite of the strenuous exertions of the critics who have not contracted this 'new species of intellectual dandyism, the evil has been daily and even hourly increasing.'

Shelley himself led some reviewers to see a relationship with Wordsworth, for in the preface to *The Cenci* he laid down some principles of language which sounded very much like Wordsworth's 'Preface' to the *Lyrical Ballads*: Shelley says, 'I entirely agree with those modern critics who assert that in order to move men to true sympathy we must use the familiar language of men. . . . But it must be the real language of men in general, and not that of any particular class to whose society the writer happens to belong.'[34] The reviewer for *The Monthly Review* (No. 43) said, 'Now what is all this but the exploded *Wordsworthean heresy*, that the language of poetry and the language of real life are the same?' In a similar vein, *The Independent* (No. 44) thought Shelley's philosophy not only objectionable, but also imitative. Byron treads the same path, but he at least 'mixes life and its scenes with its horrors; he sports and laughs at them.' And this, alas Shelley does not. The

London Magazine review (No. 40) repeats the oft heard charges of immorality, perversion of intellectual and religious qualities, and deformities of nature. But a new and now time-tested offense is added to the list. 'Like poor Tom, in Lear, whom the foul fiend has possessed for many a day, it will run through ditches, through quagmires, and through bogs, to see a man stand on his head for the exact space of half an hour. Ask the reason of this raging appetite for eccentricity, the answer is, such a thing is out of the beaten track of manhood, *ergo*, it is praiseworthy.' *The Independent, or London Literary and Political Review* (No. 44) sounded a similar warning, in an almost prophetic statement concerning the impending crisis between the artist and his public. The successful author, he says, must consult the wants, the wishes, and the interests of the many; 'and the many are not of an author's particular day—but they are the people of futurity. In this particular it is, that our modern great men fail. They write for themselves; not for the world; they feel as individuals, not as component poets of a great body.'

The individualism of these authors constitutes one important sign of this revolution, but another is the critics' comprehension that a totally new value system has taken hold. Up to this point, most of the reviewers felt that Shelley and his companions had either literally or figuratively sold their souls to the devil. Some critics hoped that, like Faustus in reverse, Shelley might yet be dragged kicking and screaming back from the fiery pit. *The Cenci* gave the reviewers an opportunity to contrast Shelley's work with the Elizabethan dramas they admired so highly, and also with ancient classical drama. Although modern critics would find their readings of these earlier tragedies difficult to accept and often facile, the reviewer for *The London Magazine* (No. 40) drew some conclusions which have since been supported by modern writers such as Murray Krieger and Morse Peckham.[35] As the *London* critic notes, the essential distinction between earlier tragedy and Shelley's version is the loss of transcendental order and supernatural authority. Writers like Shelley, he says, 'leave the nature of man bare and defenceless. . . . They render miserable man accountable for all his acts; his soul is the single source of all that occurs to him; he is forbidden to derive hope either from his own weakness or the strength of a great disposing authority, presiding over the world, and guiding it on principles that have relation to the universe.' This vision is, of course, quite unlike the classical tragic view, for 'the blackness and the storms suspended over the head of man, and which often discharged destruction on his fairest possessions, *hung from Heaven*, and above them there was light, and peace, and intelligence.' This description of a world without value except that imposed by man and originating in man coincides of course with Shelley's view that evil exists because man wills it to exist. But the description, combined with the emphasis on individualism and self-consciousness, proves that these early reviewers laid the foundation for the judgment of critics a century later.

Prometheus Unbound

Prometheus Unbound, according to *The London Magazine and Monthly Critical and Dramatic Review* (No. 51) is 'one of the most stupendous of those works which the daring and vigorous spirit of modern poetry and thought has created.' But not all reviewers agreed, and the division of critical opinion, which began immediately on publication and still haunts Shelley's reputation, is represented by the judgment of *The Quarterly Review* (No. 54). 'Mr. Shelley's poetry is, in sober sadness, drivelling prose run mad.'

In all of the reviews of *Prometheus Unbound* political and religious prejudices play a major role both in the condemnations and defenses. Although there is not unanimous praise for Shelley's genius such as he enjoyed earlier, there is substantial agreement on the significant issues. Critics on both sides recognized that *Prometheus Unbound* was an intellectual and stylistic watershed. The sympathetic *London Magazine* (No. 48) proclaimed that 'this poem is more completely the child of the *Time* than almost any other modern production: it seems immediately sprung from the throes of the great intellectual, political, and moral labour of nations.' In a long and abusive review in *The Quarterly Review* (No. 54), W. S. Walker, in contrast, held fast to the presuppositions of a previous age and literary fashion and condemned Shelley's stylistics. 'It seems to be his maxim, that reason and sound thinking are aliens in the dominions of the Muses, and that, should they ever be found wandering about the foot of Parnassus, they ought to be chased away as spies sent to discover the nakedness of the land.' The major intellectual shift represented by Shelley's handling of the Promethean theme was described by the perceptive reviewer in *The London Magazine and Monthly Critical and Dramatic Review* (No. 51). Whereas to Aeschylus the fate of Prometheus suggested the temporary predominance of brute force over intellect, the oppression of right by might, and the final deliverance of the spirit of humanity from the iron grasp of its foes, Aeschylus seems not to have placed symbolic meaning in Prometheus's deliverance. In Shelley's play, the deliverance of Prometheus is 'a symbol of the peaceful triumph of goodness over power; of the subjection of might to right ... To represent vividly and poetically this vast moral change is . . . the design of the drama.' Thus reviewers sympathetic and critical caught the intellectual and moral significance of *Prometheus Unbound*. To some, this monster need only suffer the scrutiny of public examination to be met with its deserved contempt. The reviewer for *The Literary Gazette* (No. 49) felt it his duty rather 'to stem such a tale of literary folly and corruption, than to promote its flooding over the country.' But as *Blackwood's Edinburgh Magazine* (No. 50) remarked, however men may disagree about Shelley's poetical power, 'there is one point in regard to which all must be agreed, and that is his Audacity.'

And disagree the critics did, and have ever since, about Shelley's poetical power in *Prometheus Unbound*. In place of the earlier universal praise for Shelley's genius, more reservations are voiced in these reviews than in earlier ones. *The Literary Gazette* (No. 49), using the figure of *Lear*'s Tom again, insisted that Shelley was a candidate for Bedlam. *The Monthly Review and British Register* (No. 53) repeated the inevitable pun that *Prometheus Unbound* will always remain unbound, but did affirm Shelley's genius. W. S. Walker in *The Quarterly Review* (No. 54) setting out with the avowed purpose of ending the question of Shelley's poetical merits, concluded, 'Poetical power can be shown only by writing good poetry and this Mr. Shelley has not yet done.'

Then, as now, the critical question centred on Shelley's use of similes and metaphors and the profusion of images. *Blackwood's Edinburgh Magazine* (No. 50) would not deny that Shelley demonstrated 'very extraordinary powers of language and imagination in his treatment of the allegory.' Although *Prometheus* is a pestiferous mixture, all who read carefully will agree it abounds in poetical beauties of the highest order. *The London Magazine and Monthly Critical and Dramatic Review* (No. 51) praised the 'profusion of felicitously compounded epithets' and the imagery which the reviewer feels resembles that of Aeschylus and Sophocles.

On the other hand, some sophisticated and provincial journals recognized that Shelley's style in *Prometheus Unbound* represented a new direction in English verse, a direction not to be tolerated or encouraged. *The Lonsdale Magazine or Provincial Repository* (No. 52) compared *Prometheus* to the song of the Sirens. Thomas Paine had been too low and scurrilous to attract even the illiterate, and the *Edinburgh* reviewers were too absurd and Godwin too metaphysical to attract the populace, but when writers like Byron and Shelley 'envelope their destructive theories in language, both intended and calculated to entrance the soul by its melodious richness, to act upon the passions without consulting the reason, . . . then it is that the unwary are in danger of being misled, the indifferent of being surprised, and the innocent of being seduced.' Other reviewers also thought that Shelley had abrogated reason. *The Monthly Review and British Register* (No. 53) remarked, 'There is an excess of fancy which rapidly degenerates into nonsense: if the *sublime* be clearly allied to the ridiculous, the *fanciful* is twin-sister to the foolish and really Mr. Shelley has worthily maintained the relationship.' But *The Literary Gazette* (No. 49) attacked more seriously and viciously. 'If this be genuine inspiration, and not the greatest absurdity, then is farce sublime, and maniacal raving the perfection of reasoning: then were all the bards of other times, Homer, Virgil, Horace, drivellers.' All of these reviewers thought that Shelley's poetic style was symptomatic of a new disease in the literary world.

They diagnosed the malady much as twentieth-century formalists such as Cleanth Brooks, T. S. Eliot, and John Crowe Ransom have judged Shelley and the other Romantic writers. In his 1942 essay, 'The Language of Paradox,' Brooks condemned Shelley's 'loosely decorative' and 'sometimes too gaudy' metaphor.[36] This attack was foreshadowed by the reviewer for *The Literary Gazette, and Journal of the Belles Lettres* (No. 49) who asserted that the chief secret of Shelley's poetry was 'merely opposition of words, phrases, and sentiments, so violent as to be utter nonsense.' He continues, 'The glimpses of meaning which we have here, are soon smothered by contradictory terms and metaphor carried to excess.' He also attacks Shelley's prolific use of colors, pointing out that in seventeen lines, Shelley employs seven positive colours, and nearly as many shades. He concludes, 'Surely, the author looks at nature through a prism instead of spectacles.' It is interesting to note that Brooks repeated these attacks, arguing that the Romantics were led astray by a fallacious belief that imagery was an extrinsic and external decoration, in spite of clear evidence that none of the Romantics held this view.[37]

In *The Quarterly Review* (No. 54) W. S. Walker discussed the question of Shelley's imagery in even greater detail and added another criticism which the New Critics would later repeat: the asserted lack of definiteness and concreteness in Shelley's imagery. In Walker's words, 'We are dazzled by the multitude of words which sound as if they denoted something very grand or splendid: fragments of images pass in crowds before us; but when the procession has gone by, and the tumult is over, not a trace of it remains upon the memory.' John Crowe Ransom, following T. E. Hulme, was to make the same attack in his comments on Aristotle, arguing that the accurate descriptions of things is enough for poetry.[38] Walker concluded: 'It is easy to read without attention; but it is difficult to conceive how an author, unless his intellectual habits are thoroughly depraved, should not take the trouble to observe whether his imagination has definite forms before it, or is gazing in stupid wonder on assemblages of brilliant words.' The similarity of the attacks on Shelley's imagery by contemporary reviewers and twentieth-century formalist critics, while perhaps reflecting some common aesthetic and philosophic presuppositions, demonstrates that Shelley's early reviewers were at least as astute and perhaps even less biased, considering their frequent praise of Shelley's genius, than the latter-day formalists.

In addition to the reviews and notices of specific works, in 1820 and 1821 a number of journals and periodicals discussed Shelley's reputation and contributions in general terms, attempting to survey his literary career to that point. These notices, sometimes brief, on occasion lengthy, agree, with few exceptions, that Shelley stands near the forefront of contemporary poets. Hazlitt in *The London Magazine* (No. 63) charged that Shelley had 'a fever in his blood, a maggot in his brain, a hectic flutter in his speech, which mark out the philosophic fanatic.' Other reviewers emphasized his solid position in English literary history. *The Honeycomb* (No. 58) regretted Shelley's alliance with Leigh Hunt. Shelley rises 'so far above his compeers', 'that we should never have classed Mr. Shelley with Leigh Hunt, or even with Barry Cornwall, as in power and extent of intellect, richness of imagination, and skill in numbers, he is far their superior.' The reviewer for *The Honeycomb* believed that Hunt had received 'as much encouragement as he deserves, or perhaps too much, and Barry Cornwall has gained certainly a greater reputation than he is entitled to,' but Shelley has never been adequately appreciated. The reason for this neglect, according to the reviewer, is the now familiar charge of vagueness. Shelley 'writes in a spirit which people do not comprehend: there is something too mystical in what he says—something too high or too deep for common comprehensions.' In the December 23, 1821 issue of *The Champion* (No. 64) the same charge is repeated, in nearly identical words, but prefaced with 'He writes in a spirit which the *million* do not comprehend.' Still, the reviewer recalls in a comparison with Shakespeare that there are many passages in the latter's plays which do not admit exact definition.

The *London Magazine and Theatrical Inquisitor* (No. 61) defended Shelley's views while admitting excesses of idealism. Nevertheless the reviewer believes that Shelley's prophecies of a world void of civil and religious prejudices are not unfounded, 'that the days are not far distant when the Deity shall once again be imaged in the beasts of his creations.' As a poet, Shelley 'is perhaps the most intensely sublime writer of his day, and, with the exception of Wordsworth, is more highly imaginative, than any other living poet.' While Shelley can never become a popular poet because he is too visionary, 'in intensity of description, depth of feeling, and richness of language, Mr. Shelley is infinitely superior to Lord Byron.'

By 1821, Shelley's reputation then was firmly fixed. In spite of serious reservations on the part of the conservative press about Shelley's radicalism, there was substantial agreement that *Prometheus Unbound* was Shelley's most significant work to date. They also agreed that Shelley stood near to Wordsworth and Byron although he would probably never be as popular. Time and twentieth-century critics have not seriously modified this judgment. While Shelley still claims his devoted followers who admire his profusion of imagery and the depth of his intellect, both Wordsworth and Byron have a popular appeal which Shelley has not achieved, and probably will not ever achieve. Nevertheless, no one can deny Shelley a place in the first rank of nineteenth-century English poets.

In the final year and one-half of Shelley's life, from January 1821 to July 1822, Shelley wrote and published several major pieces of poetry, particularly 'Epipsychidion,' 'Adonais,' 'Hellas,' 'The Triumph of Life,' and a host of minor poems. For whatever reason, Shelley's residence in Italy, publication difficulties, public indifference, or Shelley's sudden and tragic death which overshadowed his entire career, these later poems received relatively little critical attention.

'Epipsychidion' was noticed twice in *The Gossip*.[39] On June 23, 1821, the critic attacked what he saw to be Shelley's implied immorality and praise of free love. The second notice, a satiric attack in the form of a letter to the editor, took issue with Shelley's language and imagery. ' "It is poetry *intoxicated*," said Clementina. "It is poetry in *delirium*," said I.' A third notice in *Blackwood's Edinburgh*

Magazine (February 1822) is chiefly interesting because the reviewer rightly identifies Shelley as the anonymous author of 'Epipsychidion.'[40]

'Adonais,' because of its subject, the death of Keats, and the attacks on the reviewers for failing to recognize Keats's genius, received more attention than did 'Hellas,' but few reviewers saw the poem as the work of art Shelley claimed it was. On June 5, 1821 Shelley wrote to Gisborne: 'I have been engaged these last days in composing a poem on the death of Keats, which will shortly be finished; and I anticipate the pleasure of reading it to you, as one of the very few persons who will be interested in it and understand it. It is a highly wrought *piece of art*, perhaps better in point of composition than anything I have written.'[41] Although 'Adonais' has a place among the finest of nineteenth-century elegies, contemporary reviewers failed to see the unity and craft which Shelley believed the poem possessed. *The Literary Gazette and Journal of Belles Lettres* (No. 67) refused to repeat its earlier conviction of the author's 'incurable absurdity,' but the reviewer did assert that 'Adonais' was 'unconnected, interjectional, and nonsensical.' He continued,

The poetry of the work is *contemptible*—a mere collection of bloated words heaped on each other without order, harmony, or meaning; the refuse of a schoolboy's commonplace book, full of the vulgarisms of pastoral poetry, yellow gems and blue stars, bright Phoebus and rosy-fingered Aurora; and of this stuff is Keats's wretched Elegy compiled.

Blackwood's Edinburgh Magazine (No. 68) also found the poem absurd, not only in its contention that negative reviews had killed Keats, but also in its details. The poem proves 'that it is possible to write two sentences of pure nonsense out of every three. A more faithful calculation would bring us to ninety-nine out of every hundred, or,—as the present consists of only fifty-five stanzas,—leaving about five readable lines in the entire.' Undoubtedly Shelley's unfortunate characterizations of the reviewers as 'herded wolves' and 'obscene ravens' provoked the vicious attacks (thus ironically almost proving Shelley's assertion), but clearly both the *Quarterly* and *Blackwood's* felt that Shelley was beyond all hope, that he had hardened his heart against all that was good and decent, and that he had set his face like flint toward perdition and damnation. Leigh Hunt labored loyally in *The Examiner* to counteract this judgment, but his defenses only fanned the reviewers' fury and verified their opinions about 'the Satanic School.'

'Hellas' fared little better than 'Adonais' either in quality or quantity. *The General Weekly Register of News, Literature, Law, Politics, and Commerce* (No. 70) devoted a lengthy notice to 'Hellas,' not because it deserved so much attention but because of Shelley's reputation. While 'Hellas' is 'not entirely devoid of merit, [it] is but a bad specimen of Mr. Shelley's powers, and but ill calculated to increase the former fame of its author.'

Clearly the last works of Shelley did not receive their just notice from the reviews. The failure to devote adequate attention to these works undoubtedly stemmed in part from the religious and moral prejudices of the journals and their reviewers. On the other hand, historical accidents of delays in mail (inevitable in the transmission of correspondence from Italy into England and back) and Shelley's shocking death at the height of his genius also contributed to this neglect. However, with the exception of these last reviewers, a close reading of the entire contemporary critical literature reveals that the reviewers and critics, far from neglecting Shelley, firmly established him as one of England's finest poets in spite of a cultural and intellectual milieu which from this distance seems almost benighted. While the reviewers often opposed Shelley's religious, social and political ideas, they recognized his genius. And when they took exception to his style, their judgments have been verified by the tools and experience of the twentieth century, an age which prides itself on its use of sophisticated critical apparatus. It was the task of the mid-Victorian critics to consolidate Shelley's position in literary history and to demonstrate that Shelley's alleged radicalism was indeed the cry of a prophet in the wilderness who did not live to see the rough places made smooth.

SHELLEY IN THE TWENTIETH CENTURY

The conflicting currents and eddies which threatened Shelley's posthumous reputation in the nineteenth century mark the scholarship and criticism of the twentieth century as well. The best and most authoritative survey, co-authored by Bennett Weaver and Donald Reiman, appears in the Shelley chapter of *The English Romantic Poets: A Review of Research and Criticism* (1972) edited by Frank Jordan, Jr. No attempt to condense or spotlight key points in that survey can do justice to their work or its subject. The authors demonstrate that the judgment of Shelley's contemporary critics still stands. For the most part one is either greatly attracted or greatly repelled by Shelley's poetry. Few readers or critics remain indifferent.

The student who wishes to pursue Shelley's fortunes and his reputation in greater detail should consult Newman I. White's *The Unextinguished Hearth* and *Shelley* as well as Sylva Norman's *Flight of the Skylark: The Development of Shelley's Reputation* and Carl Woodring's 'Dip of the Skylark' (*KSJ*, 1960). The reaction to Shelley in America has been recounted in admirable detail in Julia Power's *Shelley in America in the Nineteenth Century*.

Twentieth-century readers of Shelley, like their nineteenth-century counterparts, face a serious difficulty in that no complete and scholarly edition of Shelley's works is available. If Neville Rogers's projected four volumes of Shelley's poetry meets expectations, part of the dilemma will be resolved. In the meantime, Thomas Hutchinson's edition (Oxford, 1904), which forms the basis for G. M. Matthews's Oxford Standard Authors Edition, and the ten-volume Julian Edition (1926–30) of prose and poetry edited by Ingpen and Peck are most frequently used. But none is satisfactory, for each is either incomplete or textually corrupt. For the letters, students must consult Frederick L. Jones's *Letters of Percy Bysshe Shelley*, but these volumes will have to be re-edited after Kenneth Neill Cameron's *Shelley and his Circle* has been completed. As Weaver and Reiman have emphasized, 'Shelley's text is in flux.'

The twentieth century has treated Shelley as a poet, rather harshly. The wave of 'New Criticism' which began in the 1930s and crested in the 1950s attacked Shelley's poetry for vagueness and lack of organic unity, for ambiguity, tension, and irony. Typical of these judgments are T. S. Eliot's *The Use of Poetry and the Use of Criticism* (1933), F. R. Leavis's *Revaluations*, and the criticism of John Crowe Ransom and Allen Tate. Important dissenting cries were sounded by C. S. Lewis in 'Shelley, Dryden, and Mr. Eliot' (*Rehabilitations*, 1939), by Richard Harter Fogle in *The Imagery of Keats and Shelley* (1949), and by Frederick A. Pottle in 'The Case for Shelley' (*PMLA*, 1952). Other works, particularly Carlos Baker's *Shelley's Major Poetry: The Fabric of a Vision* (1948), and the various studies by Earl R. Wasserman, did a great deal toward rescuing Shelley from the prejudices which marked the writing of the New Critics.

The debate about Shelley's personality which began while he still lived and which produced fourteen biographies by 1887, (no one of which, as Newman Ivey White pointed out, agreed with the other thirteen) was carried on into the twentieth century. N. I. White's *Shelley* (1940; revised 1947) still stands as one of the best biographies of literary men available, a model for all aspiring biographers. In the less objective stream of biography, both professional and amateur psychologists have applied whatever psychological theory is fashionable to explain Shelley's personality and behaviour. Carl Grabo's *Shelley's Eccentricities* (1950) tried to combat these less than fruitful endeavours by arguing that geniuses like Shelley are 'the only sane or relatively sane beings in a half-mad world.'

Shelley's ideas have been the subject of a number of significant and helpful studies and commentaries, many of which have helped to enhance his intellectual stature. The sources for Shelley's ideas in the cultural milieu of the late-eighteenth and early-nineteenth centuries have been found and this work has strengthened Shelley's reputation as a thinker. For example, A. M. D. Hughes's *The Nascent Mind of Shelley* (1947), and Kenneth Neill Cameron's *The Young Shelley: Genesis of a Radical* (1950) explore Shelley's early work, and find a significant intellectual foundation for the poems up to and including *Queen Mab*.

The extent of the influence of Platonism and Neo-platonism is still not settled. James A. Natopoulos found Platonic influence in nearly every line of Shelley (*The Platonism of Shelley*, 1949), while Joseph Barrell in *Shelley and the Thought of his Time* (1947) has sought to place the Platonism in broader perspective. The sum effect of these works and others, like Pulos's *The Deep Truth: A Study of Shelley's Skepticism* and Wasserman's several books, has been to restore Shelley's reputation as a thinker as well as to mitigate the popular view of a frenzied, unthinking, half-mad poet.

A promising and rewarding area of Shelley studies has been undertaken by critics who have examined recurring patterns of Shelley's poetic imagery and have sought to find the source for his imagery in the mythic memory. Richard Harter Fogle's *The Imagery of Keats and Shelley* (1949) and Peter H. Butter's *Shelley's Idols of the Cave* (1954) began this work, and Harold Bloom's two volumes, *Shelley's Mythmaking* (1959) and *The Visionary Company* (1961), have carried this movement into comparative studies with Spenser, Milton, Yeats, and Stevens. As well as shedding light on the mythic imagination, such criticism has opened new vistas into Shelley's intellectual framework and his relationship to the Anglo-American poetic tradition. Perhaps no other method of literary inquiry has done more to vitiate the attacks of the early twentieth-century critics.

In spite of the well-intentioned efforts of scholars to produce less corrupt texts of Shelley's poetry, prose, and letters, and in spite of the monumental efforts of critics to provide objective biography, to understand Shelley's poetic methodology, and to relate his work to the mythic patterns which underlie all literature, Shelley's reputation in the twentieth century does not differ greatly from what it did when he died. To some readers, he is a source of joy. To others, no amount of critical and scholarly endeavour can save him. Perhaps Shelley wrote the best judgment of all, when he complained in a letter dated September 6, 1819 to his publisher Charles Ollier, 'The ill account you give of the success of my Poetical attempts sufficiently accounts for your silence; but I believe the truth is, I write less for the public than for myself.'[42]

NOTES

1 John Wilson, *Noctes Ambrosianae* (1857), i, p. 143. Appeared in *Blackwood's Edinburgh Magazine* for March 1822.

2 *Blackwood's Edinburgh Magazine* (November 1819), vi, pp. 148–54 and (September 1820), vii, pp. 679–87.

3 E. J. Trelawney, *Recollections of the Last Days of Shelley and Byron* (1859), pp. 13–14.

4 'Conversations and Reminiscences recorded by the Bishop of Lincoln,' *The Prose Works of William Wordsworth*, ed. Grosart (1876), iii, pp. 458–67.

5 *Henry Crabb Robinson on Books and Their Writers*, ed. Edith J. Morley (1938), i, p. 351.

6 John Morley, *Life of William Ewart Gladstone* (1903), i, p. 136.

7 Edith C. Batho, *The Later Wordsworth* (1935), p. 101.

8 Frederick Maurice, *Maurice: The Life of Frederick Denison Maurice* (1804), i, p. 199.

9 *The Letters of Ralph Waldo Emerson*, ed. Rusk (1939), vi, p. 19.

10 Julia Power, *Shelley in America* (1940, 1969), p. 4.

11 Ibid.

12 July 15, 1828, pp. 245–7.

13 June 1836, xix, pp. 257–87.

14 September 1825–March 1826, i, pp. 53–4.

15 December 1843, iii, pp. 603–23.

16 April 1836, ii, pp. 326–36.

17 December 1840, vi, pp. 826–8.

18 *The Literary Panorama* (February 1811), ix, pp. 252–3.

19 Newman Ivey White, *The Unextinguished Hearth* (1966), p. 45.

20 White, p. 45.

21 In 1821, *Queen Mab* was reprinted without Shelley's permission. Shelley objected not so much to the piracy as to the fact that it was an immature work. See *The Investigator* for 1822, v, pp. 315–73 as an example of the later critical treatment of this poem.

22 The pamphlet is not reprinted for lack of space, but has been reprinted in White's *The Unextinguished Hearth*, pp. 62–95.

23 Ibid., p. 71.

24 Ibid., p. 75.

25 Ibid., p. 75.

26 See Northrop Frye, *Romanticism Reconsidered* (New York, 1963) and Harold Bloom, *The Visionary Company* (New York, 1961).

27 *Letters of Percy Bysshe Shelley*, ed. Jones (1964), II, p. 163.

28 *Complete Works of Shelley*, ed. Ingpen (1965), x, p. 134.

29 *Letters of Percy Bysshe Shelley*, II, pp. 102–3.

30 Ibid., II, p. 102.

31 Ibid., II, p. 363.

32 *The Examiner*, March 19, 1820 (no. 638, pp. 190–1).

33 *Selected Poetry of Shelley*, ed. Neville Rogers (1968), p. 436.

34 *Complete Works of Shelley*, ii, p. 73.

35 See Murray Krieger, *The Tragic Vision* (New York, 1960) and Morse Peckham, *Beyond the Tragic Vision* (New York, 1962).

36 Cleanth Brooks, 'The Language of Paradox,' *The Language of Poetry* (Princeton, 1942).

37 See the essay by R. W. Fogle, 'Romantic Bards and Metaphysical Reviewers,' *ELH*, XII (1945), pp. 221–50 for a defense of Shelley's imagery.

38 John Crowe Ransom, *The World's Body* (New York, 1938).

39 *The Gossip*, June 23, 1821 and July 14, 1821.

40 *Blackwood's Edinburgh Magazine*, February 1882, xi, pp. 237–8.

41 *Letters of Percy Bysshe Shelley*, II, pp. 293–4.

42 *Letters of Percy Bysshe Shelley*, II, p. 116.

Note on the Text

In reviews and articles typographical errors in the originals have been silently corrected and the form of reference to titles has been regularized. The spelling of the names of Shelley and Shakespeare has also been standardized. Quotations from letters and journals are reprinted exactly from the standard texts. Omissions and ellipses are marked in the text or noted in the headnotes when only extracts appear.

ORIGINAL POETRY, BY VICTOR AND CAZIRE

1810

1 Unsigned review, *The Literary Panorama*

October 1810, viii, 1063–6

Surely modern poets are the most unhappy of men! Their imaginations are perpetually haunted with terrors. While others are congratulating themselves on a beautiful day, and basking in the enlivening rays of the sun, these votaries of the Muse of misery see nothing but glooms, and listen to the pealing thunder, distant or near, as fancy dictates, 'not loud but deep.' In the evening 'black whirlwinds,' and 'yelling fiends' beset them on every side, in spite of the golden beams of the declining sun, or the cheerful azure of a cloudless day. At night,—ghosts,—hob-goblins,—shadowy forms, death, devils, disaster, and damnation dance around them, in dire dismay, till their 'souls are chilled,'—their 'blood is frozen,'—their 'heart sinks within them,' and miserable they are, to be sure! At length they commit their sorrows to paper; they publish, and the public are enraptured with their sufferings. Well, after all, the Fairy people for our money! There was something *so* blithesome and gay in the gambols of the elfin crew 'that frisked in the frolicsome round'; something *so* equitable in their rewards and punishments! We who might confidently expect to find 'sixpence in one of our shoes,' while lubber louts intent on mischief might be pinch'd and pull'd without mercy,—we regret the change. Willingly would we renounce all the phantoms and spectres of Monk Lewis and Mrs. Radcliffe, to enjoy a rencounter with a ring of these lightly tripping dancers, whether by moon light, or star light. But alas!

> Farewell rewards and fairies,
> Good housewives now may say;
> For now foul sluts in dairies
> Do fare as well as they!

41

As sung the witty Bishop Corbet, long ago. Now, under the fascination of these cheerful ideas, what can we say to such terrific meteors
of song as those which flit before us in these poems? e.g.

THE UNEXTINGUISHED HEARTH

Horror covers all the sky,
   Clouds of darkness blot the moon
Prepare, for mortal thou must die,
   Prepare to yield thy soul up soon.

Fierce the tempest raves around,
   Fierce the volleyed lightnings fly,
Crashing thunder shakes the ground,
   Fire and tumult fill the sky.—

Hark! the tolling village bell,
   Tells the hour of midnight come,
Now can blast the powers of Hell,
   Fiend-like goblins now can roam.

So, so; we cannot be frightened by a spectre without a tempest, it
seems: certainly all poets of feeling will allow that a tempest affords
a delightful opportunity for strong painting, glowing description, and
the full range of fine compound epithets: intermingled with blue
lightning, chilling blasts, howling storms, sulphurous clouds, and black
marble tombs; or gaping graves, as the case may be.

Can any thing possibly be finer—that is, more terrific—that is—
ahem!—than the following?—

The night it was bleak the fierce storm raged around,
The lightning's blue firelight flashed on the ground,
Strange forms seemed to flit,—and howl tidings of fate,
As Agnes advanced to the sepulchre gate.—

The youth struck the portal,—the echoing sound
Was fearfully rolled midst the tombstones around,
The blue lightning gleamed o'er the dark chapel spire,
And tinged were the storm clouds with sulphurous fire.

Still they gazed on the tombstone where Conrad reclined,
Yet they shrank at the cold chilling blast of the wind,
When a strange silver brilliance pervaded the scene,
And a figure advanced—tall in form—fierce in mien.

A mantle encircled his shadowy form,
As light as a gossamer borne on the storm,
Celestial terror sat throned in his gaze,
Like the midnight pestiferous meteor's blaze.

Spirit.

Thy father, Adolphus, was false, false as hell,
And Conrad has cause to remember it well,
He ruined my Mother, despised me his son,
I quitted the world ere my vengeance was done.

I was nearly expiring—'twas close of the day,—
A demon advanced to the bed where I lay,
He gave me the power from whence I was hurled,
To return to revenge, to return to the world,—

THE JUVENILE PERIOD

Now Adolphus I'll seize thy best loved in my arms,
I'll drag her to Hades, all blooming in charms,
On the black whirlwind's thundering pinion I'll ride,
And fierce yelling fiends shall exult o'er thy bride.

He spoke and extended his ghostly arms wide,
Majestic advanced with a swift, noiseless stride,
He clasped the fair Agnes—he raised her on high,
And clearing the roof sped his way to the sky—

All was now silent,—and over the tomb,
Thicker, deeper, was swiftly extended a gloom,—
Adolphus in horror sank down on the stone,
And his fleeting soul fled with a harrowing groan.

December 1809.

December! What a dismal ditty for Christmas! no, Sir:—

ever 'gainst that Season
Wherein our Saviour's birth is celebrated,
——————————no spirit dares stir abroad;
The nights are wholesome, then; no planets strike,
No fairy takes, no witch hath power to charm,
So hallow'd and so gracious is the time!

However, we must not part with our poets unkindly; we adopt their own good wishes (*numberless* though they be) in their own words and verses:

May misfortunes, dear Girl, ne'er thy happiness cloy,
May thy days glide in peace, love, comfort, and joy,

43

May thy tears with soft pity for other woes flow,
Oh dear! what sentimental stuff I've written,
Only fit to tear up and play with a kitten.
Now adieu, my dear—, I'm sure I must tire,
For if I do, you may throw it into the fire,
So accept the best love of your cousin and friend,
Which brings this nonsensical rhyme to an end.

2. Unsigned notice, *The British Critic*

April 1811, xxxvii, 408–9

When we ventured to say that poetical taste and genius abound in the present day, we by no means intended to assert, that we always meet with either the one or the other. Miserable, indeed, are the attempts which we are often doomed to encounter; so miserable sometimes that it seems quite wonderful how any individuals fancying themselves able to write should be so far behind their contemporaries. One of the unknown authors of this volume begins by complaining, most sincerely, we are convinced, of the difficulty of writing grammatically, but there is another difficulty, which seems never to have entered the lady's head (if a lady!)—that is, the difficulty of writing *metrically*. In this she is still less successful than in the other, and does not seem at all to suspect it. The verse intended to be used is that of 'The Bath Guide,' and so it is *sometimes*; but sometimes also not. For example;

> This they friendly will tell, and n'er make you blush,
> With a jeering look, taunt, or an O fie! tush!
> Then straight all your thoughts in black and white put,
> Not minding the *if's*, the *be's*, and the *but's*. P. 6.

Again,

> My excuse shall be hunble, and faithful, and true
> *Such as I fear can be made but by few.*—P. 7.

44

This *humble* and *faithful* lady lays claims *only* to 'sense, wit, and grammar!' Yet she tells her friend;

> Be not a coward, shrink not to a tense,
> But read it all over, *and make it out sense.*
> *What a tiresome girl!*—pray soon make an end. P. 9.

This last line, if not measure, contains at least truth in the first part, and a reasonable wish in the second.

Two epistles, in this exquisite style, begin the volume, which is filled up by songs of sentimental nonsense, and very absurd tales of horror. It is perfectly clear, therefore, that whatever we may say in favour of the poetry of this time, such volumes as this have no share in the commendation. One thing may be said in its favour, that the printer has done his task well; would he had been employed on something better! If he has taste as well as skill, he must dread the names of Victor and Cazire.

3. Unsigned notice, under 'Criticisms 1811,' *The Poetical Register and Repository of Fugitive Poetry for 1810–1811*

1814, 617

There is no 'original *poetry*' in this volume; there is nothing in it but downright scribble. It is really annoying to see the waste of paper which is made by such persons as the putters-together of these sixty-four pages. There is, however, one consolation for the critics who are obliged to read all this sort of trash. It is, that the crime of publishing is generally followed by condign punishment, and in the chilling tones of the booksellers, when to the questions of the anxious rhymer, how the book sells, he answers that not more than half a dozen copies have been sold.

ZASTROZZI, A ROMANCE

1810

4. Unsigned notice, *The Gentleman's Magazine and Historical Chronicle*

September 1810, lxxx, 258, part 2

A short, but well-told tale of horror, and, if we do not mistake, not from an ordinary pen. The story is so artfully conducted that the reader cannot easily anticipate the denouement, which is conducted on the principles of moral justice: and, by placing the scene on the Continent, the Author has availed himself of characters and vices which, however useful to narratives of this description, thank God, are not to be found in this country.

5. Unsigned review, *The Critical Review and Annals of Literature*

November 1810, xxi, 329–31

Zastrozzi is one of the most savage and improbable demons that ever issued from a diseased brain. His mother, who had been seduced by an Italian nobleman by the name of Verezzi, and left by him in wretchedness and want, conjures her son on her death bed, to avenge her wrongs on Verezzi and his progeny forever! Zastrozzi fulfills her diabolical injunctions, by assassinating her seducer; and pursues the young Verezzi, his son, with unrelentless and savage cruelty. The first scene which opens this *shameless* and disgusting volume represents Verezzi in a damp cell, chained to the wall.

His limbs, which not even a little straw kept from the rock, were fixed by immense staples to the flinty floor; and but one of his hands was left at liberty to take the scanty pittance of bread and water which was daily allowed him.

This beautiful youth (as he is described), is released from his confinement by the roof of the cell falling in during a most terrific storm. He is then conducted, though in a raging fever, by the emissaries of the fiend-like Zastrozzi to the cottage of an old woman which stands on a lone heath, removed from all human intercourse. From this place he contrives to escape, and we find him at another old woman's cottage near Passau. Here he saves the life of Mathilda, La Contessa di Laurentini, who, in a fit of desperation and hopeless love for the Adonis Verezzi, plunges herself into the river. The author does not think proper to account to his readers when and how these two persons had become acquainted, or how Verezzi could know the unbounded and disgusting passion which Mathilda entertains for him. It is vaguely intimated that Verezzi loves, and is beloved by, Julia Marchesa di Strobazzo, who is as amiable as Mathilda is diabolical; but we are left to conjecture how the connection between Zastrozzi and Mathilda is brought about. But these inconsistencies need not surprise us, when we reflect that a more discordant, disgusting, and despicable performance has not, we are persuaded, issued from the press for some time.

Verezzi accompanies Mathilda to Passau, with whom he remains, and by whom he is informed of the death of Julia. This intelligence throws him into another fever; on his recovery, Mathilda conveys him to a castella of her own, situated in the Venetian territory. Here she practices every art and assumes all the amiable appearances and fascinating manners she is mistress of, which she thinks most likely to wean Verezzi from his fondness for the memory of Julia, and to inspire him with an affection for herself. But all her arts prove fruitless, till Zastrozzi suggests the scheme of affecting to assassinate Verezzi, when Mathilda is to interpose and make him believe that she saves his life. Verezzi, who is a poor fool, and anything but a man, falls into the snare, forgets his Julia, indulges a vicious passion for Mathilda, which the author denominates love, but which is as far removed from that exalted passion as modesty is from indecency, and deserves a name which we shall not offend our readers by repeating. Revelling in an inordinate and bestial passion, of which the fiend Mathilda is the object, he discovers that Julia still lives. This causes momentary regret, but awakens the jealousy of Mathilda, which he calms by the most indelicate professions and whilst he is about to drink a goblet of wine to the happiness of her infamous paramour, Julia glides into the room. Verezzi is instantly seized with a frenzy, and stabs himself. Mathilda is rendered furious by this death-blow to her criminal gratifications.

'Her eyes scintillated,' (a favorite word with the author, which he introduces in almost every page) 'with fiend-like expression. She advanced to the lifeless corpse of Verezzi, she plucked the dagger from his bosom, it was stained with his life's blood, which trickled fast from the point to the floor, she raised it on high, and imperiously called upon the God of nature to doom her to endless torments should Julia survive her vengeance.'

She is as good as her word; she stabs Julia in a thousand places; and, with exulting pleasure, again and again buries her dagger in the body of the unfortunate victim of her rage. Mathilda is seized by the officers of justice, as well as Zastrozzi, who confesses that he had planned the whole business, and made Mathilda the tool by which he satiated his revenge.

The story itself, and the style in which it is told, are so truly contemptible, that we should have passed it unnoticed, had not our indignation been excited by the open and barefaced immorality and grossness displayed throughout. Mathilda's character is that of a lascivious fiend, who dignifies vicious, unrestrained passion by the appellation of love.

Does the author, whoever he may be, think his gross and wanton pages fit to meet the eye of a modest young woman? Is this the instruction to be instilled under the title of a romance? Such trash, indeed, as this work contains, is fit only for the inmates of a brothel. It is by such means of corruption as this that the tastes of our youth of both sexes become vitiated, their imaginations heated, and a foundation laid for their future misery and dishonour. When a taste for this kind of writing is imbibed, we may bid farewell to innocence, farewell to purity of thought, and all that makes youth and virtue lovely.

We know not when we have felt so much indignation as in the perusal of this execrable production. The author of it cannot be too severely reprobated. Not all his 'scintillated eyes,' his 'battling emotions,' his 'frigorific torpidity of despair,' nor his 'Lethean torpor,' with the rest of his nonsensical and stupid jargon, ought to save him from infamy, and his volume from the flames.

ST. IRVYNE: or THE ROSICRUCIAN

---

6. Unsigned notice, *The British Critic*

January 1811, xxxvii, 70–1

'Red thunder-clouds, borne on the wings of the midnight whirlwind, floated at first athwart the crimson-coloured orbit of the moon; the rising fierceness of the blast, sighed through the stunted shrubs, which bending before its violence, inclined towards the rocks whereon they grew: over the blackened expanse of heaven, at intervals, was spread the blue lightning's flash; it played upon the granite heights, and with momentary brilliancy, disclosed the terrific scenery of the Alps; whose gigantic, and misshapen summits, reddened by the transitory moon-beam, were crossed by black fleeting fragments of the tempest-cloud.'

The above is the first sentence of this Romance, by 'a gentleman of Oxford.' Some readers will, perhaps, be satisfied, and will proceed no further, they who do, will find the Cavern of Gil Blas with very little variation of circumstance, a profusion of words which no dictionary explains, such as *unerasible, Bandit, en-horrored*, descriptions wilder than are to be found in Radcliffe, and a tale more extravagant than the *St. Leon* of Godwin.

Would that this gentleman of Oxford had a taste for other and better pursuits, but as we presume him to be a *young gentleman*, this may in due time happen.

7. Unsigned review, *The Anti-Jacobin Review and Magazine*

January 1812, xli, 69–72

Had not the title-page informed us that this curious 'Romance' was the production of 'a gentleman,' a freshman of course, we should certainly have ascribed it to some 'Miss' in her teens; who, having read the beautiful and truly poetic descriptions, in the unrivalled romances of Mrs. Ratcliffe [*sic*], imagined that to admire the writings of that lady, and to imitate her style were one and the same thing. Here we have *description run mad*; every uncouth epithet, every wild expression, which either the lexicographer could supply, or the disordered imagination of the romance-writer suggest, has been pressed into the service of 'the Rosicmeian' [*sic*]. Woe and terror are heightened by the expressions used to describe them. Heroes and heroines are not merely distressed and terrified, they are 'enanguished' and 'enhorrored.'

Nor are the ordinary sensations of *joy* or even *delight*, sufficient to gratify such exalted beings. No, when the hero was pleased, not only did he experience 'a transport of delight'; *burning ecstasy revelled through his veins; pleasurable coruscations were emitted from his eyes.* Even hideous sights acquire an additional deformity under the magic of this 'gentleman's' pen. We read of 'a form more hideous than the imagination is capable of portraying, whose proportions, gigantic and deformed, were seemingly blackened by the *inerasible traces of the thunder-bolts of God.*'

From one who, disdaining the common forms and modes of language, aims at sublimity both of thought and expression, a slavish subjection to the vulgar restrictions of grammar, a tame submission to the *Jus et Norms loquendi*[1] cannot reasonably be extracted. Exalted genius ever spurns restraint; and the mind accustomed to indulge in 'a train of labyrinthic meditations' cannot very well bear up under the trammels of common sense.

Were he, however, only enthusiastic and nonsensical, we should

---

[1] 'Rule and standard of speaking'.

dismiss his book with contempt. Unfortunately he has subjected himself to censure of a severer cast. In the fervor of his illustrations he is, not infrequently, impious and blasphemous. And his notions of *innocence* and *virtue* are such as, were they to pass current in the world, would soon leave society without one innocent or virtuous being. His two heroines are represented as women of rank, family, and education; yet one of them, Megalina, is made to fall in love at first sight with a member of a company of banditti, residing in a cave in the Alps, who had just robbed and murdered her father. And to this man, who is the hero of the piece, she surrenders herself, without a struggle, and becomes his mistress. The other heroine, Eloise, who has had a religious education, and who has just buried her mother, also falls in love at first sight with a man wholly unknown to her, and whom she had seen under very suspicious circumstances. To him she, also, surrenders her virgin charms; lives with him as his mistress, becomes pregnant by him; then leaves him and becomes the mistress of another stranger.

Yet, under these circumstances, the reader is insulted with the assertion, that 'her soul was susceptible of *the most exalted virtue and expansion*.' Fitzeustace, the man with whom she lives, at length proposes to take her with him to England, when the following dialogue occurs between them.

'But before we go to England, before my father will see us, it is necessary that we should be married—nay, do not start, Eloise; I view it in the light that you do; I consider it an human institution and incapable of furnishing that bond of union by which, alone, can intellect be conjoined; I regard it as but a chain, which, although it keeps the body bound, leaves the soul unfettered: it is not so with love. But still, Eloise, to those who think like us, it is at all events harmless; 'tis but yielding to the prejudices of the world wherein we live, and procuring moral expediency, at a slight sacrifice of what we believe to be right.'

'Well, well, it shall be done, Fitzeustace,' resumed Eloise, 'but take the assurance of my promise that I cannot love you more.'

'They soon agreed on a point of, in their eyes, such trifling importance,[1] and arriving in England, tasted that happiness which love and *innocence* alone can give. Prejudice may triumph for a while, but *virtue* will be eventually the conqueror.'

His penetration must be deeper than any to which we can form

[1] Eloise, be it observed, is a Catholic, and must therefore have been taught to regard marriage, not as a 'human institution' but as a *sacrament*. (Reviewer's footnote)

pretentions, who can discover in this denouement, any thing bearing the most distant resemblance to the triumph of virtue. It exhibits, however, a tolerably fair criterion by which the standard of the writer's intellectual powers, and his peculiar system of ethics, may be estimated.

A third female character, Olympia, a young lady of the first rank in Genoa, is introduced for no other imaginable purpose than to increase the reader's contempt and abhorrence of the sex. She, setting aside all dignity and decorum, as well as every feature of virtue, seeks at night the residence of a man whom she believes to be married and courts prostitution. He, however, who has never restrained his passions in any one instance, during his whole life, and who for their gratification has committed the most enormous crimes, suddenly displays a virtue wholly foreign from his disposition and character, and resolutely resists the most powerful temptation presenting itself under the most alluring form. Olympia, thus unable to become a prostitute, commits suicide.

But 'tis not surprising that the writer, who can outrage nature and common sense in almost every page of his book, should libel a sex, of whom, we suppose, he has no knowledge, but such as may be collected in the streets or in a brothel.

Of his hero, Wolfstein, and *his* mistress, Megalina, he disposes in a very summary way. The latter is found dead in the vaults of the Castle of St. Irvyne; though how she came there we are not informed. To these vaults Wolfstein repairs for the purpose of being taught the secret of obtaining eternal life. Here the Devil himself 'borne on the pinions of hell's sulphurous whirlwind,' appears to him and calls on him to deny his Creator. Wolfstein refuses; then, 'blackened in terrible convulsions, Wolfstein expired; over him had the power of hell no influence.'—*Why* he was made to expire, and *why* hell had no power over him, we are left to conjecture. Wolfstein, be it observed, had lived in the habitual commission of atrocious crimes, and died an impenitent sinner.

Of such a rhapsody we have, perhaps, said too much. But it is a duty due from critics to the public to mark every deviation from religious and moral principle with strong reprobation; as well as to deter readers from wasting their time in the perusal of unprofitable and vicious productions, as to check silly and licentious writers at an early period of their literary career. If this duty were performed with greater punctuality, the press would be more purified than it is. As to this Oxford gentleman, we recommend him to the care of his tutor, who, after a proper *jobation* for past folly, would do well, by *imposition*, to forbid him the use of the pen until he should have taken his *bachelor's degree*.

8. Unsigned letter, *The Anti-Jacobin Review and Magazine*

February 1812, xli, 221

To the Editor of the Anti-Jacobin Review

SIR,—I am happy to say that your excellent review now begins to be much more properly appreciated, and particularly at this University, where it is gaining ground rapidly. Of late I attribute this to your very excellent critique on the Oxford University Romance, *St. Iroyne* [*sic*], on the subject of which I now trouble you with these few lines. This iniquitous and absurd romance is attributed to the pen of a very young gentleman, who I understand is heir to a title and a landed estate of ten thousand a year, which he will, if he lives, be in possession of very soon. And this reputed author was not long after the publication of this romance, expelled from the University, in consequence of the freedom with which he avowed his singularly wicked sentiments. He had a companion in the college, who was expelled at the same time. These facts appear to have been kept out of all public prints, but I think their promulgation will do good, as they will at once hold out a warning to others, and prove to the world, that a vigilant eye is still kept in this University over improprieties of conduct,

Your well-wisher

AN OXFORD COLLEGIAN.

OXFORD UNIVERSITY, Feb. 8th, 1812.

Report says that our ex-collegian, on being discountenanced by his friends, ran off with a young lady of no fortune, to Scotland, after a very sudden acquaintance, and has married her. I presume in revenge!

THE NECESSITY OF ATHEISM AND A DECLARATION OF RIGHTS

1811

9. Robert Southey, from a letter to Grosvenor Bedford

January 4, 1812

Robert Southey (1774–1843) enjoyed the friendship of the leading Romantic poets, especially Wordsworth and Coleridge. Coleridge and Southey married sisters and together they planned to settle an ideal community in the United States, a plan which never materialized. His poems and essays received high acclaim, and he was named Poet Laureate in 1813, but only his prose is much read today. The letter appears in *Robert Southey; the Story of His Life Written in His Letters*, ed. John Ennis (1887), pp. 238–9.

Here is a man at Keswick, who acts upon me as my own ghost would do. He is just what I was in 1794. His name is Shelley, son to the member for Shoreham; with 6000*l.* a year entailed upon him, and as much more in his father's power to cut off. Beginning with romances of ghosts and murder, and with poetry at Eton, he passed, at Oxford, into metaphysics; printed half-a-dozen pages which he entitled *The Necessity of Atheism*; sent one anonymously to Coplestone, in expectation, I suppose, of converting him; was expelled in consequence; married a girl of seventeen, after being turned out of doors by his father; and here they both are, in lodgings, living upon 200*l.* a year, which her father allows them. He is come to the fittest physician in the world. At present he has got to the Pantheistic stage of philosophy, and, in the course of a week, I expect he will be a Berkeleyan, for I have put him upon a course of Berkeley. It has surprised him a good deal to meet, for the first time in his life, with a man who perfectly understands him, and does him full justice. I tell him that all the difference between us is, that he is nineteen, and I am thirty-seven; and I dare say it will not be very long before I shall succeed in convincing him that he may be a true philosopher, and do a great deal of good, with 6000*l*. a year; the thought of which troubles him a great deal more at present than ever the want of sixpence (for I have known such a want) did me.

10. Unsigned review, *The Brighton Magazine*

May 1822, i, 540–5

The name of Percy Bysshe Shelley is not prefixed to these tracts, but they are well known to be the production of his pen; and we have selected them in our first notice of his works, as with them he commenced his literary career. In this view they are extraordinary, not as efforts of genius, but as indications of that bold and daring insubordination of mind, which led the writer, at a very early age, to trample both on human and divine authority. *The Necessity of Atheism* contains a distinct negation of a Deity; and the *Declaration of Rights* is an attempt to subvert the very foundations of civil government. Were not the subject far too grave for pleasantry, we might amuse ourselves with the idea of a stripling, an undergraduate, commencing hostilities against heaven and earth, and with the utmost self-satisfaction exulting that he has vanquished both.

Some of our readers are aware, that for the first of these performances, (after every persuasion from his superiors to induce him to retract it had been urged in vain,) Mr. Shelley was expelled from college; and that for posting up the second on the walls of a provincial town, his servant was imprisoned; and, from these facts, they may perhaps imagine that they are remarkably effective engines of atheism and democracy. But, in truth, they are below contempt,—they rather insult than support the bad cause to which they are devoted.

To maintain the Necessity of Atheism is, perhaps, the wildest and most extravagant effort of a perverted understanding; and to consider this as achieved by a mere boy in thirteen widely printed pages of a duodecimal pamphlet, is to conceive the performance of a miracle more stupendous than any recorded in the Scriptures. Had we not of late been accustomed to witness the arrogance and presumption of impiety; had not the acuteness of our sensibility been somewhat deadened by familiar acquaintance with the blasphemies of the school in which this young man is now become a professor, we could not trust our feelings even with a remote reference to his atrocious, yet most imbecile, production. It is difficult, on such a subject, to preserve the decorum of moral tolerance, and to avoid a severity of indignation incompatible with the office of Christian censors.

Mr. Shelley oddly enough denominates belief a passion; then he denies that it is ever active; yet he tells us that it is capable of excitement, and that the degrees of excitement are three. But lest we should be suspected of misrepresentation, Mr. Shelley shall speak for himself.

The senses are the sources of all knowledge to the mind, consequently their evidence claims the strongest assent. The decision of the mind, founded upon our experience derived from these sources, claims the next degree; the experience of others, which addresses itself to the former one, occupies the lowest degree. Consequently, no testimony can be admitted which is contrary to reason; reason is founded on the evidence of our senses.

Every proof may be referred to one of these three divisions; we are naturally led to consider what arguments we receive from each of them, to convince us of the existence of a Deity.

These sentences embrace a page of the pamphlet, and immediately succeed a general introduction occupying eight more; and, of course, the whole investigation is despatched in less than four. Its result is summed up in the following words:

From this it is evident, that having no proofs from any of the three sources of conviction, the mind cannot believe the existence of a God. It is also evident, that as belief is a passion of the mind, no degree of criminality can be attached to disbelief. *They only are reprehensible who willingly neglect to remove the false medium through which their mind views the subject.* It is almost unnecessary to observe, that the general knowledge of the deficiency of such proof cannot be prejudicial to society. Truth has always been found to promote the best interests of mankind. Every reflecting mind must allow that there is no proof of the existence of a Deity.

Such is the jargon of the new philosophy. 'The satanic school' maintains, that belief cannot be virtuous; yet, that it may be reprehensible, and therefore vicious; and that the greatest crime of which a rational creature can be guilty, is to admit the being of a God. Such is the logic of Mr. Shelley. To discuss the question at issue between atheists and theists with such a writer, would be extreme folly; nor should we have drawn from oblivion this extravagant freak of his boyhood, had he not by subsequent writings, and at a matured period of his life, avowed the same sentiments, and obtruded them upon the world with an effrontery unexampled in the annals of impiety. But on this strange intellectual and moral phenomenon we shall take occasion to offer a few remarks. In what light are we to consider the intellectual qualities and attainments of an individual, who denies the existence of a Deity, on the supposition that he has discovered a great and momentous truth? But he has explored the universe, and not only cannot find a God, but can demonstrate the impossibility of his existence. How surprisingly great must be his understanding! how stupendous and overpowering his knowledge! For as this is a fact that requires demonstration, no inferior degree of evidence can be admitted as conclusive. What wondrous Being then presents himself before us in all the confidence of absolute persuasion, founded on irrefragable evidence, declaring that there is no God? And how has he grown to this immense intelligence? Yesterday he was an infant in capacity, and humble; and now he is invested with the attributes of the very Divinity whose existence he denies. 'For unless this man is omnipresent, unless he is at this moment in every place in the universe, he cannot know but there may be in some place manifestations of a Deity, by which even *he* would be overpowered. If he does not know absolutely every agent in the universe, and does not know what is so, that which is so may be God. If he is not in absolute possession of all the propositions that constitute universal truth, the one which he wants may be, that there is a God. If he cannot, with certainty, assign the cause of all that he perceives to exist, that cause may be God. If he does not know everything that has been done in the immeasurable ages that are past, some things may have been done by a God. Thus, unless he knows all things, that is, precludes another Deity, by being one himself, he cannot know that the Being whose existence he rejects does not exist. But he must know that he does not exist, else he deserves equal contempt and compassion for the temerity with which he firmly avows his rejection, and acts accordingly.'[1] As, however, no individual can presume that he has attained this alarming superiority above his fellow-creatures; as the necessity of atheism has never been proved; but in every case where it has been pretended, it has been the result of some peculiar conjunction of disastrous influences, we are constrained to infer that the atheist must be the victim of a mental obliquity, of a strange perversion of the understanding, which renders him incapable of comprehending the laws of evidence, and the principles of right and reason.

There are certain principles on which, with a few anomalous exceptions, all men are agreed. The foundation of all reasoning concerning being and events, for instance, is a supposed or acknowledged connexion between cause and effect. By cause is meant that something, be it what it may, which produces, or causes to produce, existence, or any change of existence, and without which the existence or the change would not have been. It is universally admitted, that we have no knowledge of any existence, or any change, which has taken place without a cause. The human mind, under whatever circumstances of culture or neglect, has acknowledged, in the clearest manner, and in every way of which the subject is susceptible, the inseparable nature of this connexion. We learn it from experience, and in two ways—by the testimony of our senses, and by the inspection of our minds. We cannot realize the fact, that no existence or change can take place without a cause. The man who began by denying what is so self-evident, discovers an incapacity to reason. He holds nothing in common with the rest of mankind, and no absurdity can be greater than to attempt to argue with him. Indeed, he cannot pursue an argument on the subject without a practical refutation of the principle he assumes. In speaking, he exhibits *himself* as the cause of all the words uttered by him, and of the opinions he would communicate; and, in the act of arguing, admits you to be a similar cause. If his body be not a cause, and your eyes another, you cannot see him; if his voice and your ears be not causes, you cannot hear him; if his mind and yours be not causes, you cannot understand him. In a word, without admitting the connexion between cause and effect, you can never know that he is arguing with you, or you with him. But the sophistry which leads to Atheism, denies this first principle of all reasoning, and betrays a mental perversion, which utterly disqualifies for sober and rational investigation.

[1] Foster's *Essays*. (Reviewer's footnote)

And with this sturdy rejection of everything like evidence on the subject of a Deity, it is remarkable that Atheists are the most credulous of mankind. There is no absurdity which the human mind, in the very spirit of extravagance, has been capable of inventing, which they have not gravely maintained. The dogmas of Atheism are the most melancholy exhibition of weakness which has ever degraded the human understanding. And we are warranted in affirming, that Atheism, *in all its forms*, is a specimen of the most absolute credulity. The three grand schemes of existence, which it has devised, to get rid of the idea of one glorious, intelligent Creator; namely, that things have existed in an eternal series; that their existence is casual; and that all distinct, or separate, beings owe their existence to the powers and operations of matter; have been refuted by direct demonstrations; they have been unanswerably proved not only to be false, but to be impossible. What then can we think of the mental capacities of him, who goes on quietly with his faith in these hypotheses, and resolves to believe, in defiance of demonstration and impossibility?

But the source of Atheism is the heart rather than the head; and it is a moral phenomenon of the most portentous and appalling character. It is the child of depravity, bearing all the worst features of its parent. A tree is known by its fruits; reason never produced such a monster as Atheism; it is to be traced to the indisposition of the heart to acknowledge the existence of a Creator. He that hates the control, and dreads the inspection, judgment, and retribution of his Maker, finds no refuge from anxiety and alarm so safe, as the belief that there is no God.

To us there is something fearful and even terrific in the state of mind which can delight in the renunciation of a Deity—which can derive satisfaction from the feeling, that the infinite Spirit is gone, that the only solid foundation of virtue is wanting; which can enjoy pleasure in renouncing that system of doctrine of which a God is the great subject, and that train of affections and conduct of which He is the supreme object. The idea of a God seems essential to every pleasurable and sublime execution; without it we can conceive of nothing glorious, nothing delightful. And, could it once be exploded, in one view it would diminish to insignificance the range of thought, the circle of enjoyment. The absence of God would cover the face of nature with funereal gloom; and, he that should first make the fatal discovery, according to our apprehension, would be at once and forever the most miserable being in the universe. He would evince no eagerness to communicate the dismal search; on the contrary, he would envy his fellow-creatures the pleasant delusion which sustained their virtue, and encouraged their hope.

But 'Truth,' says Mr. Shelley, 'has always been found to promote the best interests of mankind.' We admit the proposition, and therefore maintain that that which is subversive of their best interests, cannot be truth. We may confidently ask, in what possible way can Atheism secure the well-being of society?

If we grant that the belief in a Deity operates as a very slight restraint on vice, in individual cases where the character has become utterly depraved, yet its general influence must be mighty, interwoven as it is with the whole civil and social economy of man. It must act powerfully as an incentive to whatever is good, and as a check to whatever is evil; and, it can only fail in particular instances of atrocious obduracy. But, what offences against himself or his fellow-creatures, may not an Atheist perpetrate with conscious impunity, without regret, and without a blush? What protection can his principles afford to confiding innocence and beauty? What shall deter him from dooming an amiable and lovely wife to penury, to desolation, and an untimely grave? What shall make seduction and adultery criminal in his eyes, or induce him when she is in his power, to spare the victim of unhallowed and guilty passions? What can he know of honour, of justice, and integrity? What friend will he not betray? What tradesman will he not defraud? What enemy will he not pursue to utter destruction? What lawless gratification will he not indulge, when its indulgence does not compromise his personal safety? Who, we may ask, are those that set the decencies of life at defiance, that laugh at virtue, and riot in epicurean debauchery? Are they not the base apostates from God, who boast of their impiety, and write themselves 'Atheists' to their own disgrace, and the scandal of the country that gave them birth? These are the questions which we put to what was once a conscience in the breast of Mr Shelley, with little hope, however, that they will rouse this benumbed and long-forgotten faculty, to any thing like feeling. It is well for mankind that the life of the Atheist is so just a comment upon his creed, and that none can feel a wish to join his standard, but he who has become an alien from virtue, and the enemy of his species.

We had intended to indulge in further observations, and to bring the principles of the *Declaration of Rights* more prominently and distinctly before our readers; but for the present we shall forbear. A government founded on Atheism, or conducted by Atheists, would be the greatest curse the world has ever felt. It was inflicted for a short season, as a visitation on a neighboring country, and its reign was avowedly and expressly the reign of terror. The declarers of rights, intoxicated by their sudden elevation, and freed from every restraint, became the most ferocious tyrants, and, while they shut up the temples of God, abolished his worship, and proclaimed death to be an eternal sleep, they converted, by their principles and spirit, the most polished people of Europe into a horde of assassins, the seat of voluptuous refinement, of pleasure and of arts, into a theatre of blood.

With an example so recent and so fearfully instructive before our eyes, it is not probable that we shall be deluded by Mr. Shelley or any of his school; the splendours of a poetical imagination may dazzle and delight, and they may prove a mighty engine of mischief to many who have more fancy than judgment; but they will never impose upon the sober and calculating part of the community; they will never efface the impression from our minds, that Atheism is an inhuman, bloody, and ferocious system, equally hostile to every useful restraint, and to every virtuous affection; that having nothing above us to excite awe, or around us to awaken tenderness, it wages war with Heaven, and with earth: its first object is to dethrone God; its next to destroy man. With such conviction the enlightened and virtuous inhabitants of Great Britain will not surely be tempted to their fate by such a rhapsody as the following, with which Mr. Shelley concludes his *Declaration of Rights*, and with which we take our leave of him:

Man! thou whose rights are here declared, be no longer forgetful of the loftiness of thy destination. Think of thy rights; of those possessions which will give thee virtue and wisdom, by which thou mayest arrive at happiness and freedom. They are declared to thee by one who knows thy dignity; for every hour does his heart swell with honourable pride, in the contemplation of what thou mayest attain; by one who is not forgetful of thy degeneracy, for every moment brings home to him the bitter conviction of what thou art.

Awake!—Arise!—or be forever fallen.

QUEEN MAB

1813

11. Review signed 'F.,' *The Theological Inquirer, or Polemical Magazine*

March, April, May, July 1815, 34–9; 105–10; 205–9; 358–62

To the Editor of the Theological Inquirer

SIR,

Observing in your prospectus, that it is your intention occasionally to insert criticisms on books connected with the subjects proposed, and also to give an account of scarce and valuable works in the different departments you have laid down, I take the liberty of informing you that during an excursion on the Continent, in the last summer, the celebrated Kotzebue put into my hands an English poem, which he doubted if I had seen in my own country, as he considered it too bold a production to issue from the British press. He spoke of it in the highest terms of admiration; and though I had not time then to peruse it, I afterwards purchased six copies of it at Berlin and have been amply repaid by the pleasure it has afforded me. I would send you a copy to reprint in your journal; but am afraid notwithstanding the freedom, candour, and impartiality you seem to aim at, that you would be intimidated from the publication, as our press is at present too much shackled to give vent to the many important truths it contains. I shall, however, attempt a description of this poem, and extract such passages as will serve to give a faint idea of the whole, though, I am sorry to say, I shall be under the necessity of omitting some of its greatest beauties. The author has made fiction, and the usual poetical imagery, the vehicles for his moral and philosophical opinions. It is entitled *Queen Mab*, and the attributes of that celebrated personage form the machinery of a work, in which the delightful creations of

63

fancy and the realities of truth unite to produce an indelible impression on the mind.

The fairy descends in her chariot, and hovering over this earth, confers on the soul of a beautiful female (Ianthe) the glorious boon of a complete knowledge of the past, the present, and the future; the body is lulled to sleep, the soul ascends the fairy car, and they take their flight through the immeasurable expanse of the universe. Arrived at the palace of the 'Queen of Spells,' the spirit is led by her to the 'overhanging battlement,' and thence beholds the inexpressible grandeur of that multitude of worlds among which this earth (to which her attention is especially directed) is but an insignificant speck. The fairy then proceeds to point out the ruined cities of ancient time, and her sublime descriptions, with the reflections naturally suggested by the pomp and decay of grandeur, and the rise and fall of empires, will form some of the most interesting of those extracts which I design to introduce.

Having reviewed the deeds of ages past, the fairy then expatiates on the systems of present existence; and here the author's opinions, conveyed through the lips of his visionary instrument, are bold to the highest pitch of daring; this, however, is not the theatre for their discussion; to state and to applaud would be dangerous, and to condemn would be ungenerous while a restricted press allows not of open defense.

The doctrine of *Necessity*, abstruse and dark as the subject is generally believed, forms a leading consideration in this poem, and is treated with a precision of demonstration, and illumined with a radiance of genius, far beyond expectation itself:

> The Present and the Past thou hast beheld;
> It was a desolate sight.

And the fairy then lifts the veil of an imaginary futurity, and presents to the delighted spirit the prospect of a state of human perfection, which affords illimitable range for the erratic wanderings of poetic ardour: here the fairy and the spirit revel in all the luxury of hope and joy; and having contemplated awhile with virtuous satisfaction the happy scene thus opened to mortal conception, the former declares her task completed, and conveys the latter to her earthly tenement, which her anxious lover is watching with impatient ardor for its resuscitation.

The reflections in the commencement of the poem over the inanimate body of Ianthe, are remarkably impressive. . . .

[quotes Canto I, lines 19–36]

The approach of Queen Mab is thus powerfully described:

[quotes Canto I, lines 45–58]

The description of the fairy's appearance, as

—Leaning gracefully from th' etherial car,
Long did she gaze, and silently,
Upon the slumbering maid.

is introduced in the following sublime strain of exclamation:

Oh! not the visioned poet in his dreams,
When silvery clouds float through the wildered brain,
When every sight of lovely, wild and grand
Astonishes, enraptures, elevates,
When fancy at a glance combines
The wondrous and the beautiful,—
So bright, so fair, so wild a shape
Hath ever yet beheld,
As that which reined the coursers of the air,
And poured the magic of her gaze
Upon the maiden's sleep.

Her address to the soul of Ianthe, and its effects, are marked with the most vivid beauties of poetry. . . .

[quotes Canto I, lines 114–56]

In answer to the spirit's natural inquiry of astonishment at the new feeling which pervades her, the fairy proceeds to explain her own state of being. . . .

[quotes Canto I, lines 167–87]

The magic power of this command operates instantaneously:

The strains of earth's immurement
Fell from Ianthe's spirit;
They shrank and brake like bandages of straw
Beneath a wakened giant's strength.

Satan's passage through chaos, in Milton, sublime as it is, sinks into comparative insignificance, when considered with the description of the fairy and the spirit's course through the immensity of the universe; it is lengthy, but a short extract or two will justify my opinion. . . .

[quotes Canto I, lines 222–48]

The reflections on this imposing scene, with which the first part of the poem (which is in nine divisions) concludes, must not be omitted. . . .

[quotes Canto I, lines 264–77]

If, Mr. Editor, you make your approbation of this correspondence by inserting it, I shall continue my selections from a work, the whole of which there is but small probability of the present generation becoming acquainted with. I am, Sir,

Your well-wisher, F.

[April 1815]

MR. EDITOR,

As you have gratified me, and (I trust) the public, by inserting my fine selection of specimens from *Queen Mab*, I shall continue to point out what appear to me its principal excellencies; proud of the opportunity of homaging the shrine of genius, and delighted to cull flowers from the luxuriant garden of a rich poetic imagination.

The description of the Fairy Queen's palace is introduced in a manner peculiarly calculated to arrest the attention. . . .

[quotes Canto II, lines 1–21]

The light step of beauty has been frequently the subject of fanciful description. Scott, in his *Lady of the Lake*, has it:

> Ev'n the light hare-bell raised its head
> Elastic from her airy tread.

But the following is a more sublime picture:

> The Fairy and the Spirit
> Entered the Hall of Spells:
> Those golden clouds
> That rolled in glittering billows
> Beneath the azure canopy
> With the ethereal footsteps trembled not.

In the view of the 'countless and unending orbs' of the universe,
this earth is described as:

> —a little light
> That twinkled in the misty distance;
> None but a spirit's eye
> Might ken that rolling orb.

The tombs of the lovely, the good, and the great, have always
afforded a fruitful source of reflection to the sensitive mind; even the
gibbet of the criminal excites a sigh for the perversion of human ability.

But over the records of mighty nations, fallen beneath the mad blow
of the conqueror's ambition; or decayed by the consumptive influence
of moral corruption; the sensibilities take a wider and more dignified
scope for meditation; and although the disordered relations of man are
thus martialled in dreadful array before the shrinking perception, so as
to produce a transient emotion of despair in the bosom of the philanthropist, yet is the glow of patriotism ultimately benefited, and every
virtue strengthened and improved. . . .

[quotes Canto II, lines 109–81]

The author's favourite doctrine of the eternity of matter is thus
forcibly illustrated and insisted upon. . . .

[quotes Canto II, lines 211–43]

Adverting to the rottenness of certain established systems of government, and the patient and wonderful endurance of man, the Fairy
indignantly proceeds. . . .

[quotes Canto III, lines 106–17]

How nobly contemptuous is the tone of the inquiry which follows a
deprecation of the evils of tyranny, and a fond prophecy of a period
when

> Falsehood's trade
> Shall be as hateful and unprofitable
> As that of truth is now.

[The quotation continues through lines 138–49 of Canto III]

That the author is a powerful advocate of *Necessity* is evinced by
the following extract. . . .

[quotes Canto III, lines 214–40]

Alas! how little is there in the present aspect of the world and its institutions, to warrant a hope of the speedy consummation of this anticipated state of perfection! yet does the eye of innocence receive with grateful delight the feeble ray thus stealing through the crevice of its persecuted being's dungeon.   F.

[May 1815]
The following description of a fine night in winter will strike the reader with a forcible sense of admiration.

[quotes Canto IV, lines 1–19]

Further on, the author imagines the quiet of this scene destroyed by the tumult and horror of war.

[quotes Canto IV, lines 33–69]

The Fairy, in a strain of indignant inquiry into the moral causes which produce the scenes of horror and devastation depicted above, asks . . .

[quotes Canto IV, lines 89–104]

The demon of trade, that enemy of virtue, that monster whose breath chills the ardor of sensibility, and drives the shivering soul to the inmost corner of distrustful reserve, is an object of our author's most powerful indignation.

[quotes Canto V, lines 44–63]

How lamentably true the following picture of the evils resulting from the love of gain.

[quotes Canto V, lines 166–96]

An episode, founded on the celebrated legend of the wandering Jew, forms a prominent feature in the admirable poem under analysis. The fairy thus expresses herself.

[quotes Canto VII, lines 59–82]

This is that suppositious character, who, for insulting Christ on his way to the place of execution, is said to be condemned to a restless existence on earth till the day of judgment: the vengeful acrimony of his disposition, naturally produced by this severe decree, pervades the whole of his long harrangue to the fairy and the spirit, so as to render it imprudent to submit it here; but the reader must be gratified by the sublime and impressive manner of its conclusion.

[quotes Canto VII, lines 254–75]

If, in this division of the poem, which describes the systems of the present, I have confined myself to extracts characteristic, by their power of fancy and beauty of description, of the author's ability as a poet; and have not produced those indications that he is a philosopher of the first rank, with which the volume abounds, it must be attributed to the boldness of his sentiments, which, in this country, where the freedom of the press is little more than an empty name, it would be hazardous to disseminate.

[July 1815]

Now it is that the visionary golden age bursts in full splendour on the luxurious imagination of our poet: and this favorite theme of all bards is treated in a manner which covers former descriptions with insignificance, its effects on the Spirit are rapturous.

[quotes Canto VIII, lines 11–40]

The concluding simile is inexpressibly beautiful; nor does an extensive poetical reading furnish me with any reason to doubt its originality. It is not to the blooming vales of Tempé, to the golden groves of Arcadia; or to any other favorite spot that our poet confines the happiness of his mental vision; the whole earth is the work of renovation, and the desert and the deep alike are resigned to the desirable influence.

[quotes Canto VIII, lines 70–87]

The sublime and faultless fabric of his conception being perfected, the poet exclaims with rapturous gratulation,

[quotes Canto IX, lines 1–55]

The following are striking, but, alas! unhoped-for changes:

[quotes Canto IX, lines 93–129]

Thus, Mr. Editor, have I endeavoured, like Mahomet and St. John, to give your readers a faint idea of the paradise to which I have been admitted; surely my selections must interest the soul of fancy, the heart of feeling, to such a degree, that the energies of resolution will be impelled with increased force to the accomplishment of that great object the complete freedom of the press in matters of public opinion. For the reflection must occur that this is only one of the numerous productions of genius which have perished in the bud, which have been destroyed in the womb by its oppressive restrictions.

The copious and elegant notes to the poem, it is not within my design to call your attention to.

A Paine, a Voltaire, and a Volney, have written to teach man his dignity; they have conveyed the voice of Reason to the unprejudiced ear, and have seemed monuments of fame in the gratitude of future ages, but it was reserved for the author of *Queen Mab* to show, that

'The poet's eye, in a fine frenzy rolling,'

might soar to other and to nobler objects than the domes of super-stition, and the heaven of priestly invention, and to prove the justice of Milton's beautiful ejaculation;

How charming is divine philosophy!
Not harsh and crabbed as dull fools suppose,
But musical as is Apollo's lute,
And a perpetual feast of nectared sweets
Where no crude surfeit reigns.

F.

12. Unsigned review, *John Bull's British Journal*

March 11, 1821, no. 3, 22

As the name of this poet is now become familiar to the literary world in consequence of the animadversions his *Revolt of Islam*, *The Cenci*, a tragedy, and *Prometheus*, a lyrical drama, have given rise to in the magazines and Reviews, they may perhaps feel interested in an account of a poem, written and printed (for private circulation only), but never published, some years since. It contains thoughts and sentiments so bold, no bookseller has hitherto ventured to publish it; but that is no reason why some of its beauties should not be made known to our readers. The author has made fiction and suitable poetical imagery the vehicles of his moral and philosophic opinions. The attributes of Queen Mab form the machinery of a work in which the delightful creations of fancy, and the realities of truth, unite to produce an indelible impression on the mind.

[The remainder of this review closely follows the text of 'F.'s' review in *The Theological Inquirer* (see No. 11).]

13. Unsigned review, *The London Magazine and Theatrical Inquisitor*

March 1821, iii, 278–81

Queen Mab is a poem, written (as we understand) by Mr. Shelley when at Oxford, and is one of the earliest of his productions. The sentiments contained in it gave considerable offence to the learned heads of the University, and entailed on the author some unpleasant consequences. With these, however, we have nothing to do at present. Our business is with the poetical merits of the work. With the speculative tenets of the writer we shall not intermeddle. If his opinions are palpably absurd and false, they must fall by their own absurdity and falsehood; and discussion could serve no other purpose than to invest them with an importance they do not intrinsically possess. As to the private scandal from which some critics have borrowed pungency and attraction for their disquisitions, we utterly disclaim it; we can neither conceive its connection with criticism, not its propriety from the pen of a reviewer.

The prominent features of Mr. Shelley's poetical character are energy and depth. He has not the tenderness and delicacy of some living poets, nor the fertile and soaring imagination of others. In the former he is surpassed very far indeed by Barry Cornwall, nor does he approach in the latter to Coleridge, or even to Keats. But he has an intense and overwhelming energy of manner, and if he does not present us with many original conceptions, his turn of thought, as well as expression, is strongly indicative of original genius. We apprehend, indeed, that the peculiar charm of Shelley's writing is derived from that complete conviction which he evidently entertains of the justness and importance of all he asserts. This feeling, whether a man's opinions be right or wrong, communicates a force and pointedness to diction, and an interest to composition, which mere labour can never bestow. All Mr. Shelley's thoughts are feelings. He constantly communicates to his reader the impression made upon his own mind, and gives it, even in our apprehension, all the vividness and strength with which it struck his own fancy. His figures, it is true, are often disproportioned, often terrific; but they burst upon us from the canvas in all the energy of life and motion. This gives interest to his sketches, even where the colouring is coarse, and the drawing deficient in exactitude.

Queen Mab opens with some fine reflections upon sleep and death, and allusions to a maid termed Ianthe, apparently dead. Her the poet describes as all that was pure and lovely. He proceeds to tell us that a rushing noise is heard where the body lay, and soon the fairy queen makes her appearance in a radiant car, arrayed in all the lightness and splendour of poetical decoration. She addresses the spirit of Ianthe— she declares herself to be acquainted both with the past and the future, and that it is permitted her 'to rend the veil of mortal fraility,' and to inform the human spirit how it may best accomplish those purposes for which it received its being. That this is a privilege granted only to pure sinless spirits like Ianthe's. She accordingly invites her to avail herself of it immediately, and ascend the car with her. The spirit complies, and they proceed upon their journey to the palace of the fairy. They pass by innumerable suns and worlds, and at length terminate their etherial voyage upon the very boundaries of this universe. The description of this voyage, and of the palace of her fairy majesty, is highly splendid and poetical. When arrived there, Queen Mab declares the purpose of their journey, presents the spirit with a view from the eternal battlements of her palace, of the immense universe stretched below. She takes a review of the past; dwells upon the glories and disgraces of mankind as exhibited in history: upon their crimes, their infatuations, their prejudices, and the absurdity of all received opinions and institutions. She then opens a vista of the future, clad in all the splendid anticipations of perfectibility. She tells how crime, tyranny, and war shall cease: how swords shall be turned into plough-shares, and spears into pruning-hooks; and how, in spite of the dole-ful predictions of Mr. Malthus, the increase of population, consequent on such state, will only tend to the increase of happiness and virtue. Thus the fairy's task is ended: she restores the spirit to its fleshy taber-nacle; and we discover, at the conclusion that Ianthe was not dead, but had slept, and that all was a dream!—The poetical excellence of this work may be judged from the following extracts. . . .

[quotes I, 144–56; I, 264–77; II, 225–43; III, 138–69]

Our readers, we think, will agree with us in pronouncing, that none but a man of genius could write this. At the same time it must be con-fessed, that the poem possesses many of the faults of a young writer, and a few of the affectations of that school with which the author has been classed, but from whose restrictions we trust he will soon com-pletely emancipate himself. We cannot conclude this article without earnestly exhorting Mr. Shelley to undertake something truly worthy of his great powers—something that can be read by the generality of mankind—something divested of those peculiar associations which render him at present so unpopular. Let him remember, that the most effectual mode of combating prejudice is not by direct and violent opposition, but by gentleness and inteneration. We would also tell him, that a genius like his was formed for mankind—that his home is the universe, and that he will not fulfil his high destiny by contracting himself within the narrow limits of a circle of friends, whose standard of literary excellence is regulated by certain conventional ideas pecu-liar to themselves. It is not thus that his writings will acquire that ex-tension and permanence that alone can render them truly beneficial to mankind, and productive of immortality to their author.

14. Unsigned review, *The Literary Gazette and Journal of Belles Lettres*

May 19, 1821, no. 226, 305–8

The mixture of sorrow, indignation, and loathing, with which this volume has overwhelmed us, will, we fear, deprive us of the power of expressing our sentiments upon it, in the manner best suited to the subject itself, and to the effect which we wish our criticism to have upon society. Our desire is to do justice *to* the writer's genius, and *upon* his principles: not to deny his powers, while we deplore their perversion; and above all, when we lay before our readers the examples of his poetry, to warn them against the abominable and infamous contagion with which in the sequel he poisons these splendid effusions. We have doubted whether we ought to notice this book at all; and if our silence could have prevented its being disseminated, no allusion to it should ever have stained *The Literary Gazette*. But the activity of the vile portion of the press is too great to permit this hope,[1] and on weighing every consideration presented to our minds, we have come to the conclusion to lay, as far as we are able, the bane and antidote before the public. *Queen Mab* has long been in limited and private circulation, as a duodecimo; and the first two or three cantos, under the title of *The Demon of the World*, were reprinted at the end of a poem called *Alastor*; as was also the principal note against Christianity in a detached pamphlet. Though the hellish ingredients, therefore, are now for the first time brought together into one cauldron, they have, like those of the evil beings in Macbeth, previously disgusted the world in forms of separate obsceneness.

We have spoken of Shelley's genius, and it is doubtless of a high order; but when we look at the purposes to which it is directed, and contemplate the infernal character of all its efforts, our souls revolt

---

[1] As this is a book of so blasphemous a nature, as to have no claim to the protection of copy-right it may be published by Scoundrels at all prices, to destroy the moral feeling of every class of the community. In the present instance the author has not, we imagine, been consulted. (Reviewer's footnote)

74

with tenfold horror at the energy it exhibits, and we feel as if one of the darkest of the fiends had been clothed with a human body, to enable him to gratify his enmity against the human race, and as if the supernatural atrocity of his hate were only heightened by his power to do injury. So strongly has this impression dwelt upon our minds that we absolutely asked a friend who had seen this individual, to describe him to us—as if a cloven foot, or horn, or flames from the mouth, must have marked the external appearance of so bitter an enemy to mankind. We were almost disappointed to learn that the author was only a tall, boyish looking man, with eyes of unearthly brightness, and a countenance of the wildest cast: that he strode about with hurried and impatient gait, and that a perturbed spirit seemed to preside over all his movements. It is not then in his outward semblance but in his inner man that the explicit demon is seen; and it is a frightful supposition, that his own life may have been a fearful commentary upon his principles[1]—principles, which in the balance of law and justice, happily deprived him of the superintendence of his infants, while they plunged an unfortunate wife and mother into ruin, prostitution, guilt, and suicide.

Such, alas! are the inevitable consequences of the fatal precepts enforced in this publication, which spares not one grace, one good, one ornament, nor one blessing, that can ameliorate our lot on earth; which wagers exterminating war against all that can refine, delight or improve human kind; which ridicules every thing that can contribute to our happiness here, and boldly tries to crush every hope that could point to our happiness hereafter.

As we shall, however, have to say something of these matters in detail, we shall now turn to the review of *Queen Mab*.

The rhythm is of that sort which Mr. Southey employed so forcibly in his *Thalaba*, and other poems; and it is no mean praise to observe, that in his use of it, Mr. Shelley is not inferior to his distinguished predecessor. The first Canto opens with great beauty, in the same way as *Thalaba*.

---

[1] We are aware, that ordinary criticism has little or nothing to do with the personal conduct of authors; but when the most horrible doctrines are promulgated with appalling force it is the duty of every man to expose, in every way, the abominations to which they irresistibly drive their odious professors. We declare against receiving our social impulses from a destroyer of every social virtue; our moral creed, from an incestuous wretch, or our religion from an atheist, who denied God, and reviled the purest institutes of human philosophy and divine ordination, did such a demon exist. (Reviewer's footnote)

[quotes Canto I, lines 1–113]

This is genuine poetry; and in an almost equal strain does the author proceed through forty pages, when he lapses into metaphysics of the worst kind, and becomes at once prosaic and unintelligible. The story, or vehicle for spreading his atrocious opinion, is thus framed. Mab releases the soul of Ianthe from her body, and they pass together, namely, the spirit and the fairy, to an empyreal region, where the mortal globe is made to submit its elements to the enquiry of the freed soul, and the superior being explains, according to Mr. Shelley's ideas, the depravity of the existing system and shapes out a new moral, or rather immoral world, in millennial perspective. Of course, the spirit is delighted to find that there are to be no restraints on the passions, no laws to curb vice, no customs to mark with reprobation the grossest indulgence in sensuality and crime: that in the revocated order, chastity in women, and honour in men, are to be unknown or despised: and in fine, that in the perfected creation there are to be no statesmen, no priests, no king, no God!

The pure enlightened spirit of Ianthe then returns instructed to its corporeal frame, and finds some Henry kneeling by her bedside, to begin the practice of these holy precepts.

The ascent to the visionary abode of Mab is however a piece of splendid composition.

[quotes Canto I, lines 199–277]

Thus ends the first Canto; and the second opens in nearly as sublime a strain; but speedily degenerates into affectation and bombast. New-coined words, and a detail in what may well be styled nonsense verses succeed, and the author becomes what he would call 'meaningless,' ever and anon exclaiming, 'how wonderful,' as if he were himself surprized at his own absurdities. The Mosaic account of creation is, as might be anticipated, treated with ridicule; and we are given to understand that instead of an Almighty Providence, the Creator of the Universe with all the 'rolling orbs,' was a certain power whose appellation is NECESSITY. The attributes of this Necessity are not very definite; but Mr. Shelley supposes it is enough to know and to believe that they were the cause of all nature, and are the universal soul of his precious system. And this leads us to Canto 3, in which the present wickedness and future destiny of man are unfolded. Were it turned to aught but the vilest of purposes, there might be much of excellent writing selected from this part; with which, as we have already noticed, the beauty of the poem as a poem dies. For example, the following reflections on the instability of sublunary things is finely shaped to draw a virtuous moral from; but the author only lays it as the foundation for his engine to cast a fiercer desolation among mankind.

> Where is the fame
> Which the vain-glorious mighty of the earth
> Seek to eternize? Oh! the faintest sound
> From time's light footfall, the minutest wave
> That swells the flood of ages, whelms in nothing
> The unsubstantial bubble. Aye! to-day
> Stern is the tyrant's mandate, red the gaze
> That flashes desolation, strong the arm
> That scatters multitudes. To-morrow comes!
> That mandate is a thunder-peal that died
> In ages past; that gaze, a transient flash
> On which the midnight closed, and on that arm
> The worm has made his meal.

We shall now quote what appears to us to be the noblest piece of poetry which the author ever imagined; and having done him that justice, refrain from further example, except in so far as may be necessary to show, that however gifted with talents, he has only heaped coals of fire upon his head by their perversion, and is a writer to be shunned, loathed, and execrated by every virtuous mind, as dangerous to the ignorant and weak, hateful to the lovers of social felicity, and an enemy to all that is valuable in life, or hopeful in eternity. The passage alluded to follows.

[quotes Canto IV, lines 1–70]

We are afraid that we may be obnoxious to censure, for giving nearly all the brilliant parts of this poem, as they may excite a desire to peruse the whole; but our object in so doing (besides that truth demands it, and that we cannot help indulging a slight hope that the fiend-writer may yet be struck with repentance) is, that in our pages all that curiosity could long for might be gratified, and the impious volume whence we derive these extracts, be allowed to fall into oblivion with all its deep pollutions and horrid blasphemies. For having selected the poetical beauties from the first four cantos, we have now, at page 42, reached the doctrinal inculcations of the author, which are heavy and inexplicable, having nothing to recommend them, if their heresies do not; nothing to induce any one to read them, unless he is prompted by a desire to see how daringly, as well as stupidly, a man can outrage every good feeling of the human heart, try to make life a chaos of sin and misery, and fling his filth against Omnipotence. But even if there are those whom curiosity would prompt to this, let them, we adjure them, be satisfied with what follows. The fairy instilling her poisons, thus speaks of that balm of afflicted souls, the Christian faith—

> Twin-sister of religion, selfishness!
> Rival in crime and falsehood, aping all
> The wanton horrors of her bloody play.
>
> How ludicrous the priest's dogmatic roar!
> The weight of his exterminating curse,
> How light! and his affected charity,
> To suit the pressure of the changing times,
> What palpable deceit!—but for thy aid,
> Religion! but for thee, prolific fiend,
> Who peoplest earth with demons, hell with men,
> And heaven with slaves!
> Thou taintest all thou lookest upon.[1]

And what substitute have we for piety, good-will to man, religion, and a God? The answer of this incarnate driveller is, a 'Spirit of Nature!' . . .

[Continues the quotation, Canto VI, lines 197–219]

The utter annihilation of every enjoyment which man can have on earth—the black catalogue of woes, to which so dreadful a creed as this must tend—the blank and dismaying prospect which it opens to the revolting sense—all the idiotcy of its conception, and all the villany of its avowal—deprive us of words to speak our detestation of its author. But the blaster of his race stops not here: in the very next page—we tremble while we transcribe it—he desperately, insanely asserts—

THERE IS NO GOD.

Miserable worm! Pity pleads for thee; and contempt, disgust, and horror, are tempered by compassion for thy wretched infirmity of mind. But an overwhelming passion rises when we gaze on the hideous blasphemy of thy more prolix commentary on this detestable text.

[1] This is the beginning of the mixture of poetry, bombast, and blasphemy, entitled an Ode to Superstition, in *Alastor*. (Reviewer's footnote)

We hardly dare copy it; but it is our duty to show to what monstrous extent the author carries his impious profanation.

[quotes Canto VII, lines 26–44]

We cannot proceed: pages of raving atheism, even more atrocious than what we have quoted, follow; and the blasphemer revels in all the pruriency of his disordered and diabolical fancy. For men like the writer, when they are known to exist, there are no terms of infamy sufficiently strong. We may therefore say, in the mild language of Bentley, that as 'no atheist, as such, can be a true friend, an affectionate relation, or a loyal subject,' we leave to his conscience, at some awakened hour, this contemner of every thing that is good, this sapper of every thing that is sacred,—this demoniac proscriber of his species, and insolent insulter of his Maker.

To observe that extreme madness[1] and contradiction are notorious in every paragraph, is not enough; it is the bounden duty of those to whom the conservation of public morals is entrusted, to prohibit the sale of this pernicious book—

> Deny the curst blasphemer's tongue to rage,
> And turn God's fury from an impious age.

It is hardly worth while to ask how a theorist of Mr. Shelley's class would act in the relations between man and man. It can hardly be doubted but his practice would square with his principles, and be calculated to disturb all the harmonies of nature. A disciple following his tenets, would not hesitate to debauch, or, after debauching, to abandon any woman: to such, it would be a matter of perfect indifference to rob a confiding father of his daughters, and incestuously to live with all the branches of a family whose morals were ruined by the damned sophistry of the seducer; to such it would be sport to tell a deserted wife to obtain with her pretty face support by prostitution; and, when the unhappy maniac sought refuge in self-destruction, to laugh at the fool while in the arms of associate strumpets. For what are the ties of nature, what are the pangs of humanity, to them? They are above the idle inventions of tyrants and priests—the worthless restrictions of 'morals, law, and custom,'—the delusions of virtue, and the ordinances of a deity. The key to their heaven is in the annexed lines.

[quotes Canto IX, lines 76–90]

[1] Ex. gr. the following jargon:—(Reviewer's footnote) [quotes Canto IV, lines 139–51].

79

Promiscuous intercourse of the sexes, and individual 'courage of soul,' to despise every thing but the gratification of its own appetites: this is the millenium promised by the votaries of Shelley, and the worshippers of the god Necessity!

The notes are worthy of the poem; and it is said that those distinguished by an ☞ are the production of a noble lord, who once lived in unrestrained intimacy with the author, and partook of the pleasures of his free mode of testifying to the sincerity of his professed opinions. One of these is a dialogue between Vice and Falsehood; very proper interlocutors, for Falsehood says . . .

[quotes Note IV, lines 49–53 and 89–108]

Another has the following political illustration of the new philosophy.

English reformers exclaim against sinecures,—but the true pension-list is the rentroll of the landed proprietors: wealth is a power usurped by the few, to compel the many to labour for their benefit. The laws which support this system derive their force from the ignorance and credulity of its victims: they are the result of a conspiracy of the few against the many, who are themselves obliged to purchase this pre-eminence by the loss of all real comfort.

The domestic relations are the same character.

[quotes Note V, paragraphs 2 and 4 and the first four and last two sentences of paragraph 6]

Need we go farther to justify what we have said respecting this most infamous publication? We will not stain our pages with another line; and we trust to Heaven, that in discharging as painful and difficult a duty as ever fell upon a Review, we may be pardoned if we have acted unwisely, since we are sure we have acted conscientiously.

15. Unsigned notice, *The Monthly Magazine and British Register*

June 1, 1821, li, 460–1

A poem entitled *Queen Mab*, by Mr. Percy Bysshe Shelley, was printed and distributed among his friends, about seven years ago, but has at length been published. The text of the work is in measured lines, of unequal length, which being divided into parcels, by means of Roman numerals have the appearance of so many odes, but without rhyme. It is in the *Thalaba* style, which has been so bepraised by the poetasters of the present day. 'He,' says Dr. Johnson, 'that thinks himself capable of astonishing, may write blank verse; but these that hope only to please, must condescend to rhyme.' The Author before us does, indeed, endeavour to *astonish*, by the extravagance of his paradoxes, and the incongruity of his metaphors; and may, therefore, claim the right to print his lines of such various lengths as may suit his own whim or the taste of his compositor. It is a continuous declamation without either 'rhyme or reason,' and the speaker may pause where he will without injury to the sense or interruption to the monotonous flow of the harangue. The notes occupy much more space than the text; and consist chiefly of extracts from various authors, in favour of Atheism, the equalization of property, and the unrestrained intercourse of the sexes! The French, Latin, and Greek passages, which were left in their original dress in the gratuitous edition, are here translated for the benefit of the mere English reader. Advocates, as we are, for a very extended freedom of the press, we fear commenting further on this work, lest we should, unintentionally, assist in that *powerful* criticism, to which, we fear, it will soon be subjected. We have observed, of late, a seeming design to lure the unwary author to his destruction. The public journals, not even excepting *The Quarterly Review*, have lauded Mr. Shelley as a poet,—as a genius of the highest order! The other panders of corruption speak of his 'powerful talents'! What can all this flattery mean, if it be not to decoy the witless bird, and to catch him in the snare? Either this is the case, or our Critics are a set of dunces, who cannot distinguish between sublimity and bombast,—between poetry and 'prose run mad.'

16. Unsigned notice, *The Literary Chronicle and Weekly Review*

June 2, 1821, no. 107, 344–5

Mr. Shelley furnishes one of the most striking and melancholy instances of the perversion, or rather prostitution of genius, that we ever met with. With talents that, if properly directed, might have made him universally admired and esteemed, he has made such a total wreck of his character, that he has not only armed society against him, but has almost put himself out of the pale of human laws. While we cannot but feel some portion of pity for a man of enlarged intellectual powers thus debasing himself, we feel disgust at his licentious and incestuous principles, and horror at his daring impiety; and his very name—

> Comes over our memory,
> As doth the raven o'er th' infected house,
> Boding to ill.

The history of the poem of *Queen Mab* is as curious as the subject is impious. Whether, when it was first written some years ago, a trader in blasphemy was not to be found, or that the author felt some dread at the injury a general diffusion of his work might occasion, we know not, but it was only circulated privately among the author's friends; it was afterwards, we believe, printed in the *Theological Enquirer*; and the first three cantos also appeared under the title of *The Demon of the World*, the notes being printed in a separate pamphlet. The whole are now, for the first time, brought together, and, as it would appear, without the knowledge of the author; the poem contains much powerful writing and many beautiful passages; but these make but a miserable atonement for the principles which it inculcates.

The author is an avowed Atheist, who would shake off all laws, human and divine, and have a society rioting in lust and incest, and, as he himself terms it,—

Unchecked by dull and selfish chastity.

We shall not quote another line from this baneful production, and shall only observe, that the private life of Mr. Shelley is said to be in unison with his principles; and that—

His own example strengthens all his laws;
And he's himself the *monster* that he draws.

Of the character of this poem, we might have been spared the labour of criticism, since a court of equity deemed its principles such, that the author ought not to be intrusted with the guardianship of his own children, of which he was in consequence deprived.

A man of Mr. Shelley's cultivated mind, cannot but possess strong feelings, and he must sometimes reflect on the ruin he has brought on himself, and on the probable injury he may have done to society; if he does so reflect, he must have a hell in his own conscience, which will torture him more severely than even the scorn of society and the abhorrence of all good men; and to that we consign him, sincerely wishing that this may be his only punishment, and that it may never be aggravated by the consciousness of having destroyed the happiness of others, either by his precept or example.

17. Richard Carlile, review, *The Republican*

February 1, 1822, v, 145-8

Richard Carlile published a series of radical periodicals and other liberal literature including several pirated editions of *Queen Mab*. Shelley protested at his frequent fines and imprisonments.

This beautiful poem is again in full sale at a reduced price, or at 7s. 6d. three-fifths only of its first price. The Vice Society, by an indictment, had succeeded in suppressing its public sale. They are now solicited to try what they can do again in that respect. If they please, they shall make it as common as they have made the 'Age of Reason.'

The present publisher has been called on by a person calling himself 'Consistency' (he hates all anonymous writers, particularly when they ask questions) to explain how his conduct in publishing *Queen Mab* corresponds with the objections he has taken to Mr. Benbow's publication of the *Political Works* of Paine. If 'Consistency' had been consistent in his views as in his professions, he would have seen no inconsistency on the part of the present publisher of *Queen Mab*: to explain which a short history of the publication will suffice.

In the summer of 1821, Mr. William Clark, in a shop near St. Clement's Church in the Strand, published *Queen Mab*. The author, Percy Bysshe Shelley, printed a few copies for his friends a few years back, but it was never known to be publicly sold until published by Mr. Clark. Immediately on its appearance the Vice Society pounced upon it with an indictment, against which the publisher (Mr. Clark) was not proof. He was arrested, and instead of going to the Bench Prison, or to Newgate, as he should have done, he offered to compromise the matter with the Society, and to give up the copies he had by him for their destruction; pleading ignorance of its being objectionable. This hypocrisy weighed nothing with Pritchard, the Secretary of the Society, he reminded Mr. Clark that he needed not to plead ignorance of the quality of the publication, after having so long served

God hath not promised
        Skies always blue,
Flower-strewn pathways
    All our lives through;
God hath not promised
        Sun without rain,
Joy without sorrow,
        Peace without pain.

But God hath promised
    Strength for the day,
Rest for the labor,
        Light for the way.
Grace for the trials,
        Help from above,
Unfailing sympathy
        Undying love . . .

In

Memory

as shopman in Carlile's shop in Fleet Street. 'Six Acts' proved too much for Mr. Clark: he bound himself down to good behaviour, as they call it, and found that he could not move in the sale of the work, as a second arrest took place because some other person had sold a copy in his shop. He should not have given recognizances, and he might then have bid them defiance, as has evidently and successfully been done in Fleet Street. By neglecting to do this, *Queen Mab* was suppressed without going to a Jury, without even a struggle on the part of its publisher. Here then it was certainly fair game for any person to take up, particularly for the present publisher, who has suffered from the redoubled violence of the prosecuting gangs occasioned by the scandalous compromises which have been made with them by others.

'Consistency,' says, very inconsistently, that Mr. Clark and his family are suffering from the publication of *Queen Mab*. It may be wished that it were so, and very happy would have been the writer of this, if the sufferings of Mr. Clark were not from a less honourable source than the publication of *Queen Mab*. The whole weight of the expence of paper and printing for *Queen Mab*, fell upon the shoulders of others, and not upon those of Mr. Clark, and it is partly to relieve those persons from their loss, that the publication of the same edition with a new imprint has been taken up by its present publisher.

'Consistency' should have looked at the matter before he had complained of inconsistency. He would have seen that Mr. Carlile never complained of Mr. Benbow's publishing the *Theological Works* of Mr. Paine, although he did express a wish that they had been published publicly. It was the publication of the *Theological Works* privately, and the *Political Works* publicly, about which complaint was made.

If Mr. Clark had stood his ground and kept the copies of *Queen Mab* on sale, until a Jury had given a verdict against it, the present publisher would then have taken up the public sale of it in his turn, and this is the way the warfare ought to be carried on. Mr. Clark should have published the *Age of Reason*, and Palmer's *Principles of Nature*, as well as *Queen Mab*, publicly; and after him Mr. Benbow should have done the same openly, instead of clandestinely, and then the matter would have been in a fair train for success, and prosecution would only accelerate the demand. Poor 55, in Fleet Street, has to sustain all the brunt of the battle, whilst others wish to strip it of its feathers and its laurels without assisting to fight in the same foremost rank. This shall not be done. What we earn we will keep and wear.

Our comrades shall share our success, but not so with the pirate and the poltroon.

Queen Mab is a philosophical poem in nine cantos, and is remarkably strong in its exposure and denunciation of Kingcraft and Priestcraft. Lord Byron calls it a poem of great strength and wonderful powers of imagination; and, with his Lordship, we differ from some of the Author's metaphysical opinions. However it is upon the principle of free discussion, and upon the principle of giving currency to every thing that is valuable, that the present publisher has taken up the publication. He read it twice over during his first imprisonment in the King's Bench Prison, waiting for trial for the 'Parodies,' and in the summer of 1819, he made an effort to obtain the consent of its author to its publication in the *Temple of Reason*, but did not succeed. Should the Author now wish that the publication should not be proceeded with, the present Publisher would willingly yield to his instructions, in the same manner and disposition as he first hesitated to print without them, although advised to do it by many of the Author's friends and intimate acquaintance.

In addition to the Poem itself, there are Notes by the Author, of equal bulk, equal beauties, and equal merit. Every thing that is mischievous to society is painted in this work in the highest colours. We hesitate before we give assent to the Author's views of marriage, particularly, as he strikes at the contract without modifications, and seems desirous of destroying it without defining a better system. This part of the Notes we understand forms one of the passages selected for indictment, and as war is commenced we would prefer to support the Author without coinciding with all his views, than to give the least encouragement to the hypocrites and villains who would stifle all discussion, and suppress every valuable publication, because it tends to unmask them, and to put a stop to their robberies upon the industrious multitude.

The last Note forms an essay of twenty-two pages, to encourage an abstinence from the use of animal food, and, to our knowledge, it has made a very great impression, upon that point, with many of its readers. Very powerful arguments can be brought forward on both sides of this question, but we hesitate not to say, that the laws of Nature and Necessity determine nothing regular on this point, but vary with climates and seasons. For ourselves we can say that we lean to the use of vegetable food in preference to animal, where its quantity and quality can be rendered sufficient to all the purposes of life and health.

When we say that this volume is replete with beauties, the reader will excuse the hacknied [*sic*] custom of making selections.

EDITOR.

18. William Bengo Collyer, from a review of *Queen Mab* in 'Licentious Productions in High Life,' *The Investigator,* or *Quarterly Magazine*

1822 second part, v, 315–73

Collyer's essay from which this excerpt is taken attacks seven other books including *Don Juan* and *Cain*. Ironically, later Collyer who had attacked Shelley's personal life so viciously was charged himself with moral failures.

To the last part of the painful duty which we have imposed upon ourselves we turn with pleasure, because it is the last, for nothing else could induce us to revert to that most execrable publication, *Queen Mab*, with any other feelings than those of unmingled horror and disgust. Compared with this *Don Juan* is a moral poem and *Cain* a homily. It does not merely question or sneer at revelation, nor is it satisfied with denying it—deism is too mean a flight for its author's wondrous powers—the providence of the Deity too insignificant an object of his attack,—his being therefore is denied, and the atheist-bard confidently assures us, that there is no God. Our blood curdled in our veins as we waded through nine cantos of blasphemy and impiety, such as we never thought that any one, on the outside of bedlam, could have uttered; nor dare we transcribe any portion of it in our pages, save one of the very mildest of its author's attacks upon religion, the slightest of his insults to his God, whom again and again—our hand trembles

87

as we write it—the impious wretch has dared to brand as a tyrant,
a murderer, a cheat, a demon, and a fiend.

> How ludicrous the priest's dogmatic roar!
> The weight of his exterminating curse
> How light! and his affected charity,
> To suit the pressure of the changing times,
> What palpable deceit—but for thy aid,
> Religion! but for thee, prolific fiend,
> Who peoplest earth with demons, Hell with men,
> And Heaven with slaves!
>
> Thou taintest all thou look'st upon!
>
> But now contempt is mocking thy gray hairs;
> Thou art descending to the darksome grave,
> Unhonoured and unpitied, but by those
> Whose pride is passing by like thine, and sheds,
> Like thine, a glare that fades before the sun
> Of truth, and shines but in the dreadful night
> That long has lowered above the ruined world.

But we must desist; we cannot quote the shortest passage referring
either to the Creator or the Redeemer of mankind, which is not so
awfully horrible in its blasphemy, that even to transcribe it for the
mere purpose of holding it up to the execrations of mankind, must be
in itself a sin. This atheist, like others of a tribe but few in numbers
and but rarely appearing as monstrosities of their race, dethrones one
God, whose attributes are revealed, and whose requirements are
known, to set up a strange nondescript something or nothing in his
stead, which he passionately invokes as the

> . . . Soul of the Universe,
> Spirit of Nature, all-sufficing Power,
> Necessity!

Of the person, nature, and functions of this old pseudo-divinity
newly revived, our readers will, we doubt not, be abundantly satisfied with the following very philosophical and intelligible exposition.

[quotes Canto VI, lines 198–226]

Thus much for the precious jargon of Mr. Shelley's new theology:
a word or two ere we leave him upon his morality. The tone and
character of this may be easily collected from a single extract, from the

representation given by the poet, of how the world should be governed, and would be, were he its governor.

> Then that sweet bondage which is Freedom's self,
> And rivets with sensation's softest tie
> The kindred sympathies of human souls,
> Needed no fetters of tyrannic law:
> Those delicate and timid impulses
> In Nature's primal modesty arose,
> And with undoubted confidence disclosed
> The growing longings of its dawning love,
> Unchecked by dull and selfish chastity,
> That virtue of the cheaply virtuous,
> Who pride themselves in senselessness and frost.

This, one would think, was plain and intelligible enough, but lest it should not be, it is illustrated and expanded in a long, artful, and sophistical note in which we are boldly told that

'Chastity is a monkish and evangelical superstition, a greater foe to natural temperance even than unintellectual sensuality; it strikes at the root of all domestic happiness, and consigns more than half of the human race to misery, that some few may monopolize according to law. A system could not well have been devised more studiously hostile to human happiness than marriage.'

The notes of which this extract is a very favourable specimen, as far as their delicacy and morality are concerned, form, in our opinion, the most dangerous part of this wicked and dangerous book, for they are more intelligible than the poem, which is wrapt in an obscurity and mysticism, which neither Madame Guyon nor Jacob Behmen could have surpassed. Their authors, for there were more than one, labour by them to establish and enforce such notable discoveries and propositions as these: 'all that miserable tale of the Devil and Eve is irreconcileable with the knowledge of the stars'; 'the narrow and unenlightened morality of the Christian religion is an aggravation of the evils of society'; 'utility is morality'; 'there is neither good nor evil in the universe, otherwise than as the events to which we apply these epithets, have a relation to our own peculiar mode of being'; 'the universe was not created, but existed from all eternity'; 'Jesus was an ambitious man, who aspired to the throne of Judea'; 'had the resolution of Pontius Pilate been equal to his candour, the Christian religion could never have prevailed.' Nor is there, according to these new lights of the world 'a state of future punishment'; nor, except that sublimely obscure and unintelligible principle, for being it can have none, 'necessity, the mother of the world,' can there be a God. How they demonstrate these positions to be true and shew all men, except themselves—for we hope and believe there are few other atheists, at least in the world—to be fools and madmen, two specimens of their candour and their hardihood will more than suffice to shew.

'But even that a man should raise a dead body to life before our eyes, and on this fact rest his claim to being considered the son of God;— the Humane Society restores drowned persons, and because it makes no mystery of the method it employs, its members are not mistaken for the sons of God.'

'Lord Chesterfield was never yet taken for a prophet, even by a bishop, yet he uttered this remarkable prediction: "The despotic government of France is screwed up to the highest pitch; a revolution is fast approaching; that revolution, I am convinced, will be radical and sanguinary." This appeared in the letters of the prophet long before the accomplishment of this wonderful prediction. Now, have these particulars come to pass, or have they not? If they have, how could the Earl have foreknown them without inspiration?'

Whilst we tremble at the horrid blasphemy of these passages, we cannot suppress a smile at the absurdity of the beardless philosophers, who could think for a moment to gull even their brother freshmen at the university by such ridiculous comparisons. Those who could be gulled by them must, indeed, be the veriest fools that ever walked the earth without a keeper. But these boys in reasoning, as in years, are prophets forsooth themselves, as well as interpreters of prophecy, and *arcades ambo*, are drivellers in both. Bear witness the following notable prediction to the truth of this description.

'Analogy seems to favour the opinion that as, like other systems, Christianity has arisen and augmented, so like them it will decay and perish; that as violence, darkness, and deceit, not reasoning and persuasion, have procured its admission among mankind, so, when enthusiasm has subsided, and time, that infallible controverter of false opinions has involved its pretended evidences in the darkness of antiquity, it will become obsolete; that Milton's poem alone will give permanency to the remembrance of its absurdities; and that men will laugh as heartily at grace, faith, redemption, and original sin, as they now do at the metamorphoses of Jupiter, the miracles of Romish saints, the efficacy of witchcraft, and the appearance of departed spirits.'

To complete the catalogue of absurdities thrown together in glorious confusion, through ninety pages and gleaned from all quarters, all kindreds, and all ages of the system of infidel philosophy, from the 'admirable author' of the *Inquirer* and *Political Justice* upwards, enforcing the doctrines of equality of property, and an equal division of bodily labour, is followed by a very learned and elaborate note, attributing the origin of evil and all the misery in the world to a nonadherence to vegetable diet, or rather to the pernicious practise of altering our food by fire, the natural conclusion from which is, that it had better be eaten raw. This most elaborate disquisition is enlivened by a new and very ingenious interpretation of the story of Prometheus, whose stealing fire from Heaven means, as is very learnedly shewn, that he was the first cook who 'applied that element to culinary purposes,' or, in other words, was the inventor of the palatable but most destructive arts of roasting, boiling, frying, and all those etceteras on which Dr. Kitchener, the Prometheus of modern times, displays so much erudition. We hope that in the next edition of his most popular work, the learned and most appropriately named Doctor will not omit to notice this important discovery, the omission of which, we cannot help thinking, no slight imputation upon his oracular discernment and profound research. This hint for cooks and compilers of cookery-books—in these degenerate days, a most lucrative and honourable employment—that follows concerns divines, who, in all their curious and abstruse speculations upon the fall of man, have not hit, we will undertake to say, upon so novel and ingenious an interpretation as this.

'The allegory of Adam and Eve eating from the tree of evil, and entailing upon their posterity the wrath of God and the loss of everlasting life, admits of no other explanation than the disease and crime that have flowed from unnatural diet.'

Who but, after this, must lift up his hands and eyes in astonishment, and exclaim, 'A Daniel, Yea, a second Daniel, come to judgment!' But a truce at once with jesting, and commenting of all sorts, on such stuff and nonsense. Of its authors, one was expelled from the University for printing, for private circulation, these atheistical blasphemies, and the other withdrew, to save himself from the disgrace, (for he evidently did not consider it a triumph), of sharing the same fate. The notes, which have a hand appended to them, partly original, but for the greater part extracted from older infidels, are not written by the author of the poem. They have been attributed to his early and constant friend, Lord Byron; but here we are satisfied that rumour does the noble lord some wrong, as they are the production of a much less able and obscurer man. We saw him once some years ago, but whether he is still to be seen or is no more, we know not. To have sat for an hour or two, once in your life, in company with an avowed atheist, is enough, and more than enough for any man who retains the slightest respect for religion, or veneration for the name and attributes of God. These are so habitually and so coarsely blasphemed by the individual in question, as to have shocked even those who make no profession of religion, but who are rather fond than averse to skeptical inquiries, conducted as they ought to be, when entered upon at all, with decency, —with some deference to the opinion of million upon millions of mankind, and with the solemnity due to the awful consequences which they involve. But he disposed of the existence of a God, and a future state, and with the same levity, flippancy, and frivolity as he would dismiss the merits of a play, or the dancing of his partner at last night's ball—and avows—yes, we ourselves have heard him avow, to the disgust of a large assembly—that the only thing worth living for, is the sensual enjoyment in which man participates with brute!—The brute that perishes, we add, and happy would it be for him if he so perished also. But he may yet be—for all we know to the contrary— in the land of the living, and within reach of mercy, and the possibility of repentance. But his wretched friend and co-adjutor, where is he? In the meridian of his days he died not the death of the atheist de-pictured, by the depraved yet glowing fancy of his youth.

> I was an infant when my mother went
> To see an atheist burned. She took me there;
> The dark-robed priests were met around the pile;
> The multitude was gazing silently;
> And as the culprit passed with dauntless mien,
> Tempered disdain in his unaltering eye,
> Mixed with a quiet smile, shone calmly forth:
> The thirsty fire crept round his manly limbs;
> His resolute eyes were scorched to blindness soon;
> His death-pang rent my heart! the insensate mob
> Uttered a cry of triumph, and I wept.
> 'Weep, not, child!' cried my mother, 'for that man
> Has said, There is no God.'

Embarked in a sailing boat on a lovely day upon the waves of the Adriatic, with a chosen companion of his pleasurable excursions, the fisherman marked his sails gallantly unfurled, and glittering in the sun,

—he looked again, and in a moment—in the twinkling of an eye, the boat had disappeared, and the atheist had sunk to the bottom of a fathomless abyss, either to rot into annihilation there, or but to deposit the lifeless body for whose gratification he had lived, that his disencumbered spirit might rise to the judgment of his God. That judgment we presume not to pronounce; but this we may, and this we will undertake to say, that he stood not in his presence and before his throne, to utter blasphemies he promulgated upon earth—nor when the dead shall arise—for in spite of his daring assertions and imbecile arguments to the contrary, the dead *shall* arise,—at the great day of final doom, in the face of an assembled universe, and at the bar of him whom as an imposter he villified and despised, will he venture to maintain the creed he adopted for himself, and urged upon others here:—

> There is no God
> Nature confirms the faith his death-groan sealed:
> Let heaven and earth, let man's revolving race,
> His ceaseless generations tell their tale;
> Let every part depending on the chain
> That links it to the whole, point to the hand
> That grasps its term! let every seed that falls
> In silent eloquence unfold its store
> Of argument; infinity within,
> Infinity without, belie creation;
> The exterminable spirit it contains
> Is nature's only God.

Such a death to such a man is awful in the extreme and ought to be impressive—or call it Providence—or call it chance.

'I am acquainted with a lady of considerable accomplishments, and the mother of a numerous family, whom the Christian religion has goaded to incurable insanity. A parallel case is, I believe, within the experience of every physician.'

Without attaching any credit to this representation until we have more minute particulars of the case, we can oppose to it a worse illustration of the effects of the philosophy and morality taught by *Queen Mab*. It had a disciple, the descendant and heir of an ancient, and honourable, and a titled family. That family was disgraced by his vices from youth to his death. These two, with the principles of which they were the natural offspring, most righteously deprived him of the guardianship of his children, but unhappily drove their mother to ruin, prostitution and suicide, whilst he consoled himself for the loss of a wife's society by first seducing one daughter of his friend, and afterwards living in an incestuous connection with another. For his sake we exult not, but rather would weep that he is no more, since nothing short of a greater miracle than those which whilst living he ridiculed and rejected, could snatch him from the punishment due to his crimes; but for the sake of the world, we rejoice that both he and the reviver of the principles he adopted, have run their race of impiety and sin.

19. Henry Crabb Robinson, diary entry

January 10, 1836

Robinson's illuminating diaries and journals contain numerous references to literary figures and to his reading during his lifetime, 1775–1867. This extract comes from *Henry Crabb Robinson on Books and their Writers*, ed. Morley (1938), ii, p. 479.

JAN. 10th. . . . I read at night and in the morning the notes to Shelley's *Queen Mab* as well as here and there bits of his poetry. His atheism is very repulsive, but the God he denies seems to be after all but the God of the superstitious. I suspect that he has been guilty of this fault of which I find I have all my life been guilty, though not to his extent,— inferring that there can be no truth behind the palpable falsehoods propounded to him. He draws in one of his notes a picture of Christianity, or rather he sums up the Christian doctrine, and in such a way that perhaps Wordsworth would say: 'This, I disbelieve as much as Shelley, but that is only the caricature and burlesque of Christianity.' And yet this is the Christianity most men believe. As poetry there is much very delightful in Shelley. Read till late in bed.

ALASTOR; or THE SPIRIT OF SOLITUDE: and other poems

1816

20. Unsigned notice, *The Monthly Review, or Literary Journal*

April 1816, lxxix, 433

We must candidly own that these poems are beyond our comprehension; and we did not obtain a clue to their sublime obscurity, till an address to Mr. Wordsworth explained in what school the author had formed his taste. We perceive, through the 'darkness visible' in which Mr. Shelley veils his subject, some beautiful imagery and poetical expressions: but he appears to be a poet 'whose eye, in a fine phrenzy rolling,' seeks only such objects as are 'above this visible diurnal sphere;' and therefore we entreat him, for the sake of his reviewers as well as of his other readers, (if he has any,) to subjoin to his next publication an *ordo*, a glossary, and copious notes, illustrative of his allusions and explanatory of his meaning.

21. Unsigned review, *The British Critic*

May 1816, n.s. v, 545–6

If this gentleman is not blessed with the inspiration, he may at least console himself with the madness of a poetic mind. In the course of our critical labours, we have been often condemned to pore over much profound and prosing stupidity; we are therefore not a little delighted with the nonsense which mounts, which rises, which spurns the earth, and all its dull realities; we love to fly with our author to a silent nook.

> One silent nook
> Was there. Even on the edge of that vast mountain
> Upheld by knotty roots and fallen rocks
> It overlooked in its serenity
> The dark earth and the bending vault of stars.

Tolerably high this aforesaid nook, to overlook the stars: but

> Hither the poet came. His eyes beheld
> Their own wan light through the reflected lines
> Of his thin hair, distinct in the dark depths
> Of that still fountain.

Vastly intelligible. Perhaps, if his poet had worn a wig, the case might have been clearer: for then it might have thrown some light on the passage from the ancient legend.

> By the side of a soft flowing stream
> An elderly gentleman sat;
> On the top of his head was his wig,
> On the top of his wig was his hat.

But this aforesaid hair is endowed with strange qualities.

> his scattered hair
> Sered by the autumn of strange suffering,
> Sung dirges in the wind.

This can only be interpreted by supposing, that the poet's hair was entwined in a fiddle-stick, and being seared with 'the autumn of strange

sufferings,' *alias* rosin, 'scraped discords in the wind,' for so the last
line should evidently be read. But, soft—a little philosophy, for our
poet is indubitably a vast philosopher.

> Seized by the sway of the *ascending* stream
> With dizzy swiftness round, and round, and round
> Ridge after ridge the straining boat arose,
> Till on the verge of the extremest curve
> Where through an opening of the rocky bank
> The waters overflow, and a smooth spot
> Of glassy quiet 'mid those battling tides
> Is left, the boat paused shuddering.

A very animated boat this; something resembling that of the Irish-
man, which must needs know its way to Greenwich, because it had
been down the stream so often. We cannot do sufficient justice to the
creative fancy of our poet. A man's hair singing dirges, and a boat
pausing and shuddering, are among the least of his inventions; nature
for him reverses all her laws, the streams ascend. The power of the
syphon we all know, but it is for the genius of Mr. Shelley to make the
streams run up hill. But we entreat the pardon of our readers for dwelling so long upon this *ne plus ultra* of poetical sublimity.

22. Unsigned review, *The Eclectic Review*

October 1816, n.s. v. 391–3

It is but justice to Mr. Shelley, to let him give his own explanation of
this singular production.

[quotes the first paragraph and the first sentence of the second paragraph of Shelley's Preface]

We fear that not even this commentary will enable ordinary readers
to decipher the import of the greater part of Mr. Shelley's allegory.
All is wild and specious, untangible and incoherent as a dream. We

should be utterly at a loss to convey any distinct idea of the plan or purpose of the poem. It describes the adventures of a poet who 'lived' and 'died' and 'sung in solitude'; who wanders through countries real and imaginery, in search of an unknown and undefined object; encounters perils and fatigues altogether incredible; and at length expires 'like an exhalation,' in utter solitude, leaving this world inconsolable for a loss of which it is nevertheless unconscious.

The poem is adapted to show the dangerous, the fatal tendency of that morbid ascendancy of the imagination over the other faculties, which incapacitates the mind for bestowing an adequate attention on the real objects of this 'work-day' life, and for discharging the relative and social duties. It exhibits the utter uselessness of imagination, when wholly undisciplined, and selfishly employed for the mere purposes of intellectual luxury, without reference to those moral ends to which it was designed to be subservient. This could not be better illustrated, than in a poem where we have glitter without warmth, succession without progress, excitement without purpose, and a search which terminates in annihilation. It must surely be with the view of furnishing some such inference as we have supposed, that every indication of the Author's belief in a future state of existence, and in the moral government of God, is carefully avoided, unless the following be an exception.

> O that God,
> Profuse of poisons, would concede the chalice
> Which but one living man has drained, who now,
> Vessel of deathless wrath, a slave that feels
> No proud exemption in the blighting curse
> He bears, over the world wanders forever,
> Lone as incarnate death! (p. 47.)

Our readers will be startled at the profanity of this strange exclamation, but we can assure them that it is the only reference to the Deity in the poem. It was, we presume, part of the Author's plan, to represent his hero as an atheist of that metaphysical school, which held that the universe was God, and that the powers of evil constituted a sort of demonology. He speaks in his Preface of 'the poet's self-centred seclusion' being 'avenged by the furies of an irresistible passion pursuing him to speedy ruin.' 'But *that power*,' he adds, 'which strikes the luminaries of the world with sudden darkness and extinction, by awakening them to too exquisite a perception of its influences, dooms to a slow and *poisonous* decay those meaner spirits which dare to objure its dominion.' It is a pity that in his Preface Mr. S. had not avoided such jargon.

We shall enter no further into the Author's theory, nor shall we subject his poetry to minute criticism. It cannot be denied that very considerable talent for descriptive poetry is displayed in several parts. The Author has genius which might be turned to much better account; but such heartless fictions as *Alastor*, fail in accomplishing the legitimate purposes of poetry. In justice to the Author, we subjoin the following extract.

[quotes lines 420–68]

23. Leigh Hunt on Shelley in 'Young Poets,' *The Examiner*

December 1, 1816, no. 466, 761–2, and January 19, 1817, no. 473, 41

Leigh Hunt, along with his brother John, championed liberal political causes and was imprisoned for libel of the Prince Regent. Hunt wrote prolifically to encourage Keats and Shelley, but his political reputation probably injured both poets more than it helped them. *Blackwood's Magazine* called their poetry in derision 'the Cockney School.'

In sitting down to this subject we happen to be restricted by time to a much shorter notice than we could wish; but we mean to take it up again shortly. Many of our readers however have perhaps observed for themselves, that there has been a new school of poetry rising of late, which promises to extinguish the French one that has prevailed among us since the time of Charles the 2d. It began with something excessive, like most revolutions, but this gradually wore away; and an evident

aspiration after real nature and original fancy remained, which called
to mind the finer times of the English Muse. In fact it is wrong to call
it a new school, and still more so to represent it as one of innovation,
its only object being to restore the same love of Nature, and of *thinking* instead of mere *talking*, which formerly rendered us real poets, and
not merely versifying wits, and bead-rollers of couplets.

We were delighted to see the departure of the old school acknowledged in the number of the *Edinburgh Review* just published,—a
candour the more generous and spirited, inasmuch as that work has
hitherto been the greatest surviving ornament of the same school in
prose and criticism, as it is now destined, we trust, to be still the leader
in the new....

The object of the present article is merely to notice three young
writers, who appear to us to promise a considerable addition of
strength to the new school. Of the first who came before us, we have,
it is true, yet seen only one or two specimens, and these were no sooner
sent us than we unfortunately mislaid them; but we shall procure what
he has published, and if the rest answer to what we have seen, we shall
have no hesitation in announcing him for a very striking and original
thinker. His name is PERCY BYSSHE SHELLEY, and he is the author of a
poetical work entitled *Alastor, or the Spirit of Solitude*.

[The remaining two-thirds of the article is devoted to Reynolds and
Keats. In the January 19, 1817 issue, the poem 'Hymn to Intellectual
Beauty' was printed for the first time.]

24. John Gibson Lockhart, review, *Blackwood's Edinburgh Magazine*

November 1819, vi, 148–54

In *The Unextinguished Hearth*, Newman I. White attributed this review to John Wilson, but more recent scholarship suggests that John Gibson Lockhart was the author. Lockhart, a frequent contributor to *Blackwood's*, and Scott's son-in-law, was considered one of the more influential reviewers. See Alan Strout's *A Bibliography of Articles in Blackwood's Magazine: 1817–1825* (Lubbock, Texas, 1959).

We believe this little volume to be Mr Shelley's first publication; and such of our readers as have been struck by the power and splendour of genius displayed in *The Revolt of Islam*, and by the frequent tenderness and pathos of *Rosalind and Helen*, will be glad to observe some of the earliest efforts of a mind destined, in our opinion, under due discipline and self-management, to achieve great things in poetry. It must be encouraging to those who, like us, cherish high hopes of this gifted but wayward young man, to see what advances his intellect has made within these few years, and to compare its powerful, though still imperfect display, in his principal poem with its first gleamings and irradiations throughout this production almost of his boyhood. In a short preface, written with all the enthusiasm and much of the presumption of youth, Mr Shelley gives a short explanation of the subject of *Alastor; or, the Spirit of Solitude*, which we cannot say throws any very great light upon it, but without which, the poem would be, we suspect, altogether unintelligible to ordinary readers. Mr Shelley is too fond of allegories; and a great genius like his should scorn, now that it has reached the maturity of manhood, to adopt a species of poetry in which the difficulties of the art may be so conveniently blinked, and weakness find so easy a refuge in obscurity.

[quotes the first paragraph of the Preface]

Our readers will not expect, from this somewhat dim enunciation, at all times to see the drift of this wild poem; but we think they will feel, notwithstanding, that there is the light of poetry even in the darkness of Mr Shelley's imagination. Alastor is thus first introduced to our notice.

[quotes lines 67–92]

He is then described as visiting volcanoes, lakes of bitumen, caves winding among the springs of fire, and starry domes of diamond and gold, supported by crystal columns, and adorned with shrines of pearl and thrones of chrysolite—a magnificent pilgrimage no doubt, and not the less so on account of its being rather unintelligible. On completing his mineralogical and geological observations, and on re-ascending from the interior of our earth into the upper regions, his route is, to our taste, much more interesting and worthy of a poet.

[quotes lines 106–28]

During the soul-rapt enthusiasm of these mystic and magnificent wanderings, Alastor has no time to fall in love; but we are given to understand that, wherever he roams, he inspires it. There is much beauty in this picture. . . .

There is scarcely any part of the Poem which does not partake of a character of extravagance—and probably many of our readers may have felt this to be the case in our extracts, even more than ourselves. Be this as it may, we cannot but think that there is great sublimity in the death scene.

[quotes lines 632–71]

Several of the smaller poems contain beauties of no ordinary kind— but they are almost all liable to the charge of vagueness and obscurity! —Mr Shelley's imagination is enamoured of dreams of death; and he loves to strike his harp among the tombs.

[quotes 'On Death']

There breathes over the following scene, a spirit of deep, solemn, and mournful repose.

[quotes 'A Summer Evening Churchyard']

Long as our extracts have been, we must find room for one more, from a strange and unintelligible fragment of a poem, entitled 'The Daemon of the World.' It is exceedingly beautiful.

[quotes lines 1–48]

We beg leave, in conclusion, to say a few words about the treatment which Mr Shelley has, in his poetical character, received from the public. By our periodical critics he has either been entirely overlooked, or slightingly noticed, or grossly abused. There is not so much to find fault with in the mere silence of critics; but we do not hesitate to say, with all due respect for the general character of that journal, that Mr Shelley has been infamously and stupidly treated in the *Quarterly Review*. His Reviewer there, whoever he is,[1] does not shew himself a man of such lofty principles as to entitle him to ride the high horse in company with the author of *The Revolt of Islam*. And when one compares the vis inertiae of his motionless prose with the 'eagle-winged raptures' of Mr Shelley's poetry, one does not think indeed of Satan reproving Sin, but one does think, we will say it in plain words and without a figure, of a dunce rating a man of genius. If that critic does not know that Mr Shelley is a poet, almost in the very highest sense of that mysterious word, then, we appeal to all those whom we have enabled to judge for themselves, if he be not unfit to speak of poetry before the people of England. If he does know that Mr Shelley is a great poet, what manner of man is he who, with such conviction, brings himself, with the utmost difficulty, to admit that there is any beauty at all in Mr Shelley's writings, and is happy to pass that admission off with an accidental and niggardly phrase of vague and valueless commendation. This is manifest and mean—glaring and gross injustice on the part of a man who comes forward as the champion of morality, truth, faith, and religion. This is being guilty of one of the very worst charges of which he accuses another; nor will any man who loves and honours genius, even though that genius may have occasionally suffered itself to be both stained and led astray, think but with contempt and indignation and scorn of a critic who, while he pretends to wield the weapons of honour, virtue, and truth, yet clothes himself in the armour of deceit, hypocrisy, and falsehood. He *exults* to calumniate Mr Shelley's moral character, but he *fears* to acknowledge his genius. And therefore do we, as the sincere though sometimes sorrowing friends of Mr Shelley, scruple not to say, even though it may expose

[1] Lockhart is referring to the review of Shelley's *Revolt of Islam* in *The Quarterly Review* of April 1819 (xxi, 466–71), written by John Taylor Coleridge.

us to the charge of personality from those from whom alone such a charge could at all affect our minds, that the critic shews himself by such conduct as far inferior to Mr Shelley as a man of worth, as the language in which he utters his falsehood and uncharitableness shews him to be inferior as a man of intellect.

In the present state of public feeling, with regard to poets and poetry, a critic cannot attempt to defraud a poet of his fame, without paying the penalty either of his ignorance or his injustice. So long as he confines the expression of his envy or stupidity to works of moderate or doubtful merit, he may escape punishment; but if he dare to insult the spirit of England by contumelious and scornful treatment of any one of her gifted sons, that contumely and that scorn will most certainly be flung back upon himself, till he be made to shrink and to shiver beneath the load. It is not in the power of all the critics alive to blind one true lover of poetry to the splendour of Mr Shelley's genius—and the reader who, from mere curiosity, should turn to *The Revolt of Islam* to see what sort of trash it was that so moved the wrath and the spleen and the scorn of the Reviewer, would soon feel, that to understand the greatness of the poet, and the littleness of his traducer, nothing more was necessary than to recite to his delighted sense any six successive stanzas of that poem, so full of music, imagination, intellect, and passion. We care comparatively little for injustice offered to one moving majestical in the broad day of fame—it is the injustice done to the great, while their greatness is unknown or misunderstood that a generous nature most abhors, in as much as it seems more basely wicked to wish that genius might never lift its head, than to envy the glory with which it is encircled.

There is, we firmly believe, a strong love of genius in the people of this country, and they are willing to pardon to its possessor much extravagance and error—nay, even more serious transgressions. Let both Mr Shelley and his critic think of that—let it encourage the one to walk onwards to his bright destiny, without turning into dark or doubtful or wicked ways—let it teach the other to feel a proper sense of his own insignificance, and to be ashamed, in the midst of his own weaknesses and deficiencies and meannesses, to aggravate the faults of the highly-gifted, and to gloat with a sinful satisfaction on the real or imaginery debasement of genius and intellect.

And here we ought, perhaps, to stop. But the Reviewer has dealt out a number of dark and oracular denunciations against the Poet, which the public can know nothing about, except that they imply a charge of immorality and wickedness. Let him speak out plainly, or let him hold his tongue. There are many wicked and foolish things in Mr Shelley's creed, and we have not hitherto scrupled, nor shall we henceforth scruple to expose that wickedness and that folly. But we do not think that he believes his own creed—at least, that he believes it fully and to utter conviction—and we doubt not but the scales will yet all fall from his eyes. The Reviewer, however, with a face of most laughable horror, accuses Mr Shelley in the same breath of some nameless act of atrocity, and of having been rusticated, or expelled, or warned to go away from the University of Oxford! He seems to shudder with the same holy fear at the violation of the laws of morality and the breaking of college rules. He forgets that in the world men do not wear caps and gowns as at Oriel or Exeter. He preaches not like Paul—but like a Proctor.

Once more, then we bid Mr Shelley farewell. Let him come forth from the eternal city, where, we understand, he has been sojourning,—in his strength, conquering and to conquer. Let his soul watch his soul, and listen to the voice of its own noble nature—and there is no doubt that the future will make amends for the past, whatever its errors may have been—and that the Poet may yet be good, great, and happy.

THE REVOLT OF ISLAM

1818

25. Leigh Hunt, *The Examiner*

February 1, 1818, no. 527, 75–6; February 22, no. 530, 121–2; March 1, 1818, no. 531, 139–41

This is an extraordinary production. The ignorant will not understand it; the idle will not take the pains to get acquainted with it; even the intelligent will be startled at first with its air of mysticism and wildness; the livelier man of the world will shake his head at it good naturedly; the sulkier one will cry out against it; the bigot will be shocked, terrified, and enraged; and fall to providing all that is said against himself; the negatively virtuous will resent the little quarter that is given to mere custom; the slaves of bad customs or bad passions of any sort will either seize their weapons against it, trembling with rage or conscious worthlessness, or hope to let it quietly pass by, as an enthusiasm that must end in air; finally, the hopeless, if they are ill-tempered, will envy its hopefulness,—if good tempered, will sorrowfully anticipate its disappointment,—both from self-love, though of two different sorts;—but we will venture to say, that the intelligent and the good, who are yet healthy-minded, and who have not been so far blinded by fear and self-love as to confound superstition with desert, anger and hatred with firmness, or despondency with knowledge, will find themselves amply repaid by breaking through the outer shell of this production, even if it be with the single reflection, that so much ardour for the happy virtues, and so much power to recommend them, have united in the same person. To will them with hope indeed is to create them; and to extend that will is the object of the writer before us.

The story of *The Revolt of Islam* is this. The poet, rising from 'visions of despair' occasioned by the late triumphs over the progress of mankind, goes meditating by the sea-shore, and after an awful and prophetic tempest, suddenly sees in the air the extraordinary spectacle of a combat between a serpent and an eagle:—

> The Serpent's mailed and many-coloured skin
> Shone through the plumes its coils were twined within
> By many a swollen and knotted fold; and high
> And far, the neck, receding light and thin,
> Sustained a crested head, which warily
> Shifted and glanced before the Eagle's steadfast eye.

The Serpent is defeated, and falls into the sea, from whence he is received into the bosom of a beautiful woman who sits lamenting upon the shore. She invites the poet to go somewhere across the sea with them in a boat. He consents, more in fear for her than for himself; and in the course of the voyage she tells him that the Serpent and the Eagle are the powers of Good and Evil who combat with each other at intervals; that the Serpent, or Power of Good, has again been defeated; and that she herself is his selected companion, whom in his more radiant shape he appeared to once at night, and announced his having fallen in love with. The Serpent all this while lies still, recovering from the effects of the combat; and at last the voyagers come to a magnificent temple beyond the polar ocean in which

> —There sat on many a sapphire throne
> The Great, who had departed from mankind,
> A mighty Senate;—some, whose white hair shone
> Like mountain snow, mild, beautiful, and blind.
> Some female forms, whose gestures beamed with mind;
> And ardent youths, and children bright and fair;
> And some had lyres, whose strings were intertwined
> With pale and clinging flames, which ever there,
> Waked faint yet thrilling sounds that pierced the chrystal air.

A magic and obscure circumstance then takes place, the result of which is: that the woman and Serpent are seen no more, but that a cloud opens asunder and a bright and beautiful shape, which seems compounded of both, is beheld sitting on a throne—a circumstance apparently imitated from Milton:

[quotes Canto I, lines 640–54, omitting lines 645–7]

This is a fine Grecian feeling of what may be called the sentiment of shape. The two strangers are the hero and heroine of the poem: and here the more human part of the story commences. *Laon*, the hero, relates it. He was an ardent and speculative youth, born in modern Greece; and grew up with great admiration of the beauties and kindnesses of external nature, and a great horror of the superstitions and other oppressions with which his country and mankind in general were afflicted. A beautiful female orphan under the care of his parents shared these feelings with him; and a mutual love was the consequence. She even speculated upon taking some extraordinary though gentle step to deliver the world from its thraldom; when she was torn away from him by some slaves of the Grand Turk's Seraglio; and he himself, for endeavouring to rescue her, and for taking that opportunity of proclaiming freedom, was shut up in a prison in a rock, where his senses forsook him. The effect of the circumstance however is not lost. He is delivered from his dungeon by an old man, and after a second but milder insanity, is informed by his preserver that the people had been awakened to new ideas, and that there was a maiden who went about exciting them to a bloodless freedom. It was his love *Cythna*, after having been made a victim of the tyrant's lust, and having been likewise imprisoned, and robbed of her senses. A considerable interval elapses while *Laon* recovers his reason, but on so doing, and hearing of the exploits of her whom he justly supposed to be his lovely friend, he takes leave of the old man, and journeys for Constantinople, or the Golden City, where he finds the people risen, the tyrant fallen, and *Cythna* the predominant spirit of the change. He goes with others to the palace, and sees the 'sceptered wretch' sitting silent and sullen on the footstool of his throne,—

> Alone, but for one child, who led before him
> A graceful dance:—*weeping and murmuring*
> *'Mid her sad task of unregarded love,*
> *That to no smiles it might his speechless sadness move.*

She clasps the tyrant's feet, and then stands up when the strangers come nigh;—

> Her lips and cheeks seemed very pale and wan,
> But on her forehead, and within her eye
> Lay beauty, which makes hearts that feed thereon
> Sick with excess of sweetness; on the throne
> She leaned; the King, with gathered brow, and lips
> *Wreathed by long scorn*, did inly sneer and frown
> *With hue like that when some great painter dips*
> *His pencil in the gloom of earthquake and eclipse.*

108

Laon saves his life from the fury of the crowd; a festival is held at which *Cythna* presides like a visible angel, and every thing seems happiness and security. The Revolters however are suddenly assailed by the allies of the tyrant; and the fortune of the contest is changed. *Cythna* reaches *Laon* through the lost battle on a huge black Tartarian horse, 'whose path makes a solitude'; and they fly to a distance through a desolate village, in the dwellings of which the flames and human beings were now dead:—

> But the wide sky,
> Flooded with lightning, *was ribbed overhead*
> *By the black rafters;* and around did lie
> Women, and babes, and men, slaughtered confusedly.

The only survivor is a female, who has gone mad, and fancies herself the Plague. The description of her desperate laughter and actions is appalling, though not without a tendency, we think, to something overwrought and artificial. When the travellers arrive at a place of rest, *Cythna* tells *Laon* her adventures. They have been briefly alluded to, and include a finely-fancied and pathetic account of a child which she had in her dungeon, and which was taken from her. *Laon* goes out from the retreat occasionally to get food and intelligence, and finds that Revenge, and subsequently Pestilence and Famine, have been making terrible havoc in the city. The tyrant and his slaves, in their terror, make frightened addresses to heaven, and a priest advises them to expiate its 'vengeance' by sacrificing *Laon* and *Cythna*. He according-ly dispatches members to hunt them out; upon which *Laon* comes for-ward disguised and offers to give up the man provided the woman be spared. They take an oath to do so, and he declares himself; but it is then declared impious to have made the oath; and at last, *Cythna* comes voluntarily forward, and shares the funeral pyre with her be-loved friend, from which they find themselves suddenly sailing on a beautiful sea to the Paradise in which the Spirit of Good resides, where *Cythna* meets with her child who had died of the plague; and the poem concludes.

We gave the fine description of the preparation for the sacrifice last week; we shall pursue our criticism next, with further extracts, an account of the particular views of the author, and a summary of the poetical character of the work in general.

We have given the story of this extraordinary book, and some ex-tracts by which the reader can easily judge of its general merits. We have some remarks however to make on the particular qualities of its poetry, and on the deep social interests upon which it speculates; but as we are much pressed for room now the Parliament are sitting, and yet do not wish to pass over the work lightly, we had better occupy our present article at once with some extracts we intended to make from the author's preface. He explains in them the general object of his poem, and touches in a masterly manner upon the great political point of it, and indeed of the age in which we live.

'The poem,' says he, 'which I now present to the world, is an attempt from which I scarcely dare to expect success, and in which a writer of established fame might fail without disgrace. It is an experiment on the temper of the public mind, as to *how far a thirst for a happier condition of moral and political society survives, among the enlightened and refined, the tempests which have shaken the age in which we live.* I have sought to enlist the harmony of metrical language, the ethereal combinations of the fancy, the rapid and subtle transitions of human passion, all those elements which essentially compose a Poem, in the cause of a liberal and comprehensive morality, and in the view of kindling within the bosoms of my readers, a virtuous enthusiasm for those doctrines of liberty and justice, *that faith and hope in something good,* which neither violence, nor misrepresentation, nor prejudice, can ever totally extinguish among mankind.'

After dilating a little more on the subjects of his poem, Mr. Shelley, with the feeling that ever seems to be at the bottom of his warmth, gives the following placid and easy solution of a difficulty, which the world, we believe, is also instinctively solving, but which, as he says, has been the 'moral ruin' of some eminent spirits among us. If the Lake School, as they are called, were not as dogmatic in their despair as they used to be in their hope, we should earnestly recommend the passage to their attention. They might see in it, at any rate, how it becomes an antagonist to talk; and how charitable and consistent the mind can be, that really inquires into the philosophical causes of things. Mr. Shelley does not say that Mr. Southey is 'no better than a housebreaker'; nor does he exclaim with Mr. Wordsworth, in the ill-concealed melancholy of a strange piety, which would be still stranger if it were really cheerful, that 'Carnage is God's daughter,' He is not in the habit, evidently, of begging the question against the low and uneducated; nor has he the least respect for that very sweeping lady, Miss Theodosia Carnage;—but stop; we must not be violating the charity of his philosophy.

'The panic,' says our author . . .

[quotes paragraphs four and five of Shelley's Preface]

The reader has seen the fable as well as some passages of this poem, and heard the author's own account of his intentions in extracts from the preface. It remains for us to give a general criticism upon it, interspersed with a few more specimens; and as the object of the work is decidedly philosophical, we shall begin with the philosophy.

Mr. Shelley is of opinion with many others that the world is a very beautiful one externally, but wants a good deal of mending with respect to its mind and habits; and for this purpose he would quash as many cold and selfish passions as possible, and rouse up the general element of Love, till it set our earth rolling more harmoniously. The answer made to a writer, who sets out with endeavours like these, is that he is idly aiming at perfection; but Mr. Shelley has no such aim, neither have nine hundred and ninety-nine out of a thousand of the persons who have ever been taunted with it. Such a charge, in truth, is only the first answer which egotism makes to any one who thinks he can go beyond its own ideas of the possible. If this however be done away, the next answer is, that you are attempting something wild and romantic,—that you will get disliked for it as well as lose your trouble, —and that you had better coquet, or rather play the prude, with things as they are. The wordly sceptic smiles, and says 'Hah!'—the dull rogues wonder, or laugh out;—the disappointed egotist gives you a sneering admonition, having made up his mind about all these things because he and his friends could not alter them; the hypocrite affects to be shocked: the bigot anticipates the punishment that awaits you for daring to say that God's creation is not a vile world, nor his creatures bound to be miserable;—and even the more amiable compromiser with superstition expresses alarm for you,—does not know what you may be hazarding, though he believes nevertheless that God is all good and just,—refers you to the fate of Adam, to shew you that because he introduced the knowledge of evil, you must not attempt to do it away again,—and finally, advises you to comfort yourself with *faith*, and to secure a life in the next world because *this* is a bad business, and *that*, of course, you may find a worse. It seems forgotten all this while, that Jesus Christ himself recommended Love as the great law that was to supersede others; and recommended it too to an extreme, which has been held impracticable. How far it has been found impractible, in consequence of his doctrines having been mixed up with contradictions and threatening dogmas, and with a system of after-life which contradicts all its principles, may be left to the consideration. Will theologians never discover, that men, in order to be good and just to each other, must either think well of a Divine Being, really and not pretendingly or not think of him at all? That they must worship Goodness and a total absence of the revengeful and malignant passions, if not Omnipotence? or else that they must act upon this quality for themselves, and agree with a devout and amiable Pagan, that 'it were better men should say there was no such being as Plutarch, than that there was one Plutarch who eat his own children?' Instead of the alarms about searches after happiness being wise and salutary, when the world is confessedly discordant, they would seem, if we believed in such things, the most fatal and ingenious invention of an enemy of mankind. But it is only so much begging of the question, fatal indeed as far as it goes, and refusing in the strangest manner to look after good, because there is a necessity for it. And as to the Eastern apologue of Adam and Eve (for so many Christians as well as others have thought it), it would be merely shocking to humanity and to a sense of justice in any other light; but it is, in fact, a very deep though not wisely managed al-legory, deprecating the folly of mankind in losing their simplicity and enjoyment, and in taking to those very mistakes about vice and virtue, which it is the object of such authors as the one before us to do away again. Faith! It is the very object they have in view; not indeed faiths in endless terrors and contradictions, but 'a faith and hope,' as Mr. Shelley says, 'in something good,'—that faith in the power of men to be kinder and happier, which other faiths take so much pains, and professed pains, to render unbelievable even while they recommend it! 'Have faith,' says the theologian, 'and bear your wretchedness, and escape the wrath to come.' 'Have faith,' says the philosopher, 'and begin to be happier now, and do not attribute odious qualities to any one.'

People get into more inconsistencies in opposing the hopes and efforts of a philosophical enthusiasm than on any other subject. They say 'use your reason, instead of your expectations'; and yet this is the reverse of what they do in their own beliefs. They say, take care how you contradict custom;—yet Milton, whom they admire, set about ridiculing it, and paying his addresses to another woman in his wife's lifetime, till the latter treated him better. They say it is im-possible the world should alter; and yet it has often altered. They say possible, at any rate, it should mend; yet people are no longer burnt at the stake. They say, but it is too old to alter to any great purpose of happiness,—that all its experience goes to the contrary; and yet they talk at other times of the brief life and shortsighted knowledge of man, and of the nothingness of 'a thousand years.' The experience of a man and an ephemeris are in fact just on a par in all that regards the impossibility of change. But one man,—they say—what can one man do? Let a glorious living person answer,—let Clarkson answer; who sitting down in his youth by a road-side, thought upon the horrors of the Slave Trade, and vowed he would dedicate his life to endeavour at overthrowing it. He was laughed at; he was violently opposed; he was called presumptuous and even irreligious; he was thought out of his senses; he made a noble sacrifice of his own health and strength; and he has *lived* to see the Slave Trade, aye, even the slavery of the descendants of the 'cursed' Ham, made a Felony.

We have taken up so much room in noticing these objections, that we have left ourselves none for entering into a further account of Mr. Shelley's views than he himself has given; and we have missed any more quotations at last. But we are sure that he will be much better pleased to see obstructions cleared away from the progress of such opinions as his, than the most minute account given of them in particular. It may be briefly repeated, that they are at war with injustice, violence, and selfishness of every species, however disguised;—that they represent, in a very striking light, the folly and misery of systems, either practical or theoretical, which go upon penal and resentful grounds, and add 'pain to pain'; and that they would have men, instead of worshipping tyrannies and terrors of any sort, worship goodness and gladness, diminish the vices and sorrows made by custom only, encourage the virtues and enjoyments which mutual benevolence may realize; and in short, make the best and utmost of this world, as well as hope for another.

The beauties of the poem consist in depth of sentiment, in grandeur of imagery, and a versification remarkably sweet, various, and noble, like the placid playing of a great organ. If the author's genius reminds us of any other poets, it is of two very opposite ones, Lucretius and Dante. The former he resembles in the Daedalian part of it, in the boldness of his speculations, and in his love of virtue, of external nature, and of love itself. It is his gloomier or more imaginative passages that sometimes remind us of Dante. The sort of supernatural architecture in which he delights has in particular the grandeur as well as obscurity of that great genius, to whom however he presents this remarkable and instructive contrast, that superstition and pain and injustice go hand in hand even in the pleasantest parts of Dante, like the three Furies, while philosophy, pleasure, and justice, smile through the most painful passages of our author, like the three Graces.

Mr. Shelley's defects as a poet are obscurity, inartificial and yet not natural economy, violation of costume, and too great a sameness and gratuitousness of image and metaphor, and of image and metaphor too drawn from the elements, particularly the sea. The book is full of humanity; and yet it certainly does not go the best way to work of appealing to it, because it does not appeal to it through the medium of its common knowledges. It is for this reason that we must say something, which we would willingly leave unsaid, both from admiration of Mr. Shelley's genius and love of his benevolence; and this is, that the work cannot possibly become popular. It may set others thinking and writing, and we have no doubt will do so; and those who can understand and relish it, will relish it exceedingly; but the author must forget his metaphysics and sea-sides a little more in his future works, and give full effect to that nice knowledge of men and things which he otherwise really possesses to an extraordinary degree. We have no doubt he is destined to be one of the leading spirits of his age, and indeed has already fallen into his place as such; but however resolute as to his object, he will only be doing it justice to take the most effectual means in his power to forward it.

We have only to observe in conclusion, as another hint to the hopeless, that although the art of printing is not new, yet the Press in any great and true sense of the word is a modern engine in the comparison, and the changeful times of society have never yet been accompanied with so mighty a one. *Books* did what was done before; they have now a million times the range and power; and the Press, which has got hold of Superstition, and given it some irrecoverable wounds already, will, we hope and believe, finally draw it in altogether, and crush it as a steam-engine would a great serpent.

26. John Gibson Lockhart, unsigned review, *Blackwood's Edinburgh Magazine*

January 1819, iv, 475–82

A pernicious system of opinion concerning man and his moral government, a superficial audacity of unbelief, an overflowing abundance of uncharitableness towards almost the whole of his race, and a disagreeable measure of assurance and self-conceit—each of these things is bad, and the combination of the whole of them in the character of any one person might, at first sight, be considered as more than sufficient to render that one person utterly and entirely contemptible. Nor has the fact, in general, been otherwise. In every age, the sure ultimate reward of the sophistical and phantastical enemies of religion and good order among mankind, has been found in the contempt and the disgust of those against whose true interests their weapons had been employed. From this doom the most exquisite elegance of wit, and of words, the most perfect keenness of intellect, the most flattering despotism over contemporary opinion—all have not been able to preserve the inimitable Voltaire. In this doom, those wretched sophists of the present day, who would fain attempt to lift the load of oppressing infamy from off the memory of Voltaire, find their own living beings already entangled, 'fold above fold, inextricable coil.' Well may they despair:—we can almost pardon the bitterness of their disappointed malice. Their sentence was pronounced without hesitation, almost without pity—for there was nothing in them to redeem their evil. They derived no benefit from that natural, universal, and proper feeling, which influences men to be slow in harshly, or suddenly, or irrevocably condemning intellects that bear upon them the stamp of power,—they had no part in that just spirit of respectfulness which makes men to contemplate, with an unwilling and unsteady eye, the aberrations of genius. The brand of inexpiable execration was ready in a moment to scar their fronts, and they have long wandered neglected about the earth—perhaps saved from extinction, like the fratricide, by the very mark of their ignominy.

Mr. Shelley is devoting his mind to the same pernicious purposes which have recoiled in vengeance upon so many of his contemporaries; but he possesses the qualities of a powerful and vigorous intellect, and therefore his fate cannot be sealed so speedily as theirs. He is also of the 'COCKNEY SCHOOL,' so far as his opinions are concerned; but the base opinions of the sect have not as yet been able entirely to obscure in him the character, or take away from him the privileges of the genius born within him. Hunt and Keats, and some others of the School, are indeed men of considerable cleverness, but as poets, they are worthy of sheer and instant contempt, and therefore their opinions are in little danger of being widely or deeply circulated by their means. But the system, which found better champions than it deserved even in them, has now, it would appear, been taken up by one, of whom it is far more seriously, and deeply, and lamentably unworthy; and the poem before us bears unfortunately the clearest marks of its author's execrable system, but it is impressed every where with the more noble and majestic footsteps of his genius. It is to the operation of the painful feeling above alluded to, which attends the contemplation of perverted power—that we chiefly ascribe the silence observed by our professional critics, in regard to *The Revolt of Islam*. Some have held back in the fear that, by giving to his genius its due praise, they might only be lending the means of currency to the opinions in whose service he has unwisely enlisted its energies; while others, less able to appreciate his genius, and less likely to be anxious about suppressing his opinions, have been silent, by reason of their selfish fears—dreading, it may be, that by praising *The Revolt of Islam*, they might draw down upon their own heads some additional marks of that public disgust which followed their praises of 'Rimini'.

Another cause which may be assigned for the silence of the critics should perhaps have operated more effectually upon ourselves; and this is, that *The Revolt of Islam*, although a fine, is, without all doubt, an obscure poem. Not that the main drift of the narrative is obscure, or even that there is any great difficulty in understanding the tendency of the undercurrent of its allegory—but the author has composed his poem in much haste, and he has inadvertently left many detached parts, both of his story and his allusion, to be made out as the reader best can, from very inadequate data. The swing of his inspiration may be allowed to have hurried his own eye, *pro tempore*, over many chasms; but Mr. Shelley has no excuse for printing a very unfinished piece—an error which he does not confess,—or indeed for many minor errors which he does confess in his very arrogant preface. The unskillful manner in which the allegory is brought out, and the doubt in which the reader is every now and then left, whether or no there be any allegory at all in the case; these alone are sufficient to render the perusal of this poem painful to persons of an active and ardent turn of mind; and, great as we conceive the merits of Mr. Shelley's poetry to be, these alone, we venture to prophesy, will be found sufficient to prevent *The Revolt of Islam* from ever becoming any thing like a favourite with the multitude.

At present, having entered our general protest against the creed of the author, and sufficiently indicated to our readers of what species its errors are,—we are very willing to save ourselves the unwelcome task of dwelling at any greater length upon these disagreeable parts of our subject. We are very willing to pass in silence the many faults of Mr. Shelley's opinions, and to attend to nothing but the vehicle in which these opinions are conveyed. As a philosopher, our author is weak and worthless;—our business is with him as a poet, and, as such, he is strong, nervous, original; well entitled to take his place near to the great creative masters, whose works have shed its truest glory around the age wherein we live. As a political and infidel treatise, *The Revolt of Islam* is contemptible;—happily a great part of it has no necessary connexion either with politics or with infidelity. The native splendour of Mr. Shelley's faculties has been his safeguard from universal degradation, and a part, at least, of his genius, has been consecrated to themes worthy of it and of him. In truth, what he probably conceives to be the most exquisite ornaments of his poetry, appear, in our eyes, the chief deformities upon its texture; and had the whole been framed like the passages which we shall quote,—as *The Revolt of Islam* would have been a purer, so we have no doubt, would it have been a nobler, a loftier, a more majestic, and a more beautiful poem.

We shall pass over, then, without comment, the opening part of this work, and the confused unsatisfactory allegories with which it is chiefly filled. It is sufficient to mention, that, at the close of the first canto, the poet supposes himself to be placed for a time in the regions of eternal repose, where the good and great of mankind are represented as detailing, before the throne of the Spirit of Good, those earthly sufferings and labours which had prepared them for the possession and enjoyment of so blissful an abode. Among these are two, a man and a woman of Argolis, who, after rescuing their country for a brief space from the tyranny of the house of Othman, and accomplishing this great revolution by the force of persuasive eloquence and the sympathies of human love alone, without violence, bloodshed, or revenge,

—had seen the fruit of all their toils blasted by foreign invasion, and the dethroned but not insulted tyrant replaced upon his seat; and who, finally, amidst all the darkness of their country's horizon, had died, without fear, the death of heroic martyrdom, gathering consolation, in the last pangs of their expiring nature, from the hope and the confidence that their faith and example might yet raise up successors to their labours, and that they had neither lived nor died in vain.

In the persons of these martyrs, the poet has striven to embody his ideas of the power and loveliness of human affections; and, in their history, he has set forth a series of splendid pictures, illustrating the efficacy of these affections in overcoming the evils of private and of public life. It is in the portraying of that passionate love, which had been woven from infancy in the hearts of Laon and Cythna, and which, binding together all their impulses in one hope and one struggle, had rendered them through life no more than two different tenements for the inhabitation of the same enthusiastic spirit;—it is in the portraying of this intense, overmastering, unfearing, unfading love, that Mr. Shelley has proved himself to be a great poet. Around his lovers, moreover, in the midst of all their fervours, he has shed an air of calm gracefulness, a certain majestic monumental stillness, which blends them harmoniously with the scene of their earthly existence, and realizes in them our ideas of Greeks struggling for freedom in the best spirit of their fathers.—We speak of the general effect—there are unhappily not a few passages in which the poet quits his vantage ground, and mars the beauty of his personifications by an intermixture of thoughts, feelings, and passions, with which, of right, they have nothing to do.

It is thus that Laon narrates the beginning of his love for Cythna,—if, indeed, his love can be said to have had any beginning, separate from that of his own intellectual and passionate life.

[quotes Canto II, lines 847–73, 883–918]

While the life of this happy pair is gliding away in day-dreams and night-dreams of delight, the arm of oppression is suddenly stretched forth against them. Their innocent repose is dissolved by the rude touch of savages, who come to bear the beautiful Cythna to the Harem of the tyrant, Othman,—as food

> To the hyena lust, who, among graves,
> Over his loathed meal, laughing in agony, raves—

Laon, in his phrenzy, slays three of the ravishers, and is forthwith dragged by the rest of them to await the punishment of his violence in a strange prison.

[quotes Canto III, lines 1218–51]

But the 'peace of madness is' of long endurance, and Laon, wakening from thirst and hunger to a sense of his own condition, forgets that again in the remembrance of Cythna. A white sail is set on the bay far below him, and he feels that the vessel is destined to bear the maiden from the shore. The thought of this turns the stream of his mind to a darker channel, and the agonies of fierce madness succeed to the lethargy out of which he had arisen. The fourth day finds him raving on the summit of his pillar, when there arives at the foot of it a venerable hermit, who had heard of the cause of his affliction—of his generous nature and lofty aspirations. This visitor sets him free from his chain, and conveys him to a small bark below, while entirely insensible to what is passing around him; but he learns long afterwards, that the old man's eloquence had subdued his keepers, and that they had consented, at their own peril, to his escape. He is conveyed across the sea to a lonely island, where for seven years he is tended by his aged benefactor, whose kind and compassionate wisdom, and that long space, are not more than sufficient to win back the mind of Laon to entire self-possession.

In the first moments of the patient's perfect recovery, he is informed by the old man, that during the years of his illness the cause of liberty had been slowly gaining ground in the 'Golden city'—that he himself would fain assist in the Revolution which had now actually commenced there, but that he felt himself too old and too subdued in his spirit and language to be an effectual leader,—

> While Laon's name to the tumultuous throng
> Were like the star whose beams the waves compel,
> And tempests; and his soul-subduing tongue
> Were as a lance to quell the mailed crest of wrong.

Laon accepts with eagerness the proposal of the old man, and they depart in their bark for the Revolutionized city.

On their arrival they find the work apparently well-nigh completed. An immense multitude of the people—of men weary of political, and women sick of domestic slavery—are assembled in the fields without the walls. Laon and his friend walk into the encampment, and are received as friends. The host already acknowledge a leader and a presiding spirit in the person of a female, whom they reverence under the name of LAONE. Laon and this heroine are attracted to each other by some unknown sympathy; the tones of her voice stir up all the depths of his spirit; but her countenance is veiled, and scarcely dares he wish to have the covering removed. The palace of the tyrant Othman, is, meantime, surrounded by the multitude; and Laon entering it, finds him sitting alone in his hall, deserted by all but one little child, whose affection has been won to him by previous commendations and caresses. Nothing can be more touching than the picture of this innocent. Thus speaks Laon:

[quotes Canto V, lines 1909–26]

The monarch is quietly removed from his palace, none following him but this child; and on this consummation of their triumph, the multitude join in holding a high festival, of which Laone is the priestess. Laon sits near her in her pyramid; but he is withheld, by a strange impulse, from speaking to her, and he retires to pass the night in repose at a distance from where she sleeps.

At break of day, Laon is awakened by sounds of tumults; the multitude, lately so firm and collected, are seen flying in every direction; and he learns that the cause of their disarray is the arrival of a foreign army, sent by some of his brother princes to the relief of Othman. Laon, and a few of the more heroic spirits, withdraw to the side of a hill, where, ill-armed and outnumbered, they are slaughtered till the evening by their enemies. The carnage, and the confidence of the sufferers, are painted with a power and energy altogether admirable; but we have room to quote only the deliverance of Laon.

[quotes Canto VI, lines 2493–527]

They take up their abode in a lonely ruin, and many hours are wasted in the transports of a recognition—which, even in such circumstances, to them is joyful.

[quotes Canto VI, lines 2615–58]

They remain for some time in this retreat, communicating to each other the long histories of their suffering.—Cythna, according to her own wild tale, being carried away from Laon at the moment when he slew three of the slaves that surrounded her, had been conveyed to the tyrant's palace, and had suffered all the insults, and almost all the injuries to which its inmates were exposed. Her high spirit had, however, offended at last her oppressor, and she was sent to a submarine cavern, near the Symplegades, to which strange dungeon she was borne through the waves by a slave, 'made dumb by poison,'

A diver lean and strong, of Oman's coral sea.

Here she was supplied with a daily pittance of food by an eagle, trained to hover over the only crevice through which the air had access to the captive. She sank into a melancholy phrenzy, and was aroused to consciousness by strange feelings which taught her to expect that she was about to be a mother. It is so, and for a while all the sorrows of her prison are soothed by the caresses of her child; but the child disappears suddenly, and the bewildered mother half suspects that its existence has been but a dream of her madness. At last an earthquake changes the position of the cavern, and Cythna is released by some passing mariners, who convey her to the city of Othman, and are prepared by her discourses during the voyage to take a part in the insurrection, which Cythna arrives in time to lead. But to come to the main story—it is the custom of Laon to ride forth every night on the Tartar horse to procure food for Cythna. By this means their retreat is at last discovered, Laon is seized, led before the tyrant, and sentenced to be burned alive before his eyes, on the very scene of his treason. The guards, the priests, and the slaves, are gathered around the throne of Othman.

[quotes Canto XII, lines 4465–521]

This is Cythna come to partake the fate of her lord.

[quotes Canto XII, lines 4567–647]

We forbear from making any comments on this strange narrative; because we could not do so without entering upon other points which we have already professed our intention of waiving for the present. It will easily be seen, indeed, that neither the main interest nor the main merit of the poet at all consists in the conception of his plot or in the arrangements of his incidents. His praise is, in our judgment, that of having poured over his narrative a very rare strength and abundance of poetic imagery and feeling—of having steeped every word in the essence of his inspiration. *The Revolt of Islam* contains no detached passages at all comparable with some which our readers recollect in the works of the great poets our contemporaries; but neither does it contain any such intermixture of prosaic materials as disfigure even the greatest of them. Mr. Shelley has displayed his possession of a mind intensely poetical, and of an exuberance of poetic language, perpetually strong and perpetually varied. In spite, moreover, of a certain perversion in all his modes of thinking, which, unless he gets rid of it, will ever prevent him from being acceptable to any considerable or respectable body of readers, he has displayed many glimpses of right understanding and generous feeling, which must save him from the unmingled condemnation even of the most rigorous judges. His destiny is entirely in his own hands; if he acts wisely, it cannot fail to be a glorious one; if he continues to pervert his talents, by making them the instruments of a base sophistry, their splendour will only contribute to render his disgrace the more conspicuous. Mr. Shelley, whatever his errors may have been, is a scholar, a gentleman, and a poet; and he must therefore dispise from his soul the only eulogies to which he has hitherto been accustomed—paragraphs from the *Examiner*, and sonnets from Johnny Keats. He has it in his power to select better companions; and if he does so, he may very securely promise himself abundance of better praise.

27. Unsigned review, *The Monthly Review*

March 1819, lxxxviii, 323–4

The wild burst of the French Revolution called out ten thousand corresponding fancies and furies in the human heart; and no department of civil and military life, no branch of science, or region of taste and literature, was untouched or uninfluenced by this general concussion. Not only were politics rhapsodized in the course of that tremendous occurrence, but rhapsodies became political; and in the midst of the gravest ratiocination on the 'universal economy,' appeared the strangest vagaries of versification, to answer to the Pindaric flights of some unfledged philosopher in government.

A singular compound of all these qualities is presented in *The Revolt of Islam*. It is lamentable, indeed, to see the waste of so much capability of better things as the present volume exhibits. The author has many poetical talents, but he does not seem to have rendered a just account of a single one. His command of language is so thoroughly abused as to become a mere snare for loose and unmeaning expression; and his facility of writing, even in Spenser's stanza, leads him into a licentiousness of rhythm and of rhyme that is truly contemptible. His theories also are pushed to so extravagant a length, that no 'Theophilanthropist' or 'Spencean' of the day would be disposed to follow him into his religious or his political speculations; and his dreams of the perfection of the world, in which the *eagle of evil* will finally be conquered by the *serpent of good*,' partake too much of poetical phrenzy for our comprehension. Mr. Percy Bysshe Shelley seems to be one of those obdurate dreamers, whose imaginations are *hardened* rather than *reproved* by the frequent exposure of their follies; and he goes on rhyming without reason, and reasoning without rhyme, in spite of the manifest advantages of education and society which his work displays. We subjoin a specimen of this *demi-maniac* composition:

[quotes Canto III, lines 1297–314]

28. John Taylor Coleridge, review, *The Quarterly Review*

April 1819, xxi, 460–71

John Taylor Coleridge, nephew of the poet, wrote this review which Peacock later called 'one of the most malignant effusions of the *odium theologicum* that ever appeared, even in those days and in that periodical.' In his letters Shelley acknowledges having read this review.

This is one of that industrious knot of authors, the tendency of whose works we have in our late Numbers exposed to the caution of our readers—novel, poem, romance, letters, tours, critique, lecture and essay follow one another, framed to the same measure, and in subjection to the same key-note, while the sweet undersong of the weekly journal, filling up all pauses, strengthening all weaknesses, smoothing all abruptnesses, harmonizes the whole strain. Of all his brethren Mr. Shelley carries to the greatest length the doctrines of the sect. He is, for this and other reasons, by far the least pernicious of them; indeed there is a naiveté and openness in his manner of laying down the most extravagant positions, which in some measure deprives them of their venom; and when he enlarges on what certainly are but necessary results of opinions more guardedly delivered by others, he might almost be mistaken for some artful advocate of civil order and religious institutions. This benefit indeed may be drawn from his book, for there is scarcely any more persuasive argument for truth than to carry out to all their legitimate consequences, the doctrines of error. But this is not Mr. Shelley's intention; he is, we are sorry to say, in sober earnest:—with perfect deliberation and the steadiest perseverance he perverts all the gifts of his nature, and does all the injury, both public and private, which his faculties enable him to perpetrate.

Laon and Cythna is the same poem with *The Revolt of Islam*—under the first name it exhibited some features which made 'the experiment on the temper of the public mind,' as the author calls it, somewhat too bold and hazardous. This knight-errant in the cause of 'a liberal and comprehensive morality' had already sustained some 'perilous handling' in his encounters with Prejudice and Error, and acquired in consequence of it a small portion of *the better part of valour*. Accordingly *Laon and Cythna* withdrew from circulation; and happy had it been for Mr. Shelley if he had been contented with his failure, and closed his experiments. But with minds of a certain class, notoriety, infamy, anything is better than obscurity; baffled in a thousand attempts after fame, they will still make one more at whatever risk,—and they end commonly like an awkward chemist who perseveres in tampering with his ingredients, till, in an unlucky moment, they take fire, and he is blown up by the explosion.

Laon and Cythna has accordingly re-appeared with a new name, and a few slight alterations. If we could trace in these any signs of an altered spirit, we should have hailed with the sincerest pleasure the return of one whom nature intended for better things, to the ranks of virtue and religion. But Mr. Shelley is no penitent; he has reproduced the same poison, a little, and but a little, more cautiously disguised, and as it is thus intended only to do the more mischief at less personal risk to the author, our duty requires us to use his own evidence against himself, to interpret him where he is obscure now, by himself where he was plain before, and to exhibit the 'fearful consequences' to which he would bring us, as he drew them in the boldness of his first conception.

Before, however, we do this, we will discharge our duty to Mr. Shelley as poetical critics—in a case like the present, indeed, where the freight is so pernicious, it is but a secondary duty to consider the 'build' of the vessel which bears it: but it is a duty too peculiarly our own to be wholly neglected. Though we should be sorry to see *The Revolt of Islam* in our readers' hands, we are bound to say that it is not without beautiful passages, that the language is in general free from errors of taste, and the versification smooth and harmonious. In these respects it resembles the latter productions of Mr. Southey, though the tone is less subdued, and the copy altogether more luxuriant and ornate than the original. Mr. Shelley indeed is an unsparing imitator; and he draws largely on the rich stores of another mountain poet, to whose religious mind it must be matter, we think, of perpetual sorrow to see the philosophy which comes pure and holy from his pen, degraded and perverted, as it continually is, by this miserable crew of atheists or pantheists, who have just sense enough to abuse its terms, but neither heart nor principle to comprehend its import, or follow its application. We shall cite one of the passages to which we alluded above, in support of our opinion: perhaps it is that which has pleased us more than any other in the whole poem.

[quotes Canto II, lines 847–82]

These, with all their imperfections, are beautiful stanzas; they are, however, of rare occurrence:—had the poem many more such, it could never, we are persuaded, become popular. Its merits and its faults equally conspire against it; it has not much ribaldry or voluptuousness for prurient imaginations, and no personal scandal for the malicious; and even those on whom it might be expected to act most dangerously by its semblance of enthusiasm, will have stout hearts to proceed beyond the first canto. As a whole, it is insupportably dull, and laboriously obscure; its absurdities are not of the kind which provoke laughter; the story is almost wholly devoid of interest, and very meagre; nor can we admire Mr. Shelley's mode of making up for this defect;—as he has but one incident where he should have ten, he tells that one so intricately, that it takes the time of ten to comprehend it.

Mr. Shelley is a philosopher by the courtesy of the age, and has a theory of course respecting the government of the world; we will state in as few words as we can the general outlines of that theory, the manner in which he demonstrates it, and the practical consequences which he proposes to deduce from it. It is to the second of these divisions that we would beg his attention; we despair of convincing him directly that he has taken up false and pernicious notions; but if he pays any deference to the common laws of reasoning, we hope to show him that, let the goodness of his cause be what it may, his manner of advocating it is false and unsound. This may be mortifying to a teacher of mankind; but a philosopher seeks the truth, and has no vanity to be mortified.

The existence of evil, physical and moral, is the grand problem of all philosophy; the humble find it a trial, the proud make it a stumbling-block; Mr. Shelley refers it to the faults of those civil institutions and religious creeds which are designed to regulate the conduct of man here, and his hopes in a hereafter. In these he seems to make no distinction, but considers them all as bottomed upon principles pernicious to man and unworthy of God, carried into details the most cruel, and upheld only by the stupidity of the many on the one hand, and the selfish conspiracy of the few on the other. According to him the earth is a boon garden needing little care or cultivation, but pouring forth spontaneously and inexhaustibly all innocent delights and luxuries to her innumerable children; the seasons have no inclemencies, the air no pestilences for man in his proper state of wisdom and liberty; his business here is to enjoy himself, to abstain from no gratification, to repent of no sin, hate no crime, but be wise, happy and free, with plenty of 'lawless love.' This is man's natural state, the state to which Mr. Shelley will bring us, if we will but break up the 'crust of our outworn opinions,' as he calls them, and put them into his magic cauldron. But kings have introduced war, legislators crime, priests sin; the dreadful consequences have been that the earth has lost her fertility, the seasons their mildness, the air its salubrity, man his freedom and happiness. We have become a foul-feeding carnivorous race, are foolish enough to feel uncomfortable after the commission of sin; some of us even go so far as to consider vice odious; and we all groan under a multiplied burden of crimes, *merely conventional*; among which Mr. Shelley specifies with great *sang froid* the commission of *incest*!

We said that our philosopher makes no distinction in his condemnation of creeds; we should rather have said, that he makes no exception; distinction he does make, and it is to the prejudice of that which we hold. In one place indeed he assembles a number of names of the founders of religions, to treat them all with equal disrespect.

> And through the host contention wild befell,
> As each of his own God the wonderous works did tell;
> [1]And Oromaze and Christ and Mahomet,
> Moses and Buddh, Zerdusht, and Brahm and Foh,
> A tumult of strange names, &c.—p. 227.

But in many other places he manifests a dislike to Christianity which is frantic, and would be, if in such a case any thing could be, ridiculous. When the votaries of all religions are assembled with one accord (this unanimity by the bye is in a vision of the *nineteenth* century) to stifle the first breathings of liberty, and execute the revenge of a ruthless tyrant, he selects a Christian priest to be the organ of sentiments outrageously and pre-eminently cruel. The two characteristic principles upon which Christianity may be said to be built are repentance and faith. Of repentance he speaks thus:—

> Reproach not thine own soul, but know thyself;
> *Nor hate another's crime, nor loathe thine own.*

[1] 'And Oromaze, Joshua and Mahomet.' p. 227. *Revolt of Islam*. This is a very fair specimen of Mr. Shelley's alterations, which we see are wholly prudential, and artfully so, as the blasphemy is still preserved entire. (Reviewer's footnote.)

It is the dark idolatry of self
Which, when our thoughts and actions once are gone,
Demands that we should weep and bleed and groan;
O vacant expiation! be at rest—
The past is death's—the future is thine own;
And love and joy can make the *foulest* breast
A paradise of flowers where peace might build her nest.—p. 188.

Repentance then is selfishness in an extreme which amounts to idolatry! but what is Faith? our readers can hardly be prepared for the odious accumulation of sin and sorrow which Mr. Shelley conceives under his word. 'Faith is the Python, the Ogress, the Evil Genius, the Wicked Fairy, the Giantess of our children's tales;' whenever any thing bad is to be accounted for, any hard name to be used, this convenient monosyllable fills up the blank.

> Beneath his feet, 'mong ghastliest forms, represt
> Lay Faith, *an obscene worm.*—p. 118.

> ————————sleeping there
> With lidless eyes lie Faith, and Plague, and Slaughter,
> A ghastly brood conceived of Lethe's sullen water.—p. 220.

> And underneath thy feet writhe Faith and Folly,
> Custom and Hell, and mortal Melancholy.—p. 119.

> Smiled on the flowery grave, in which were lain
> Fear, Faith and Slavery.—p. 172.

Enough of Mr. Shelley's theory.—We proceed to examine the manner in which the argument is conducted, and this we cannot do better than by putting a case.

Let us suppose a man entertaining Mr. Shelley's opinions as to the causes of existing evil, and convinced of the necessity of a change in all the institutions of society, of his own ability to produce and conduct it, and of the excellence of that system which he would substitute in their place. These indeed are bold convictions for a young and inexperienced man, imperfectly educated, irregular in his application, and shamefully dissolute in his conduct; but let us suppose them to be sincere;—the change, if brought about at all, must be effected by a concurrent will, and that, Mr. Shelley will of course tell us, must be produced by an enlightened conviction. How then would a skilful reasoner, assured of the strength of his own ground, have proceeded in composing a tale of fiction for this purpose? Undoubtedly he would have taken the best laws, the best constitution, and the best religion in the known world; such at least as they most loved and venerated whom he was addressing; when he had put all these together, and developed their principles candidly, he would have shown that under all favourable circumstances, and with all the best propensities of our nature to boot, still the natural effect of this combination would be to corrupt and degrade the human race. He would then have drawn a probable inference, that if the most approved systems and creeds under circumstances more advantageous than could ever be expected to concur in reality, still produced only vice and misery, the fault lay in them, or at least mankind could lose nothing by adventuring on a change. We say with confidence that a skilful combatant would and must have acted thus; not merely to make victory final, but to gain it in any shape. For if he reasons from what we acknowledge to be bad against what we believe to be good; if he puts a government confessedly despotic, a religion monstrous and false, if he places on the throne a cruel tyrant, and at the altar a bigoted and corrupt priesthood, how can his argument have any weight with those who think they live under a paternal government and a pure faith, who look up with love and gratitude to a beneficent monarch, and reverence a zealous and upright priesthood? The laws and government on which Mr. Shelley's reasoning proceeds, are the Turkish, administered by a lawless despot; his religion is the Mahommedan, maintained by servile hypocrites; and his scene for their joint operation, Greece, the land full beyond all others of recollections of former glory and independence, now covered with shame and sunk in slavery. We are Englishmen, Christians, free, and independent; we ask Mr. Shelley how his case applies to *us*? or what *we* learn from it to the prejudice of our own institutions?

His residence at Oxford was a short one, and, if we mistake not, rather *abruptly* terminated; yet we should have thought that even in a freshman's term he might have learned from Aldrick not to reason from a particular to an universal; and any one of our fair readers we imagine who never heard of Aldrick, would see the absurdity of inferring that all of her own sex were the victims of the lust and tyranny of the other, from the fact, if it be a fact, that young women of Greece were carried off by force to the seraglio of Constantinople. This, however, is the sum and substance of the argument, as far as it attempts to prove the causes of existing evil. Mr. Shelley is neither a dull, nor, considering all his disadvantages, a very ignorant man; we will frankly confess, that with every disposition to judge him charitably, we find it hard to convince ourselves of his belief in his own conclusions.

We have seen how Mr. Shelley argues for the necessity of a change; we must bestow a word or two upon the manner in which he brings the change about, before we come to the consequences which he derives from it. Laon and Cythna, his hero and heroine, are the principal, indeed, almost the sole agents. The latter by her eloquence rouses all of her own sex to assert their liberty and independence; this perhaps was no difficult task; a female tongue in such a cause may be supposed to have spoken fluently at least, and to have found a willing audience; by the same instrument, however, she disarms the soldiers who are sent to seize and destroy her,—

> even the torturer who had bound
> Her meek calm frame, ere yet it was impaled
> Loosened her weeping then, nor could be found
> One human hand to harm her.—p. 84.

The influence of her voice is not confined to the Golden City, it travels over the land, stirring and swaying all hearts to its purpose:—

> in hamlets and in towns
> The multitudes collect tumultuously,—
> Blood soon, although unwillingly, to shed.—p. 85.

These peaceable and tender advocates for 'Universal Suffrage and *no* representation' assemble in battle-array under the walls of the Golden City, keeping night and day strict blockade (which Mr. Shelley calls 'a watch of love,') around the desperate bands who still adhere to the maintenance of the iron-hearted monarch on the throne. Why the eloquence of Cythna had no power over *them*, or how the monarch himself, who had been a slave to her beauty, and to whom this model of purity and virtue, *had borne a child*, was able to resist the spell of her voice, Mr. Shelley leaves his readers to find out for themselves. In this pause of affairs Laon makes his appearance to complete the revolution; Cythna's voice had done wonders, but Laon's was still more powerful; the 'sanguine slaves' of page 96, who stabbed ten thousand in their sleep, are turned in page 99 to fraternal bands, the power of the throne crumbles into dust and the united hosts enter the city in triumph. A good deal of mummery follows, of national fêtes, reasonable rites, altars of federation, &c. borrowed from that store-house of cast-off mummeries and abominations, the French revolution. In the mean time all the kings of the earth, pagan and Christian, send more sanguine slaves, who slaughter the sons of freedom in the midst of their merry-making; Plague and Famine come to slaughter them in return; and Laon and Cythna, who had chosen this auspicious moment in a ruined tower for the commencement of their 'reign of love,' surrender themselves to the monarch and are burnt alive.

Such is Mr. Shelley's victory, such its security, and such the means of obtaining it! These last, we confess, are calculated to throw a damp upon our spirits, for if the hopes of mankind must depend upon the exertion of super-eminent eloquence, we have the authority of one who had well considered the subject, for believing that they could scarcely depend upon anything of more rare occurrence. *Plures in omnibus rebus, quàm in dicendo admirabiles*,[1] was the remark of Cicero a great many ages ago, and the experience of all those ages has served but to confirm the truth of it.

Mr. Shelley, however, is not a man to propose a difficult remedy without suggesting the means of procuring it. If we mistake not, Laon and Cythna, and even the sage, (for there is a sort of good stupid Archimago in the poem) are already provided, and intent to begin their mission if we will but give them hearing. In short Mr. Shelley is his own Laon: this is clear from many passages of the preface and dedication. The lady to whom the poem is addressed is certainly the original of Cythna: we have more consideration for her than she has had for herself, and will either mortify her vanity, or spare her feelings, by not producing her before the public; it is enough for the philanthropist to know that when the season arrives, she will be forthcoming. Mr. Shelley says of himself and her, in a simile picturesque in itself, but laughable in its application,—

> thou and I,
> Sweet friend, can look from our tranquillity,
> Like lamps, into the world's tempestuous night—
> Two tranquil stars, while clouds are passing by
> Which wrap them from the foundering seaman's sight,
> That burn from year to year with unextinguished light.—p. xxxii.

Neither will the reader be much at a loss to discover what sapient personage is dimly shadowed out in Archimago; but a clue is afforded even to the uninitiate by a note in the preface, in which we are told that Mr. Malthus by his last edition has reduced the *Essay on Population* to a commentary illustrative of the unanswerableness of *Political Justice*.

[1] 'The majority (of people) are distinguished in all things except in speaking'. An allusion to Cicero, *De Oratore*, 1.2.6.

With such instruments doubtless the glorious task will be speedily accomplished—and what will be the issue? This indeed is a serious question, but, as in most schemes of reform, it is easier to say what is to be removed, and destroyed, than what is to be put in its place. Mr. Shelley would abrogate our laws—this would put an end to felonies and misdemeanours at a blow; he would abolish the rights of property, of course there could thenceforward be no violations of them, no heart-burnings between the poor and the rich, no disputed wills, no litigated inheritances, no food in short for sophistical judges, or hireling lawyers; he would overthrow the constitution, and then we should have no expensive court, no pensions or sinecures, no silken lords or corrupt commoners, no slavish and enslaving army or navy; he would pull down our churches, level our Establishment, and burn our bibles— then we should pay no tithes, be enslaved by no superstitions, abused by no priestly artifices: marriage he cannot endure, and there would at once be a stop put to the lamented increase of adulterous connections amongst us, whilst by repealing the canon of heaven against incest, he would add to the purity, and heighten the ardour of those feelings with which brother and sister now regard each other; finally, as the basis of the whole scheme, he would have us renounce our belief in our religion, extinguish, if we can, the light of conscience within us, which embitters our joys here, and drown in oblivion the hopes and fears that hang over our hereafter. This at least intelligible; but it is not so easy to describe the structure, which Mr. Shelley would build upon this vast heap of ruins. 'Love,' he says, 'is to be the sole law which shall govern the moral world;' but Love is a wide word with many significations, and we are at a loss as to which of them he would have it now bear. We are loath to understand it in its lowest sense, though we believe that as to the issue this would be the correctest mode of interpreting it; but this at least is clear, that Mr. Shelley does not mean it in its highest sense: he does not mean that love, which is the fulfilling of the law, and which walks after the commandments, for he would erase the Deca-logue, and every other code of laws; not the love which is said to be of God, and which is beautifully coupled with 'joy, peace, long suffering, gentleness, goodness, faith, meekness, temperance,' for he pre-eminently abhors that religion, which is built on that love and incul-cates it as the essence of all duties, and its own fulfilment.

It is time to draw to an end.—We have examined Mr. Shelley's system slightly, but, we hope, dispassionately; there will be those, who will say that we have done so coldly. He has indeed, to the best of his ability, wounded us in the tenderest part.—As far as in him lay, he has loosened the hold of our protecting laws, and sapped the principles of our venerable polity; he has invaded the purity and chilled the un-suspecting ardour of our fireside intimacies; he has slandered, ridiculed and blasphemed our holy religion; yet these are all too sacred objects to be defended bitterly or unfairly. We have learned, too, though not in Mr. Shelley's school, to discriminate between a man and his opinions, and while we shew no mercy to the sin, we can regard the sinner with allowance and pity. It is in this spirit, that we conclude with a few lines, which may serve for a warning to others, and for reproof, admonition, and even if he so pleases of encouragement to himself. We have already said what we think of his powers as a poet, and doubtless, with those powers, he might have risen to respectability in any honourable path, which he had chosen to pursue, if to his talents he had added industry, subordination, and good principles. But of Mr. Shelley much may be said with truth, which we not long since said of his friend and leader Mr. Hunt: he has not, indeed, all that is odious and contemptible in the character of that person; so far as we have seen he has never exhibited the bustling vulgarity, the ludicrous affectation, the factious flippancy, or the selfish heartlessness, which it is hard for our feelings to treat with the mere contempt they merit. Like him, however, Mr. Shelley is a very vain man; and like most very vain men, he is but half instructed in knowledge, and less than half-disciplined in his reasoning powers; his vanity, wanting the control of the faith which he derides, has been his ruin; it has made him too impatient of applause and distinction to earn them in the fair course of labour; like a speculator in trade, he would be rich without capital and without delay, and, as might have been anticipated, his speculations have ended only in disappointments. They both began, his speculations and his disappointments, in early child-hood, and even from that period he has carried about with him a soured and discontented spirit—unteachable in boyhood, unamiable in youth, querulous and unmanly in manhood,—singularly unhappy in all three. He speaks of his school as 'a world of woes,' of his masters 'as tyrants,' of his school-fellows as 'enemies,'—alas! what is this, but to bear evidence against himself? every one who knows what a public school ordinarily must be, will only trace in these lines the language of an insubordinate, a vain, a mortified spirit.

We would venture to hope that the past may suffice for the specula-tions in which Mr. Shelley has hitherto engaged; they have brought him neither honour abroad nor peace at home, and after so fair a trial it seems but common prudence to change them for some new venture. He is still a young man, and though his account be assuredly black and heavy, he may yet hope to redeem his time, and wipe it out. He may and he should retain all the love for his fellow-creatures, all the zeal for their improvement in virtue and happiness which he now professes, but let that zeal be armed with knowledge and regulated by judgment. Let him not be offended at our freedom, but he is really too young, too ignorant, too inexperienced, and too vicious to undertake the task of reforming any world, but the little world within his own breast; that task will be a good preparation for the difficulties which he is more anxious at once to encounter. There is a book which will help him to this preparation, which has more poetry in it than Lucretius, more interest than Godwin, and far more philosophy than both. But it is a sealed book to a proud spirit; if he would read it with effect, he must be humble where he is now vain, he must examine and doubt himself where now he boldly condemns others, and instead of relying on his own powers, he must feel and acknowledge his weakness, and pray for strength from above.

We had closed our remarks on *Laon and Cythna*, when *Rosalind and Helen* was put into our hands: after having devoted so much more space to the former than its own importance merited, a single sentence will suffice for the latter. Though not without some marks of the same ability, which is occasionally manifested in Mr. Shelley's earlier production, the present poem is very inferior to it in positive merit, and far more abundant in faults: it is less interesting, less vigorous and chaste in language, less harmonious in versification, and less pure in thought; more rambling and diffuse, more palpably and consciously sophistical, more offensive and vulgar, more unintelligible. So it ever is and must be in the downward course of infidelity and immorality;—we can no more blot out the noblest objects of contemplation, and the most heart-stirring sources of gratitude from the creation without injury to our intellectual and moral nature, than we can refuse to walk by the light of the sun without impairing our ocular vision. Scarcely any man ever set himself in array against the cause of social order and religion, but from a proud and rebel mind, or a corrupt and undisciplined heart: where these are, true knowledge cannot grow. In the enthusiasm of youth, indeed, a man like Mr. Shelley may cheat himself with the imagined loftiness and independence of his theory, and it is easy to invent a thousand sophisms, to reconcile his conscience to the impurity of his practice: but this lasts only long enough to lead him on beyond the power of return; he ceases to be the dupe, but with desperate malignity he becomes the deceiver of others. Like the Egyptian of old, the wheels of his chariot are broken, the path of 'mighty waters' closes in upon him behind, and a still deepening ocean is before him:—for a short time, are seen his impotent struggles against a resistless power, his blasphemous execrations are heard, his despair but poorly assumes the tone of triumph and defiance, and he calls ineffectually on others to follow him to the same ruin—finally, he sinks 'like lead' to the bottom, and is forgotten. So it is now in part, so shortly will it be entirely with Mr. Shelley: if we might withdraw the veil of private life, and tell what we *now* know about him, it would be indeed a disgusting picture that we should exhibit, but it would be an unanswerable comment on our text; it is not easy for those who *read only*, to conceive how much low pride, how much cold selfishness, how much unmanly cruelty are consistent with the laws of this 'universal' and 'lawless love.' But we must only use our knowledge to check the groundless hopes which we were once prone to entertain of him.

29. Leigh Hunt, '*The Quarterly Review* and *The Revolt of Islam*', *The Examiner*

September 26, 1819, no. 613, 620–1; October 3, 1819, no. 614, 635–6; October 10, 1819, no. 615, 652–53

Since our last paper, we have met with the *Quarterly Review*; and we shall beg our reader's disgust at that publication to be patient a little, while we say something upon its present number.—The *Quarterly Review itself* (for there are one or two deeper articles in it, this time, than usual[1]) ought to be ashamed of the one it has written upon Mr. Shelley. Heavy, and swelling, and soft with venom, it creeps through the middle of it like a skulking toad. The Editor, and the other more malignant

[1] See particularly the article on the Italian Poets, which is the best piece of English criticism we have yet seen upon that subject, as well as a singularly liberal one, in its general remarks, for the *Review* in question. There is also some deeper writing than ordinary in the article on the Greek comedy and philosophy; though it is edifying enough to see such an elabor-

writers in this Review, (for we know too much of such publications to confound all the writers together), have grown a little more cunning in their mode of attack. They only missed their aim, and pitched themselves headlong, with their blind fury, in such articles as that on the *Story of Rimini*. They have since undertaken to be more candid and acknowledging; and accordingly, by a ludicrous effort of virtue, they now make a point of praising some *one* thing, or rather giving some *one* extract, which they find rather praiseworthy than otherwise; and then they set to, sharper than ever, and reward their new morals with a double draught of malignity.

They are always too impatient however, not to betray themselves at the outset. They begin their article on Mr. Shelley's *Revolt of Islam* by referring to the same book under another title, which that gentleman suppressed. He suppressed it by the advice of his friends, because in the ardour of his sincerity he had carried one of his theories to an excess which they thought would injure the perusal of it. Perhaps but two or three copies of that first impression were sold. The public at large certainly knew nothing of it. And yet the *Quarterly* Reviewers, who think these theories so pernicious, drag forth the impression, in order to abuse what he has not used. If on the other hand, he had not suppressed it, then the cry would have been—Surely he ought at least to have suppressed this;—and he would have been reproached for what he did use.

We are not going to nauseate the reader with all the half-sighted and whole-clawed meanness of the article in question. It is, in truth, a dull as well as a malicious endeavour; and to anybody acquainted with the speculations which it undertakes to handle, talks quite as much against itself as for. We will content ourselves with a short specimen or two. Mr. Shelley, in endeavouring to shew the perniciousness of superstition in general, from which the perniciousness of its family members is to be deduced, lays the scene of his philosophical poem among the Mahometans:—upon which the Reviewer after blessing himself upon our present happy government, and expressing his own infinite content with it (which we have no doubt is great) calls upon the author to witness his triumph in the following manner:—

'The laws and government on which Mr. Shelley's reasoning proceeds, are the Turkish, administered by a lawless despot; his religion is

---

ate case made out in the *Quarterly Review* for Aristophanes *versus* Socrates. This article seems touched or noted by different hands, as is often the case. If not, we are much mistaken; or some people are strangely acquiescent; some others more strangely improved in writing. (Hunt's footnote.)

the Mohammedan, maintained by servile hypocrites; and his scene for
their joint operation Greece, the land full beyond all others of recollections of former glory and independence, now covered with shame
and sunk in slavery. We are Englishmen, Christians, free, and independent: we ask Mr. Shelley how his case applies to *us*? Or what *we*
learn from it to the prejudice of our own constitution?'—The Reviewer might as well ask what we learnt from any other fiction, which
was to apply without being literal. Mr. Shelley is not bound to answer
for his critic's stupidity. The reader of *Gulliver's Travels* might as well
ask how the big or little men applied to *him*, he being neither as tall as a
church nor as short as a molehill. The Editor of the *Review* himself, for
instance, might as well ask how Mr. Hazlitt's appellation of *Grildrig*
applied to him,—his name being not *Grildrig*, but *Gifford*; and he never
having stood in the hand of an enormous prince, though he has licked
the feet of petty ones, and thrown stones at their discarded mistresses'
crutches.

Another,—and we have done with specimens. Mr. Shelley, says the
Reviewer, 'speaks of his school as "a world of woes," of his masters as
"tyrants," of his school-fellows as "enemies":—Alas! what is this but to
bear evidence against himself? Every one who knows what a public
school ordinarily must be, can only trace in these lines the language of
an insubordinate, a vain, a mortified spirit.'[1]

Now, Reader, take the following lines:—

> . . . *Public schools 'tis public folly feeds.*
> *The slaves of custom and establish'd mode,*
> With pack-horse constancy we keep the road,
> Crooked or strait, through quags or thorny dells,
> True to the jingling of our leader's bells.
> To follow foolish precedents, and wink
> With both our eyes, is easier than to think.

. . . Speaking of the worldly views with which even future priests are sent
to these schools, the Poet says,

> Egregious purpose worthily begun,
> In barb'rous prostitution of your son;
> Press'd on *his* part by means, that would disgrace

[1] We are much mistaken if anti-despotic opinions have not since taken more root in the
school Mr. Shelley was brought up in than these writers are aware. The boys, we are quite
sure, will be happier, wiser, gentler, and at the same time more truly courageous, in proportion as they do; though some of their old tyrants may see with alarm and rage their
new tyrannies threatened by them. (Hunt's footnote.)

A scriv'ner's clerk, or footman out of place;
And ending, if at last its end be gained,
In sacrilege, in God's own house profan'd.

The *royal letters* are a thing of course;
A King, that would, might recommend his horse;
And Deans,[1] no doubt, and Chapters, with one voice,
As bound in duty, would confirm the choice.

And lastly:—

Would you your son should be a sot, or dunce,
Lascivious, headstrong, or all these at once;
That in good time the stripling's finished taste
For loose expense, and fashionable waste,
Should prove your ruin, and his own at last,
Train him in public with a mob of boys.

Reader, these are not the profane Mr. Shelley's verses, but the pious Cowper's;—Cowper, the all-applauded as well as the deserving, who in these lines, according to the *Quarterly* Reviewer, 'bears evidence against himself,' and proves that there is nothing to be traced in them but the 'language of an insubordinate, a vain, a mortified spirit';—Cowper, in short, the independent, the good, and the sensible,—who, because he had not callousness enough to reconcile his faith in the dreadful dogmas of the Church to his notions of the Supreme Goodness, like these reviewing worshippers of power,—nor courage enough to wage war with them, like Mr. Shelley,—finally lost his senses; and withered away in the very imagination of 'blasts from hell,' like a child on the altar of Moloch.

Our reviewing Scribes and Pharisees beg the question against Mr. Shelley's theories because he does not believe in their own creed. As if they had any creed but that which is established; and the better spirit of which they, and men like them, have ever prevented from appearing! They cannot affect meekness itself, but out of hostility. In the course of an article, full of anger, scandal, and bigotry, they put on little pale-lipped airs of serenity like a vixenish woman; and during one of these they say they would recommend Mr. Shelley to read the Bible, only it is 'a sealed book to a proud spirit.' We will undertake to say that Mr.

1 We recommend this to the criticism of that illustrious obscure, Dean Ireland, whom Mr. Gifford, in the very midst of his rage against 'pretensions' of all sorts, is continually thrusting before the public, and nobody will attend to. (Hunt's footnote.)

Shelley knows more of the Bible, than all the priests who have any thing to do with the *Review* or its writers. He does not abjure 'the pomps and vanities of this wicked world,' only to put them on with the greater relish. To them, undoubtedly, the Bible is not a sealed book, in one sense. They open it to good profit enough. But in the sense which the Reviewer means, they contrive to have it sealed wherever the doctrines are inconvenient. What do they say to the injunctions against 'judging others that ye be not judged,'—against revenge—against tale-bearing,—against lying, hypocrisy, partiality, riches, pomps and vanities, swearing, perjury (videlicet, Nolo-Episcopation), Pharisaical scorn, and every species of worldliness and malignity? Was Mr. Canning (the parodist) a worthy follower of him that condoled with the lame and blind, when he joked upon a man's disease? Was Mr. Croker, (emphatically called 'the Admiralty Scribe') a worthy follower of him who denounced Scribes, Pharisees, and 'devourers of widows' houses,' when he swallowed up all those widows' pensions? Was Mr. Gifford a worthy follower of him who was the forgiver and friend of Mary Magdalen, when he ridiculed the very lameness and crutches of a Prince's discarded mistress! Men of this description are incapable of their own religion. If Christianity is compatible with all that they do and write, it is a precious thing. But if it means something much better,—which we really believe it does mean, in spite both of such men and of much more reverenced and ancient authorities, then is the spirit of it to be found in the aspiration of the very philosophies which they are most likely to ill treat. The Reviewer for instance quotes, with horrified Italics, such lines as these—

> Nor hate another's crime, nor loathe thine own.
> And love of joy can make the foulest breast
> A paradise of flowers, where peace might build her nest.

What is this first passage but the story of the woman taken in adultery? And what the second, but the story of Mary Magdalen, 'out of whom went seven devils,' and who was forgiven because 'she loved much'? Mr. SHELLEY may think that the sexual intercourse might be altered much for the better, so as to diminish the dreadful evils to which it is now subject. His opinions on that matter, however denounced or mis-represented, he shares in common with some of the best and wisest names in philosophy, from Plato down to Condorcet. It has been doubted by Doctors of the Church, whether Christ himself thought on these matters as the Jews did. But be this as it may, it does not hurt the parallel spirit of the passages. The Jews were told 'not to hate another's crime.' The woman was not told to loathe her sin, but simply not to repeat it; and was dismissed gently with these remarkable words,— 'Has any man condemned thee? No, Lord. Neither do I condemn thee.' Meaning, on the most impartial construction, that if no man had brought her before a judge to be condemned, neither would he be the judge to condemn her. She sinned, because she violated the conventional ideas of virtue, and thus hazarded unhappiness to others, who had not been educated in a different opinion; but the goodness of the opinion itself is left doubtful. It is to the spirit of Christ's actions and theories that we look, and not to the comments or contradictions even of apostles. It was a very general spirit, if it was any thing, going upon the sympathetic excess, instead of the antipathetic—notoriously opposed to existing establishments, and reviled with every term of opprobrium by the Scribes and Pharisees then flourishing. If Mr. Shelley's theological notions run counter to those which have been built upon the supposed notions of Christ, we have no hesitation in saying that the moral spirit of his philosophy approaches infinitely nearer to that Christian benevolence so much preached and so little practised, than any the most orthodox dogmas ever published. The Reviewers with their usual anti-christian falsehood say that he recommends people to 'hate no crime' and 'abstain from no gratification.' In the Christian sense he *does* tell them to 'hate no crime'; and in a sense as benevolent, he does tell them to 'abstain from no gratification.' But a world of gratification is shut out from his code, which the Reviewer would hate to be debarred from; and which he instinctively hates him for denouncing already. Hear the end of the Preface to *The Revolt of Islam*. 'I have avoided all *flattery* to those violent and malignant passions of our nature, which are ever on the watch to mingle with and to alloy the most beneficial innovations. *There is no quarter given to Revenge, Envy, or Prejudice*. Love is celebrated every where as the sole law which should govern the moral world.' Now, if Envy is rather tormenting to ye, Messieurs Reviewers, there is some little gratification, is there not, in Revenge? and some little gratifying profit or so in Prejudice? 'Speak, Grildrig.'

Failing in the attempt to refute Mr. Shelley's philosophy, the Reviewers attack his private life. What is the argument of this? or what right have they to know any thing of the private life of an author? or how would they like to have the same argument used against themselves? Mr. Shelley is now seven and twenty years of age. He entered life about 17; and every body knows, and every candid person will allow, that a young man at that time of life, upon the very strength of a warm and trusting nature, especially with theories to which the world are not accustomed, may render himself liable to the misrepresentations of the worldly. But what have the *Quarterly* Reviewers to do with this? What is Mr. Shelley's private life to the *Quarterly Review*, any more than Mr. GIFFORD's or Mr. CROKER's, or any other *Quarterly* Reviewer's private life is to the *Examiner*, or the *Morning Chronicle*, or to the *Edinburgh Review*,—a work, by the bye, as superior to the *Quarterly*, in all the humanities of social intercourse, as in the liberality of its opinions in general. The Reviewer talks of what he '*now*' knows of Mr. Shelley. What does this pretended *judge* and actual male-gossip, this willing listener to scandal, this minister to the petty wants of excitement, now know more than he ever knew, of an absent man, whose own side of whatever stories have been told him he has never heard? Suppose the opponents of the *Quarterly Review* were to listen to all the scandals that have been reported of writers in it, and to proclaim this man by name as a pimp, another as a scamp, and another as a place or pulpit-hunting slave made out of a schoolboy tyrant? If the use of private matters in public criticism is not to be incompatible with the decencies and charities of life, let it be proved so; and we know who would be the sufferers. We have experienced, in our own persons, what monstrous misrepresentations can be given of a man, even with regard to the most difficult and unselfish actions of his life, and solely because others just knew enough of delicacy, to avail themselves of the inflexible love of it in others.[1]

We shall therefore respect the silence hitherto observed publicly by Mr. Shelley respecting such matters, leaving him when he returns to England to take such notice or otherwise of his calumniators as may seem best to him. But we cannot resist the impulse to speak of one particular calumny of this Reviewer, the falsehood of which is doubly impressed upon us in consequence of our own personal and repeated

[1] The Reviewer in question, always true to his paltry trade, is pleased, in speaking of the Editor of this paper, to denounce his 'bustling vulgarity, the ludicrous affection, the factious flippancy, and the selfish heartlessness, which it is hard for the Reviewer's feelings to treat with the mere contempt they merit.' Indeed! The saying is a borrowed one, and much the worse for its shabby wear. Oh, good God! how applicable are all these charges but the political one, to some of those we could tell the world! Applied as they are, they have only excited a contemptuous mirth against the Reviewer among the companions of the Editor, who hereby, with a more than exemplary fairness of dealing, repays his mock-contempt with real. (Hunt's footnote.)

knowledge of the reverse. He says Mr. Shelley 'is shamefully dissolute in his conduct.' We laugh the scandalmonger to scorn. Mr. Shelley has theories, as we have said before, with regard to the regulation of society, very different certainly from those of the *Quarterly* Reviewers, and very like opinions which have been held by some of the greatest and best men, ancient and modern. And be it observed that all the greatest and best men who have ever attempted to alter the condition of sexual intercourse at *all* have been calumniated as profligates, the devout Milton not excepted. A man should undoubtedly carry these theories into practice with caution, as well as any other new ones, however good, which tend to hurt the artificial notions of virtue, before reasoning and education have prepared them. We differ with Mr. Shelley in some particulars of his theory, but we agree in all the spirit of it; and the consequence has partly been to us, what it has been to him:—those who have only a belief, or an acquiescence, and no real principle at all; —or who prefer being rigid theorists and lax practisers, with the zest of hypocrisy first and penitence afterwards;—or who love to confound conventional agreements and reputations with all that is to be wished for in human nature, and hate, and persecute, and delight to scandalize any body who, with the kindest intentions, would win them out of the hard crust of their egotism, however wretched,—or lastly, those who, having acted with the most abominable selfishness and unfeelingness themselves, rejoice in the least opportunity of making a case out to the world against those they have injured,—these, and such persons as these, have chosen to assume from our theories all which they think the world would least like in point of practice; and because we disdained to notice them, or chose to spare not only the best feelings of others, whom they should have been the last to wound, but even their own bad, false, and malignant ones, would have continued to turn that merciful silence against us, had they not unfortunately run beyond their mark and shown their own fear and horror at being called upon to come forward. But to return to Mr. Shelley. The Reviewer asserts that he 'is shamefully dissolute in his conduct.' We heard of similar assertions, when we resided in the same house with Mr. Shelley for nearly three months; and how was he living all that time? As much like Plato himself, as any of his theories resemble Plato,—or rather still more like a Pythagorean. This was the round of his daily life:—He was up early; breakfasted sparingly; wrote this *Revolt of Islam* all the morning; went out in his boat or into the woods with some Greek author or the *Bible* in his hands; came home to a dinner of vegetables (for he took neither meat nor wine); visited (if necessary) *the sick and the fatherless,* whom others gave Bibles to and no help; wrote or studied again, or read to his wife and friends the whole evening; took a crust of bread or a glass of whey for his supper; and went early to bed. This is literally the whole of the life he led, or that we believe he now leads in Italy; nor have we ever known him, in spite of the malignant and ludicrous exaggerations on this point, deviate, notwithstanding his theories, even into a single action which those who differ with him might think blameable. We do not say, that he would always square his conduct by their opinions as a matter of principle: we only say, that he acted just as if he did so square them. We forbear, out of regard for the very bloom of their beauty, to touch upon numberless other charities and generosities which we have known him exercise; but this we must say in general, that we never lived with a man who gave so complete an idea of an ardent and principled aspirant in philosophy as Percy Shelley; and that we believe him, from the bottom of our hearts, to be one of the noblest hearts as well as heads which the world has seen for a long time. We never met in short with a being who came nearer, perhaps so near, to that height of humanity mentioned in the conclusion of an essay of Lord Bacon's, where he speaks of excess in Charity and of its not being in the power of 'man or angel to come in danger by it.'

'If a man be gracious and courteous to strangers,' continues this wise man of the world, in opening the final-stop of his high worship of a greater and diviner wisdom,—'If a man be gracious towards strangers, it shews he is a citizen of the world, and that his heart is no island cut off from other lands, but a continent that joins to them. If he be compassionate towards the afflictions of others, it shews that his heart is like the noble tree that is wounded itself when it gives the balm. If he easily pardons and remits offences, it shews that his mind is planted above injuries, so that he cannot be shot. If he be thankful for small benefits, it shews that he weighs men's minds, and not their trash. But, above all, if he have St. Paul's perfection, that he would wish to be an anathema from Christ, for the salvation of his brethren, it shews much of a divine nature, and a kind of conformity with Christ himself.'

We could talk, after this, of the manner in which natures of this kind are ever destined to be treated by the Scribes, Pharisees, and Hypocrites of all times and nations; but what room can we have for further indignation, when the ideas of benevolence and wisdom unite to fill one's imagination?—Blessings be upon thee, friend; and a part of the spirit which ye profess to serve, upon ye, enemies.

ROSALIND AND HELEN

1819

30. Leigh Hunt, review, *The Examiner*

May 9, 1819, no. 593, 302–3

This is another poem in behalf of liberality of sentiment and the deification of love, by the author of *The Revolt of Islam*. It is 'not an attempt,' says the writer, 'in the highest style of poetry. It is in no degree calculated to excite profound meditation; and if, by interesting the affections and amusing the imagination, it awaken a certain ideal melancholy favourable to the reception of more important impressions, it will produce in the reader all that the writer experienced in the composition. I resigned myself, as I wrote, to the impulse of the feelings which moulded the conception of the story; and this impulse determined the pauses of a measure, which only pretends to be regular inasmuch as it corresponds with, and expresses the irregularity of the imaginations which inspired it.'

Mr. Shelley has eminently succeeded in all that he thus wished to do. The speakers, who tell each other their stories, are two fine-hearted women, who have been unhappy in their loves,—the one having seen her partner in life die of a disappointed sympathy with mankind in consequence of the late great political changes; and the other, having for the sake of her reduced family accepted a hard, cold-blooded man for her husband, after she had been on the eve of marrying a beloved friend, who turned out at the altar to be her brother. The father

> . . . came from a distant land
> And with a loud and fearful cry
> Rushed between us suddenly.
> *I saw the stream of his thin grey hair,*
> *I saw his lean and lifted hand,*
> And heard his words,—and live: Oh God!
> Wherefore do I live?—'Hold, hold!'
> He cried,—'I tell thee 'tis her brother!'

The couplet marked in Italics, especially the first line, is very striking and fearful. He comes between them like a spirit grown old.—There is something very beautiful in the way in which the two heroines meet. It is in Italy, whither they have both gone, like solitary birds of passage, from a climate every way colder; and *Rosalind*, who it seems is a legitimate widow, turns away from her old friend, who had adopted Mary Wollstonecraft's opinion in those matters. This fortune however, coming in aid of her former tenderness, melted her heart; and it again ran into that of *Helen* with tears. They unite their fortunes, and have the pleasure of seeing their children, a girl and boy, grow up in love with each other, till in their union they saw

> The shadow of the peace denied to them.

This little publication, in form and appearance resembling the one we criticised last week, presents a curious contrast with it in every other respect. It is in as finer a moral taste, as *Rosalind* and *Helen* are pleasanter names than *Peter Bell*. The object of Mr. Wordsworth's administrations of melancholy is to make men timid, servile, and (considering his religion) selfish;—that of Mr. Shelley's, to render them fearless, independent, affectionate, infinitely social. You might be made to worship a devil by the process of Mr. Wordsworth's philosophy; by that of Mr. Shelley, you might re-seat a dethroned goodness. The Poet of the Lakes always carries his egotism and 'saving knowledge' about with him, and unless he has the settlement of the matter, will go in a pet and plant himself by the side of the oldest tyrannies and slaveries;—our Cosmopolite-Poet would evidently die with pleasure to all personal identity, could he but see his fellow-creatures reasonable and happy. He has no sort of respect, real or sullen, for mere power and success. It does not affect him in its most powerful shapes; and he is inclined to come to no compromise with it; he wants others happy, not himself privileged. —But comparisons are never so odious, as when they serve to contrast two spirits who ought to have agreed. Mr. Wordsworth has become hopeless of this world, and therefore would make everybody else so;— Mr. Shelley is superior to hopelessness itself; and does not see why all happiness and all strength is to be bounded by what he himself can feel or can effect.

But we shall again be tempted to transgress the limits of our Literary Notices. We must give some further specimens of the poetry. The following is a passage which will go to every true woman's heart. . . .

[quotes lines 338–70]

Of *Helen's* lover *Lionel*, in his happier times, it is said that

> A winged band
> Of bright persuasions, which had fed
> On his sweet lips and liquid eyes,
> *Kept their swift pinions half outspread*
> To do on men his least command.

The gentle noise arising from the earth during a still summer evening is thus delightfully described:—but we must go back, and make a larger extract than we intended. *Lionel* comes out of a prison, into which he had been cast for his opinions; and so, says his fond survivor,

[quotes lines 953–76]

A picture follows, which we were going to say would be appreciated by none but the most delicate minded; but Mr. Shelley can make his infinite earnestness and sincerity understood even by critics of a very different cast, who happen to have no personal pique with him; though we understand also that they take care to abuse him enough, in order to shew the time-serving bigotry of their opinions in general.

To the chief poem succeeds a smaller one entitled 'Lines written among the Euganean Hills.' Some of them are among the grandest if not the deepest that Mr. Shelley has produced, with a stately stepping in the measure. But we have not space to quote any,[1] not even a noble compliment which he introduces to his friend Lord Byron. We must also abstain from many other passages which tempt us in the poem we have criticised.

Upon the whole, with all our admiration of *The Revolt of Islam*, we think that *Rosalind and Helen* contains, for the size, a still finer and more various, as well as a more popular, style of poetry. The humanity is brought nearer to us, while the abstractions remain as lofty and noble. Mr. Shelley seems to look at Nature with such an earnest and intense love, that at last if she does not break her ancient silence, she returns him look for look. She seems to say to him, 'You know me, if others do not.' For him, if for any poet that ever lived, the beauty of the external world has an answering heart, and the very whispers of the wind a meaning. Things, with mankind in general, are mere words; they have only a few paltry commonplaces about them, and see only the surface of those. To Mr. Shelley, all that exists, exists indeed,—colour, sound

[1] Hunt's footnote includes 'Lines Written among the Euganean Hills' quoted in full.

motion, thought, sentiment, the lofty and the humble, great and small, detail and generality,—from the beauties of a blade of grass or the most evanescent tint of a cloud, to the heart of man which he would elevate, and the mysterious spirit of the universe which he would seat above worship itself.

31. Unsigned review, *The Commercial Chronicle*

June 3, 1819, no. 2979, 1

This review, with a few minor changes, also appears in *The London Chronicle* of June 1, 1819 and *The Gentleman's Magazine*, Supplement for 1819 (lxxxix, 625–6, part I).

We speak our sincere opinion in saying, that if we desired to bring a poetic sanction to the basest passions of the human heart, or the most odious, revolting, and unnameable crimes of human society, we should seek it in the works of certain Poets who have lately visited the Lake of Geneva.

Rosalind and *Helen* are two unfortunates, who meet on the shores of another lake, that of Como, a place which appears singularly favoured by the unfortunates of the world. But their ill-luck has come upon those weepers in different forms. *Rosalind* was a wife, with a passion for an earlier lover, and *Helen* simply a kept mistress, but of remarkably delicate sentiment, seduced, it is true, but seduceable by only one man in the world, and that man *Lionel*, the laboured portraiture of the 'poetic Peer.' The partners of both the Ladies have died, and the desolate fair shed tears in deluges—*Helen* for her *protector*, and *Rosalind* to see *Helen* shed tears. In this mournful conference, common sense points out that they cannot stand for ever, and they accordingly first select a place to sit down in.

> There,
>> Let us sit on that grey stone,
>> Till our mournful talk be done.

Helen objects to this location for the following weighty reasons:—

>> Alas! not there; I cannot bear
>> The murmur of this Lake to hear.
>> A sound from thee, Rosalind dear,
>> Which never yet I heard elsewhere,
>> But in our native land, recurs,
>> Even here where now we meet, it stirs
>> Too much of suffocating sorrow.

Rosalind consents, and they change their position under the guidance of Helen's child.

> A Mamma's Dialogue

>> Henry
>>> 'Tis Fenici's seat
>> Where you are going? This is not the way,
>> Mamma! It leads behind those trees that grow
>> Close to the little river.

>> Helen
>>> Yes, I know.
>> I was bewildered. Kiss me and be gay,
>> Dear boy; why do you sob?

>> Henry
>>> I do not know;
>> But it might break any one's heart to see
>> You and the lady cry so bitterly.

>> Helen
>> It is a gentle child, my friend. Go home,
>> Henry, and play with Lilla till I come.
>> We only cried with joy to see each other;
>> We are quite merry now. Good night.

This we recommend to all amateurs as one of the most perfect specimens of 'lisping in numbers.' It is worthy of the purest periods of the nursery. But the Poet knows, that without a terrific story now and then,

the cradle republic might lie in 'commotion rude,' and he has his horror
forthcoming with the readiness of a genuine gossip.

> With tremulous lips he told
> That a hellish shape at midnight led
> The ghost of a youth with hoary hair,
> And sate on the seat beside him—there
> When the fiend would change to a lady fair.

The Poets of this school have the original merit of conceiving that
the higher emotions of the heart are to be roused in their highest
degree by deformity, physical and moral; they have found out a new
source of the sublime—disgust; and with them the more sickening the
circumstance, the more exquisite the sensibility. The gossip horror is
wound up by telling us that the parties were incestuous. But the innocent enthusiasts who perpetrated this poetic crime were unhappily
victims to the mob, and that most terrible of manslayers, the priest.
The multitude killed the mother and the child,

> But the youth, for God's most holy grace
> A priest saved to burn in the market place.

> Infantine Sports
> He was a gentle boy
> And in all gentle sports took joy,
> Oft in a dry leaf for a boat
> With a small feather for a sail,
> His fancy on that spring would float.

> Accommodating Sorrow
> (for the loss of a husband)
> Oh, I could not weep:
> The sources whence such blessings flow
> Were not to be approached by me!
> But I could smile, and I could sleep.

> Filial Feelings
> My children knew their Sire was gone,
> But when I told them 'he is dead,'
> They laugh'd aloud in frantic glee
> They clapp'd their hands and leap'd about,
> Answering each other's ecstasy
> With many a prank and merry shout.

Rosalind's tale hangs on the favorite and horrid incident of the new
school. She has loved a brother, unconscious indeed of the relationship,

but the poet could not afford to spare the disgust connected with the simple suggestion. On the altar steps her father forbids the marriage; she is overwhelmed obviously less by the crime than the prohibition, and forthwith neither dies nor goes distracted, but does the last thing that natural feeling would do, and marries another. *Helen's* turn now comes, and she thus disburthens her spirit and her magnanimous contempt for the vulgar opinions against harlotry.

> Thou well
> Rememberest when we met no more,
> And though I dwelt with Lionel,
> That friendless caution pierc'd me sore
> With grief—a wound my spirit bore
> Indignantly.

Lionel, meant as a fac-simile of Lord Byron, for Mr. Shelley writes himself down as the Noble Bard's friend, appears to have started into vigour in that prolific period, the French Revolution, when

> ... Men dreamed the aged earth
> Was labouring in that mighty birth
> Which many a poet and a sage
> Has aye forseen—the happy age
> When truth and love shall dwell below.

Lionel advances rapidly in his universal love for the happiness of man, and his resolute opposition to the old bug-bears of priestcraft and superstition.

> That poor and hungry men should break
> The laws which wreak them toil and scorn,
> We understand; but Lionel
> We know is rich and nobly born.
> So wondered they: yet all men loved
> Young Lionel, though few approved;
> All but the priests, whose hatred fell
> Like the unseen blight of a smiling day.

Yet we suspect that with all his imagination Mr. Percy Shelley has some slight jealousy of the noble Lord's pen, for this is the description of his poetry:—

> For he made verses wild and queer
> On the strange creeds priests hold so dear,
> Because they bring them land and gold.
> Of devils and saints and all such gear,

> He made tales which whoso heard or read
> Would laugh till he were almost dead.
> So this grew a proverb: 'Don't get old
> Till Lionel's "Banquet in Hell" you hear,
> And then you will laugh yourself young again.'
> So the priests hated him, and he
> Repaid their hate with cheerful glee.

All this seems to us barbarous nonsense, however jealous it may be; yet Lord Byron may be reconciled by looking on it as the 'Puff Preliminary' for his dormant *Il Don Giovanni*. Helen then gives the following succint and happy history of her seduction. She and her Lionel had a habit of walking at sunset on the seashore:—

> And so we loved, and did unite
> All in us that was yet divided:
> For when he said, that many a rite,
> By men to bind but once provided,
> Could not be shared by him and me,
> Or they would kill him in their glee,
> I shuddered, and then laughing said—
> 'We will have rites our faith to bind,
> But our church shall be the starry night,
> Our altar the grassy earth outspread.'

Such, with the wind for the priest, is the formula of a philosophical marriage. But Lionel is captured for the originality of his opinions, and sent to Newgate:

> The ministers of misrule sent,
> Seized upon Lionel, and bore
> His chained limbs to a dreary tower,
> In the midst of a city vast and wide.
> For he, they said, from his mind had bent
> Against their gods keen blasphemy,
> For which, though his soul must roasted be
> In hell's red lakes immortally,
> Yet even on earth must he abide
> The vengeance of their slaves: a trial,
> I think, men call it.

Lionel is released, but dies of a consumption; Rosalind goes the way of all weepers, and is buried on 'Chiavenna's precipice,' in the hope that her soul may become a 'part of its storms.' Helen

> Whose spirit is of softer mould,

151

as is evinced by her greater atrocities and longer life

> Dies among her kindred, being old.

This work may seem utterly unworthy of criticism; but the character of the school gives importance to the nonsense of the writer. Mr. Shelley is understood to be the person who, after gazing on Mont Blanc, registered himself in the Album as Percy Bysshe Shelley, Atheist; which gross and cheap bravado he, with the natural tact of the new school, took for a display of philosophic courage; and his obscure muse has since constantly been spreading all her foulness on those doctrines which a decent infidel would treat with respect, and in which the wise and honourable have in all ages found the perfection of wisdom and virtue.

32. John Wilson, review, *Blackwood's Edinburgh Magazine*

June 1819, v, 268–74

John Wilson (1785–1854), professor of moral philosophy at the University of Edinburgh, contributed regularly to *Blackwood's* under the pseudonym 'Christopher North.' Although he was a talented and well-educated critic, his inability to restrain himself and a degree of recklessness led him into absurdities which damaged his reputation as a balanced critic. Alan Strout attributes this review to John Gibson Lockhart. See his *A Bibliography of Articles in Blackwood's Magazine (1817–1825)* (1959).

We have already expressed our belief that Mr. Shelley is a true poet, and that it will be his own fault if his name does not hold a conspicuous place in the literature of his country. With our high hopes of him are mingled, however, many disheartening fears, which, we lament to say, are far from being weakened by the spirit of his new poem. For, while this modern eclogue breathes throughout strong feeling, and strong passion, and strong imagination, it exhibits at the same time a strange perversion of moral principle—a wilful misrepresentation of the influence of the laws of human society on human virtue and happiness—and a fierce and contemptuous scorn of those sacred institutions which nature protects and guards for the sake of her own worth and dignity. Indeed, Mr. Shelley does not write like a conscientious man, sinking into fatal error through the imbecility of his intellect—nor like an enthusiastic man hurried away into fatal error by the violence of his passions—but he often writes like a man angry and dissatisfied with the world, because he is angry and dissatisfied with himself—impotently striving to break those bonds which he yet feels are riveted by a higher power—and because his own headstrong and unhappy will frets and fevers within the salutary confinement of nature's gracious laws, impiously scheming to bring these laws into disrepute, by representing them as the inventions and juggleries of tyranny and priestcraft. We are willing to attribute this monstrous perversity in a man of genius and talents like Mr. Shelley, to causes that are external, and that, therefore, will pass away. We leave it to others to speak of him in the bitterness of anger and scorn—to others again to speak of him in the exultation of sympathy and praise. We claim no kindred with either set of critics—seeing in this highly-gifted man much to admire—nay much to love—but much also to move to pity and to sorrow. For what can be more mournful than the degradation of youthful genius involving in its fall virtue, respectability, and happiness?

Rosalind and Helen are two ladies, whom the events of a disastrous life have driven from their native land, and who, after a long discontinuance of their youthful friendship, meet in their distress, one calm summer evening, on the shore of the lake of Como. They retire into the forest's solitude, to communicate to each other the story of their lives—and in these confessions consist almost the whole poem.

[quotes lines 97–111 and 146–54]

Helen had directed the steps of her friend Rosalind to this spot,

> From the wrecks of a tale of wilder sorrow,
> So much of sympathy to borrow
> As soothed her own dark lot.

And what may be this tale, of power to soften or elevate grief?

> A fearful tale! The truth was worse:
> For here a sister and a brother
> Had solemnized a monstrous curse,

Meeting in this fair solitude:
For beneath yon very sky,
Had they resigned to one another
Body and soul.

Leaving for the present without any comment on this worse than needless picture of unnatural guilt, let us attend to the heroines.

Silent they sate, for evening
And the power its glimpses bring
Had, with one awful shadow, quelled
The passion of their grief—

In that profound solitude Rosalind tells the story of her griefs to her melancholy friend. When at the altar stair with her lover, her father, who had come from a distant land, rushed in between them, and forbade the marriage, declaring the youth to be *her brother*!

Then with a laugh both long and wild
The youth upon the pavement fell:
They found him dead! All looked on me,
The spasms of my despair to see:
But I was calm. I went away:
I was clammy-cold like clay!
I did not weep: I did not speak:
But day by day, week after week,
I walked about like a corpse alive!
Alas! sweet friend, you must believe
This heart is stone: it did not break.

On her father's death her mother fell into poverty, and Rosalind, for her sake, married a withered, bloodless, cruel miser, whom her heart abhorred. Her description of her joy on feeling that a babe was to be born to comfort her dark and sullen lot, is exceedingly beautiful, and reminds us of the strains of Wordsworth.

[quotes lines 360–99]

These fair shadows interposed between her loathing soul and her husband, whom she thus describes. . . .

[quotes lines 261–75]

At last worn out with the feverish and quenchless thirst of gold, and with the selfish cares and cruel thoughts that eat into a miser's heart, this man of sin dies.

[quotes lines 436–56]

Having seen and brooded over his wife's loathing, and disgust, and hatred, the shrivelled miser had laid up revenge in his heart.

> After the funeral all our kin
> Assembled, and the will was read.
> My friend, I tell thee, even the dead
> Have strength, their putrid shrouds within,
> To blast and torture. Those who live
> Still fear the living, but a corpse
> Is merciless, and power doth give
> To such pale tyrants half the spoil
> He rends from those who groan and toil,
> Because they blush not with remorse
> Among their crawling worms.

The will imported that, unless Rosalind instantly abandoned her birthplace and her children for ever, they should be disinherited, and all his property go to

> A sallow lawyer, cruel and cold,
> Who watched me, as the will was read,
> With eyes askance, which sought to see
> The secrets of my agony;
> And with close lips and anxious brow
> Stood canvassing still to and fro
> The chance of my resolve, and all
> The dead man's caution just did call.

The effect of this iniquitous last will and testament was to throw over the character of Rosalind the suspicion of adultery and infidelity, the first of which crimes she indignantly denies; but

> As to the Christian creed, if true
> Or false, I never questioned it:
> I took it as the vulgar do:
> Nor my vext soul had leisure yet
> To doubt the things men say, or deem
> That they are other than a dream!!!

Rather than reduce her children to beggary, the widow resolves to endure expatriation and solitary death.

[quotes lines 518–35]

Such is the outline of the Tale of Rosalind, distinguished by great animation and force of passion, and containing much beautiful description of external nature, which we regret it is not possible for us to quote. She then requests Helen 'to take up weeping on the mountains wild.'

> Yes, speak. The faintest stars are scarcely shorn
> Of their thin beams by that delusive morn
> Which sinks again in darkness, like the light
> Of early love, soon lost in total night.

Helen then gives a long, laboured, and to us not very interesting account of her lover, whose whole soul in youth had been absorbed and swallowed up in schemes for the amelioration of the political state of mankind. He seems, first of all, to have revelled in the delight of the French revolution; and finally, if we mistake not, to have fallen into a consumption out of pure grief at the battle of Waterloo and the dethronement of Buonaparte.

[quotes lines 732–55]

Lionel and Helen now become lovers.

> He dwelt beside me near the sea:
> And oft in evening did we meet,
> When the waves, beneath the starlight, flee
> O'er the yellow sands with silver feet,
> And talked: our talk was sad and sweet.

The progress of their love is then described as terminating in a sort of wedding, without benefit of clergy.

On the very night of these moonlight nuptials, however, Lionel is seized 'by the ministers of misrule,' and committed to prison. Helen tells this in a very silly manner.

> For he, they said, from his mind had bent
> Against their gods keen blasphemy,
> For which, though his soul must roasted be
> In hell's red lakes immortally,
> Yet even on earth must he abide
> The vengeance of their slaves: *a trial*
> *I think, men call it!!*

With all the fidelity of a wife, and all the passion of a mistress, Helen, who is refused admittance to his cell, takes a lodging beside the prison-gate, and on his release, (whether he had been acquitted, condemned, or not tried at all, we are not told,) accompanies him to the seat of his ancestors.

[quotes lines 949–92]

His imprisonment, however, had entirely destroyed a constitution already shaken by the agitation of so many disappointed passions, and the gradual decay of life is painted by Mr. Shelley with great power and pathos. The closing scene, though somewhat fantastic, as indeed the whole of Helen's history is, could have been written by none but a genuine poet. Lionel's mother had built a temple in memory and honour of a god (the only saint in her calendar), that had rescued her from drowning, to which we are told she often resorted, and . . .

[quotes lines 1,099–186]

With all its beauty, we feel that the above passage may, to many minds, seem forced and extravagant, but there can be but one opinion of the following one, than which Byron himself never wrote any thing finer.

[quotes lines 1,195–227]

Our extracts have been already long—but it is our anxious desire to bring the genius of this poet fairly before the public, and therefore we quote the conclusion of the poem.

[quotes lines 1,240–318]

Mr. Shelley's writings have, we believe, hitherto had but a very limited circulation, and few of our periodical brethren have condescended to occupy their pages with his poetry. It is one of the great objects of this journal to support the cause of genius and of imagination—and we are confident that our readers will think we have done so in this number, by the full and abundant specimens of fine poetry we have selected from Percy Bysshe Shelley and Barry Cornwall. We trust that the time will soon come when the writings of such men will stand in no need of our patronage.—Meanwhile we give them ours, such as it is worth, and that it is worth more than certain persons are willing to allow, is proved by nothing more decidedly than the constant irritation and fretfulness of those on whom we cannot in conscience bestow it.

But we cannot leave Mr. Shelley without expressing ourselves in

terms of the most decided reprobation of many of his principles, if, indeed, such vague indefinite and crude vagaries can, by any latitude of
language, be so designated. And, first of all, because priests have been
bloody and intolerant, is it worthy of a man of liberal education and
great endowments, to talk with uniform scorn and contempt of the
ministers of religion? Can any thing be more puerile in taste, more
vulgar in feeling, more unfounded in fact, or more false in philosophy?
Mr. Shelley goes out of his way—out of the way of the leading passion
of his poetry to indulge in the gratification of this low and senseless
abuse—and independently of all higher considerations, such ribaldry
utterly destroys all impassioned emotion in the hearts of his readers,
and too frequently converts Mr. Shelley from a poet into a satirist, from
a being who ought, in his own pure atmosphere, to be above all mean
prejudices, into a slave, basely walking in voluntary trammels.

From his hatred and contempt of priests, the step is but a short one to
something very like hatred and contempt of all religion—and accordingly superstition is a word eternally upon his lips. How many fine,
pure, and noble spirits does he thus exclude from his audience? And
how many sympathies does he thus dry up in his own heart? If the
christian faith be all fable and delusion, what does this infatuated young
man wish to substitute in its stead? One seeks, in vain, through his
poetry, fine as it often is, for any principles of action in the characters
who move before us. They are at all times fighting against the law of
the world, the law of nature, and the law of God—there is nothing
satisfactory in their happiness, and always something wilful in their
misery. Nor could Mr. Shelley's best friend and most warm admirer do
otherwise than confess that he is ever an obscure and cheerless moralist,
even when his sentiments are most lofty, and when he declaims with
greatest eloquence against the delusions of religious faith. That a poet
should be blind, deaf, and insensible to the divine beauty of Christianity,
is wonderful and deplorable, when, at the same time, he is so alive to
the beauty of the external world, and, in many instances, to that of the
human soul. If Mr. Shelley were a settled—a confirmed disbeliever, we
should give him up as a man of whom no high hopes could rationally
be held—but we think him only an inconsiderate and thoughtless
scoffer, who will not open his eyes to a sense of his wickedness and folly
—and therefore it is that we express ourselves thus strongly, not out of
anger or scorn, but real sorrow, and sincere affection.

It is also but too evident, from Mr. Shelley's poetry, that he looks
with an evil eye on many of the most venerable institutions of civil

polity. His creed seems to be the same, in many points, as that once held by a celebrated political writer and novelist, who has lived to abjure it. But in all that Godwin wrote, one felt the perfect sincerity of the man —whereas Mr. Shelley seems to have adopted such opinions, not from any deep conviction of their truth, but from waywardness and caprice, from the love of singularity, and, perhaps, as a vain defence against the reproaches of his own conscience. His opinions, therefore, carry no authority along with them to others—nay, they seem not to carry any authority with them to himself. The finer essence of his poetry never penetrates them—the hues of his imagination never clothes [sic] them with attractive beauty. The cold, bald, clumsy, and lifeless parts of this poem are those in which he obtrudes upon us his contemptible and long-exploded dogmas. Then his inspiration deserts him. He never stops nor stumbles in his career, except when he himself seems previously to have laid blocks before the wheels of his chariot.

Accordingly there is no great moral flow in his poetry. Thus, for example, what lesson are we taught by this eclogue, *Rosalind and Helen*? Does Mr. Shelley mean to prove that marriage is an evil institution, because by it youth and beauty may be condemned to the palsied grasp of age, avarice and cruelty? Does he mean to shew the injustice of law, because a man may by it bequeath his property to strangers, and leave his wife and children beggars? Does he mean to shew the wickedness of that law by which illegitimate children do not succeed to the paternal and hereditary estates of their father? The wickedness lay with Lionel and with Helen, who, aware of them all, indulged their own passion, in violation of such awful restraints—and gave life to innocent creatures for whom this world was in all probability to be a world of poverty, sorrow, and humiliation.

But we have stronger charges still—even than these—against this poet. What is it that he can propose to himself by his everlasting allusions to the unnatural loves of brothers and sisters? In this poem there are two stories of this sort—altogether gratuitous—and, as far as we can discover, illustrative of nothing. Why then introduce such thoughts, merely to dash, confound, and horrify? Such monstrosities betoken a diseased mind;—but be this as it may—it is most certain that such revolting passages coming suddenly upon us, in the midst of so much exquisite beauty, startle us out of our dream of real human life, and not only break in upon, but put to flight all the emotions of pleasure and of pathos with which we were following its disturbed discourses. God knows there is enough of evil and of guilt in this world, without our seeking to raise up such hideous and unnatural phantasms of wickedness—but thus to mix them up for no earthly purpose with the ordinary events of human calamity and crime, is the last employment which a man of genius would desire—for there seems to be really no inducement to it, but a diseased desire of degrading and brutifying humanity.

We hope ere long to see the day when Mr. Shelley, having shaken himself free from these faults—faults so devoid of any essential or fundamental alliance with his masterly genius—will take his place as he ought to do, not far from the first poets of his time. It is impossible to read a page of his *Revolt of Islam*, without perceiving that in nerve and pith of conception he approaches more nearly to Scott and Byron than any other of their contemporaries—while in this last little eclogue, he touches with equal mastery the same softer strings of pathos and tenderness which had before responded so delightfully to the more gentle inspirations of Wordsworth, Coleridge, and Wilson.[1] His fame will yet be a glorious plant if he does not blast its expanding leaves by the suicidal chillings of immorality—a poison that cannot be resisted long by any product of the soil of England.

33. Unsigned review, *The Monthly Review, or Literary Journal*

October 1819, xc, 207–9

We are here presented with another specimen of the modern school of *poetical metaphysics*. Indistinct, however, and absolutely unmeaning, as Mr. Shelley usually is, he has, in his lucid intervals, a power of composition that raises him much above many of his fellows. We regret, indeed, to see so considerable a portion of real genius wasted in merely desultory fires; and still more do we lament to observe such extensive

[1] If John Wilson (i.e. 'Christopher North') wrote this review, this audacious reference is almost unparalleled in English literature.

infidelity in the mind of a writer who is evidently capable of better things. The practical influence, which his scepticism would seem to have on the poet, is a subject of sincere commiseration. We can over-look a few general sallies of a thoughtless nature: but, when a man comes to such a degree of perverseness, as to represent the vicious union of two individuals of different sexes as equally sacred with the nuptial tie, we really should be wanting in our duty not to reprobate so gross an immorality.

> We will have rites our faith to bind,
> But our church shall be the starry night,
> Our altar the grassy earth outspread,
> And our priest the muttering wind.

So speaks the modern *Helen*; who seems about as chaste as her antient namesake and prototype; and this is not the only passage in which such sentiments are clothed in the author's best garb of words, or put into the mouth of some interesting and amiable being.

When this writer speaks of the 'bloody faith,' we well know *what faith* he means; and to charge the wicked abuses of darker ages, and of false professors of religion, on *the spirit itself* of the mildest of creeds, is no common degree of audacity. We shall not, however, waste any valuable time on an author who, we fear, is quite incorrigible in this respect; and we shall rather turn to his poetical merits; which, with the drawback of obscurity overclouding almost all that he writes, are, on some occasions, of no common stamp.

The following description of a delightful journey, taken by a lover (just released from prison) with his happy love, certainly manifests much force and feeling:

[quotes lines 936–77]

We would, in a friendly manner, admonish this poet to *stop in time*.

The death of Lionel is very striking, but occasionally disfigured by extravagant *conceits*, and throughout pervaded by *mysticism*.

In the 'Lines written among the Euganean Hills', (as Mr. Shelley bar-barously calls them,—*Euganea quantumvis mollior agna*,[1]) a spirited, handsome, and deserved compliment is paid to Lord Byron. We extract the best part of it. The poet is addressing Venice:

> As the ghost of Homer clings
> Round Scamander's wasting springs;
> As divinest Shakespeare's might

[1] 'However much softer than a Euganean lamb!' (Juvenal, *Satires*, 8.15).

Fills Avon and the world with light
Like omniscient power, which he
Imaged 'mid mortality;
As the love from Petrarch's urn,
Yet amid yon hills doth burn,
A quenchless lamp, by which the heart
Sees things unearthly; so thou art,
Mighty spirit: so shall be
The city that did refuge thee.

A sublime volley of bombast is uttered by the hero, in defiance of his gaolers, at p. 47:

Fear not, the tyrants shall rule for ever,
Or the priests of the bloody faith;
They stand on the brink of that mighty river,
Whose waves they have tainted with death;
It is fed from the depths of a thousand dells,
Around them it foams, and rages, and swells,
And their swords and their sceptres I floating see,
Like wrecks in the surge of eternity.

Yield, Nathaniel Lee! and hide thy diminish'd head!

THE CENCI

September 1819

34. Unsigned notice, *The Monthly Magazine, or British Register*

April 1, 1820, xlix, 260

We observe with pleasure, not unmingled with disgust, a new publication from the pen of Mr. Percy Bysshe Shelley, whose original and extensive genius has so frequently favoured the poetical world with productions of no ordinary merit. In this instance it has assumed a dramatic form, in a singular and wild composition, called *The Cenci*, a family of Italy, whose terrific history seems well adapted to the death-like atmosphere, and unwholesome regions, in which Mr. Shelley's muse delights to tag its wings. We cannot here explain the incestuous story on which it turns; but must content ourselves with observing, that in the attempt to throw a terror over the whole piece, he has transgressed one of the first rules of the master of criticism; and, instead of terror, succeeded only in inspiring us with sentiments of horror and disgust. In the action he has not only 'overstepped the bounds of modesty and nature,' but absolutely turned sentiment into nonsense, and grief into raving, while we endeavour in vain to persuade ourselves, that such faults can be redeemed by occasional bursts of energy and true poetry.

35. Unsigned review, *The Literary Gazette, and Journal of Belles Lettres, Arts, Sciences*

April 1, 1820, clxvii, 209–10

Of all the abominations which intellectual perversion, and poetical atheism, have produced in our times, this tragedy appears to us to be the most abominable. We have much doubted whether we ought to notice it; but, as watchmen place a light over the common sewer which has been opened in a way dangerous to passengers, so have we concluded it to be our duty to set up a beacon on this noisome and noxious publication. We have heard of Mr. Shelley's genius; and were it exercised upon any subject not utterly revolting to human nature, we might acknowledge it. But there are topics so disgusting . . . and this is one of them; there are themes so vile . . . as this is; there are descriptions so abhorrent to mankind . . . and this drama is full of them; there are crimes so beastly and demoniac . . . in which *The Cenci* riots and luxuriates, that no feelings can be excited by their obtrusion but those of detestation at the choice, and horror at the elaboration. We protest most solemnly, that when we reached the last page of this play, our minds were so impressed with its odious and infernal character, that we could not believe it to be written by a mortal being for the gratification of his fellow-creatures on this earth: it seemed to be the production of a fiend, and calculated for the entertainment of devils in hell.

That monsters of wickedness have been seen in the world, is too true; but not to speak of the diseased appetite which would delight to revel in their deeds, we will affirm that depravity so damnable as that of Count Cenci, in the minute portraiture of which Mr. S. takes so much pains, and guilt so atrocious as that which he paints in every one of his dramatic personages, never had either individual or aggregate existence. No; the whole design, and every part of it, is a libel upon humanity; the conception of a brain not only distempered, but familiar with infamous images, and accursed contemplations. What adds to the shocking effect is the perpetual use of the sacred name of God, and incessant appeals to the Saviour of the universe. The foul mixture of religion and blasphemy, and the dreadful association of virtuous principles with incest, parricide, and every deadly sin, form a picture which, 'Too look upon we dare not.'

Having said, and unwillingly said, this much on a composition which we cannot view without inexpressible dislike, it will not be expected from us to go into particulars farther than is merely sufficient to enforce our warning. If we quote a passage of poetic power, it must be to bring tenfold condemnation on the head of the author—for awful is the responsibility where the head condemns the heart, and the gift of talent is so great, as to remind us of Satanic knowledge and lusts, and of 'archangel fallen.'

The story, we are told, in a preface where the writer classes himself with Shakespeare and Sophocles, although two centuries old, cannot be 'mentioned in Italian society without awakening a deep and breathless interest.' We have no high opinion of the morality of Italy; but we can well believe, that even in that country, such a story must, if hinted at, be repressed by general indignation, which Mr. Shelley may, if he pleases, call breathless interest. It is indeed, as he himself confesses, 'Eminently fearful and monstrous; any thing like a dry exhibition of it upon the stage would be insupportable' (Preface, p. ix). And yet he presumes to think that that of which even a dry exhibition upon the stage could not be endured, may be relished when arrayed in all the most forcible colouring which his pencil can supply, in all the minute details of his graphic art, in all the congenial embellishments of his inflamed imagination. Wretched delusion! and worthy of the person who ventures to tell us that, 'Religion in Italy is not, *as in Protestant countries*, a cloak to be worn on particular days; or a passport which those who do not wish to be railed at carry with them to exhibit; or a gloomy passion for penetrating the impenetrable mysteries of our being, which terrifies its possessor at the darkness of the abyss to which it has conducted him:' worthy of the person who, treating of dramatic imagery, blasphemously and senselessly says, that 'imagination is as the immortal God, which should assume flesh for the redemption of mortal passion.'

The characters are Count Cenci, an old grey haired man, a horrible fiendish incarnation, who invites an illustrious company to a jubilee entertainment on the occasion of the violent death of two of his sons; who delights in nothing but the wretchedness of all the human race, and causes all the misery in his power; who, out of sheer malignity, forcibly destroys the innocency of his only daughter; and is, in short, such a miracle of atrocity, as only this author, we think, could have conceived. Lucretia, the second wife of the Count, a most virtuous and

amiable lady, who joins in a plot to murder her husband; Giacomo, his
son, who because his parent has cheated him of his wife's dowry, plots
his assassination; Beatrice the daughter, a pattern of beauty, integrity,
grace, and sensibility, who takes the lead in all the schemes to murder
her father; Orsino, a prelate, sworn of course to celibacy, and in love
with Beatrice, who enters with gusto into the conspiracy, for the
sound reason, that the fair one will not dare to refuse to marry an
accomplice in such a transaction; Cardinal Camillo, a vacillating demi-
profligate; two bravos, who strangle the Count in his sleep; execu-
tioners, torturers, and other delectable under-parts. The action consists
simply of the rout in honour of the loss of two children, of the incest, of
the murderous plot, of its commission, and of its punishment by the
torture and execution of the wife, son, and daughter. This is the dish of
carrion, seasoned with sulphur as spice, which Mr. Shelley serves up to
his friend Mr. Leigh Hunt, with a dedication, by way of grace, in
which he eulogizes his 'gentle, tolerant, brave, honourable, innocent,
simple, pure,' &c. &c. &c. disposition. What food for a humane,
sypathizing creature, like Mr. Hunt! if, indeed, his tender-hearted-
ness be not of a peculiar kind, prone to feast on 'gruel thick and slab,'
which 'like a hell-broth boils and bubbles.'[1]

We will now transcribe a portion of the entertainment scene, to
show how far the writer out herods Herod, and outrages possibility in
his personation of villany, by making Count Cenci a character which
transforms a Richard III. an Iago, a Sir Giles Overreach, comparatively
into angels of light.

[quotes Act I, Scene iii, lines 1–99]

This single example, which is far from being the most obnoxious, unnatural, and infernal in the play, would fully justify the reprobation we
have pronounced. Mr. Shelley, nor no man, can pretend that any good
effect can be produced by the delineation of such diabolism; the bare
suggestions are a heinous offence; and whoever may be the author of
such a piece, we will assert, that Beelzebub alone is fit to be the prompter. The obscenity too becomes more refinedly vicious when Beatrice,
whose 'crimes and miseries,' forsooth, are as 'the mask and the mantle

[1] We are led to this remark by having accidentally read in one of Mr. Hunt's late political
essays, an ardent prayer that Buonaparte might be released from St. Helena, were it only to
fight another Waterloo against Wellington, on *more equal terms*. A strange wish for a
Briton, and stranger still for a pseudo philanthropist, whether arising from a desire to have
his countrymen defeated, or a slaughter productive of so much woe and desolation repeated. (Reviewer's footnote)

in which *circumstances clothed her* for her impersonation on the scenes of world'[1] is brought prominently forward. But we cannot dwell on this. We pass to a quotation which will prove that Mr. Shelley is capable of powerful writing: the description of sylvan scenery would be grand, and Salvator-like, were it not put into the mouth of a child pointing out the site for the murder of the author of her being, 'unfit to live, but more unfit to die.'

[quotes Act III, Scene i, lines 245–74]

It will readily be felt by our readers why we do not multiply our extracts. In truth there are very few passages which will bear transplanting to a page emulous of being read in decent and social life. The lamentable obliquity of the writer's mind pervades every sentiment, and 'corruption mining all within,' renders his florid tints and imitations of beauty only the more loathsome. Are loveliness and wisdom incompatible? Mr. Shelley makes one say of Beatrice, that

> Men wondered how such loveliness and wisdom
> Did not destroy each other!

Cenci's imprecation on his daughter, though an imitation of Lear, and one of a multitude of direct plagiarisms, is absolutely too shocking for perusal; and the dying infidelity of that paragon of parricides, is all we dare to venture to lay before the public.

> Whatever comes, my heart shall sink no more.
> And yet, I know not why, your words strike chill:
> How tedious, false and cold seem all things. I
> Have met with much injustice in this world;
> No difference has been made by God or man,
> Or any power moulding my wretched lot,
> 'Twixt good or evil as regarded me.
> I am cut off from the only world I know,
> From light, and life, and love, in youth's sweet prime.
> You do well telling me to trust in God,
> I hope I do trust in him. In whom else
> Can any trust? And yet my heart is cold.

[1] Preface, p. xiii, and a sentence, which, if not nonsense, is a most pernicious sophistry. There is some foundation for the story, as the Cenci family were devoured by a terrible catastrophe; and a picture of the daughter by Guido, is still in the Colonna Palace. (Reviewer's footnote)

We now most gladly take leave of this work; and sincerely hope, that should we continue our literary pursuits for fifty years, we shall never need again to look into one so stamped with pollution, impiousness, and infamy.

36. Unsigned review, *The London Magazine and Monthly Critical and Dramatic Review*

April 1820, i, 401–7

There has lately arisen a new-fangled style of poetry, facetiously yclept the Cockney School, that it would really be worth any one's while to enter as a candidate. The qualifications are so easy, that he need never doubt the chance of his success, for he has only to knock, and it shall be opened unto him. The principal requisites for admission, in a literary point of view, are as follows. First, an inordinate share of affectation and conceit, with a few occasional good things sprinkled, like green spots of verdure in a wilderness, with a '*parcâ quod satis est manu.*'[1] Secondly, a prodigious quantity of assurance, that neither God nor man can daunt, founded on the honest principle of 'who is like unto me?' and lastly, a contempt for all institutions, moral and divine, with secret yearnings for aught that is degrading to human nature, or revolting to decency. These qualifications ensured, a regular initiation into the Cockney mysteries follows as a matter of course, and the novice enlists himself under their banners, proud of his newly-acquired honors, and starched up to the very throat in all the prim stiffness of his intellect. A few symptoms of this literary malady appeared as early as the year 1795, but it then assumed the guise of simplicity and pathos. It was a poetical Lord Fanny. It wept its pretty self to death by murmuring brooks, and rippling cascades, it heaved delicious sighs over sentimental lambs, and love-lorn sheep, apostrophized donkies in the innocence of primæval nature; sung tender songs to tender nightingales; went to bed without

'That which is enough with a sparing hand.'

a candle, that it might gaze on the chubby faces of the stars; discoursed sweet nothings to all who would listen to its nonsense; and displayed (*horrendum dictu*) the acute profundity of its grief in ponderous folios and spiral duodecimos. The literary world, little suspecting the dangerous consequences of this distressing malady, suffered it to germinate in silence; and not until they became thoroughly convinced that the disorder was of an epidemical nature, did they start from their long continued lethargy. But it was then too late! The evil was incurable; it branched out into the most vigorous ramifications, and following the scriptural admonition, 'Increase and multiply,' disseminated its poetry and its prose throughout a great part of England. As a dog, when once completely mad, is never satisfied until he has bitten half a dozen more, so the Cockney professors, in laudable zeal for the propagation of their creed, were never at rest until they had spread their own doctrines around them. They stood on the house tops and preached, 'till of a verity they were black in the face with the heating quality of their arguments; they stationed themselves by the bye roads and hedges, to discuss the beauties of the country; they looked out from their garrett [*sic*] windows in Grub-street, and exclaimed, '*O! rus, quando ego te aspiciam;*'[1] and gave such afflicting tokens of insanity, that the different reviewers and satirists of the day kindly laced them in the strait jackets of their criticism. 'But all this availeth *us* nothing,' exclaimed the critics, 'so long as *we* see Mordecai the Jew sitting at the gate of the Temple; that *is* to say, as long as there is one Cockney pericranium left unscalped by the tomahawks of our satire.' But notwithstanding the strenuous exertions of all those whose brains have not been cast in the mould of this new species of intellectual dandyism, the evil has been daily and even hourly increasing; and so prodigious is the progressive ratio of its march, that the *worthy* Society for the Suppression of Vice should be called upon to eradicate it. It now no longer masks its real intentions under affected purity of sentiment; its countenance has recently acquired a considerable addition of brass, the glitter of which has often been mistaken for sterling coin, and incest, adultery, murder, blasphemy, are among other favourite topics of its discussion. It seems to delight in an utter perversion of all moral, intellectual, and religious qualities. It gluts over the monstrous deformities of nature; finds gratification in proportion to the magnitude of the crime it extolls; and sees no virtue but in vice; no sin, but in true feeling. Like poor Tom, in *Lear*, whom the foul fiend has possessed for many a day, it will run

[1] 'O country! when shall I look upon you?' (Horace, *Satires*, 2.60).

through ditches, through quagmires, and through bogs, to see a man stand on his head for the exact space of half an hour. Ask the reason of this raging appetite for eccentricity, the answer is, such a thing is out of the beaten track of manhood, *ergo*, it is praiseworthy.

Among the professors of the Cockney school, Mr. Percy Bysshe Shelley is one of the most conspicuous. With more fervid imagination and splendid talents than nine-tenths of the community, he yet prostitutes those talents by the utter degradation to which he unequivocally consigns them. His *Rosalind and Helen*, his *Revolt of Islam*, and his *Alastor, or the Spirit of Solitude*, while they possess beauties of a superior order, are lamentably deficient in morality and religion. The doctrines they inculcate are of the most evil tendency; the characters they depict are of the most horrible description; but in the midst of these disgraceful passages, there are beauties of such exquisite, such redeeming qualities, that we adore while we pity—we admire while we execrate—and are tempted to exclaim with the last of the Romans, 'Oh! what a fall is *here*, my countrymen.' In the modern Eclogue of *Rosalind and Helen* in particular, there is a pensive sadness, a delicious melancholy, nurst in the purest, the deepest recesses of the heart, and springing up like a fountain in the desert, that pervades the poem, and forms its principal attraction. The rich yet delicate imagery that is every where scattered over it, is like the glowing splendor of the setting sun, when he retires to rest, amid the blessings of exulting nature. It is the balmy breath of the summer breeze, the twilight's last and holiest sigh. In the dramatic poem before us, the interest is of a different nature; it is dark—wild, and unearthly. The characters that appear in it are of no mortal stamp; they are dæmons in human guise, inscrutable in their actions, subtle in their revenge. Each has his smile of awful meaning—his purport of hellish tendency. The tempest that rages in his bosom is irrepressible but by death. The phrenzied groan that diseased imagination extorts from his perverted soul, is as the thunder-clap that reverberates amid the cloud-capt summits of the Alps. It is the storm that convulses all nature—that lays bare the face of heaven, and gives transient glimpses of destruction yet to be. Then in the midst of all these accumulated horrors comes the gentle Beatrice,

Who in the gentleness of thy sweet youth
Hast never trodden on a worm, or bruised
A living flower, but thou hast pitied it
With needless tears. Page 50.

She walks in the light of innocence; in the unclouded sunshine of loveliness and modesty; but her felicity is transient as the calm that precedes the tempest; and in the very whispers of her virtue, you hear the indistinct muttering of the distant thunder. She is conceived in the true master spirit of genius; and in the very instant of her parricide, comes home to our imagination fresh in the spring time of innocence—hallowed in the deepest recesses of melancholy. But notwithstanding all these transcendant qualities, there are numerous passages that warrant our introductory observations respecting the Cockney school, and plunge 'full fathom five,' into the profoundest depths of the Bathos. While, therefore, we do justice to the abilities of the author, we shall bestow a passing smile or two on his unfortunate Cockney propensities.

The following are the principal incidents of the play. Count Cenci, the *dæmon* of the piece, delighted with the intelligence of the death of two of his sons, recounts at a large assembly, specially invited for the purpose, the circumstances of the dreadful transaction. Lucretia, his wife, Beatrice, his daughter, and the other guests, are of course startled at his transports; but when they hear his awful imprecations,

> Oh, thou bright wine whose purple splendour leaps
> And bubbles gaily in this golden bowl
> Under the lamp light, as my spirits do,
> To hear the death of my accursed sons!
> Could I believe thou wert their mingled blood,
> Then would I taste thee like a sacrament,
> And pledge with thee the mighty Devil in Hell,
> Who, if a father's curses, as men say,
> Climb with swift wings after their children's souls,
> And drag them from the very throne of Heaven,
> Now triumphs in my triumph!—But thou art
> Superfluous; I have drunken deep of joy
> And I will taste no other wine tonight—

their horror induces them to leave the room. Beatrice, in the meantime, who has been rating her parent for his cruelty, is subjected to every species of insult; and he sends her to her own apartment, with the hellish intention of prostituting her innocence, and contaminating, as he pithily expresses it, 'both body and soul.' The second act introduces us to a tête-a-tête between Bernardo (another of Cenci's sons) and Lucretia; when their conference is suddenly broken off, by the abrupt entrance of Beatrice, who has escaped from the pursuit of the Count. She recapitulates the injuries she has received from her father, the most atrocious of which appear to be, that he has given them all 'ditch water' to drink, and 'buffalos' to eat. But before we proceed further, we have a word or two respecting this same ditch water, and buffalo's flesh, which we shall mention, as a piece of advice to the author. It is well known, we believe, in a case of lunacy, that the first thing considered is, whether the patient has done any thing sufficiently foolish, to induce his relatives to apply for a statute against him: now any malicious, evil-minded person, were he so disposed, might make successful application to the court against the luckless author of *The Cenci, a Tragedy in Five Acts.* Upon which the judge with all the solemnity suitable to so melancholy a circumstance as the decay of the mental faculties, would ask for proofs of the defendant's lunacy; upon which the plaintiff would produce the affecting episode of the ditch water and buffalo flesh; upon which the judge would shake his head, and acknowledge the insanity; upon which the defendant would be incarcerated in Bedlam.

To return from this digression, we are next introduced to Giacomo, another of Cenci's hopeful progeny, who, like the rest, has a dreadful tale to unfold of his father's cruelty towards him. Orsino, the favored lover of Beatrice, enters at the moment of his irritation; and by the most artful pleading ultimately incites him to the murder of his father, in which he is to be joined by the rest of the family. The plot, after one unlucky attempt, succeeds; and at the moment of its accomplishment, is discovered by a messenger, who is despatched to the lonely castle of Petrella (one of the Count's family residences), with a summons of attendance from the Pope. We need hardly say that the criminals are condemned; and not even the lovely Beatrice is able to escape the punishment of the law. The agitation she experiences after the commission of the incest, is powerfully descriptive.

[quotes Act III, Scene i, lines 6–23]

At first she concludes that she is mad; but then pathetically checks herself by saying, 'No, I am dead.' Lucretia naturally enough inquires into the cause of her disquietude, and but too soon discovers, by the broken hints of the victim, the source of her mental agitation. Terrified at their defenceless state, they then mutually conspire with Orsino against the Count; and Beatrice proposes to way-lay him (a plot, however, which fails) in a *deep and dark ravine*, as he journeys to Petrella.

[quotes Act III, Scene i, lines 244–66]

Giacomo, meanwhile, who was privy to the transaction, awaits the arrival of Orsino, with intelligence of the murder, in a state of the most fearful torture and suspence.

[quotes Act III, Scene ii, lines 1–31]

We envy not the feelings of any one who can read the curses that Cenci invokes on his daughter, when she refuses to repeat her guilt, without the strongest disgust, notwithstanding the intense vigor of the imprecations.

[quotes Act IV, Scene i, lines 114–67]

Ohé! jam satis est!![1]—The *minutiæ* of this *affectionate* parent's curses forcibly remind us of the equally minute excommunication so admirably recorded in *Tristram Shandy*. But Sterne has the start of him; for though Percy Bysshe Shelley, Esquire, has contrived to include in the imprecations of Cenci, the eyes, head, lips, and limbs of his daughter, the other has anticipated his measures, in formally and specifically anathematizing the lights, lungs, liver, and *all odd joints*, without excepting even the great toe of his victim.—To proceed in our review; the dying expostulations of poor Beatrice, are beautiful and affecting, though occasionally tinged with the Cockney style of burlesque; for instance, Bernado asks, when they tear him from the embraces of his sister,

Would ye divide body from soul?

On which the judge sturdily replies—'That is the headsman's business.' The idea of approaching execution paralyses the soul of Beatrice, and she thus frantically expresses her horror.

[quotes Act V, Scene V, lines 47–67]

The author, in his preface, observes that he has committed only one plagiarism in his play. But with all the triumph of vanity, we here stoutly convict him of having wilfully, maliciously and despitefully stolen, the pleasing idea of the repetition of 'down, down, down,' from the equally pathetic and instructive ditty of 'up, up, up,' in 'Tom Thumb'; the exordium or prolegomena to which floweth *sweetly* and *poetically* thus:—

Here we go up, up, up,
And here we go *down, down, down!*

[1] 'Alas! now it is enough.'

In taking leave of Mr. Shelley, we have a few observations to whisper in his ear. That he has the seedlings of poetry in his composition no one can deny, after the perusal of many of our extracts; that he employs them worthily, is more than can be advanced. His style, though disgraced by occasional puerilities, and simpering affectations, is in general bold, vigorous, and manly; but the disgraceful fault to which we object in his writings, is the scorn he every where evinces for all that is moral or religious. If he must be skeptical—if he must be lax in his human codes of excellence, let him be so; but in God's name let him not publish his principles, and cram them down the throats of others. Existence in its present state is heavy enough; and if we take away the idea of eternal happiness, however visionary it may appear to some, who or what is to recompence us for the loss we have sustained? Will scepticism lighten the bed of death?—Will vice soothe the pillow of declining age? If so! let us all be sceptics, let us all be vicious; but until their admirable efficacy is proved, let us jog on the beaten course of life, neither influenced by the scoff of infidelity, nor fascinated by the dazzling but flimsy garb of licentiousness and immorality.

37. Review signed 'B.,' *The Theatrical Inquisitor and Monthly Mirror*

April 1820, xvi, 205–18

We are not familiar with the writings of Mr. Shelley, and shall therefore discharge a strict critical duty in considering this, 'the latest of his literary efforts,' upon independent grounds; as neither depreciated nor enhanced by his former productions; but as the offering of a muse that demands our deep, serious, and impartial investigation, to whatever praise or censure it may be ultimately entitled.

This tragedy is founded upon a narrative of facts, preserved in the archives of the 'Cenci' palace at Rome, which contains a detailed account of the horrors that ended in the extinction of a rich and noble family of that place, during the pontificate of Clement VIII., in the year 1599. To this manuscript Mr. Shelley obtained access in the course of his travels through Italy, and having found, on his return to Rome, that the story was not to be told in Italian society without a deep and breathless interest, he imbibed his conception of its fitness for a dramatic purpose. The subject of *The Cenci* is, indeed, replete with materials for terrific effect, and when it has been laid before our readers in the words of Mr. Shelley, we feel assured of their adherence to that opinion.

[quotes Shelley's summary of the story]

From a knowledge of the power inherited by this tale to awaken the sympathy of its hearers, Mr. Shelley determined to clothe it in such language and action as would adjust with the perceptions of his countrymen and 'bring it home to their hearts.' A dry exhibition of it on the stage, he observes, would be insupportable, and we fully coincide in the justice of that remark. Audiences are universally the dupes of feeling and that feeling is too often a wrong one. Alive only to the intricacies of an elaborate plot, without taste for poetical diction, or judgment for powerful character, their sanction and dissent are equally valueless—can establish no merit, and attribute no distinction. The patent puppet-shows of this mighty metropolis are swayed and supplied by individuals who have no emulation but in the race of gain; rash, ignorant, and rapacious, they have rendered the stage a medium of senseless amusement, and if their sordid earnings could be secured by a parricidal sacrifice of the drama itself, we do not scruple to confess our belief that such a detestable sacrifice would be readily effected. If Mr. Shelley has ever speculated in the remotest manner upon an appeal to the stage, we urge him, most earnestly, to renounce that intention. There is something like latent evidence that the tragedy before us was not meant exclusively for the closet; such a purpose is by no means explicitly avowed; but we are glad, however, to perceive that Mr. Shelley, in the structure of his present poem, has not evinced a single claim to the loathsome honours of play-house approbation.

The Cenci opens with an interview between Count Cenci and Cardinal Camillo, in which the latter alludes to the remission of a great recent offense, on the payment of an enormous forfeiture. In the course of this conversation Count Cenci's appetite for lust and blood are vividly enforced; he spurns the humane counsels of his priestly adviser, who having watched him from his 'dark and fiery youth' through 'desperate and remorseless manhood' to 'dishonoured age' had

repeatedly screened him from punishment, and throws out a dark hint
of silencing even him by assassination:

> Cardinal,
> One thing, I pray you, recollect henceforth,
> And so we shall converse with less restraint.
> A man you knew spoke of my wife and daughter;
> He was accustomed to frequent my house;
> So the next day his wife and daughter came
> And asked if I had seen him; and I smiled.
> I think they never saw him any more.

This trait of ferocity is still farther heightened by the complete development of Cenci's moral system, which is built up of the most bold and
flagitious materials that can help render him a paragon of depravity:

[quotes Act I, Scene i, lines 66–120]

Cenci appears soon after at a sumptuous feast given to his kindred
and many other nobles of Rome. Elated most unnaturally at the intelligence, he communicates to this assembly the death of his two elder sons,
Rocco and Cristofano, whom he had removed from Rome to Sala-
manca,

> Hoping some accident would cut them off,
> And meaning, if he could, to starve them there.

In the height of his horrid joy, Cenci thus describes these disastrous
events:

> Rocco
> Was kneeling at the mass, with sixteen others,
> When the church fell and crushed him to a mummy,
> The rest escaped unhurt. Cristofano
> Was stabbed in error by a jealous man,
> Whilst she he loved was sleeping with his rival;
> All in the self-same hour of the same night;
> Which shows that Heaven has special care of me.

The guests impute this exaltation to some really agreeable news, till
Cenci confirms the tidings he has just delivered, by the following
atrocious though sublime ejaculation:

[quotes Act I, Scene iii, lines 77–90]

Beatrice then steps forward, and adjures the various members of her
family to curb the tyranny of Cenci, by removing both her and her

step-mother, Lucretia, beyond the reach of his cruel treatment. The effect of Cenci's rigour is thus beautifully illustrated:

> O God! That I were buried with my brothers!
> And that the flowers of this departed spring
> Were fading on my grave!

The danger of exciting Cenci's animosity deters her relatives from interfering, and they depart with a sincere but spiritless commiseration of the wrongs it was their duty to relieve. Cenci then revokes his determination of not drinking, and, having quaffed a bowl of wine, bursts into a dark but desperate announcement of some impending villainy, which, under the influence of his exhilarating draught, he rushes out to achieve.

At the opening of Act II., a partial disclosure is made by Beatrice of the execrable crime that her father has resolved to perpetrate, and in advance toward which, he has determined on removing to an ancient castle among the rocks of Apulia. His meditations upon this arrangement are as follows:

[quotes Act II, Scene i, lines 174–93]

In the meantime Orsino, a wily prelate, who, previous to his embracing a state of sordid celibacy, had won the affections of Beatrice, under the mask of friendship but from designs of a most offensive nature, has urged her to petition the Pope against her father's brutality, which, however, he perpetuates by keeping her petition back, and pretending it has failed. In the same spirit he sympathises with Giacomo, the son and heir of Count Cenci, whom that hoary sinner by his duplicity and slander has plunged into the deepest shades of domestic distress. The nature and result of Orsino's machinations are unravelled with great adroitness in the following soliloquy:

[quotes Act II, Scene ii, lines 147–61]

The dreadful outrage contemplated by Cenci is at length completed, and Beatrice reels in with the most appalling marks of his incestuous enormity. The circumstances that lead to this crime are not more remarkable for their horror than their extravagance. That 'one with white hair and imperious brow' should satiate his hatred by an expedient of this sort, it is impossible to believe, and yet there is something so devilishly malignant in such a consummation, so rashly wicked, and immeasurably fearful, that it contributes more than any other feature of this tragedy to feed the dark splendour and extent of Mr. Shelley's genius. We feel 'sick with hate' at this picture of atrocity, and yet what finer compliment can be paid to its power, than the excess of such a painful sensation? We have enjoyed the same gloomy delight while gazing at the works of Spagnoletto, in one of which, the 'Flaying of St. Bartholomew,' he represents an executioner as he jags down the stubborn skin with a knife between his teeth, from which the blood of the writhing martyr is seen distinctly to drip. It is ridiculous to object that the point of horror is here carried to excess. Horror was the artist's aim, and unless we mean to quarrel at once with the choice of his subject, we have no right to impeach its execution. His volcanic bosom bubbled over in its own way, pouring out columns of smoke and flame without caution or restraint; and gross, indeed, must be the folly that would search for molten gold among its streams of radiant lava.

We are throwing up this ponderous specimen of Mr. Shelley's power, to return most probably with double violence upon our heedless heads and beat us to the very ground from which we have dared urge its ascension. There is something, however, so shudderingly awful in the scene where this mysterious event is described, that we shall make a copious quotation to corroborate our argument:

[quotes Act III, Scene i, lines 1–102]

This passage is, perhaps, a fairer specimen of the present drama than any other extract could afford. It has no broken bursts of passion, but proceeds in a tone of fierce equability to the point at which we have concluded. We see the victim of Cenci's destructive hatred rushing from his serpent coil, her veins swollen with the venom of his infectious guilt, her heart bruised in her very bosom by his merciless pressure. She utters no rhapsody of words, though her exclamations are fraught with the strangest phenomena of which nature is susceptible. As her griefs are dark and dreadful, so her lamentation is earnest and excessive; it borders upon frenzy; but when her reason has surmounted the shock that displaced it, she drops at once from the day-dreams of an unsettled fancy, to the sorrows of immovable conviction and the bitterness of unqualified despair. Her thoughts are then devoted to vengeance, and yet could her father's crime be atoned for by the blood he has polluted, she would freely expend it; that, however, cannot happen; and therefore, after a reproachful glance at the laxity of heaven, she resumes her innate piety, and returns to a gloomy speculation of revenge.

Orsino, the crafty tempter to deeds of death, now enters, and, in the true spirit of priestliness, incenses the very passions he ought in duty to allay. The murder of Cenci is concerted to the vindictive delight of Beatrice, and with the timid assent of Lucretia. The approaching journey to Petrella is selected for this purpose, and the spot pointed out for its commission is thus impressively described. . . .

[quotes Act III, Scene i, lines 244–65]

The unscrupulous villainy of the monster thus about to be summarily despatched, is still further blazoned by the injuries of his son, Giacomo, who, having narrated the wrongs he has sustained, accedes to Orsino's plan of retribution. It fails, however, and Cenci reaches his Apulian fort, where fresh and final matters of cruelty engage his attention. . . .

[quotes Act IV, Scene i, lines 45–69]

In this march of mischief he is quickly cut off by Olimpio, the castellan of Petrella, a man who

> hated
> Old Cenci so, that in his silent rage
> His lips grew white only to see him pass;

And Marzio, a common stabber, from whom Cenci, though 'well-earned and due,' had withheld the guerdon of assassination. These ruffians are loth at first to kill 'an old and sleeping man,'

> His veined hands crossed on his heaving breast,

till Beatrice, with unconquerable fierceness, by offering to immolate him herself, incites them to the task. They strangle him and throw his body out of the window where it catches in the branches of a pine-tree, and is speedily discovered. The Pope's legate, Savella, arrives with an order for Cenci's apprehension, and on detecting the manner in which he has been dealt with, leads away Beatrice, Lucretia, and Marzio to Rome, where they are arraigned for his imputed murder. Marzio, subdued by torture, confesses the crime, and implicates his abettors, upon which Beatrice, with astonishing hardihood, maintains her innocence and succeeds in persuading Marzio to recant his accusation. Giacomo, who had been betrayed by Orsino to facilitate his own escape, and Lucretia are at length tormented to confession, and adjudged to death with Beatrice, who, when her fate is declared, utters this pathetic exclamation: . . .

[quotes Act V, Scene iv, lines 48–67]

Much intercession is used to avert the fulfillment of her sentence, and when counselled to hope for a favorable issue, Beatrice thus repulses the specious delusion. . . .

[quotes Act V, Scene iv, lines 97–111]

Her faithful and devoted brother, Bernardo, who has prayed like a 'wreck-devoted seaman' to the pontiff for mercy, now rushes in wildly to proclaim the failure of his hopeless errand. . . .

[quotes Act V, Scene iv, lines 121–37]

Beatrice, turning from the prospect of her premature death and blasted honour, abandons the bitterness, obstinacy, and dissimulation those evils had occasioned. She takes a touching leave of her young and kind brother, does a little familiar office for Lucretia, and placidly follows her guards to the place of execution.

We have now rendered to this tragedy such tokens of our admiration, as a hasty perusal and restricted limits would allow us to afford. The worshippers of old, who with pious inclinations had but imperfect means, when they could not give wine to their gods, offered water, and laid a leaf upon that shrine to which others brought its fruit or its flower. If purity of praise can atone to Mr. Shelley for the rough terms in which it is delivered, we beg him to believe us sincere, though unpolished, in its application. As a first dramatic effort *The Cenci* is unparalleled for the beauty of every attribute with which drama can be endowed. It has few errors but such as time will amend, and many beauties that time can neither strengthen nor abate. The poetical lilies of Mr. Shelley have sprung up much sooner than more common blossoms, and by their blossoms, and by their beauty at the break of the morning, we may speculate upon the fragrance they will yield for the rest of the day.

38. Unsigned review,
The New Monthly Magazine and Universal Register

May 1, 1820, xiii, 550–3

Whatever may be the variety of opinion respecting the poetical genius displayed in this work, there can be but one sentiment of wonder and disgust in every honest heart, at the strange perversity of taste which selected its theme. It is the story of a wretch grown old in crime, whose passions are concentrated at last in quenchless hate towards his children, especially his innocent and lovely daughter, against whom he perpetrates the most fearful of outrages, which leads to his own death by her contrivance, and her own execution for the almost blameless parricide. The narrative, we believe is 'extant in choice Italian'; but that is no excuse for making its awful circumstances the groundwork of a tragedy. If such things have been, it is the part of a wise moralist decently to cover them. There is nothing in the circumstance of a tale being true which renders it fit for the general ear. The exposure of a crime too often pollutes the very soul which shudders at its recital, and destroys that unconsciousness of ill which most safely preserves its sanctities. There can be little doubt that the horrible details of murder, which are too minutely given in our public journals, lead men to dwell on horrors till they cease to petrify, and gradually prepare them for that which once they trembled to think on. 'Direness familiar to their slaughterous thoughts cannot once start them.' One suicide is usually followed by others, because men of distempered imaginations brood over the thoughts of the deed, until their diseased and fevered minds are ready to embrace it. It is sometimes true in more than one sense, that 'where there is no law there is no transgression.' All know that for many centuries there was no punishment provided at Rome for parricide, and that not an instance occurred to make the people repent of this omission. And may it not be supposed that this absence of crime was owing to the absence of the law—that the subject was thrown far back from the imagination—that the offense was impossible because it was believed so—and that the regarding it as out of all human calculation gave to it a distant awfulness far more fearful than the severest of earthly penalties? We know well, indeed, that crimes like those intimated in *The Cenci* can never be diffused by any mistaken attempt to drag them forth to the world. But if the mind turns from their loathsomeness, as the sun refused to shine on the horrible banquet of Thyestes, they may still do it irreparable evil. There is no small encouragement to vice in gazing into the dark pits of fathomless infamy. The ordinary wicked regard themselves as on a pinnacle of virtue, while they look into the fearful depth beneath them. The reader of this play, however intense his hatred of crime, feels in its perusal that the sting is taken from offences which usually chill the blood with horror, by the far-removed atrocity which it discloses. The more ordinary vices of the hero become reliefs to us; his cruelties seem to link him to humanity; and his murders are pillows upon which the imagination reposes. It would be well if those who are disposed to exhibit as a spectacle the most awful anomalies of our nature, reflected on the noble reasoning of Sir Thomas Browne in the last chapter of his *Enquiries into Vulgar Errors*: 'For of sins heteroclital, and such as want either name or precedent, there is oft-times a sin even in their histories. We desire no records of such enormities: sins should be accounted new, so that they may be esteemed monstrous. The pens of men may sufficiently expatiate without these singularities of villainy; for as they increase the hatred of vice in some, so do they enlarge the theory of wickedness in all. And this is one thing that may make latter ages worse than the former; for the vicious examples of ages past poison the curiosity of these present, affording a hint of sin unto seduceable spirits, and soliciting those unto the imitation of them, whose heads were never so perversely principled as to invent them. In this kind we recommend the wisdom and goodness of Galen, who would not leave unto the world so subtle a theory of poisons; unarming thereby the malice of venomous spirits, whose ignorance must be contended with sublimate and arsenic. For surely there are subtler venenations, such as will invisibly destroy, and like the basilisks of heaven. In things of this nature, silence commendeth history; 'tis the veniable part of things lost, wherein there must never rise a Pancirollus,[1] nor remain any register but that of Hell!'

If the story of the drama before us is unfit to be told as mere matter of historic truth, still further is it from being suited to the uses of poetry. It is doubtless one of the finest properties of the imagination to soften

[1] Who wrote *De Antiquis Perditis* or of *Inventions Lost*. (Reviewer's footnote)

away the asperities of sorrow, and to reconcile by its mediating power, the high faculties of man and the mournful vicissitudes and brief duration of his career in this world. But the distress which can thus be charmed away, or even rendered the source of pensive joy, must not be of a nature totally repulsive and loathsome. If the tender hues of fancy cannot blend with those of the grief to which they are directed, instead of softening them by harmonious influence, they will only serve to set their blackness in a light still more clear and fearful. Mr. Shelley acknowledges that 'anything like a dry exhibition of his tale on the stage would be insupportable,' and that 'the person who would treat such a subject must increase the ideal, and diminish the actual horror of events, so that the pleasure which arises from the poetry which exists in these stupendous sufferings and crimes, may mitigate the pain of the contemplation of the moral deformity from which they spring.' But in the most prominent of these sufferings and crimes there is no poetry, nor can poetry do aught to lessen the weight of superfluous misery they cast on the soul. Beauties may be thrown around them; but as they cannot mingle with their essence they will but increase their horrors, as flowers fantastically braided round a corpse, instead of lending their bloom to the cheek, render its lividness more sickening. In justice to Mr. Shelley we must observe that he has not been guilty of attempting to realize his own fancy. There is no attempt to lessen the horror of the crime, no endeavour to redeem its perpetrator by intellectual superiority, no thin veil thrown over the atrocities of his life. He stands, base as he is odious, and, as we have hinted already, is only thought of as a man when he softens into a murderer.

We are far from denying that there is great power in many parts of this shocking tragedy. Its author has at least shown himself capable of leaving these cold abstractions which he has usually chosen to embody, and of endowing human characters with life, sympathy, and passion. With the exception of Cenci, who is half maniac and half fiend, his persons speak and act like creatures of flesh and blood, not like the problems of strange philosophy set in motion by galvanic art. The heroine, Beatrice is, however, distinguished only from the multitude of her sex by her singular beauty and sufferings. In destroying her father she seems impelled by madness rather than will, and in her fate excites pity more by her situation than her virtues. Instead of avowing the deed, and asserting its justice, as would be strictly natural for one who had committed such a crime for such a cause—she tries to avoid death by the meanest arts of falsehood and encourages her accomplice to endure the extremities of torture rather than implicate her by confession. The banquet given by Cenci to all the cardinals and nobles of Rome, in order to give expression to his delight on the violent deaths of his sons, is a wanton piece of absurdity, which could have nothing but its improbability to recommend it for its adoption. The earlier scenes of the play are tame—the middle ones petrifying—and the last scene of all affecting and gentle. Some may object to the final speech of Beatrice, as she and her mother are going out to die, where she requests the companion of her fate to 'tie her girdle for her, and bind up her hair in any simple knot,' and refers to the many times they had done this for each other, which they should do no more, as too poor and trifling for the close of a tragedy. But the play, from the commencement of the third act, is one catastrophe, and the quiet pathos of the last lines is welcome as breaking the iron spell which so long has bound the currents of sympathy.

The diction of the whole piece is strictly dramatic—that is, it is nearly confined to the expression of present feeling, and scarcely ever overloaded with imagery which the passion does not naturally create. The following beautiful description of the chasm appointed by Beatrice for the murder of her father, is truly asserted by the author to be the only instance of isolated poetry in the drama:

[quotes Act III, Scene i, lines 243–65]

The speeches of Cenci are hardly of this world. His curses on his child—extending, as they do, the view of the reader beyond the subject into a frightful vista of polluting horrors—are terrific, almost beyond example, but we dare not place them before the eyes of our readers. There is one touch, however, in them, singularly profound and sublime to which we may refer. The wretch, debased as he is, asserts his indissoluble relation of father, as giving him a potency to execrate his child, which the universe must unite to support and heaven allow—leaning upon this one sacred right which cannot sink from under him even while he curses! The bewildered ravings of Beatrice are awful, but their subject will not allow of their quotation. We give the following soliloquy of Cenci's son, when he expects to hear news of his father's murder, because, though not the most striking, it is almost the only unexceptionable instance which we can give of Mr. Shelley's power to develop human passion.

[quotes Act III, Scene ii, lines 1–30]

We must make one more remark on this strange instance of perverted genius, and we shall then gladly fly from its remembrance forever. It seems at first sight wonderful that Mr. Shelley, of all men, should have perpetrated this offense against taste and morals. He professes to look almost wholly on the brightest side of humanity—to 'bid the lovely scenes at distance hail'—and live in fond and disinterested expectation of a 'progeny of golden years' hereafter to bless the world. We sympathize with him in these anticipations, though we differ widely from him as to the means by which the gradual advancement of the species will be effected. But there is matter for anxious inquiry, when one, richly gifted, and often looking to the full triumph of happiness and virtue, chooses to drag into public gaze the most awful crimes, and luxuriates in the inmost and most pestilential caverns of the soul. To a mind, thus strangely inconsistent, something must be wanting. The lamentable solution is, that Mr. Shelley, with noble feelings, with far-reaching hopes, and with a high and emphatic imagination, has no power of religious truth fitly to balance and rightly to direct his energies. Hence a restless activity prompts him to the boldest and most fearful excursions—sometimes almost touching on the portals of heaven, and, at others, sinking a thousand fathoms deep in the cloudy chain of cold fantasy, into regions of chaos and eternal night. Thus will he continue to vibrate until he shall learn that there are sanctities in his nature as well as rights, and that these venerable relations which he despises, instead of contracting the soul, nurture its most extended charities, and cherish its purest aspirations for universal good. Then will he feel that his imaginations, beautiful as ever in shape, are not cold, but breathing with genial life, and that the most ravishing prospects of human improvement, can only be contemplated steadily from those immortal pillars which Heaven has provided Faith to lean upon.

39. Unsigned review,
The Edinburgh Monthly Review

May 1820, iii, 591–604

In the Colonna palace at Rome, there is a small picture, a masterpiece of Guido, which those who have looked upon it can never forget. It is the portrait of a young pale golden-haired melancholy female—her countenance wears the stamp of settled and mild grief—her hands are folded in the firmness of gentle despair—all around her is black as the night of a prison. It represents Beatrice, a lady of the once illustrious house of Cenci, and was painted two hundred years ago, while she lay under sentence of death for the crime of parricide.

Tradition reports, and those that put any faith in physiognomy will easily believe the tradition, that the crime for which this fair creature suffered the last severity of the law, was alien to her original nature, and that her mind, formed to be of the meekest and most merciful order, had been wrought up to the point of bloody resolution, only by the accumulated horrors of paternal cruelty, continued through all the brief series of her opening years, and terminated at last in one deed of outrage so dark, that it ought forever to be without a name—so atrocious, that if any injury could justify parricide, that worst injury was this.

To choose, as the subject of dramatic embellishment, a story so revolting to all human hearts, as that of which this painting has long been the only memorial—to lavish, in the calm possession of intellectual power, the splendours of a rich and lovely imagination, upon the portraiture of deeds and thoughts so horrible, and the development of characters, so warped from the simplicity of nature as those involved in its delineation—was an idea which, we are firmly persuaded, could never have entered into the head of any man of genius besides Mr. Percy Bysshe Shelley. With the private history of this gentleman we have nothing to do, but we must be permitted to say, that the deliberate conception and the elaborate execution of a tragedy, founded on such a plot, is, to our judgment, an abundant proof that he has embraced some pernicious and sophistical system of moral belief—that he has taught himself to regard, with a sinful indifference, the brightest and darkest places of our frail and imperfect nature—that he delights in deepening, by artificial gloom, those mysteries in the government of this passing world, which it is the part and privilege of Faith alone to lighten—that, confident in the possession of talents which were not given or won to him by himself, he disdains to confess the existence of any thing beyond his reach of understanding, and rashly rejoices, in considering as an arena, whereon to display his own strength, that which, as a man, even if not as a Christian, it might have better become him to contemplate with the humility of conscious weakness. In an evil hour does the pleasure of exhibiting might, first tempt the hand of genius to withdraw the veil from things that ought for ever to remain concealed, and Mr. Shelley should consider (and he has an abundance of time to do so, for he is yet a very young man,) that the perpetration of actual guilt, may possibly be to some natures a pastime of scarcely a different essence from that which is afforded to himself, and some others of his less-gifted contemporaries, by the scrutinizing and anatomizing discovery of things so monstrous. In two poems which have already rendered his name well known to the public, the same lamentable perverseness of thought and belief was sufficiently visible, although the allegorical and mystical strain in which these were composed, prevented the fault from coming before the eye of the reader in the whole of its naked fulness. But now that he has departed from his aerial, and, indeed, not very intelligible impersonations, and ventured to embody the lamentable errors of his system in a plain unvarnished picture of real human and domestic atrocities, we are mistaken in our notion of the British public, if he will not find that he has very far overshot the mark within which some measure of toleration might be permitted to the rashness and intoxication of a youthful fancy. It is absolutely impossible that any man in his sober mind should believe the dwelling upon such scenes of unnatural crime and horror can be productive of any good to any one person in the world—and, when Mr. Shelley has advanced a little farther in life and experience, he will probably learn, that in literature, as in all other human things, that which cannot do good, must, of necessity, tend to do evil. The delicacy of the moral sense of man—what then shall we say of that of woman?—was not a thing made to be tampered with upon such terms of artist-like coolness and indifference as these. He that presumes to make his intellect address a voice to the world, should know that this voice must either harmonize or jar with the universal music of life and wisdom. The lightnings of genius are, indeed, always beautiful, but it should be remembered, that although their business is to purify the air, they may easily, unless reason lift her conducting rod, be converted into the swiftest and surest instruments of death and desolation. In that case, the measure of the peril answers to the brightness of the flash. And had Mr. Shelley's powers appeared to us to be less, we should not have said so much concerning the wickedness of their perversion.

Of a poem the whole essence and structure of which are so radically wrong, it is impossible that we should give any thing like an analysis, without repeating in some sense the offence already committed by its author. Not a few of our contemporaries, however, and some of these not of the lowest authority, seem to us to labor under a foolish timidity, which prevents them from doing justice to the genius, at the same time that they inflict due chastisement on the errors of this remarkable young man. Therefore it is that we think ourselves called upon to justify, by several extracts, the high opinion we have expressed of his capacity, and the consequent seriousness of our reproof. We shall endeavour to select such passages as may give least offence—but this is, in truth, no easy task. The play opens with this conversation between old Cenci, the cruel and brutal father, and Cardinal Camillo, the nephew of the Pope.

[quotes the whole of the first scene]

In the last act—the intervening ones are too full of loathsomeness to be quoted—(although it is there, after all, that the poetry is most powerful—), Beatrice, the injured daughter of the old ruffian—Giacomo her brother—and Lucretia, their step-mother, but to them in all things else a mother, as well as in the participation of their sufferings,—are found guilty of the murder, being betrayed by the weakness of two hired assassins. The fear of death, and the consciousness of original purity of intention, render Beatrice bold in presence of her accuser and her judge.

[quotes Act V, Scene ii, lines 81–194]

Cardinal Camillo intercedes for mercy from the Pope, and Bernardo, a younger brother of Beatrice, is also sent to kneel at his feet; but although the full extent of the provocation is made known, all solicitation is in vain. We give the whole of the last scene.

[quotes the last scene]

Mr. Shelley mentions in his preface, that he has only very lately begun to turn his attention to the literature of the drama. From the language of these extracts, beautiful as they are, it might indeed be gathered that he has not yet mastered the very difficult art of English dramatic versification. But that is a trivial matter. His genius is rich to overflowing in all the nobler requisites for tragic excellence, and were he to choose and manage his themes with some decent measure of regard for the just opinions of the world, we have no doubt he might easily and triumphantly overtop all that has been written during the last century for the English stage.

40. Unsigned review, *The London Magazine*

May 1820, i, 546–55

A miscellaneous writer of the present time urges it, as an objection against some of the second-rate dramatists of the Elizabethan age, that 'they seemed to regard the decomposition of the common affections, and the dissolution of the strict bonds of society, as an agreeable study and a careless pastime.' On the other hand, he observes, 'the tone of Shakespeare's writings is manly and bracing; while theirs is at once insipid and meretricious in the comparison. Shakespeare never disturbs the ground of moral principle; but leaves his characters (after doing them heaped justice on all sides) to be judged by our common sense and natural feelings. Beaumont and Fletcher constantly bring in equivocal sentiments and characters, as if to set them up to be debated by sophistical casuistry, or varnished over with the colours of poetical ingenuity. Or Shakespeare may be said to "cast the diseases of the mind, only to restore it to a sound and pristine health"; the dramatic paradoxes of Beaumont and Fletcher are, to all appearance, *tinctured with an infusion of personal vanity* and laxity of principle.'

We have put in Italics the words at the conclusion of the above paragraph, which appear, to us most completely to indicate the con-

stitutional cause of that unhappy and offensive taste in literary composition, censured by the above author in writers that might be deemed
innocent of it, were we to judge of them only by a comparison with
some recent and present examples. *Personal vanity* rather than vicious
propensity, is the secret source of that morbid irritation, which vents
itself in fretfulness against 'the strict bonds of society'; which seeks
gratification in conjuring up, or presenting, the image or idea of something abhorrent to feelings of the general standard;—which causes the
patient to regard with a jaundiced eye the genuine workings of nature
in vice as well as in virtue;—which gives to desire the character of rank
disease; and so depraves the fancy as to lead it to take mere nuisances for
crimes, and hideous or indecent chimaeras for striking objects and
incidents. Whatever can in any way be converted into a mirror, to
reflect back *self* on the consciousness of him who is thus infatuated, is
preferable, in his estimation, to what would turn his admiration to
something nobler and better, open fields of speculation that have far
wider bounds than his own habits, and a range from which his self-love
is excluded. Hence his itch to finger forbidden things; he has these
entirely to himself; the disgust of mankind secures him from rivalry or
competition. The very fact of a feeling's having been respected, or that
a sentiment has prevailed for ages of the world, rouses his anger against
it; and, while he cants down all approved practical wisdom, with the
offensive protection of philosophy, he would fain make even nature
herself truckle to his egotism, by reversing her instincts in the human
breast in favour of the triumph of his own absurd systems, or perhaps to
mitigate the pain of a certain secret tormenting consciousness. One of
this stamp will propose lending his wife to his friend, and expect
praises of an enlarged and liberal style of thinking, when he is only insulting decency, and outraging manly feeling, under the influence of a
weak intellect, slight affections, and probably corrupted appetite. Such
persons must evidently be deemed notorious offenders, if they are not
recognised for reformers and regenerators; they can only preserve
themselves from disgrace, by throwing it on the surest and most sacred
of these principles which have hitherto preserved the social union from
total dishonour, and on which must be founded that improvement of
our social institutions which, in the present day, is so generally desired
and expected.

Yet, though thus peculiar in their tastes, these vain sophists are very
profuse of compliments, in conversation or in writing, as their opportunities may be. Their friends and associates are all *innocent, and brave,*

and pure; and this is saying no little for themselves. We happen at this moment to have on our table Lyly's *Euphues*, which the Monastery has now rendered known by name to many thousands who never before suspected its existence;—it was put there for another purpose, but it will also help to serve our present one. The quaint author excellently describes the trick above-mentioned. 'One flattereth another by his own folly, and *layeth cushions under the elbow of his fellow* when he seeth him take a nap with fancie; *and as their wit wresteth them to vice, so it forgeth them* some *feate excuse to cloake* their vanitie.' By the same rule, an opponent is ever a rascal, and the most extravagant and absurd assumptions are made with equal readiness, whether the object be to cast lustre on their intimacies, or lay a flattering unction to a wound inflicted by some justly severe hand. All that is foreign, or adverse to themselves, in short, is base, weak, selfish, or mischievous; that is the principle on which are founded their *patient and irreconcilable enmities*; and, on the other hand, the happiness of their *fortunate friendships* is exactly proportionate to the subserviency of these friendships to their habits of indolent self-indulgence, and the intolerance of their round self-conceit. What ever would annoy their consciousness must, without fail, be proscribed by their *dear friends* as a prejudice or a piece of hypocrisy; and on these conditions Charles, and James, and John receive each a sonnet apiece, garnished perhaps with a garland. These amiable goings-on, however, form a curious and far from dignified spectacle in the eyes of the public; and most judicious persons are inclined to think, that such fulsome display of parlour-fooleries is as inconsistent with staunchness of sentiment, as it is offensive to good taste. The firm base of independence, and the strong cement of a manly disposition, are wanting to these constructions for the shelter of inferior talent, and the pampering of roughly-treated pretention: they are, therefore, as frail in their substance, as fantastic and ridiculous in their appearance. Disgust is, in a little time, the natural consequence of such an intercourse as we have been describing, where there exists either intellect or feeling enough to be so affected; and infidelity naturally occurs pretty frequently amongst the inferior retainers, who, having been only received because of the tribute they brought, are free, as with some reason they seem to think, to carry it when they please elsewhere.

These remarks are (not altogether) but principally, suggested by the Preface, Poems, and Dedication contained in the volume under our review:—yet it is no more than fair towards Mr. Shelley to state, that the *style* of his writings betrays but little affectation, and that their matter evinces much real power of intellect, great vivacity of fancy, and a quick, deep, serious feeling, responding readily and harmoniously, to every call made on the sensibility by the imagery and incidents of this variegated world. So far Mr. Shelley has considerable advantages over some of those with whom he shares many grave faults. In the extraordinary work now under notice, he, in particular, preserves throughout a vigorous, clear, manly turn of expression, of which he makes excellent use to give force and even sublimity to the flashes of passion and of phrenzy,—and wildness and horror to the darkness of cruelty and guilt. His language, as he travels through the most exaggerated incidents, retains its correctness and simplicity;—and the most beautiful images, the most delicate and finished ornaments of sentiment and description, the most touching tenderness, graceful sorrow, and solemn appalling misery, constitute the very genius of poetry, present and powerful in these pages, but, strange and lamentable to say, closely connected with the signs of a depraved, nay mawkish, or rather emasculated moral taste, craving after trash, filth, and poison, and sickening at wholesome nutriment. There can be little doubt but that *vanity* is at the bottom of this, and that weakness of *character* (which is a different thing from what is called weakness of *talent*) is also concerned. Mr. Shelley likes to carry about with him the consciousness of his own peculiarities; and a tinge of disease, probably existing in a certain part of his constitution, gives to these peculiarities a very offensive cast. This unlucky tendency of his is at once his pride and his shame; he is tormented by suspicions that the general sentiment of society is against him—and, at the same time, he is induced by irritation to keep on harping on sore subjects. Hence his stories, which he selects or contrives under a systematic predisposition as it were,—are unusually marked by some anti-social, unnatural, and offensive feature:—whatever 'is not to be named amongst men' Mr. Shelley seems to think has a peculiar claim to celebration in poetry;—and he turns from war, rapine, murder, seduction, and infidelity—the vices and calamities with the description of which our common nature and common experience permit the generality of persons to sympathise—to cull some morbid and maniac sin of rare and doubtful occurrence, and sometimes to found a *system* of practical purity and peace on violations which it is disgraceful even to contemplate.

His present work (*The Cenci*) we think a case in point. We shall furnish the reader with the story on which this Drama is founded, as it is given by Mr. Shelley in his preface. . . .

[quotes first three paragraphs of Preface]

In this extract we have considerable incoherency, and more improbability, to begin with. What are we to understand by an old man conceiving 'an implacable hatred against his children, which showed itself towards one daughter in the shape of an incestuous *passion*'? A passion resulting from hatred, as well as a hatred showing itself in a passion, must be considered quite new at least. Luckily the language of common sense is not applicable to these monstrous infamies: they are not reducible even to the forms of rational communication: they are so essentially absurd that their very description slides necessarily into nonsense; and a person of talent who has taken to this sort of *fancy*, is sure to stultify himself in committing the atrocious act of insulting the soul of man which is the image of his maker. If it be really true that an individual once existed who really hated his children, and, under the impulse of hatred, committed an outrage on his daughter, that individual was *mad*; and will any who are not the same, or worse, pretend that the horrors of madness, the revolting acts of a creature stripped of its being's best part, can properly furnish the principal interest of a dramatic composition, claiming the sympathy of mankind as a representation of human nature? The author informs us, with reference to his present work, that 'the person who would treat such a subject must *increase the ideal, and diminish the actual horror* of the events, so that the *pleasure which arises from the poetry that exists in these tempestuous sufferings and crimes,* may mitigate the pain of the contemplation of the moral deformity from which they spring.' Now the necessity which Mr. Shelley here admits finally condemns his attempt; for it is a hopeless one. It is quite impossible to increase the ideal, or to diminish the actual horror of *such* events: they are therefore altogether out of the Muse's province. The Ancients were free to select them, because the superior presence and awful hand of Destiny were visible, all the way through, to the minds at least of the spectators. These could see also, by the help of the Poet's allusions, all Olympus looking on at the terrible but unequal struggle. Man, in their compositions, was not the agent but the sufferer: and the excellence of his endowments, and the noble nature of his faculties only served to give dignity to the scene on which he was played with by Powers whose decrees and purposes were not liable to be affected by his qualities or his will. The woes of the house of Tantalus are the acts of Destiny, not the offspring of human character or conduct:—individual character, in fact, has no concern with them,— and no moral lesson is in any way involved in them, except that of reverencing the gods, and submitting implicitly to the manifestations of their sovereign pleasure. No other question, either practical or philosophical, was mooted: the order and institutions of society were not affected by the representation; it only showed that the thunder of heaven might fall on the fairest edifices of human virtue and fortune. The luckless victim of the wrath of Jove might be lashed to the commission of heart-freezing enormities, without human nature appearing degraded; for it was seen that he was under a direct possession, too powerful for his nature, driving him down a steep place into the abyss of ruin. The only reasonable deduction from this was, that the anger of Jove was to be averted, if possible, by duly respecting the ministers of religion, carefully observing the rites of worship, and keeping the mind in an humble, confiding temper towards the will and interference of heaven. This, at least, is clear,—that no indulgence towards the practise of such denaturalizing depravities, could harbour even in the most secret mental recesses of those who were in the habit of seeing the occurrence represented as the immediate work of howling Furies. It was these latter that scourged the doomed person to the commission of such acts, in despite of himself,—in despite of the shriekings of his soul, and the revoltings of poor human nature! The hissing of preternatural serpents accompanied the perpetration of unnatural acts and thus the human heart was saved from corrupting degradation, and human feeling preserved from being contaminated by a familiarity with evil things.

Mr. Shelley, as author, acts on the principle most immediately opposed to this: his object, he says, is 'the teaching the human heart the knowledge of itself,' in proportion to the possession of which knowledge every human being is wise, just, sincere, *tolerant*, and kind. p. ix. He therefore considers that his work, *The Cenci*, is 'subservient to a moral purpose.' We think he is mistaken in every respect. His work does not teach the human heart, but insults it:—a father who invites guests to a splendid feast, and then informs them of the events they are called together to celebrate, in such lines as the following, has neither heart nor brains, neither human reason nor human affections, nor human passions of any kind:—nothing, in short, of human about him but the external form, which, however, in such a state of demoniac frenzy, must flash the wild beast from its eyes rather than the man.

> Oh, thou bright wine whose purple splendour leaps
> And bubbles gaily in this golden bowl
> Under the lamplight, as my spirits do,
> To hear the death of my accursed sons!

Could I believe thou wert their mingled blood,
Then would I taste thee like a sacrament,
And pledge with thee the mighty Devil in Hell,
Who, if a father's curses, as men say,
Climb with swift wings after their children's souls,
And drag them from the very throne of Heaven,
Now triumphs in my triumph!—But thou art
Superfluous; I have drunken deep of joy,
And I will taste no other wine to-night,
Here, Andrea! Bear the bowl around.

In this way Mr. Shelley proposes to *teach* the human heart, and thus to effect 'the highest moral purpose!' His precepts are conveyed in the cries of Bedlam; and the outrage of a wretched old maniac, long past the years of appetite, perpetrated on his miserable child, under motives that are inconsistent with reason, and circumstances impossible in fact, is presented to us as a mirror in which we may contemplate a portion, at least, of our common nature! How far this disposition to rake in the lazar-house of humanity for examples of human life and action, is consistent with a spirit of *tolerance* for the real faults and infirmities of human nature, on which Mr. Shelley lays so much stress, we may discover in one of his own absurd illusions. The murder of the Count Cenci he suggests, in the first quotation we have given from his preface, was punished by the Pope, *chiefly* because the numerous assassinations committed by this insane man were a copious source of papal revenue, which his death dried up forever. The atrocity involved in this supposition is, we hesitate not to say, extravagant and ridiculous. That a Pope of those times might be inclined to make money of a committed murder is not only likely, but consistent with history: but at what epoch, under what possible combination of circumstances of government and society, could it be a rational speculation in the breast of a ruler to preserve a particular nobleman with peculiar care, that his daily murders, committed in the face of the public, he himself, in the meantime, walking about a crowded city, might continue to be a source of personal profit to the sovereign! Nor would the paltriness of such a calculation, contrasted with its excessive guilt, permit it to be seriously made in any breast that can justly be adduced as an example of the heart of man. It would be intolerable to the consciousness of any one invested with the symbols of dignity and the means of authority. It would be for such an one to commit murders himself, not to wait in sordid expectation of the bribery to follow their commission by others.

It requires the 'enlarged liberality' of Mr. Shelley and his friends to fashion their chimaeras of infamy, and then display them as specimens of Princes, Priests, and Ministers. The truth is, that we see few or no signs of their *toleration*, but in regard to cases of incest, adultery, idleness and improvidence:—towards a class of abuses and enormities, falling too surely within the range of human nature and human history, but from which they are far removed by the circumstances of their conditions in life, and equally so, perhaps, by the qualities of their personal characters, they have neither tolerance nor common sense. Their sympathies then lead them to degrade and misrepresent humanity in two ways: by extenuating the commission of unnatural vices, and aggravating the guilt of natural ones:—and as it forms one of their principal objects to dissipate all the *dogmas* of religion, it is further to be observed, that they thus leave the nature of man bare and defenceless, without refuge or subterfuge—let them call it which they please. They render miserable man accountable for all his acts; his soul is the single source of all that occurs to him; he is forbidden to derive hope either from his own weakness or the strength of a great disposing authority, presiding over the world, and guiding it on principles that have relation to the universe. This is a very different basis from that of the Ancient Drama:—in it, the blackness and the storms suspended over the head of man, and which often discharged destruction on his fairest possessions, *hung from Heaven*, and above them there was light, and peace, and intelligence.

The radical foulness of moral composition, characterizing such compositions as this one now before us, we shall never let escape unnoticed or unexposed, when examples of it offer themselves. It is at once disgusting and dangerous; our duty, therefore, is here at unison with our taste. In *The Cenci*, however, the fault in question is almost redeemed, by uncommon force of poetical sentiment and very considerable purity of poetical style. There are gross exceptions to the latter quality, and we have quoted one; but the praise we have given will apply generally to the work. The story on which it is founded has already been explained. We shall proceed to give, by some extracts from the Drama itself, an idea of its execution.

The accounts which the hoary Cenci gives of himself—his character, feelings, etc.—are generally overstrained and repulsive: but in the following lines, put into the mouth of one who remonstrates with him, we have a fearful and masterly portrait.

[quotes Act I, Scene i, lines 34–56]

What follows by Cenci himself is not so good.

> I love
> The sight of agony, and the sense of joy,
> When this shall be another's, and that mine.
> And I have no remorse and little fear,
> Which are, I think, the checks of other men.
> This mood has grown upon me, until now
> Any design my captious fancy makes
> The picture of its wish, and it forms none
> But such as men like you would start to know,
> Is as my natural food and rest debarred
> Until it be accomplished.

Beatrice, the unhappy daughter of this man is, almost through the whole of the piece, sustained in beauty, delicacy, and refinement, unsullied by incidents of the most odious and contaminating kind. She is introduced in a lame, ill-executed scene, so far as Orsino, a treacherous priest and her lover, is concerned; but at the conclusion of it we find ourselves powerfully interested by the intimation she gives of what is about to take place in her father's house. . . .

[quotes Act I, Scene ii, lines 47–63]

The banquet scene itself, though strained by the maniac extravagance of Cenci, is yet drawn by the hand of a first-rate master. Lucretia, the miserable wife, flatters herself that these signs of festivity and good humour bode well: the superior intellect of her daughter enables her to divine the truth.

> *Beatr.* Ah! My blood runs cold.
> I fear that wicked laughter round his eye
> Which wrinkles up the skin even to the hair.

Cenci avows the cause of his joy in the hearing of his astounded guests and agonized family.

> Here are the letters brought from Salamanca;
> Beatrice, read them to your mother. God!
> I thank thee! In one night didst thou perform,
> By ways inscrutable, the thing I sought.
> My disobedient and rebellious sons
> Are dead!—Why, dead!—What means this change of cheer?

You hear me not, I tell you they are dead;
And they will need no food or raiment more:
The tapers that did light them the dark way
Are their last cost. The Pope, I think, will not
Expect I should maintain them in their coffins.
Rejoice with me—my heart is wondrous glad.

A movement of indignation makes itself manifest among the company: this part, we think, would *act* with great effect.

    A Guest (rising).   Thou wretch!
Will none among this noble company
Check the abandoned villain?
Camillo.   For God's sake
Let me dismiss the guests! You are insane,
Some ill will come of this.
Second Guest.   Seize, silence him!
First Guest.   I will!
Third Guest.   And I!
Cenci (addressing those who rise with a threatening gesture).
   Who moves? Who speaks? (*turning to the company*) 'tis nothing,
Enjoy yourselves.—Beware! For my revenge
Is as the sealed commission of a king
That kills, and none dare name the murderer.

Kean may covet the opportunity that would be afforded him by the words—"tis nothing—enjoy yourselves!'

Beatrice, unsuccessful in her appeal to the noble and powerful persons present, for protection for herself and her mother, exclaims, in the bitterness of her heart:

     Oh God! that I were buried with my brothers!
     And that the flowers of this departed spring
     Were fading on my grave! And that my father
     Were celebrating now one feast for all!

The unnatural father gives dark intimation of the dreadful design fermenting in his soul in what follows:

[quotes Act I, Scene iii, lines 160–78]

The first scene of the second act is so characteristic of the tragedy and so impressive in its ability, that we shall give a long extract from it, as the best method of enabling the reader to judge fairly of Mr. Shelley's power as a poet. . . .

[quotes lines 1–122]

The dreadful and disgusting crime on which the tragedy is founded has been perpetrated, when Beatrice again makes her appearance.

[quotes Act III, Scene i, lines 1–32]

We cannot follow step by step the progress of the Drama, suffice it to say, that the murder of Cenci is plotted by his wife and daughter with Orsino, a priest, who has base views on the person of Beatrice and who, after abetting the assassination, withdraws himself from its consequences at the expense of his partners in the act. Cenci retires to his castle of Petrella, where he studies new inflictions of suffering on his wretched victims: the bad taste into which Mr. Shelley inevitably falls, whenever he is led to certain allusions, is strikingly exemplified in the following lines put into his mouth:

> 'Tis plain I have been favoured from above,
> For when I cursed my sons they died.—Ay . . . so . . .
> As to the right or wrong, that's talk . . . repentance . . .
> Repentance is an easy moment's work
> And more depends on God than me. Well . . . well . . .
> I must give up the greater point, which was
> To poison and corrupt her soul.

The scene where the wife and daughter are represented, expecting the consummation of the deed by the assassins, has a creeping horror about it:

> *Lucretia.* They are about it now.
> *Beatrice.*   Nay, it is done.
> *Lucretia.* I have not heard him groan.
> *Beatrice.*   He will not groan.
> *Lucretia.* What sound is that?
> *Beatrice.*   List! 'tis the tread of feet
> About his bed.
> *Lucretia.* My God!
> If he be now a cold stiff corpse . . .
> *Beatrice.*   O, fear not
> What may be done, but what is left undone:
> The act seals all.

The means by which the murder was discovered need not be detailed. Beatrice, and her mother, and brother are tortured to extract confession, then condemned; and the tragedy thus concludes. . . .

[quotes Act V, Scene iv, lines 141–65]

Here the Drama closes, but our excited imaginations follow the parties to the scaffold of death. This tragedy is the production of a man of great genius, and of a most unhappy moral constitution.

41. Leigh Hunt, review, *The Indicator*

July 26, 1820, xlii, 329–37

'The highest moral purpose aimed at in the highest species of the drama, is the teaching the human heart, through its sympathies and antipathies, the knowledge of itself; in proportion to the possession of which knowledge, every human being is wise, just, sincere, tolerant, and kind. If dogmas can do more, it is well: but a drama is no fit place for the enforcement of them. Undoubtedly, no person can be truly dishonoured by the act of another; and the fit return to make to the most enormous injuries is kindness and forbearance, and a resolution to convert the injurer from his dark passions by love and peace. Revenge, retaliation, atonement, are pernicious mistakes. If Beatrice had thought in this manner, she would have been wiser and better; but she would never have been a tragic character: the few whom such an exposition would have interested, could never have been sufficiently interested for a domestic purpose, from the want of finding sympathy in their interest among the mass who surround them. It is in the restless and anatomizing casuistry with which men seek the justification of Beatrice, yet feel that she has done what needs justification; it is in the superstitious horror with which they contemplate alike her wrongs and revenge; that the dramatic character of what she did and suffered, consists.'

Thus speaks Mr. Shelley, in the Preface to his tragedy of *The Cenci*,— a preface beautiful for the majestic sweetness of its diction, and still more lovely for the sentiments that flow forth with it. There is no living author, who writes a preface like Mr. Shelley. The intense interest which he takes in his subject, the consciousness he has upon him nevertheless of the interests of the surrounding world, and the natural dignity with which a poet and philosopher, sure of his own motives, presents himself to the chance of being doubted by those whom he would benefit, casts about it an inexpressible air of amiableness and power. To be able to read such a preface, and differ with it, is not easy; but to be able to read it, and then go and abuse the author's intentions, shews a deplorable habit of being in the wrong.

Mr. Shelley says that he has 'endeavoured as nearly as possible to represent the characters as they really were, and has sought to avoid the error of making them actuated by his own conceptions of right or wrong, false or true, thus under a thin veil converting names and actions of the sixteenth century into cold impersonations of his own mind.' He has done so. He has only added so much poetry and imagination as is requisite to refresh the spirit, when a story so appalling is told at such length as to become a book. Accordingly, such of our readers as are acquainted with our last week's narrative of the Cenci and not with Mr. Shelley's tragedy, or with the tragedy and not with the narrative, will find in either account that they are well acquainted with the characters of the other. It is the same with the incidents, except that the legal proceedings are represented as briefer, and Beatrice is visited with a temporary madness; but this the author had a right to suppose, in probability as well as poetry. The curtain falls on the parties as they go forth to execution,—an ending which would hardly have done well on the stage, though for different reasons, any more than the nature of the main story. But through the medium of perusal, it has a very good as well as novel effect. The execution seems a supererogation, compared with it. The patience, that has followed upon the excess of the sorrow, has put the tragedy of it at rest. 'The bitterness of death is past,' as Lord Russell said when he had taken leave of his wife.

We omitted to mention last week, that the greatest crime of which Cenci had been guilty, in the opinion of the author of the Manuscript, was atheism. The reader will smile to see so foolish and depraved a man thus put on a level with Spinoza, Giordano Bruno, and other spirits of undoubted genius and integrity, who have been accused of the same opinion. But the same word means very different things to those who look into it; and it does here, though the author of the MS. might not know it. The atheism of men like Spinoza is nothing but a vivid sense of the universe about them, trying to distinguish the mystery of its opinions from the ordinary, and as they think pernicious anthropomorphism, in which our egotism envelopes it. But the atheism of such men as Cenci is the only real atheism; that is to say, it is the only real disbelief in any great and good thing, physical or moral. For the same reason, there is more atheism, to all intents and purposes of virtuous and useful belief, in some bad religions however devout, than in some supposed absences of religion: for the god they propose to themselves does not rise above the level of the world they live in, except in power like a Roman Emperor; so that there is nothing to them really outside of this world, at last. The god, for instance, of the Mussulman, is nothing but a sublimated Grand Signior; and so much the worse, as men generally are, in proportion to his power. One act of kindness, one impulse of universal benevolence, as recommended by the true spirit of Jesus, is more grand and godlike than all the degrading ideas of the Supreme Being, which fear and slavery have tried to build up to heaven. It is a greater going out of ourselves; a higher and wider resemblance to the all-embracing placidity of the universe. The Catholic author of the MS. says that Cenci was an atheist, though he built a chapel in his garden. The chapel, he tells us, was only to bury his family in. Mr. Shelley on the other hand, can suppose Cenci to have been a Catholic, well enough, considering the nature and tendency of the Catholic faith. In fact, he might have been either. He might equally have been the man he was, in those times, and under all the circumstances of his power and impunity. The vices of his atheism and the vices of his superstition would, in a spirit of his temper and education, have alike been the result of a pernicious system of religious faith, which rendered the Divine Being gross enough to be disbelieved by any one, and imitated and bribed by the wicked. Neither his scepticism nor his devotion would have run into charity. He wanted knowledge to make the first do so, and temper and privation to make the second. But perhaps the most likely thing is, that he thought as little about religion as most men of the world do at all times;—that he despised and availed himself of it in the mercenary person of the Pope, scarcely thought of it but at such times, and would only have believed in it out of fear at his last hour. Be this however as it might, still the habitual instinct of his conduct is justly traceable to the prevailing feeling respecting religion, especially as it appears that he 'established masses for the peace of his soul.' Mr. Shelley, in a striking part of his preface, informs us that even in our own times 'religion co-exists, as it were, in the mind of an Italian Catholic, with a faith in that, of which all men have the most certain knowledge. It is adoration, faith, submission, penitence, blind admiration; not a rule for moral conduct. It has no necessary connexion with any one virtue. The most atrocious villain may be rigidly devout; and without any shock to established faith, confess himself to be so. Religion pervades intensely the whole frame of society, and is according to the temper of the mind which it inhabits, a passion, a persuasion, an excuse; never a check.' We shall only add to this, that such religions in furnishing men with excuse and absolution, do but behave with something like decent kindness; for they are bound to do what they can for the vices they produce. And we may say it with gravity too. Forgiveness will make its way somehow every where, and it is lucky that it will do so. But it would be luckier, if systems made less to forgive.

The character of Beatrice is admirably managed by our author. She is what the MS. describes her, with the addition of all the living grace and presence which the re-creativeness of poetry can give her. We see the maddened loveliness of her nature walking among us, and make way with an aweful sympathy. It is thought by some, that she ought not to deny her guilt as she does;—that she ought not, at any rate, to deny the deed, whatever she may think of the guilt. But this, in our opinion, is one of the author's happiest subtleties. She is naturally so abhorrent from guilt,—she feels it to have been so impossible a thing to have killed a FATHER, truly so called, that what with her horror of the deed and of the infamy attending it, she would almost persuade herself as well as others, that no such thing had actually taken place,—that it was a notion, a horrid dream, a thing to be gratuitously cancelled from people's minds, a necessity which they were all to agree had existed but was not to be spoken of, a crime which to punish was to proclaim and make real,—any thing, in short, but that a daughter had killed her father. It is a lie told, as it were, for the sake of nature, to save it the shame of a greater contradiction. If any feeling less great and spiritual, any dread of a pettier pain, appears at last to be suffered by the author to mingle with it, a little common frailty and inconsistency only renders the character more human, and may be allowed a young creature about to be cut off in the bloom of life, who shews such an agonized wish that virtue should survive guilt and despair. She does not sacrifice the man who is put to the torture. He was apprehended without her being able to help it, would have committed her by his confession, and would have died at all events. She only reproaches him for including a daughter in the confession of his guilt; and the man, be it observed, appears to have had a light let into his mind to this effect, for her behaviour made him retract his accusations, and filled him so with a pity above his self-interest, that he chose rather to die in torture than repeat them. It is a remarkable instance of the respect with which Beatrice was regarded in Rome, in spite of the catastrophe into which she had been maddened, that Guido painted her portrait from the life, while she was in prison. He could not have done this, as a common artist might take the likeness of a common criminal, to satisfy vulgar curiosity. Her family was of too great rank and importance, and retained them too much in its reverses. He must have waited on her by permission, and accompanied the sitting with all those attentions which artists on such occasions are accustomed to pay to the great and beautiful. Perhaps he was intimate with her, for he was a painter in great request. In order to complete our accounts respecting her, as well as to indulge ourselves in copying out a beautiful piece of writing, we will give Mr. Shelley's description of this portrait, and masterly summary of her character.

[quotes Shelley's description of the portrait of Beatrice in the Colonna Palace]

The beauties of a dramatic poem, of all others, are best appreciated by a survey of the whole work itself, and of the manner in which it is composed and hangs together. We shall content ourselves therefore, in this place, with pointing out some detached beauties; and we will begin, as in the grounds of an old castle, with an account of a rocky chasm on the road to Petrella.

[quotes Act III, Scene i, lines 238–65]

With what a generous and dignified sincerity does Beatrice shew at once her own character and that of the prelate her lover.

[quotes Act I, Scene ii, lines 14–29]

The following is one of the gravest and grandest lines we ever read. It is the sum total of completeness. Orsino says, while he is meditating Cenci's murder, and its consequences,

> I see, as from a tower, the end of all.

The terrible imaginations which Beatrice pours forth during her frenzy, are only to be read in connexion with the outrage that produced them. Yet take the following, where the excess of the agony is softened to us by the wild and striking excuse which it brings for the guilt.

> What hideous thought was that I had even now?
> 'Tis gone; and yet its burthen remains still
> O'er these dull eyes—upon this weary heart.

> O, world! O, life! O, day! O, misery!
>   *Lucr.* What ails thee, my poor child? She answers not:
> Her spirit apprehends the sense of pain,
> But not its cause: suffering has dried away
> The source from which it sprung.
>   *Beatr.* (Franticly). Like Parricide,
> Misery has killed its father.

When she recovers, she 'approaches solemnly' Orsino, who comes in, and announces to him with an aweful obscurity, the wrong she has endured. Observe the last line.

> Welcome, friend!
> I have to tell you, that since last we met,
> I have endured a wrong so great and strange
> That neither life nor death can give me rest.
> Ask me not what it is, for there are deeds
> Which have no form, sufferings which have no tongue.
>   *Ors.* And what is he that has thus injured you?
>   *Beatr.* The man they call my father; a dread name.

The line of exclamations in the previous extract is in the taste of the Greek dramatists; from whom Mr. Shelley, who is a scholar, has caught also his happy feeling for compounds, such as 'the all-communi-cating air,' the 'mercy-winged lightning,' 'sin-chastising dreams,' 'wind-walking pestilence,' the 'palace-walking devil, gold,' &c. Gold, in another place, is finely called 'the old man's sword.'

Cenci's angry description of the glare of day is very striking.

> The all-beholding sun yet shines: I hear
> A busy stir of men about the streets;
> I see the bright sky through the window panes:
> It is a garish, broad, and peering day;
> Loud, light, suspicious, full of eyes and ears,
> And every little corner, nook, and hole
> Is penetrated with the insolent light.
> Come darkness!

The following is edifying:—

> The eldest son of a rich nobleman
> Is heir to all his incapacities;
> He has wide wants, and narrow powers.

We are aware of no passage in the modern or ancient drama, in which the effect of bodily torture is expressed in a more brief, comprehensive, imaginative manner, than in an observation made by a judge

SHELLEY

to one of the assassins. The pleasure belonging to the original image
renders it intensely painful.

> *Marzio.* My God! I did not kill him; I know nothing:
> Olimpio sold the robe to me, from which
> You would infer my guilt.
> > *2d Judge.* Away with him!
> > *1st Judge.* Dare you, with lips yet white from the rack's kiss,
> Speak false?

Beatrice's thoughts upon what she might and might not find in the
other world are very terrible; but we prefer concluding our extracts
with the close of the play, which is deliciously patient and affectionate.
How triumphant is the gentleness of virtue in its most mortal defeats!

[quotes Act V, Scene iv, lines 137–65]

Mr. Shelley, in this work, reminds us of some of the most strenuous
and daring of our old dramatists, not by any means as an imitator,
though he has studied them, but as a bold, elemental imagination, and a
framer of 'mighty lines.' He possesses also however, what those to
whom we more particularly allude did not possess, great sweetness of
nature, and enthusiasm for good; and his style is, as it ought to be, the
offspring of this high mixture. It disproves the adage of the Latin poet.
Majesty and Love do sit on one throne in the lofty buildings of his
poetry; and they will be found there, at a late and we trust a happier
day, on a seat immortal as themselves.

42. John Keats, letter

August 16, 1820

From a letter of John Keats (1795–1821) to Percy Bysshe Shelley, printed with notes in *The Letters of John Keats*, ed. Hyder E. Rollins (1958), ii, pp 322–3.

I received a copy of *The Cenci*,[1] as from yourself from Hunt. There is only one part of it I am judge of; the Poetry, and dramatic effect, which by many spirits now a days is considered the mammon. A modern work it is said must have a purpose, which may be the God—*an artist must serve Mammon*[2]—he must have 'self concentration' selfishness perhaps. You I am sure will forgive me for sincerely remarking that you might curb your magnanimity and be more of an artist, and 'load every rift' of your subject with ore.[3] The thought of such discipline must fall like cold chains upon you, who perhaps never sat with your wings furl'd for six Months together. And is not this extraordina[r]y talk for the writer of *Endymion*?[4] whose mind was like a pack of scattered cards—I am pick'd up and—sorted to a pip.[5] My Imagination is a Monastry and I am its Monk—you must explain my metap^{es}[6] to yourself. I am in expectation of *Prometheus* every day. Could I have my own wish for its interest effected you would have it still in manuscript—or be but now putting an end to the second act. I remember you advising me not to publish my first-flights, on Hampstead heath[7]—I am returning advice upon your hands. Most of the Poems in the volume I send

---

[1] Fanny Brawne Lindon wrote to Mrs Delke in November 1848 (Rollins, *HLB*, V 1951, 375), that she had '*The Cenci* by Shelley marked with many of Keats notes.' The whereabouts of the volume are now unknown.
[2] Matthew vi.24; Luke xvi.13.
[3] *The Faerie Queene*, II.vii.28, line 5, 'with rich metall loaded every rifte.'
[4] The point is doubtful.
[5] Arranged in orderly fashion with all the cards matched.
[6] For *metaphysics*. (MBF has 'metap^{es}' and Grylls, 'metap^r.')
[7] N. I. White, *Shelley* (New York, 1904), I, 504, says that Shelley gave this advice in 1817 but 'helped him print his volume after advising against it.'

you[1] have been written above two years, and would never have been publish'd but from a hope of gain; so you see I am inclined enough to take your advice now.

43. Unsigned review, *The Monthly Review*

February 1821, xciv, 161–8

As the genius of this writer grows on us, most heartily do we wish that we were able to say, his good sense and judgment grow with it!—but, alas! for the imperfections of the brightest minds, the reverse in this instance is the case; and the extravagance and wildness of Mr. Shelley's first flights yield to the present, not only in their own excentric [*sic*] character but in other most objectionable points.

Without any *mealy-mouthedness*, or pretences to be more delicate than our neighbours, we honestly confess that the story of the Cenci, chosen as a subject for tragedy in the twentieth [*sic*] century, does indeed astonish and revolt us: for it involves incest committed by a father, and murder perpetrated by a daughter. In the early days of our own drama, we know, great atrocities were suffered to form the subjects of some scenes; and whatever natural decency may have been observed in treating such offensive subjects, we cannot but consider the introduction of them in any way as a manifest proof of the rudeness and barbarism of a newly-born, or lately-reviving, literature. In truth, we do not see how any man of sense can view them in any other light, to whatever extent false theories, concerning the sublime awakening of the passions and the deep utterance of the secrets of the human heart, &c. &c. may mislead the vulgar. Yet such a bias towards the older school of poetry, and

1 In his *Autobiography* ([1850], III, 15) Hunt wrote of Shelley's corpse: 'Keats's last volume also (the *Lamia*, &c.), was found open in the jacket pocket. He had probably been reading it, when surprised by the storm. It was my copy. I had told him to keep it till he gave it me again with his own hands. So I would not have it from any other. It was burnt with his remains.'

all its faults, exists at this moment in England, that every champion of common sense, who strives to oppose the prejudice, is at once branded with the imputation of a narrow understanding, a defective imagination and a French taste. Be it so. The friends of Reason, we are assured, will stand or fall with her; and if she be quite extinct, why then a cheerful good night to her survivors!

Among the most devoted adherents to the style and manner of the antient English drama,—among the persons who, from all that they write, whether as critics or authors, it would seem were afflicted with a sort of *old-play-insanity*,—may be numbered Mr. Percy Shelley. He tells us in his preface that, in order 'to move men to true sympathy, we must use the *familiar language* of men;' and then, as a happy illustration of this profound axiom, he observes that the 'study of the ancient English poets is to incite us to do that for our own age, which they have done for theirs!' He adds that 'it must be the *real language* of men in general, and not of any particular class,' &c. Now what is all this but the exploded *Wordsworthian heresy*, that the language of poetry and the language of real life are the same? and this, too, when the *tragic* drama is in question! Oh, vain Horace, who dreamt of the '*os magna sona-turum*,' as combined with the '*mens sublimior!*'[1] Oh, vain Shakespeare, (for of all poets he is the most *imaginative* in language, in his loftier passages,) who fancied that passion might be poetical when ideally re-presented; and whose invariable pursuit, when not descending to the sparkling dust that strewed the arena of his *comedy*, was that *ideal beauty*, that charm, which has been embodied by the scenic representa-tions of two and only two performers[2] of our own times! Oh, for-gotten Otway and Rowe,[3] condemned to utter neglect and contempt by our wise and worthy contemporaries; because, forsooth, they *occasionally* sin by too much poetry, and too little reality of exhibition; because they, *in a few instances*, fall into misplaced similes and unnatural ornaments of verse!—We talk, however, to the desperately deaf;—we hold colours up for the judgment of the incurably blind;—we display the armour of the warrior in a conclave of *damsels*, among whom lurks no atom of the masculine spirit of old;—of that age which they dis-

[1] 'Mouth (that is) going to speak great things,' 'rather sublime mind'.
[2] Need we mention the great theatrical names of John Kemble and Mrs. Siddons? (Reviewer's footnote)
[3] Thomas Otway, a late-seventeenth-century dramatist, is best known for his tragedy *Venice Preserved*. Nicholas Rowe, a contemporary of Pope and Addison, wrote numerous plays for the eighteenth-century stage, but his major achievement was an edition of Shakespeare.

grace by their gross indiscriminate panegyric, and profane by their feeble unhallowed imitation.

Mr. Shelley is worthy of better things: but it is not merely the daemon of bad Taste which is to be laid in his gifted mind. *There* also inhabits, to all visible appearance, a deeper and darker daemon, the joint offspring of Doubt and Vanity:—of Doubt, far from thoroughly exercised in its established process of metaphysical reasoning; of Vanity, venial while young, and merely trying its wings in the atmosphere of its own limbo. Mr. Shelley, like an unfledged and unpractised giant, attempts to scale heaven on a chicken's pinion; and, little only when he is sceptical, he betrays *such* littleness in his attempts to climb and to shake Olympus, that spectators less biassed in his favour than ourselves would cease either to laugh or to behold. His imagination chiefly dwells on some filmy gossamery vision of his own brain, representing an aerial contest between the powers and princes of the air, in which the principle of evil overcomes, for a long and weary time, the principle of good. Such are the Snake and Eagle (if we recollect the *examples* rightly—we are sure of the *precept*,) of his earliest poem; and such are the Jupiter and Prometheus of that *painful* work which we shall next be called to notice.

We now return to *The Cenci*; and what a return! The spirit of the author will be best seen by a prose-extract, elucidatory of his state of feeling when he published this tragedy. Speaking of the characters of this drama, Mr. Shelley says:

They are represented as Catholics, and as Catholics deeply tinged with religion. To a Protestant apprehension there will appear something unnatural in the earnest and perpetual sentiment of the relations between God and man which pervade the tragedy of the Cenci. It will especially be startled at the combination of an undoubting persuasion of the truth of the popular religion with a cool and determined perseverance in enormous gilt. But religion in Italy is not, as in Protestant countries, a cloak to be worn on particular days; or a passport which those who do not wish to be railed at carry with them to exhibit; or a gloomy passion for penetrating the impenetrable mysteries of our being, which terrifies its possessor at the darkness of the abyss to the brink of which it has conducted him. Religion co-exists, as it were, in the mind of an Italian Catholic with a faith in that of which all men have the most certain knowledge. It is interwoven with the whole fabric of life. It is adoration, faith, submission, penitence, blind admiration; not a rule for moral conduct. It has no necessary connexion with any one virtue. The most atrocious villain may be richly devout, and without any shock to established faith, confess himself to be so. Religion pervades intensely the whole frame of society, and is according to the temper of the mind which it inhabits, a passion, a persuasion, an excuse, a refuge; never a check.

As *Protestants*, we disdain to reply to the insinuations of this passage: but, for our Catholic brethren, we must *protest* against this most uncharitable charge. '*Never a check!*'—We do trust that Mr. Shelley will not be much older ere he regrets this unchristian and unphilosophical remark. How perfectly he falls within the censure of the poet, we need scarcely remind him;

> And deal damnation round the land,
> On each I judge thy foe;

for who is the foe of God like the *religious hypocrite*?

Thus unhappily prepared, Mr. Shelley entered on his dangerous dramatic task, and wonderously has he acquitted himself in it. We cordially hope that *nothing* may ever prevent us from rendering due homage to genius, wherever it be found; for, however man may pervert it, still it bears the indication and retains the sound of the voice of Heaven within us. We grant, then, that a plain proof is afforded of Mr. Shelley's powers in almost every scene of this drama; and one or two such examples we shall endeavour to select.

In the preface, we are thus informed of the story on which the tragedy is founded. . . .

[quotes the first five sentences of Shelley's Preface]

The dreadful display of wickedness at the feast, where the father rejoices in the death of his two sons, we shall omit; as well as the base cowardice of the guests, even when invoked by the firm and lovely Beatrice, *La* Cenci; of whose picture Mr. Shelley tells us he possesses a copy, from the original in the Colonna palace:—but we shall present our readers with the impressive scene in which Beatrice first intimates to Lucretia, her innocent mother-in-law, the horrors that have passed. Carefully and feelingly touched are these horrors.

[quotes Act II, Scene i, lines 28–97]

The next scene which we can quote without injustice to the course of the story, we think, is the following. Beatrice is condemned to die, for suborning the murder of her execrable father; and thus, in the language of Claudio in *Measure for Measure*, (and we say it not in detraction from genius, although in condemnation of taste,) she deplores her fate. . . .

[quotes Act V, Scene iv, lines 47–89]

Here we must take leave of *The Cenci*; earnestly requesting Mr. Shelley to consider well the remarks which we have made in the spirit of honest applause and honest censure; and particularly exhorting him to reflect on all the gifts of Providence, and on the last words which we have quoted,

And yet my heart is cold.

44. Unsigned review, *The Independent, a London Literary and Political Review*

February 17, 1821, i, 99–103

Mr. Shelley writes with vigor, sublimity, and pathos; but we do not admire his train of thought or feeling. He deals too much with abstractions and high imaginings—and forgets the world to which he writes, and by whom he must expect to be read. Abstractions suit not with life—nor are the bulk of readers capable of valuing them. Their value to life and its business is little worth; and when they are coupled with subtractions from our hopes and fears of an hereafter, they become eminently injurious. Mr. Shelley's mind is contemplative: and did he turn his contemplations to the benefit of his fellow men, his superior powers would not be worse than wasted on the world.

The great writers of our time deal too much with the gloomy—they dissect with skill the worst affections of the heart, and dwell too fondly on vicious passions and aberrations of the mind.

This passion should be checked—its consequences are fearful. We are not sorry that Mr. Shelley is not read, or if read not rewarded. We could pardon much to youth, and make allowance for the first ebullitions of fancy—the first daring of a master mind, even though that daring were, in some degree misdirected. But the systematic abuse of power, and reviling of religion are unpardonable crimes. No man can be insensible to the abandonment of virtue too often visible in rulers and priests: but after all, they are but schoolboy themes, the target for unbearded free thinking to point its arrows at. In manhood we look for something more:—where we find great powers, we look to their development to useful purposes; but extravagance never will pass with us for superior genius. In manhood we may be, as Mr. Shelley says, both cold and subtle; but the coldness results from an exercise of judgment, and the subtlety cannot exist without some power of reflection. Judgment and reflection should lead us to wiser things than the wholesale contempt for power, and the indiscriminate censure of the sacred office. To check the abuses of either, he should not hold them up as useless or criminal. In all cases they are not so; and authors in their vagaries or false estimates too often assume that they are. Did we live in an ideal world it would be quite a different matter. Had we the power of framing and adjusting our faculties and feelings by some Utopian Standard, writers like Mr. Shelley might be tolerated and approved; but did they write till 'the last eventful day,' while our nature is constituted as it now is, and has been and ever will be, all their efforts would prove nugatory and useless. Perfection is not for man, however much Madame de Stael's philosophy the other way would lead enthusiasts to believe. We can admire this sort of abstract idealism—this system of perfectibility; but our flesh and blood—nature stares us in the face, and we see at once the folly of attempting to regulate it by those simple, yet unknown, rules that govern the rise and fall of the vegetable or mineral world. Philosophy is but wisdom, and the highest wisdom cannot always act with equal power, and bend itself in the same direction. If men were all philosophers, life would be but a dull monotony—and as all men are not equally gifted—as all men are not organized after the same fashion—equal perfectibility is beyond their attainment.

The many are fools and will continue to be so—they think at second hand, and take their faith and their code as they do their inheritances from those who went before them. Perhaps they would be wiser if they did not:—more happy, none but dreamers of wisdom and happiness will imagine. With all our neatness and refinement in literature, common sense still acts its part. The older pedantry may have yielded to modern dandyism; but perfumery and coarseness are equally repulsive to strength of intellect, and correct judgment.

It is impossible to read Mr. Shelley's works without admiration at the richness of his language and the extent of his powers; but we revolt at his doctrines, and our nature shudders at his conclusions. He must evidently forget the great objects of poetry. Improvement and innocent pleasure should be its aim; with our author—gilded atrocity—

anointed vice—horror in its gloom—iniquity in its precarious triumph are omnipotent, and omnipresent. The most splendid picturings of crime are not equal to the descriptions of its naked deformity—

> Vice is a monster of such odious mien
> That to be hated—needs but to be seen.

Mr. Shelley's philosophy is objectionable—his reasoning is all directed by the assumption of criminality and passion directing our best actions; and this is making the worse appear the better reason. We cannot argue fairly from abuses to uses; and this is the grand object of this superior young man. He would seem to be unhappy with himself, and, therefore, unreconciled to the world; this is but an imitative feeling. Byron and Maturin tread the same path; but the former mixes life and its scenes with its horrors, he sports and laughs at them; the latter opens the resources of his extraordinary powers in the mention of the terrific—pursues the spectre—anatomizes and disgusts us with his overladen portraitures:—and while we are astonished at his fancy, his language, and his landscape, we loathe and deprecate them all in proportion of our disappointment.

Here we catch ourselves wandering from our more sober duty; but we could not, in justice to ourselves and readers, abstain from entering our humble protest against, we had said, the wanton abuse of powers not given to many men even in this age of intelligence and mind. We think highly of Mr. Shelley—he has nerve and sensibility; his thinking is deep, and his very pathos masculine. His works cannot be read without filling our thoughts—and we could only wish his thoughts had a more human and religious direction. The improvement of morals does not merely result from a condemnation of vice, any more than the advancement of science takes place from the mere exposure of former absurdities. The high colouring of danger will not lead to its avoidance; nor the well-meant eulogy of virtue lead to its general practice. To write successfully authors must proceed on the first principles of justice, religion, and nature. Nature must not be narrowed, religion constrained, nor justice suited to isolated abstract views; the wants, the wishes, and the interests of the many must be consulted; and the many are not of an author's particular day—but they are the people of futurity. In this particular it is, that our modern great men fail. They write for themselves; not for the world; they feel as individuals, not as component parts of a great body. Their closet is their horizon, and not 'the visible diurnal sphere.' Hence must they fail in their object, however, laudable; and be insecure in reputation or usefulness however well intended their ambitionings may be.

The Cenci is addressed to Mr. Leigh Hunt, and our author gives the following outline of its monstrous history.

[quotes Shelley's Preface, paragraphs 1–6]

It would be impossible for us to convey an adequate idea of this production to our readers; nor could any isolated extracts convey the force of Mr. Shelley's muse. Its mere history as above narrated is its history in verse—without the charm or terror assumed by the latter. The Cenci is a man monster, as will be seen from the following passage.

[quotes Act I, Scene i, lines 77–117]

He seems only to live in others' miseries. The character of Beatrice his daughter is admirably drawn, and reminds one forcibly of Lady Macbeth. She has all her resolution, more of her amiability; and we pity the evil destiny which prompted her to the very conception of a deed at which humanity revolts. She depicts the causes of her alienation from her unnatural father in these terms, at a festival given for the purpose of celebrating a monstrous filicide.

[quotes Act I, Scene iii, lines 99–125]

The Cenci, in the second act, charges his wife Lucretia with being the cause of the disturbance at the last night's feast—which she denies; but it rankles in the Cenci's mind, and his purpose of revenge is heightened. His son Giacomo now feels all the weight of his father's ill-treatment—and resolves as the only means of obtaining redress to put him out of the world. Orsino, a wily prelate, urges him on in his fell purpose—with the hope that his sister Beatrice may be his recompense. He thus reconciles himself to his own conduct.

[quotes Act II, Scene ii, lines 120–61]

The first scene of the third act is really appalling, its interest is powerfully dramatic and intense,—it is overwhelming. Beatrice becomes frantic at the thought which has seized possession of her mind—and never was frenzy directed to a more terrible deed, but withall a conscience not dead to remorse, more ably pourtrayed than by our author.

[quotes Act III, Scene i, lines 137–206]

Beatrice at length puts Orsino's fidelity to the test, and he pledges himself to obtain the means of taking away the Cenci's life. In the

Apulian Apennines a passage lies toward Petrella, one of the country seats of the Cenci, and a part of the way to it is thus admirably sketched.

[quotes Act III, Scene i, lines 243–65]

Giacomo thus accounts for his hatred to his father, and with this able passage we shall close our extracts.

[quotes Act III, Scene i, lines 298–334]

The death of the Cenci is finally fixed, assassins are hired, but on the first attempt their courage droops. They are taunted and inspirited to the deed almost in the same breath by Beatrice; they screw their courage to the sticking place, and the parricidal murder is committed. Just at this moment a legate from the Pope arrives, supposed to be a bearer of a charge against the Cenci. His murder is discovered—and the wife, daughter, and son are summoned to Rome to abide their trial, together with the actual assassin. Brought before the tribunal, the guilty assassin reveals his crime and his instigators. Confronted, however, with Beatrice, he hesitates—is led to the torture, and declaring himself guilty, dies. The trial of the others is suspended by the interference of Camillo who also wished to espouse the Lady Beatrice, and she is conducted to prison. While in her cell, she is visited by her brother and a judge, who urges her to confess her guilt, and so die at once. We cannot resist extracting the replies of this extraordinary lady to the judge.

[quotes Act V, Scene iii, lines 60–92]

Camillo next visits the cell—his entreaties with the Pope having proved fruitless. The manner in which Beatrice is made to receive the news of her hastening doom, has all the most passionate feeling and awakening interest of Mr. Shelley's highest efforts; the calm resolution with which she prepares to leave this world, is, perhaps, to be considered the less improbable, when we contemplate the whole of a character, which has altogether no parallel in our dramatic annals. There might have been one Beatrice—we scarcely believe another exists or can have existed. The execrable Orsino is seen to have escaped, contrary to all rules of poetic justice.

45. Unsigned review, *The British Review and London Critical Journal*

June 1821, xvii, 380–9

The Cenci is the best, because it is by far the most intelligible, of Mr. Shelley's works. It is probably indebted for this advantage to the class of compositions to which it belongs. A tragedy must have a story, and cannot be conducted without men and women: so that its very nature imposes a check on the vagabond excursions of a writer, who imagines that he can find the perfection of poetry in incoherent dreams or in the ravings of bedlam. In speaking of *The Cenci*, however, as a tragedy, we must add, that we do so only out of courtesy and in imitation of the example of the author, whose right to call his work by what name he pleases we shall never dispute. It has, in fact, nothing really dramatic about it. It is a series of dialogues in verse; and mere versified dialogue will never make a drama. A drama must, in the course of a few scenes, place before us such a succession of natural incidents, as shall lead gradually to the final catastrophe, and develope the characters and passions of the individuals, for whom our interest or our sympathy is to be awakened: these incidents give occasion to the dialogue, which, in its turn, must help forward the progression of events, lay open to us the souls of the agents, move our feelings by the contemplation of their mental agitations, and sooth us with the charms of poetical beauty. It is from the number and nature of the ends which the poet has to accomplish, as compared with the means which he employs, that the glory and difficulty of the dramatic art arise. If the only object of a writer is to tell a story, or to express a succession of various feelings, the form of dialogue, far from adding to the arduousness of the task, is the easiest that can be adopted. It is a sort of drag net, which enables him to introduce and find a place for every thing that his wildest reveries suggest to him.

The fable of *The Cenci* is taken from an incident which occurred at Rome towards the end of the sixteenth century. An aged father committed the most unnatural and horrible outrages on his daughter; his wife and daughter avenged the crime by procuring the assassination of the perpetrator, and became in their turns the victims of public justice. The incident is still recollected, and often related at Rome. Hence Mr. Shelley infers, 'that it is, in fact, a tragedy which has already received, from its capacity of awakening and sustaining the sympathy of man, approbation and success.' It is remembered and related, because it is extraordinary—because it is horrible—because it is, in truth, *undramatic*. A murder, attended with circumstances of peculiar atrocity, is scarcely ever forgotten on the spot where it happened; but it is not for that reason a fit subject for dramatic poetry. The catastrophe of Marrs' family will be long recollected in London; the assassination of Fualdes will not soon be forgotten in Rhodes; yet who would ever dream of bringing either event upon the stage? Incestuous rape, murder, the rack, and the scaffold, are not the proper materials of the tragic Muse: crimes and punishments are not in themselves dramatic, though the conflict of passions which they occasion, and from which they arise, often is so. The pollution of a daughter by a father—the murder of a father by his wife and daughter, are events too disgusting to be moulded into any form capable even of awakening our interest. Mr. Shelley himself seems to have been aware of this. 'The story of *The Cenci*,' says he, 'is indeed eminently fearful and monstrous; any thing like a dry exhibition of it on the stage would be insupportable. The person who would treat such a subject must increase the ideal, and diminish the actual, horror of the events, so that the pleasure which arises from the poetry, which exists in these tempestuous sufferings and crimes, may mitigate the pain of the contemplation of the moral deformity from which they spring.' Without presuming to comprehend these observations completely (for we know not what poetry exists in rape and murder, or what pleasure is to be derived from it), we are sure, that whatever may be thought as to the possibility of overcoming by any management the inherent defects of the tale, Mr. Shelley, far from having even palliated its moral and its dramatic improprieties, has rendered the story infinitely more horrible and more disgusting than he found it, and has kept whatever in it is most revolting constantly before our eyes. A dialogue in which Cenci makes an open confession to a Cardinal of a supreme love of every thing bad merely for its own sake, and of living only to commit murder—a banquet given by him to the Roman nobility and dignitaries, to celebrate an event of which he has just received the news,—the death of two of his sons—and declarations of gratuitous uncaused hatred against all his relations, not excepting that daughter whom he resolves to make the victim of his brutal outrage for no other reason than because his imagination is unable to devise any more horrible crime, fill up the first two acts. Cenci has accomplished the deed of horror before the opening of the third act, in which the resolution to murder him is taken. In the fourth he again comes before us, expressing no passion, no desire, but pure abstract depravity and impiety. The murder follows, with the immediate apprehension of the members of the family by the officers of justice. The last act is occupied with the judicial proceedings at Rome. Cenci is never out of our sight, and, from first to last, he is a mere personification of wickedness and insanity. His bosom is ruffled by no passion; he is made up exclusively of inveterate hatred, directed not against some individuals, but against all mankind, and operating with a strength proportioned to the love which each relation usually excites in other men. There is no mode of expressing depravity in words which Mr. Shelley has not ransacked his imagination to ascribe to this wretch. His depravity is not even that of human nature; for it is depravity without passion, without aim, without temptation: it is depravity seeking gratification, first, in the perpetration of all that is most repulsive to human feelings, and next in making a display of its atrocity to the whole world. The following dialogue, for example, (and it is one of the gentler passages of the play) takes place in the presence of, and is in part addressed to, the Roman nobles and cardinals assembled at a banquet:—

[quotes Act I, Scene iii, lines 21–90]

The first time he alludes to the deed, which constitutes the substance of the plot, is in the following words addressed to a cardinal:—

——I am what your theologians call
Hardened; which they must be in impudence,
So to revile a man's peculiar taste. . . .
But that there yet remains a deed to act
Whose horror might make sharp an appetite
Duller than mine—I'd do—I know not what.—(P. 6, 7.)

After the unnatural outrage has been committed, he aims at something still more extravagent in inquity:—

Might I not drag her by the golden hair?
Stamp on her? Keep her sleepless, till her brain
Be overworn? Tame her with chains and famine?
Less would suffice. *Yet so to leave undone*
What I most seek! No, 'tis her stubborn will,
Which, by its own consent, shall stoop as low
As that which drags it down.—(P. 56.)

His wife tries to terrify him by pretending that his death has been announced by a supernatural voice; his reply is in these words:

> ———Why—such things are—
> No doubt divine revealings may be made.
> 'Tis plain I have been favoured from above,
> For when I cursed my sons, they died. Aye—so
> *As to the right or wrong, that's talk*—repentance,
> Repentance is an easy moment's work,
> And more depends on God than me. Well—well,
> I must give up the greater point, which was
> To poison and corrupt her soul.—(P. 57, 58.)

Such blasphemous ravings cannot be poetry, for they are neither sense nor nature. No such being as Cenci ever existed; none such could exist. The historical fact was in itself disgustingly shocking; and, in Mr. Shelley's hands, the fable becomes even more loathsome and less dramatic than the fact. It is true that there are tragedies of the highest order (the *Œdipus Tyrannus* for instance) where the catastrophe turns upon an event from which nature recoils; but the deed is done unwittingly; it is a misfortune, not a crime; it is kept back as much as possible from our view; the hopes, and fears, and sufferings of the parties occupy our thoughts, and all that is revolting to purity of mind is only slightly hinted at. Here the deed is done with premeditation; it is done from a wanton love of producing misery; it is constantly obtruded upon us in its most disgusting aspect; the most hateful forms of vice and suffering, preceded by involuntary pollution and followed by voluntary parricide, are the materials of this miscalled tragedy. They who can find dramatic poetry in such representations of human life must excuse us for wondering of what materials their minds are composed. Delineations like these are worse than unpoetical; they are unholy and immoral. But 'they are as lights,' if we believe Mr. Shelley, 'to make apparent some of the most dark and secret caverns of the human heart.' No, no; they teach nothing; and, if they did, knowledge must not be bought at too high a price. There is a knowledge which is death and pollution. Is knowledge any compensation for the injury sustained by being made familiar with that which ought to be to us all as if it were not? If such feelings, such ideas, exist in the world, (we cannot believe they do, for the Cenci of the Roman tradition is very different from the Cenci of Mr. Shelley) let them remain concealed. Our corporeal frames moulder into dust after death: are putrefying bodies, therefore, to be exposed in the public ways, that, forsooth, we may know what we are to be hereafter? The ties of father and daughter, of husband and wife, ought not to be profaned as they are in this poem. It is in vain to plead, that the delineations are meant to excite our hatred; they ought not to be presented to the mind at all; still less, pressed upon it long and perseveringly.

The technical structure of the piece is as faulty as its subject matter is blameable. The first two acts serve only to explain the relative situation of the parties, and do not in the least promote the action of the play; the fifth, containing the judicial proceedings at Rome, is a mere excrescence. The whole plot, therefore, is comprised in the incestuous outrage and in the subsequent assassination of the perpetrator; the former enormity occurs in the interval between the second act and the third; the latter in the fourth act. Thus the play has, properly speaking, no plot except in the third and fourth acts. But the incurable radical defects of the original conception of this drama render a minute examination of its structure superfluous.

The language is loose and disjointed; sometimes it is ambitious of simplicity, and it then becomes bald, inelegant, and prosaic. Words sometimes occur to which our ears are not accustomed; thus an 'un-appealable God' means a God from whom there is no appeal. We have a great deal of confused and not very intelligible imagery. A crag is 'huge as despair;' Cenci

> ——Bears a gloom duller
> Than the earth's shade or interlunar air:

And he describes his soul as a scourage, which will not be demanded of him till *'the lash be broken in its last and deepest wound:'*

> My soul, which is a scourge, will I resign
> Into the hands of him who wielded it;
> Be it for its own punishment or theirs,
> He will not ask it of me till the lash
> Be broken in its last and deepest wound;
> Until its hate be all inflicted.—(P. 58.)

We extract the following lines, because we have heard them much admired:—

> ——If there should be
> No God, no Heaven, no Earth in the void world;
> The wide, grey, lampless, deep, unpeopled world!
> If all things then should be—my father's spirit,
> His eye, his voice, his touch, surrounding me;

221

The atmosphere and breath of my dead life!
If sometimes, as a shape more like himself,
Even the form which tortured me on earth,
Masked in grey hairs and wrinkles, he should come
And wind me in his hellish arms, and fix
His eyes on mine, and drag me down, down, down!
For was he not alone omnipotent
On Earth, and ever present? Even tho' dead,
Does not his spirit live in all that breathe,
And work for me and mine still the same ruin,
Scorn, pain, despair? (P. 99, 100.)

We confess that to us this seems metaphysical jargon in substance'
dressed out in much flaunting half-worn finery.

The following is another of the admired passages in this tissue of
versified dialogue:—

[quotes Act III, Scene i, lines 6–38]

We say nothing of the conceit of misery killing its own father [line
37], because we wish to direct our observations, not to the imperfections of particular passages, but to the general want of fidelity to nature
which pervades the whole performance. In the crowd of images here
put into the mouth of Beatrice, there is neither novelty, nor truth, nor
poetical beauty. Misery like hers is too intensely occupied with its own
pangs to dwell so much on extraneous ideas. It does not cause the pavement to sink, or the wall to spin round, or the sunshine to become
black; it does not stain the heaven with blood; it does not change the
qualities of the air, nor does it clothe itself in a mist which glues the
limbs together, eats into the sinews, and dissolves the flesh; still less does
it suppose itself dead. This is not the language either of extreme misery
or of incipient madness; it is the bombast of a declamation, straining to
be energetic, and falling into extravagant and unnatural rant.

[quotes Act IV, Scene i, lines 78–111]

This passage exemplifies the furious exaggeration of Mr. Shelley's
caricatures, as well as of the strange mode in which, throughout the
whole play, religious thoughts and atrocious deeds are brought together.
There is something extremely shocking in finding the truths, the threats,
and the precepts of religion in the mouth of a wretch, at the very
moment that he is planning or perpetrating crimes at which nature

shudders. In this intermixture of things, sacred and impure, Mr. Shelley is not inconsistent if he believes that religion is in Protestant countries hypocrisy, and that it is in Roman Catholic countries 'adoration, faith, submission, penitence, blind admiration; not a rule for moral conduct, and that it has no necessary connexion with any one virtue.'—(Preface, p. 13.) Mr. Shelley is in an error: men act wrongly in spite of religion; but it is because they have no steady belief of it, or because their notions of it are erroneous, or because its precepts do not occur to them at the moment some vicious passion prevails. A Christian murderer does not amuse his fancy with the precepts and denunciations of his faith at the very moment of perpetrating the deed.

The moral errors of this book prevent us from quarrelling with its literary sins.

46. Henry Crabb Robinson, diary entries

March 22 and 23, 1845

From *Henry Crabb Robinson on Books and their Writers*, ed. Morley, (1938), ii, p. 652.

MARCH 22nd. . . . I came home between ten and eleven, and then I took up Shelley's *Poems*, and set about *The Cenci*, of which I read two acts in bed.

MARCH 23rd. I continued the tragedy in bed, and have now finished it. I have read it with great delight. I find but one fault in it. There is no motive suggested for the unparalleled atrocity of Cenci, the father. Shakespeare has never given a villain without enabling us to see why he is a villain; or, if not, he lets us see that he is not a mere monster. All his worst characters have something human about them and some redeeming quality. Now, Cenci has none. It is absolutely against nature that a father should so hate his children. It is more hate than lust that leads him to violate Beatrice. But then, on the other hand, how exquisite is that Beatrice; she is as perfect as he is monstrous. All is well-conceived and the tragedy is a perfect whole, and leaves the just feeling of repose after the conflict of guilt. In Beatrice's submission to death is the tragic purification. At first I objected to her wilful denial of the truth, but her motive is the allowable infirmity of noble minds. To save the family honour she lied to the last. I was led for the sake of comparison to read Coleridge's *Remorse*, which I thought beautiful, and with some very fine passages, but in significance far beneath *The Cenci*. It has a romantic interest and might attract an ordinary playgoer.

47. James Russell Lowell, 'The Imagination,' *The Function of the Poet*

James Russell Lowell (1819–91), poet, essayist and editor. Printed in *The Function of the Poet*, ed. Albert Mordell (1968), pp. 170–2.

In Shelley's *Cenci*, on the other hand, we have an instance of the poet's imagination giving away its own consciousness to the object contemplated, in this case an inanimate one.

> Do you not see that rock there which appeareth
> To hold itself up with a throe appalling,
> And, through the very pang of what it feareth,
> So many ages hath been falling, falling?

You will observe that in the last instance quoted the poet substitutes his own *impression* of the thing for the thing itself; he forces his own consciousness upon it, and herein is the very root of all sentimentalism. Herein lies the fault of that subjective tendency whose excess is so lamented by Goethe and Schiller, and which is one of the main distinctions between ancient and modern poetry.

PROMETHEUS UNBOUND

September 1820

48. Extract, unsigned review, *The London Magazine*, under 'Literary and Scientific Intelligence'

June 1820, i, 706

MR SHELLEY's announced dramatic poem, entitled *Prometheus Unbound*, will be found to be a very noble effort of a high and commanding imagination: it is not yet published, but we have seen some parts of it which have struck us very forcibly. The poet may perhaps be accused of taking a wild view of the latent powers and future fortunes of the human race; but its tendency is one of a far more inspiriting and magnanimous nature than that of *The Cenci*. The soul of man, instead of being degraded by the supposition of improbable and impossible vice, is elevated to the highest point of the poetical Pisgah, from whence a land of promise, rich with blessings of every kind, is pointed out to its delighted contemplation. This poem is more completely the child of the *Time* than almost any other modern production: it seems immediately sprung from the throes of the great intellectual, political, and moral *labour* of nations. Like the Time, its parent, too, it is unsettled, irregular, but magnificent. The following extract from Mr. Shelley's Preface, is, we think, a fine specimen of the power of his prose writings:

'We owe to Milton the progress and development of the same spirit: the sacred Milton was, be it remembered, a republican, a bold enquirer into morals and religion. The great writers of our own age, are, we have reason to suppose, the companions and forerunners of some unimagined change in our social condition, or the opinions which cement it. *The cloud of mind is discharging its collected lightning, and the equilibrium between institutions and opinions is now restoring, or is about to be restored.'*

49. Unsigned review, *The Literary Gazette, and Journal of the Belles Lettres*

September 9, 1820, no. 190, 580–2

It has been said, that none ought to attempt to criticise that which they do not understand; and we beg to be considered as the acknowledged transgressors of this rule, in the observations which we venture to offer on *Prometheus Unbound*. After a very diligent and careful perusal, reading many passages over and over again, in the hopes that the reward of our perseverance would be to comprehend what the writer meant, we are compelled to confess, that they remained to us inflexibly unintelligible, and are so to the present hour, when it is our duty to explain them *pro bono publico*.[1] This is a perplexing state for reviewers to be placed in; and all we can do is to extract some of these refractory combinations of words, the most of which are known to the English language, and submit them to the ingenuity of our readers, especially of such as are conversant with those interesting compositions which grace certain periodicals, under the titles of enigmas, rebuses, charades, and riddles. To them Mr. Shelley's poem may be what it is not to us (*Davus sum non Œdipus*)[2]—explicable; and their solutions shall, as is usual, be thankfully received. To our apprehensions, *Prometheus* is little else but absolute raving; and were we not assured to the contrary, we should take it for granted that the author was lunatic—as his principles are ludicrously wicked, and his poetry a melange of nonsense, cockneyism, poverty, and pedantry.

These may seem harsh terms; but it is our bounden duty rather to

[1] 'For the public good.'
[2] 'I am Davus not Oedipus,' Davus being a name given to Roman slaves (Terence, *Andria*, 1.2.24).

stem such a tide of literary folly and corruption, than to promote its flooding over the country. It is for the advantage of sterling productions, to discountenance counterfeits; and moral feeling, as well as taste, inexorably condemns the stupid trash of this delirious dreamer. But, in justice to him, and to ourselves, we shall cite his performance.

There is a preface, nearly as mystical and mysterious as the drama, which states Mr. Shelley's ideas in bad prose, and prepares us, by its unintelligibility, for the aggravated absurdity which follows. Speaking of his obligation to contemporary writings, he says, 'It is impossible that any one who *inhabits* the same *age*, with such writers as those who stand in the foremost ranks of our own, can conscientiously assure himself, that his language and tone of thought may not have been modified by the study of the productions of those extraordinary intellects.' (Mr. S. may rest assured, that neither his language, nor tone of thought, is modified by the study of productions of extraordinary intellects, in the *age* which he *inhabits*, or in any other.) He adds, 'It is true, that, not the spirit of their genius, but the forms in which it has manifested itself, are *due* less to the peculiarities of their own minds, than to the peculiarity of the moral and intellectual condition of the minds among which they have been produced. Thus, a number of writers possess the form, whilst they want the spirit of those whom, it is alleged, they imitate; because the former is the endowment of the age in which they live, and the latter must be the uncommunicated lightning of their own mind.' We have, upon honour, quoted verbatim: and though we have tried to construe these two periods at least seven times, we avow that we cannot discern their drift. Neither can we collect the import of the following general axiom, or paradox.—'As to imitation, poetry is a mimetic art. It creates, but it *creates* by combination and *representation*.' What kind of creation the creation by representation is, puzzles us grievously. But Mr. Shelley, no doubt, knows his own meaning; and according to honest Sancho Panza, 'that is enough.' In his next edition, therefore, we shall be glad of a more distinct definition than this—'*A poet is the combined product of such internal powers as modify the nature of others; and of such external influences as excite and sustain these powers; he is not one but both.*' We fear our readers will imagine we are vulgarly quizzing; but we assure them, that these identical words are to be found at page xiii. In the next page, Mr. S. speaks more plainly of himself; and plumply, though profanely, declares, 'For my part, I had rather be damned with Plato and Lord Bacon, than go to heaven with Paley and Malthus.'—

Poor man! how he moves concern and pity, to supersede the feelings of contempt and disgust. But such as he is, his 'object has hitherto been *simply* to familiarise the highly refined imagination of the more select classes of poetical readers with beautiful idealisms of moral excellence' —such, to wit, as the preference of damnation with certain beings, to beatitude with others!

But of this preface, more than enough:—return to *Prometheus Unbound*; humbly conceiving that this punning title-page is the soothest in the book—as no one can ever think him worth binding.

The *dramatis impersonae* are Prometheus, Jupiter, Demogorgon, the Earth, the Ocean, Apollo, Mercury, Hercules, Asia, Panthea, Ione, the phantasm of Jupiter, the Spirit of the Earth, Spirits of the Hours, other Spirits of all sorts and sizes, Echoes, substantial and spiritual, Fawns, Furies, Voices, and other monstrous personifications. The plot is, that Prometheus, after being three thousand years tormented by Jupiter, obtains the ascendancy, and restores happiness to the earth—*redeunt Saturnia regna*.[1] We shall not follow the long accounts of the hero's tortures, nor the longer rhapsodies about the blissful effects of his restoration; but produce a few of the brilliant emanations of the mind modified on the study of *extraordinary* intellects. The play opens with a speech of several pages, very acutely delivered by Signior Prometheus, from an icy rock in the Indian Caucasus, to which he is '*nailed*' by *chains* of '*burning cold.*' He invokes all the elements, *seriatim*,[2] to inform him what it was he originally said against Jupiter to provoke his ire; and, among the rest—

> Ye icy Springs, *stagnant* with wrinkling frost,
> Which *vibrated* to hear me: and then *crept*
> *Shuddering* through India.
> And ye, *swift* Whirlwinds, who, on *poised* wings
> Hung *mute* and *moveless* o'er yon hushed abyss,
> As thunder, *louder* than your own, made rock
> The orbed world.

This first extract will let our readers into the chief secret of Mr. Shelley's poetry; which is merely opposition of words, phrases, and sentiments, so violent as to be utter nonsense: *ex. gr.* the vibration of stagnant springs, and their creeping shuddering;—the swift moveless (*i.e.* motionless) whirlwinds, on poised wings, which hung mute over a hushed abyss as thunder louder than their own!! In the same strain,

---

[1] 'The kingdoms of Saturn are returning.' An allusion to Virgil, *Eclogues*, 4.6.
[2] 'In a series.'

Prometheus, who ought to have been called Sphynx, when answered in a *whisper*, says,

> 'Tis scarce like sound: it tingles thro' the frame
> As lightning tingles, *hovering ere it strike*.

Common bards would have thought the tingling was felt when it struck, and not before,—when it was hovering too, of all things for lightning to be guilty of! A 'melancholy voice' now enters into the dialogue, and turns out to be 'the Earth.' 'Melancholy Voice' tells a melancholy story, about the time—

> When plague had fallen on man, and beast, and worm
> And Famine;

She also advises her son Prometheus to use a spell,—

> . . . . So the revenge
> Of the Supreme may sweep thro' vacant shades,
> As rainy wind thro' the abandoned *gate*
> Of a fallen *palace*.

Mr. Shelley's buildings, having still gates to them! Then the Furies are sent to give the sturdy Titan a taste of their office; and they hold as odd a colloquy with him, as ever we read.
The first tells him,

> Thou thinkest we will rend thee bone from bone,
> And nerve from nerve, working like fire within:

The second,

> Dost imagine
> We will but laugh into thy lidless eyes?

And *the third*, more funnily inclined than her worthy sisters—

> Thou think'st we will live thro' thee, one by one
> Like animal life, and though we can obscure not
> The soul which burns within, that we will dwell
> Beside it, like a vain loud multitude
> Vexing the self-content of wisest men—

This is a pozer! and only paralleled by the speech of the 'Sixth Spirit,' of a lot of these beings, which arrive after the Furies. She, for these spirits are feminine, says,

> Ah, sister! *Desolation* is a *delicate thing*;
> It walks not on the earth, it floats not on the air,

But treads with *silent footsteps*, and fans with silent wing
The tender hopes which in their hearts the best and gentlest bear;
Who, soothed to false repose by the fanning plumes above,
And the *music-stirring motion* of its soft and busy *feet*,
Dream visions of aerial joy, and call the monster, *Love*,
And wake, and find the shadow pain.

The glimpses of meaning which we have here, are soon smothered by contradictory terms and metaphor carried to excess. There is another part of Mr. Shelley's art of poetry, which deserves notice; it is his fancy, that by bestowing *colouring* epithets on every thing he mentions, he thereby renders his diction and descriptions vividly poetical. Some of this will appear hereafter; but we shall select one passage, as illustrative of the ridiculous extent to which the folly is wrought.

Asia is longing for her sister's annual visit; and after talking of Spring clothing with *golden* clouds the desert of life, she goes on:

This is the season, this the day, the hour;
At sunrise thou shouldst come, sweet sister mine,
Too long desired, too long delaying, come!
How like death-worms the wingless moments crawl!
The point of one *white* star is quivering still
Deep in the *orange* light of widening morn
Beyond the *purple* mountains: thro' a chasm
Of wind-divided mist the *darker* lake
Reflects it: now it wanes: it gleams again
As the waves fade, and as the burning threads
Of woven cloud unravel in *pale* air:
'Tis lost! and thro' yon peaks of cloudlike snow
The *roseate* sun-light quivers: hear I not
The Æolian music of her *sea-green* plumes
Winnowing the *crimson* dawn?

Here in seventeen lines, we have no fewer than seven positive colours, and nearly as many shades; not to insist upon the everlasting confusion of this rainbow landscape, with *white* stars quivering in the *orange* light, beyond *purple* mountains; of *fading waves*, and clouds made of *burning threads*, which *unravel* in the *pale* air; of cloudlike snow through which *roseate* sunlight also quivers, and *sea-green* plumes winnowing *crimson* dawn. Surely, the author looks at nature through a prism instead of spectacles. Next to his colorific powers, we may rank the author's talent for manufacturing 'villainous compounds.' *Ecce signum*,[1] of a Mist.

> Beneath is a wide plain of billowy mist,
> As a *lake*, paving in the morning sky,
> With azure waves which *burst* in *silver* light,
> Some Indian vale. Behold it, rolling on
> Under the curdling winds, and *islanding*
> The *peak* whereon we stand, *midway, around*,
> Encinctured by the *dark* and *blooming* forests,
> Dim *twilight-lawns*, and *stream-illumed* caves,
> And *wind-enchanted* shapes of wandering mist;
> And far on high the keen *sky-cleaving* mountains
> From icy spires of sun-like radiance fling
> The dawn, as lifted Ocean's dazzling spray,
> From some Atlantic islet scattered up,
> Spangles the wind with *lamp-like water-drops*.
> The vale is girdled with their walls, a howl
> Of cataracts from their *thaw-cloven* ravines
> Satiates the listening wind, continuous, vast,
> Awful as silence.

This is really like Sir Sidney Smith's plan to teach morality to Musselmans by scraps of the Koran in kaleidoscopes—only that each scrap has a meaning; Mr. Shelley's lines none.

We now come to a part which quite throws Milton into the shade, with his 'darkness visible'; and as Mr. Shelley professes to admire that poet, we cannot but suspect that he prides himself on having out-done him. Only listen to Panthea's description of Demogorgon. This lady, whose mind is evidently unsettled, exclaims,

> I see a *mighty darkness*
> Filling the seat of power, and *rays of gloom*
> Dart round, as *light* from the *meridian sun*,
> *Ungazed upon* and *shapeless*—

We yield ourselves, miserable hum-drum devils that we are, to this high imaginative faculty of the modern muse. We acknowledge that hyperbola [sic], extravagance, and irreconcileable terms, may be poetry. We admit that common sense has nothing to do with 'the beautiful idealisms' of Mr. Shelley. And we only add, that if this be genuine inspiration, and not the grossest absurdity, then is farce sublime, and

[1] 'Behold the symbol.'

maniacal raving the perfection of reasoning: then were all the bards of other times, Homer, Virgil, Horace, drivellers; for their foundations were laid no lower than the capacities of the herd of mankind; and even their noblest elevations were susceptible of appreciation by the very multitude among the Greeks and Romans.

We shall be very concise with what remains: Prometheus, according to Mr. Percy Bysshe Shelley—

Gave man speech, and *speech created thought*—which is exactly, in our opinion, the cart creating the horse; the sign creating the inn; the effect creating the cause. No wonder that when such a master gave lessons in *astronomy*, he did it thus—

He taught the *implicated orbits woven*

> *Of the wide-wandering stars;* and how the sun
> Changes his *lair*, and by what *secret spell*
> The pale moon is transformed, when *her broad eye*
> Gazes not on the *interlunar sea.*

This, Promethean, beats all the systems of astronomy with which we are acquainted: Shakespeare, it was said, 'exhausted worlds and then imagined new'; but he never imagined aught so new as this. Newton was a wonderful philosopher; but, for the view of the heavenly bodies, Shelley double distances him. And not merely in the preceding, but in the following improved edition of his astronomical notions, he describes—

> A sphere, which is as many thousand spheres,
> Solid as crystal, yet through all its mass
> Flow, as through empty space, music and light:
> Ten thousand orbs involving and involved,
> Purple and azure, white, green, and golden,
> Sphere within sphere; and every space between
> Peopled with unimaginable shapes,
> Such as ghosts dream dwell in the lampless deep,
> Yet each inter-transpicuous, and they whirl
> Over each other with a thousand motions,
> Upon a thousand sightless axles spinning,
> And with the force of self-destroying swiftness,
> Intensely, slowly, solemnly roll on,
> Kindling with mingled sounds, and many tones,
> Intelligible words and music wild.
> With mighty whirl the multitudinous orb
> Grinds the bright brook into an azure mist

Of elemental subtlety, like light;
And the wild odour of the forest flowers,
The music of the living grass and air,
The emerald light of leaf-entangled beams
Round its intense yet self-conflicting speed,
Seem kneaded into one aerial mass
Which drowns the sense.

Did ever the walls of Bedlam display more insane stuff than this?

When our worthy old pagan acquaintance, Jupiter, is disposed of, his sinking to the 'void abyss,' is thus pourtrayed by his son Apollo—

An eagle so caught in some bursting cloud
On Caucasus, his *thunder-baffled wings*
Entangled in the whirlwind! &c.

An' these extracts do not entitle the author to a cell, clean straw, bread and water, a strait waistcoat, and phlebotomy, there is no madness in scribbling. It is hardly requisite to adduce a sample of the adjectives in this poem to prove the writer's condign abhorrence of any relation between that part of speech and substantives: sleep-unsheltered hours; gentle darkness; horny eyes; keen faint eyes; faint wings; fading waves; crawling glaciers, toads, agony, time, &c.; belated and noontide plumes; milky arms; many-folded mountains; a lake-surrounding flute; veiled lightening asleep (as well as hovering); unbewailing flowers; odour-faded blooms; semi-vital worms; windless pools, windless abodes, and windless air; unerasing waves; unpavilioned skies; rivetted wounds; and void abysms, are parcel of the Babylonish jargon which is found in every wearisome page of this tissue of insufferable buffoonery. After our quotations, we need not say that the verse is without measure, proportions, or elegance; that the similes are numberless and utterly inapplicable; and that the instances of ludicrous nonsense are not fewer than the pages of the Drama. Should examples be demanded, the following, additional, are brief. Of the heroic line:—

Ah me! alas, pain, pain ever, for ever—

Of the simile:—

We will entangle buds and flowers and beams
Which twinkle on the fountain's brim, and make
Strange combinations out of common things,
Like human babes in their brief innocence.—

Of the pure nonsensical:—

> Our *feet* now, every *palm*
> Are *sandalled* with *calm*,
> And the *dew* of our wings is a rain of balm;
> And *beyond* our eyes,
> The human love lies
> Which makes all it gazes on Paradise.
>
> We'll pass the eyes
> Of the starry skies
> Into the hoar deep to *colonise*:
> Death, Chaos, and Night,
> From the sound of our flight,
> Shall flee, like mist from a tempest's might.
>
> And Earth, Air, and Light,
> And the Spirit of Night,
> Which drives round the stars in their fiery flight;
> And Love, Thought, and Breath,
> The powers that quell Death,
> Wherever we soar shall assemble beneath.
>
> And our singing shall *build*
> In the *void's loose field*,
> A world for the Spirit of Wisdom to *wield*;
> We will take our plan
> From the new world of man,
> And our work shall be called the Promethean.

Alas, gentle reader! for poor Tom, whom the foul fiend hath (thus) led o'er bog and quagmire; and blisse thee from whirle-windes, starre-blasting, and taking. Would that Mr. Shelley made it his study, like this his prototype.

> How to prevent the fiend, and to kill vermin.

Poor Tom's affected want of wits is inferior to Shelley's genuine wandering with his 'father of the hours' and 'mother of the months'; and his dialogue of ten pages between *The Earth* and *The Moon*, assuredly the most arrant and gravest burlesque that it ever entered into the heart of man to conceive. We cannot resist its opening . . .

> *The Earth.* The joy, the triumph, the delight, the madness!
> The boundless, overflowing, bursting gladness,
> The vapourous exultation not to be confined!
> Ha! ha! the animation of delight

Which wraps me, like an atmosphere of light,
And bears me as a cloud is borne by its own wind.
The Moon. Brother mine, calm wanderer,
     Happy globe of land and air,
Some Spirit is darted like a beam from thee,
  Which penetrates my frozen frame,
  And passes with the warmth of flame,
With love, and odour, and deep melody
  Through me, through me!
The Earth. Ha! ha! the caverns of my hollow mountains,
My cloven fire-crags, sound-exulting fountains
Laugh with a vast and inextinguishable laughter,
  The oceans, and the deserts, and the abysses,
  And the deep air's unmeasured wildernesses,
Answer from all their clouds and billows, echoing after.

This is but the first of the ten pages: the sequel, though it may seem impossible to sustain such 'exquisite fooling,' does not fall off. But we shall waste our own and our readers' time no longer. We have but to repeat, that when the finest specimens of inspired composition may be derived from the white-washed walls of St. Lukes or Hoxton, the author of *Prometheus Unbound*, being himself among these bound writers, and chained like his subject, will have a chance of classing with foremost poets of the place.

50. John Gibson Lockhart, review, *Blackwood's Edinburgh Magazine*

September 1820, vii, 679–87

In *The Unextinguished Hearth*, N. I. White assigned this anonymous review to John Wilson and W. S. Lockhart, but Alan Strout in *A Bibliography of Articles in Blackwood's Magazine, 1817–1821* (1959) ascribed the piece to John Gibson Lockhart.

Whatever may be the difference of men's opinions concerning the measure of Mr. Shelley's poetical power, there is one point in regard to which all must be agreed, and that is his Audacity. In the old days of the exulting genius of Greece, Aeschylus dared two things which astonished all men, and which still astonish them—to exalt contemporary men into the personages of majestic tragedies—and to call down and embody into tragedy, without degradation, the elemental spirits of nature and the deeper essences of Divinity. We scarcely know whether to consider the *Persians* or the *Prometheus Bound* as the most extraordinary display of what has always been esteemed the most audacious spirit that ever expressed its workings in poetry. But what shall we say of the young English poet who has now attempted, not only a flight as high as the highest of Aeschylus, but the very flight of that father of tragedy— who has dared once more to dramatise Prometheus—and, most wonderful of all, to dramatise the *deliverance* of Prometheus—which is known to have formed the subject of a lost tragedy of Aeschylus no ways inferior in mystic elevation to that of the *Desmotēs*.[1]

Although a fragment of that perished master-piece be still extant in the Latin version of Attius—it is quite impossible to conjecture what were the personages introduced in the tragedy of Aeschylus, or by what train of passions and events he was able to sustain himself on the height of that awful scene with which his surviving *Prometheus* termin- ates. It is impossible, after reading what is left of that famous trilogy,[2] to suspect that the Greek poet symbolized any thing whatever by the person of Prometheus, except the native strength of human intellect itself—its strength of endurance above all others—its sublime power of patience. STRENGTH and FORCE are the two agents who appear on this darkened theatre to bind the too benevolent Titan—*Wit and Treachery*, under the forms of Mercury and Oceanus, endeavour to prevail upon him to make himself free by giving up his dreadful secret;—but *Strength* and *Force*, and *Wit* and *Treason*, are all alike powerless to overcome the resolution of that suffering divinity, or to win from him any acknowledgement of the new tyrant of the skies. Such was this simple and sublime allegory in the hands of Aeschylus. As to what had been the original purpose of the framers of the allegory, that is a very different question, and would carry us back into the most hidden places of the history of mythology. No one, however, who compares the mythological systems of different races and countries, can fail to

---

[1] 'Bound One.' The word is part of the Greek title of Aeschylus' *Prometheus Bound*.
[2] There was another and an earlier play of Aeschylus, *Prometheus the Fire-Stealer*, which is commonly supposed to have made part of the series; but the best critics, we think, are of opinion, that that was entirely a satirical piece. (Reviewer's footnote)

observe the frequent occurrence of certain great leading Ideas and leading Symbolisations of ideas too—which Christians are taught to
contemplate with a knowledge that is the knowledge of reverence.
Such, among others, are unquestionably the ideas of an Incarnate
Divinity suffering on account of mankind—conferring benefits on
mankind at the expense of his own suffering;—the general idea of
vicarious atonement itself—and the idea of the dignity of suffering as
an exertion of intellectual might—all of which may be found, more
or less obscurely shadowed forth, in the original *Mythos*[1] of Prometheus
the Titan, the enemy of the successful rebel and usurper Jove. We
might have also mentioned the idea of a *deliverer*, waited for patiently
through ages of darkness, and at last arriving in the person of the child
of Io—but, in truth, there is no pleasure, and would be little propriety,
in seeking to explain all this at greater length, considering, what we
cannot consider without deepest pain, the very different views which
have been taken of the original allegory by Mr. Percy Bysshe Shelley.

It would be highly absurd to deny, that this gentleman has manifested
very extraordinary powers of language and imagination in his treatment of the allegory, however grossly and miserably he may have tried
to pervert its purpose and meaning. But of this more anon. In the meantime, what can be more deserving of reprobation than the course
which he is allowing his intellect to take, and that too at the very
time when he ought to be laying the foundations of a lasting and
honourable name. There is no occasion for going round about the
bush to hint what the poet himself so unblushingly and sinfully blazoned
forth in every part of his production. With him, it is quite evident
that the Jupiter whose downfall has been predicted by Prometheus,
means nothing more than Religion in general, that is, every human
system of religious belief; and that, with the fall of this, he considers
it perfectly necessary (as indeed we also believe, though with far
different feelings) that every system of human government also should
give way and perish. The patience of the contemplative spirit in
Prometheus is to be followed by the daring of the active Demogorgon,
at whose touch all 'old thrones' are at once and for ever to be cast down
into the dust. It appears too plainly, from the luscious pictures with
which his play terminates, that Mr. Shelley looks forward to an unusual relaxation of all moral *rules*—or rather, indeed, to the extinction
of all moral feelings, except that of a certain mysterious indefinable
kindliness, as the natural and necessary result of the overthrow of all

[1] 'Mythos,' meaning the narrative account of the myth, the plot.

civil government and religious belief. It appears, still more wonderfully, that he contemplates this state of things as the ideal SUMMUM BONUM. In short it is quite impossible that there should exist a more pestiferous mixture of blasphemy, sedition, and sensuality, than is visible in the whole structure and strain of this poem—which, nevertheless, and notwithstanding all the detestation its principles excite, must and will be considered by all that read it attentively, as abounding in poetical beauties of the highest order—as presenting many specimens not easily to be surpassed, of the moral sublime of eloquence —as overflowing with pathos, and most magnificent in description. Where can be found a spectacle more worthy of sorrow than such a man performing and glorying in the performance of such things? His evil ambition,—from all he has yet written, but most of all, from what he has last and best written, his *Prometheus*,—appears to be no other, than that of obtaining the highest place among those poets,— enemies, not friends, of their species,—who, as a great and virtuous poet has well said (putting evil consequence close after evil cause).

> Profane the God-given strength, and *mar the lofty line*.

We should hold ourselves very ill employed, however, were we to enter at any length into the reprehensible parts of this remarkable production. It is sufficient to shew, that we have not been misrepresenting the purpose of the poet's mind, when we mention, that the whole tragedy ends with a mysterious sort of dance, and chorus of elemental spirits, and other indefinable beings, and that the SPIRIT OF THE HOUR, one of the most singular of these choral personages tells us:

> I wandering went
> Among the haunts and dwellings of mankind,
> And first was disappointed not to see
> Such mighty change as I had felt within
> Expressed in other things; but soon I looked,
> And behold! THRONES WERE KINGLESS, and men walked
> One with the other, even as spirits do, &c.

Again—

[quotes Act III, Scene iv, lines 164–97]

Last of all, and to complete the picture:—

> And women, too, *frank, beautiful,* and *kind*
> As the free heaven which rains fresh light and dew
> On the wide earth, past; gentle radiant forms,

From CUSTOM's evil taint exempt and pure;
Speaking the wisdom once they dared not think,
Looking emotions once they dared not feel,
And *changed to all which once they dared not be,*
Yet being now, made earth like heaven; nor pride
Nor jealousy, nor envy, nor ill shame,
The bitterest of those drops of treasured gall,
Spoilt the sweet taste of the Nepenthe, Love!

It is delightful to turn from the audacious spleen and ill-veiled abominations of such passages as these, to those parts of the production, in which it is possible to separate the poet from the allegorist—where the modern is content to write in the spirit of the ancient—and one might almost fancy that we had recovered some of the lost sublimities of Aeschylus. Such is the magnificent opening scene, which presents a ravine of icy rocks in the Indian Caucasus—Prometheus bound to the precipice—Panthea and Ione seated at his feet. The time is night; but, during the scene, morning slowly breaks upon the bleak and desolate majesty of the region.

[quotes Act I, lines 1–210]

Or the following beautiful chorus, which has all the soft and tender gracefulness of Euripides, and breathes, at the same time, the very spirit of one of the grandest odes of Pindar.

[quotes Act II, scene ii, lines 1–40]

We could easily select from the *Prometheus Unbound*, many pages of as fine poetry as this; but we are sure our readers will be better pleased with a few specimens of Mr. Shelley's style in his miscellaneous pieces, several of which are comprised in the volume. The following is the commencement of a magnificent 'VISION OF THE SEA.'

[quotes 'A Vision of the Sea,' lines 1–58; 66–79]

There is an 'Ode to the West-Wind,' another 'To a Sky-Lark,' and several smaller pieces, all of them abounding in richest melody of versification, and great tenderness of feeling. But the most affecting of all is 'The Sensitive Plant,' which is the history of a beautiful garden, that after brightening and blossoming under the eye of its lovely young mistress, shares in the calamity of her fate, and dies because she is no more there to tend its beauties. It begins thus. . . .

[quotes lines 1–40]

Then for the sad reverse—take the morning of the funeral of the young lady. . . .

[quotes Part III, lines 1–50]

We cannot conclude without saying a word or two in regard to an accusation which we have lately seen brought against ourselves in some one of the London Magazines; we forget which at this moment. We are pretty sure we know who the author of that most false accusation is—of which more hereafter. He has the audacious insolence to say, that we praise Mr. Shelley, although we dislike his principles, just because we know that he is not in a situation of life to be in any danger of suffering pecuniary inconveniences from being run down by critics; and, *vice versa*, abuse Hunt, Keats, and Hazlitt, and so forth, because we know that they are poor men; a fouler imputation could not be thrown on any writer than this creature has dared to throw on us; nor a more utterly false one; we repeat the word again—than this is when thrown upon us.

We have no personal acquaintance with any of these men, and no personal feelings in regard to any one of them, good or bad. We never even saw any one of their faces. As for Mr. Keats, we are informed that he is in a very bad state of health, and that his friends attribute a great deal of it to the pain he has suffered from the critical castigation his *Endymion* drew down on him in this magazine. If it be so, we are most heartily sorry for it, and have no hesitation in saying, that had we suspected that young author, of being so delicately nerved, we should have administered our reproof in a much more lenient shape and style. The truth is, we from the beginning saw marks of feeling and power in Mr. Keats' verses, which made us think it very likely, he might become a real poet of England, provided he could be persuaded to give up all the tricks of Cockneyism, and forswear forever the thin potations of Mr. Leigh Hunt. We, therefore, rated him as roundly as we decently could do, for the flagrant affectations of those early productions of his. In the last volume he has published, we find more beauties than in the former, both of language and of thought, but we are sorry to say, we find abundance of the same absurd affectations also, and superficial conceits, which first displeased us in his writings;—and which we are again very sorry to say, must in our opinion, if persisted in, utterly and entirely prevent Mr. Keats from ever taking his place among the pure and classical poets of his mother tongue. It is quite ridiculous to see how the vanity of these Cockneys makes them over-rate their own importance, even in the eyes of us, that have always expressed such plain unvarnished contempt for them, and who do feel for them all, a contempt too calm and profound, to admit of any admixture of any thing like anger or personal spleen. We should just as soon think of being wroth with vermin, independently of their coming into our apartments, as we should of having any feelings at all about any of these people, other than what are excited by seeing them in the shape of authors. Many of them, considered in any other character than that of authors, are, we have no doubt, entitled to be considered as very worthy people in their own way. Mr. Hunt is said to be a very amiable man in his own sphere, and we believe him to be so willingly. Mr. Keats we have often heard spoken of in terms of greater kindness, and we have no doubt his manners and feelings are calculated to make his friends love him. But what has all this to do with our opinion of their poetry? What, in the name of wonder, does it concern us, whether these men sit among themselves, with mild or with sulky faces, eating their mutton steaks, and drinking their porter at Highgate, Hampstead, or Lisson Green? What is there that should prevent us, or any other person, that happens not to have been educated in the University of Little Britain, from expressing a simple, undisguised, and impartial opinion, concerning the merits or demerits of men that we never saw, nor thought of for one moment, otherwise than as in the capacity of authors? What should hinder us from saying, since we think so, that Mr. Leigh Hunt is a clever wrong-headed man, whose vanities have got inwoven so deeply into him, that he has no chance of ever writing one line of classical English, or thinking one genuine English thought, either about poetry or politics? What is the spell that must seal our lips, from uttering an opinion equally plain and perspicuous concerning Mr. John Keats, viz. that nature possibly meant him to be a much better poet than Mr. Leigh Hunt ever could have been, but that, if he persisted in imitating the faults of that writer, he must be contented to share his fate, and be like him forgotten? Last of all, what should forbid us to announce our opinion, that Mr. Shelley, as a man of genius, is not merely superior, either to Mr. Hunt, or to Mr. Keats, but altogether out of their sphere, and totally incapable of ever being brought into the most distant comparison with either of them. It is very possible, that Mr. Shelley himself might not be inclined to place himself so high above these men as we do, but that is his affair, not ours. We are afraid that he shares, (at least with one of them) in an abominable system of belief, concerning Man and the World, the sympathy arising out of which common belief, may probably sway more than it ought to do on both sides. But the truth of the matter is this, and it is impossible to conceal it were we willing to do so, that Mr. Shelley is destined to leave a great name behind him, and that we, as lovers of true genius, are most anxious that this name should ultimately be pure as well as great.

As for the principles and purposes of Mr. Shelley's poetry, since we must again recur to that dark part of the subject, we think they are on the whole, more undisguisedly pernicious in this volume, than even in his *Revolt of Islam*. There is an 'Ode to Liberty' at the end of the volume, which contains passages of the most splendid beauty, but which, in point of meaning, is just as wicked as any thing that ever reached the world under the name of Mr. Hunt himself. It is not difficult to fill up the blank which has been left by the prudent bookseller, in one of the stanzas beginning:

> O that the free would stamp the impious name,
> Of —— into the dust! Or write it there
> So that this blot upon the page of fame,
> Were as a serpent's path, which the light air
> Erases, &c. &c.

but the next speaks still more plainly,

> O that the WISE from their bright minds would kindle
> Such lamps within the dome of this wide world,
> That the pale name of PRIEST might shrink and dwindle
> Into the HELL from which it first was hurled!

This is exactly a versification of the foulest sentence that ever issued from the lips of Voltaire. Let us hope that Percy Bysshe Shelley is not destined to leave behind him, like that great genius, a name for ever detestable to the truly FREE and the truly WISE. He talks in his preface about MILTON, as a 'Republican,' and a 'bold inquirer into Morals and religion.' Could any thing make us despise Mr. Shelley's understanding, it would be such an instance of voluntary blindness as this! Let us hope, that ere long a lamp of genuine truth may be kindled within his 'bright mind'; and that he may walk in its light the path of the true demigods of English genius, having, like them, learned to 'fear God and honour the king.'

51. Unsigned review, *The London Magazine and Monthly Critical and Dramatic Review*

September and October 1820, ii, 306–8 and 382–91

This book has made its appearance so extremely late in the month, that, although we profess to give as early and as satisfactory notices of new works as are any where to be met with, it has fairly puzzled even our most consummate ingenuity. 'Something must be done, and that right quickly, friend Bardolph'; this is our opinion as well as honest Jack Falstaff's; and with this quotation we buckle to our task. Of *Prometheus Unbound*, the principal poem in this beautiful collection, we profess to give no account. It must be reserved for our second series, as it requires more than ordinary attention. The minor pieces are stamped throughout with all the vigorous peculiarities of the writer's mind, and are everywhere strongly impregnated with the alchymical properties of genius. But what we principally admire in them is their strong and healthy freshness, and the tone of interest that they elicit. They possess the fever and flush of poetry; the fragrant perfume and sunshine of a summer's morning, with its genial and kindly benevolence. It is impossible to peruse them without admiring the peculiar property of the author's mind, which can doff in an instant the cumbersome garments of metaphysical speculations, and throw itself naked as it were into the arms of nature and humanity. The beautiful and singularly original poem of 'The Cloud' will evince proofs of our opinion, and show the extreme force and freshness with which the writer can impregnate his poetry.

[quotes 'The Cloud' in full. The review of *Prometheus Unbound* which follows appeared in the October number.]

This is one of the most stupendous of those works which the daring and vigorous spirit of modern poetry and thought has created. We despair of conveying to our readers, either by analysis or description, any idea of its gigantic outlines, or of its innumerable sweetnesses. It is a vast wilderness of beauty, which at first seems stretching out on all sides into infinitude, yet the boundaries of which are all cast by the poet; in which the wildest paths have a certain and noble direction; and the strangest shapes which haunt its recesses, voices of gentleness and of wisdom. It presents us with the oldest forms of Greek mythology, informed with the spirit of fresh enthusiasm and of youngest hope; and mingles with these the creatures of a new mythology, in which earth, and the hosts of heaven, spirits of time and of eternity, are embodied and vivified, to unite in the rapturous celebration of the reign of Love over the universe.

This work is not, as the title would lead us to anticipate, a mere attempt to imitate the old tragedy of the Greeks. In the language, indeed, there is often a profusion of felicitously compounded epithets; and in the imagery, there are many of those clear and lucid shapes, which distinguish the works of Æschylus and of Sophocles. But the subject is so treated, that we lose sight of persons in principles, and soon feel that all the splendid machinery around us is but the shadow of things unseen, the outward panoply of bright expectations and theories, which appear to the author's mind instinct with eternal and eternally progressive blessings. The fate of Prometheus probably suggested, even to the heroic bard by whom it was celebrated in older time, the temporary predominance of brute force over intellect; the oppression of right by might; and the final deliverance of the spirit of humanity from the iron grasp of its foes. But, in so far as we can judge from the mighty fragment which time has spared, he was contented with exhibiting the visible picture of the magnanimous victim, and with representing his deliverance, by means of Hercules, as a mere personal event, having no symbolical meaning. In Mr. Shelley's piece, the deliverance of Prometheus, which is attended by the dethroning of Jupiter, is scarcely other than a symbol of the peaceful triumph of goodness over power; of the subjection of might to right; and the restoration of love to the full exercise of its benign and all-penetrating sympathies. To represent vividly and poetically this vast moral change, is, we conceive, the design of this drama, with all its inward depths of mystical gloom, its pregnant clouds of imagination, its spiry eminences of icy splendour, and its fair regions overspread by a light 'which never was by sea or land,' which consecrates and harmonizes all things.

To the ultimate prospect exhibited by that philosophical system which Mr. Shelley's piece embodies, we have no objection. There is nothing pernicious in the belief that, even on earth, man is destined to attain a high degree of happiness and of virtue. The greatest and wisest have ever trusted with the most confiding faith to that nature,

with whose best qualities they were so richly gifted. They have felt that
in man were undeveloped capabilities of excellence; stores of greatness,
suffered to lie hidden beneath basest lumber; sealed up fountains,
whence a brighter day might loosen streams of fresh and ever-living
joys. In the worst and most degraded minds, vestiges of goodness are
not wanting; some old recollections of early virtue; some feeling of
wild generosity or unconquerable love; some divine instinct; some
fragments of lofty principle; some unextinguishable longings after
nobleness and peace, indicate that there is good in man which can never
yield to the storms of passion or the decays of time. On these divine
instances of pure and holy virtue; on history; on science; on imagination; on the essences of love and hope; we may safely rest, in the expectation that a softer and tenderer light will ultimately dawn on our
species. We further agree with Mr. Shelley, that Revenge is not the
weapon with which men should oppose the erring and the guilty.
He only speaks in accordance with every wise writer on legislation,
when he deprecates the infliction of one vibration of *unnecessary* pain
on the most criminal. He only echoes the feeling of every genuine
Christian, when he contends for looking with deep-thoughted pity
on the vicious, or regarding them tenderly as the unfortunate, and for
striving 'not to be overcome of evil, but to overcome evil with good.'
He only coincides with every friend of his species, when he deplores
the obstacles which individuals and systems have too often opposed to
human progress. But when he would attempt to realize in an instant
his glorious visions; when he would treat men as though they are now
the fit inhabitants of an earthly paradise; when he would cast down all
restraint and authority as enormous evils; and would leave mankind to
the guidance of passions yet unsubdued, and of desires yet unregulated,
we must protest against his wishes, as tending fearfully to retard the
good which he would precipitate. Happy, indeed, will be that time, of
which our great philosophical poet, Wordsworth, speaks, when love
shall be an 'unclouded light, and joy its own security.' But we shall
not hasten this glorious era by destroying those forms and dignities
of the social state, which are essential to the restraint of the worst
passions, and serviceable to the nurture of the kindliest affections. The
stream of human energy is gathering strength; but it would only be
scattered in vain, were we rashly to destroy the boundaries which now
confine it in its deep channel; and it can only be impeded by the impatient attempt to strike the shores with its agitated waters.

Although there are some things in Mr. Shelley's philosophy against which we feel it a duty thus to protest, we must not suffer our difference of opinion to make us insensible to his genius. As a poem, the work before us is replete with clear, pure, and majestical imagery, accompanied by a harmony as rich and various as that of the loftiest of our English poets. The piece first exhibits a ravine of icy rocks in the Indian Caucasus, where Prometheus is bound to the precipice, and Panthea and Ione sit at his feet to soothe his agonies. He thus energetically describes his miseries, and calls on the mountains, springs, and winds, to repeat to him the curse which he once pronounced on his foe, whom he now regards only with pity:

[quotes Act I, Scene i, lines 31–73]

The voices reply only in vague terms, and the Earth answers that they dare not tell it; when the following tremendous dialogue follows:

[quotes Act I, Scene i, lines 131–86]

. . . Mercury next enters with the Furies sent by Jupiter to inflict new pangs on his victim. This they effect, by placing before his soul pictures of the agonies to be borne by that race for whom he is suffering. The Earth afterwards consoles him, by calling up forms who are rather dimly described as

> ————Subtle and fair spirits,
> Whose homes are the dim caves of human thought,
> And who inhabit, as birds wing the wind,
> Its world surrounding ether.—

We give part of their lovely chaunt in preference to the ravings of the Furies, though these last are intensely terrible:

[quotes Act I, Scene i, lines 694–751]

The second Act introduces the glorious indications throughout nature of the deliverance of Prometheus from his sufferings. Panthea visits her sister Asia in a lonely vale in the Indian Caucasus, where they relate to each other sweet and mystic dreams betokening the approaching change. When they have ceased Echo calls on them to follow:

> O, follow, follow!
> Thro' the caverns hollow,
> As the song floats thou pursue,
> Where the wild bee never flew,

246

> Thro' the noontide darkness deep,
> By the odour-breathing sleep
> Of faint night-flowers, and the waves
> At the fountain-lighted caves,
> While our music, wild and sweet,
> Mocks thy gently falling feet,
> Child of Ocean!

The two sisters link their hands and follow the dying voices. They pass into a forest, at the entrance of which two young Fauns are sitting listening, while the Spirits of the Wood in a choral song thus magnificently describe its recesses:

[quotes Act II, Scene ii, lines 1–63]

Asia and Panthea follow the sounds into the realm of Demogorgon, into whose cave they descend from a pinnacle among the mountains. Here Asia, after an obscure metaphysical dialogue, sets forth the blessing bestowed by Prometheus on the world in the richest colouring, and asks the hour of his freedom. On this question the rocks are cloven and the Hours are seen flying in the heavens. With one of these the sisters ascend in the radiant Car; and Asia becomes encircled with lustre, which inspires Panthea thus rapturously to address her:—

[quotes Act II, Scene v, lines 16–47]

Another voice is heard in the air, and Asia bursts into the following strain, which is more liquidly harmonious, and of a beauty more ravishing and paradisaical, than any passage which we can remember in modern poetry:—

[quotes the 'enchanted boat' lyric entire, Act II, Scene v, lines 73–110

In the third act, Jupiter is dethroned by Demogorgon, and Prometheus is unchained by Hercules. The rest of the Drama is a celebration of the joyous results of this triumph, and anticipations of the reign of Love. Our readers will probably prefer reposing on the exquisite description given by Prometheus of the cave which he designs for his dwelling, to expatiating on the wide and brilliant prospects which the poet discloses:—

[quotes Act III, Scene vii, lines 10–56]

We have left ourselves no room to expatiate on the minor Poems of this volume. The 'Vision of the Sea' is one of the most awful pictures which poetry has set before us. In the 'Ode to Liberty,' there are passages of a political bearing, which, for the poet's sake, we heartily wish had been omitted. It is not, however, addressed to minds whom it is likely to injure. In the whole work there is a spirit of good— of gentleness, humanity, and even of religion, which has excited in us a deep admiration of its author, and a fond regret that he should ever attempt to adorn cold and dangerous paradoxes with the beauties which could only have been produced by a mind instinctively pious and reverential.

52. Unsigned review, *The Lonsdale Magazine or Provincial Repository*

November 1820, i, 498–501

Among all the fictions of early poetry, there was not perhaps a more expressive one than that of the Syrens—they assailed the eye by their beauty, and the ear by the sweetness of their music. But the heedless voyager who was captivated by these allurements, found, when too late, that the most melodious tongue might be connected with the most rapacious heart. As it was in the days of Eneas, it is in our own— those whom Heaven has formed to 'wake the living lyre,' are too often found to pervert the celestial bounty, and endeavour to allure others by the flowers of rhetoric and music of oratory—to wander from the paths of virtue and innocence—to pursue the bubble, happiness, through the gratifications of sense—to feed on the fancied visions of an ideal perfection, which is to result from an unrestrained indulgence of all our baser passions and propensities—to revel in a prospective state of human felicity, which is to crown the subversion of all social order—and to figure to themselves an earthly paradise, which is to be planted among the ashes of that pure and holy religion which the Deity himself has revealed to his creatures.

Among the pestiferous herd of those who have essayed to destroy man's last and highest hope, some, like Paine, have been so exceedingly low and scurrilous, that even the illiterate could not be induced to drink the filthy poison. Others, like the *Edinburgh* Reviewers, have been so *exquisitely* absurd, that nothing but the ignorant could possibly be misled by their flimsy sophistry. Others again, like Godwin, have been so metaphysical, that those who were capable of comprehending their sophisms, and developing their complicated hypotheses, were well qualified to confute their logical nonsense, and expose their preposterous philosophy.

But, when writers, like Byron and Shelley, envelope their destructive theories in language, both intended and calculated to entrance the soul by its melodious richness, to act upon the passions without consulting the reason, and to soothe and overwhelm the finest feelings of our nature;—then it is that the unwary are in danger of being misled, the indifferent of being surprised, and the innocent of being seduced.

Mr. Shelley is a man of such poetic powers, as, if he had employed them in the cause of virtue, honour, and truth, would have entitled him to a distinguished niche in the temple of fame. And painful it must be for every admirer of genius and talent, to see one, whose fingers can so sweetly touch the poetic lyre, prostituting his abilities in a manner which must at some future period, embitter the important moment, and throw an awful shade over the gloomy retrospect.

That we may stand justified in the opinion we have given of Mr. Shelley's superior talents as an author, we will quote a few lines from one of his fugitive pieces, entitled 'A Vision of the Sea.' A piece which for grandeur of expression, originality of thought, and magnificence of description, stands almost unrivalled.

[quotes lines 1–57, omitting 34–45]

Had all the productions of our author been, like the above, calculated only to 'soften and soothe the soul,' we should have rejoiced in adding our humble tribute of applause to the numerous encomiums which have greeted him. But alas! he has drunk deeply of the two poisonous and kindred streams—infidelity and sedition. We shall not enter into an analysis of his great work, *Prometheus Unbound*, as our principal intention is to *recommend* it to the *neglect* of our readers.—The chief design of the piece, which is a dramatic poem after the manner of the old school, is to charm the unsuspecting heart of youth and innocence, with a luscious picture of the felicities which would succeed the subversion of social, religious, and political order—and which he denominates LIBERTY.

At this happy period when

> Thrones were kingless, and men walked
> One with the other, even as spirits do . . .

After, 'Thrones, altars, judgment-seats, and prisons' shall have been destroyed, men shall

> Look forth
> In triumph o'er the palaces and tombs
> Of those who were their conquerors, mouldering around.

Religion, too, will then have vanished, which he characterizes,

> A dark yet mighty faith, a power as wide
> *As is the world it wasted. . . .*

In his ardour to anticipate the joyous period, he breaks out in an exclamation, as though he beheld it present.

> The painted veil . . . .
> . . . . is torn aside;
> The loathsome mask has fallen; the man remains
> *Sceptreless, free, uncircumscrib'd, but man*
> *Equal, unclass'd, tribeless, and nationless,*
> *Exempt from awe, worship,—the king over himself.*

But this is not all, the very decencies of our nature are to vanish beneath the magic wand of this licentious REFORMER. Every modest feeling, which now constitutes the sweetest charm of society is to be annihilated—and women are to be—*what God and nature never designed them.* But his own description alone can point the lasciviousness of his own heart:—

> And women too, *frank*, beautiful, and kind,
> *As the free heaven*, which rains fresh light and dew
> On the wide earth;—*gentle* radiant form,
> From *custom's evil taint exempt* and pure;
> Speaking the wisdom once they dar'd not think,
> *Looking emotions once they dar'd not feel,*
> And *changed to all which once they dared not be,*
> *Yet being now*, make earth like heaven; nor pride
> Nor jealousy, nor envy, *nor ill-shame,*
> The bitterest of these drops of treasured gall,
> *Spoil the sweet taste of the Nepenthe*, Love.

After having excited his own vicious imagination with this luscious picture of fancied bliss, he seems to have lost all patience with the tardy disciples of this *precious philosophy*; and feels indignant that they do not remove by force the kings and priests and other *trifling* obstacles to the completion of his burning wishes. He thirsts to be transported at once to this ecstatic *Utopia*. For in the same volume, we find an 'Ode to Liberty,' where he exclaims;—

> O, that the free would stamp the impious name
> Of —— into the dust! Or write it there;
> So that this blot upon the page of fame,
> Were as a serpent's path, which the light air
> Erases—
> O, that the wise for their bright minds would kindle
> Such lamps within the dome of the wide world,
> That the pale name of PRIEST might shrink and dwindle,
> Into the HELL from which it first was hurl'd.

Further remarks on sentiments like these, are unnecessary. The beast requires only to be dragged into public light, to meet its merited contempt. We can only express our pity for the author, and regret that so fine a poet should have espoused so detestable a cause.

53. Unsigned review, *The Monthly Review and British Register*

February 1821, xciv, 168–73

There is an excess of fancy which rapidly degenerates into nonsense: if the *sublime* be closely allied to the ridiculous, the *fanciful* is twin-sister to the *foolish*; and really Mr. Shelley has worthily maintained the relationship. What, in the name of wonder on one side, and of common sense on the other, is the meaning of this metaphysical rhapsody about the unbinding of Prometheus? Greek plays, Mr. Shelley tells us in his preface, have been his study; and from them he has caught—what?—any thing but the tone and character of his story; which as little exhibits the distinct imaginations of the heathen mythology as it resembles the virtuous realities of the Christian faith. It is only *nonsense, pure unmixed nonsense,* that Mr. Shelley has derived from his various lucubrations, and combined in the laudable work before us.

We are so far from denying, that we are most ready to acknowledge, the great merit of detached passages in the *Prometheus Unbound*: but this sort of praise, we fear from expressions in his prose advertisements, the poet before us will be most unwilling to receive; for he says on one occasion, (preface to *The Cenci,*) 'I have avoided, *with great care,* in writing this play, the introduction of what is commonly called *mere poetry*; and I imagine there will scarcely be found *a detached simile, or a single isolated description,*'!! &c. Charming prospect, indeed! 'I could find it in my heart,' says Dogberry, 'to bestow all my tediousness upon your Worship'; and so his anti-type, the author of *Prometheus Unbound,* (which, a punster might say, will always remain *unbound,*) studiously excludes from his play everything like 'mere poetry,' (*merum sal,*) or a 'single isolated description.' This speaks for itself; and we should have thought that we had been reading a burlesque preface of Fielding to one of his *mock tragedies,* rather than a real introduction by a serious dramatist to one of his *tragic plays.* We may be told, however, that we must consider the *Prometheus Unbound* as a philosophical work. 'We cry you mercy, cousin Richard!' Where are the things, then, 'not dreamt of in *our* philosophy?' The '*Prometheus Unbound*' is amply stored with such things. First, there is a *wicked supreme deity.*—Secondly, there is a Demogorgon; superior, in process of time, to that *supreme wickedness.*—Thirdly, there are nymphs, naiads, nereids, spirits of flood and fell, depth and height, the four elements, and fifty-four imaginary places of creation and residence.— Now, to what does all this tend? To nothing, positively to nothing. Like Dandie Dinmont's unproduceable child, the author cannot, in any part of his work, '*behave distinctly.*' How should he? His Manichean absurdities, his eternally indwelling notion of a good and an evil principle fighting like furies on all occasions with their whole *posse comitatus* together, cross his clearer fancy, and lay the buildings of his better mind in glittering gorgeous ruins. Let his readers observe the manner in which he talks of death, and hope, and all the thrilling interests of man; and let us also attend to what follows:—'For my part I had rather be damned with Plato and Lord Bacon than go to Heaven with Paley and Malthus.' Preface to *Prometheus*, p. 14. This appears to us to be nothing but hatred of contemporaries; not admiration of the antients. *This* 'offence is rank;—it smells to Heaven.'

The benevolent opposition of Prometheus to the oppressive and atrocious rule of Jupiter forms the main object, as far as it can be understood, of this generally unintelligible work; though some of it can be understood too plainly; and the passage beginning, 'A woful sight,' at page 49, and ending, 'It hath become a curse,' must be most offensive, as it too evidently seems to have been intended to be, to every sect of Christians.

We must cease, however, to expostulate with Mr. Shelley, if we may hope to render him or his admirers any service; and most assuredly we have a sincere desire to be thus serviceable, for he has power to do good, or evil, on an extensive scale;—and whether from admiration of genius, or from a prudent wish to conciliate its efforts, we are disposed to welcome all that is good and useful in him, as well as prepared to condemn all that is the contrary. We turn, then, to other matters, and point out what we think is unexceptionably, or fairly, poetical in the strange book before us.

[quotes Act II, Scene iv, lines 7–86]

The most imaginative of our readers must, we think, be disposed to allow that there is much *nonsense* in all this, however fanciful: yet there is much poetry also,—much benevolent feeling, beautiful language, and powerful versification.

We will take one other extract; and it shall be from the lyric portion of the drama.

[quotes Act IV, Scene i, lines 1–55]

Such a quotation as this affords ample opportunity for fair judgment; and what is the verdict? With a great portion of uncommon merit, much more absurdity is mixed; and, how great soever the author's genius may be, it is not great enough to bear him out, when he so plainly and heartily laughs in his reader's face as so clever a writer *must do* in this and many other passages.

The 'Miscellaneous Poems,' which follow *Prometheus*, display also both his fancy and his peculiarities.

54. W. S. Walker, review, *The Quarterly Review*

October 1821, xxvi, 168–80

Attributed to W. S. Walker by Hill and Helen Shine in *The Quarterly Review under Gifford* (Chapel Hill, N.C., 1949). If so, he certainly changed his mind by 1824 when he again reviewed Shelley's poetry.

A great lawyer of the present day is said to boast of practising three different modes of writing: one which any body can read; another which only himself can read; and a third, which neither he nor any body else can read. So Mr. Shelley may plume himself upon writing in three different styles: one which can be generally understood; another which can be understood only by the author; and a third which is absolutely and intrinsically unintelligible. Whatever his command may be of the first and second of these styles, this volume is a most satisfactory testimonial of his proficiency in the last.

If we might venture to express a general opinion of what far surpasses our comprehension, we should compare the poems contained in this volume to the visions of gay colours mingled with darkness, which often in childhood, when we shut our eyes, seem to revolve at an immense distance around us. In Mr. Shelley's poetry all is brilliance, vacuity, and confusion. We are dazzled by the multitude of words which sound as if they denoted something very grand or splendid: fragments of images pass in crowds before us; but when the procession has gone by, and the tumult of it is over, not a trace of it remains upon the memory. The mind, fatigued and perplexed, is mortified by the consciousness that its labour has not been rewarded by the acquisition of a single distinct conception; the ear, too, is dissatisfied: for the rhythm of the verse is often harsh and unmusical; and both the ear and the understanding are disgusted by new and uncouth words, and by the awkward, and intricate construction of the sentences.

The predominating characteristic of Mr. Shelley's poetry, however, is its frequent and total want of meaning. Far be it from us to call for strict reasoning, or the precision of logical deductions, in poetry; but we have a right to demand clear, distinct conceptions. The colouring of the pictures may be brighter or more variegated than that of reality; elements may be combined which do not in fact exist in a state of union; but there must be no confusion in the forms presented to us. Upon a question of mere beauty, there may be a difference of taste. That may be deemed energetic or sublime, which is in fact unnatural or bombastic; and yet there may be much difficulty in making the difference sensible to those who do not preserve an habitual and exclusive intimacy with the best models of composition. But the question of meaning, or no meaning, is a matter of fact on which common sense, with common attention, is adequate to decide; and the decision to which we may come will not be impugned, whatever be the want of taste, or insensibility to poetical excellence, which it may please Mr. Shelley, or any of his coterie, to impute to us. We permit them to assume, that they alone possess all sound taste and all genuine feeling of the beauties of nature and art: still they must grant that it belongs only to the judgment to determine, whether certain passages convey any signification or none; and that, if we are in error ourselves, at least we can mislead nobody else, since the very quotations which we must adduce as examples of nonsense, will, if our charge be not well founded, prove the futility of our accusation at the very time that it is made. If, however, we should completely establish this charge, we look upon the question of Mr. Shelley's poetical merits as at an end; for he who has the trick of writing very showy verses without ideas, or without coherent ideas, can contribute to the instruction of none, and can please only those who have learned to read without having ever learned to think.

The want of meaning in Mr. Shelley's poetry takes different shapes. Sometimes it is impossible to attach any signification to his words; sometimes they hover on the verge between meaning and no meaning, so that a meaning may be obscurely conjectured by the reader, though none is expressed by the writer; and sometimes they convey ideas, which, taken separately, are sufficiently clear, but, when connected, are altogether incongruous. We shall begin with a passage which exhibits in some parts the first species of nonsense, and in others the third.

Lovely apparitions, dim at first,
Then radiant, as the mind, arising bright

> From the embrace of beauty, whence the forms
> Of which these are the phantoms, casts on them
> The gathered rays which are reality,
> Shall visit us, the immortal progeny
> Of painting, sculpture, and wrapt poesy,
> And arts, tho' unimagined, yet to be.—p. 105.

The verses are very sonorous; and so many fine words are played off upon us, such as, *painting, sculpture, poesy, phantoms, radiance, the embrace of beauty, immortal progeny,* &c. that a careless reader, influenced by his habit of associating such phrases with lofty or agreeable ideas, may possibly have his fancy tickled into a transient feeling of satisfaction. But let any man try to ascertain what is really said, and he will immediately discover the imposition that has been practised. From beauty, or the embrace of beauty, (we know not which, for ambiguity of phrase is a very frequent companion of nonsense,) certain forms proceed: of these forms there are phantoms; these phantoms are dim; but the mind arises from the embrace of beauty, and casts on them the gathered rays which are reality; they are then baptized by the name of immortal progeny of the arts, and in that character proceed to visit Prometheus. This *galimatias* (for it goes far beyond simple nonsense) is rivalled by the following description of something that is done by a cloud.

> I am the daughter of earth and water,
>   And the nursling of the sky;
> I pass through the pores of the oceans and shores,
>   I change, but I cannot die.
> For after the rain, when with never a stain
>   The pavilion of heaven is bare,
> And the winds and sunbeams with their convex gleams,
>   Build up the blue dome of air.
> I silently laugh at my own cenotaph,
>   And out of the caverns of rain,
> Like a child from the womb, like a ghost from the tomb,
>   I arise, and unbuild it again.—pp. 199, 200.[1]

There is a love-sick lady, who 'dwells under the glaucous caverns of ocean,' and '*wears the shadow of Prometheus' soul,*' without which (she declares) she cannot *go to sleep.* The rest of her story is utterly incomprehensible; we therefore pass on to the *debut* of the Spirit of the earth.

[1] Lines 73–84 of 'The Cloud'. (Reviewer's footnote)

And from the other opening in the wood
Rushes, with loud and whirlwind harmony,
A sphere, which is as many thousand spheres,
Solid as chrystal, yet through all its mass
Flow, as through empty space, music and light:
Ten thousand orbs involving and involved,
Purple and azure, white, green, and golden,
Sphere within sphere; and every space between
Peopled with unimaginable shapes,
Such as ghosts dream dwell in the lampless deep,
Yet each inter-transpicuous, and they whirl
Over each other with a thousand motions,
Upon a thousand sightless axles spinning,
And with the force of self-destroying swiftness,
Intensely, slowly, solemnly, roll on,
Kindling with mingled sounds, and many tones,
Intelligible words and music wild.
With mighty whirl the multitudinous orb
Grinds the bright brook into an azure mist
Of elemental subtlety, like light;
And the wild odour of the forest flowers,
The music of the living grass and air,
The emerald light of leaf-entangled beams
Round its intense yet self-conflicting speed,
Seem kneaded into one aerial mass
Which drowns the sense.

We have neither leisure nor room to develope all the absurdities here
accumulated, in defiance of common sense, and even of grammar;
whirlwind harmony, a solid sphere which is as many thousand spheres,
and contains ten thousand orbs or spheres, with inter-transpicuous
spaces between them, whirling over each other on a thousand sightless
(alias invisible) axles; self-destroying swiftness; intelligible words and
wild music, kindled by the said sphere, which also grinds a bright
brook into an azure mist of elemental subtlety; odour, music, and light,
kneaded into one aërial mass, and the sense drowned by it!

Oh quanta species! et cerebrum non habet.[1]

One of the personages in the *Prometheus* is Demogorgon. As he is
the only agent in the whole drama, and effects the only change of
situation and feeling which befals the other personages; and as he is

[1] 'Oh, what beauty, but no brains!' (Reviewer's footnote)

likewise employed to sing or say divers hymns, we have endeavoured to find some intelligible account of him. The following is the most perspicuous which we have been able to discover:—

> ———A mighty power, which is as darkness,
> Is rising out of earth, and from the sky,
> Is showered like night, and from within the air
> Bursts, *like eclipse which had been gathered up*
> *Into the pores of sun-light.*—p. 149.

Love, as might be expected, is made to perform a variety of very extraordinary functions. It fills 'the void annihilation of a sceptred curse' (p. 140); and, not to mention the other purposes to which it is applied, it is in the following lines dissolved in air and sun-light, and then folded round the world.

> ———The impalpable thin air,
> And the all circling sun-light were transformed,
> As if the sense of love dissolved in them,
> Had folded itself round the sphered world.—p. 116.

Metaphors and similes can scarcely be regarded as ornaments of Mr. Shelley's compositions; for his poetry is in general a mere jumble of words and heterogeneous ideas, connected by slight and accidental associations, among which it is impossible to distinguish the principal object from the accessory. In illustrating the incoherency which prevails in his metaphors, as well as in the other ingredients of his verses, we shall take our first example, not from that great storehouse of the obscure and the unintelligible—the *Prometheus*, but from the opening of a poem, entitled, 'A Vision of the Sea,' which we have often heard praised as a splendid work of imagination.

> ———The rags of the sail
> Are flickering in ribbons within the fierce gale:
> From the stark night of vapours the dim rain is driven,
> And when lightning is loosed, like a deluge from heaven,
> She sees the black trunks of the water-spouts spin,
> And bend, as if heaven was raining in,
> Which they seem'd to sustain with their terrible mass
> As if ocean had sunk from beneath them: they pass
> To their graves in the deep with an earthquake of sound,
> And the waves and the thunders made silent around
> Leave the wind to its echo.—p. 174.

At present we say nothing of the cumbrous and uncouth style of these verses, nor do we ask who this 'she' is, who sees the water-spouts; but the funeral of the water-spouts is curious enough: 'They pass to their graves with an earthquake of sound.' The sound of an earthquake is intelligible, and we suspect that this is what Mr. Shelley meant to say: but an earthquake of sound is as difficult to comprehend as a cannon of sound, or a fiddle of sound. The same vision presents us with a battle between a tiger and a sea-snake; of course we have—

> ———The whirl and the splash
> As of some hideous engine, whose brazen teeth smash
> The thin winds and soft waves into thunder; the screams
> And hissings crawl fast o'er the smooth ocean streams,
> Each sound like a centipede.—p. 180.

The comparison of sound to a centipede would be no small addition to a cabinet of poetical monstrosities: but it sinks into tame common-place before the engine, whose brazen teeth pound thin winds and soft waves into thunder.

Sometimes Mr. Shelley's love of the unintelligible yields to his preference for the disgusting and the impious. Thus the bodies of the dead sailors are thrown out of the ship:

> And the sharks and the dog-fish their grave-cloths unbound,
> And were glutted, like Jews, with this manna rained down
> From God on their wilderness.—p. 177.

Asia turns her soul into an enchanted boat, in which she performs a wonderful voyage:

> My soul is an enchanted boat,
> Which, like a sleeping swan, doth float
> Upon the silver waves of thy sweet singing:
> And thine doth like an angel sit
> Beside the helm conducting it,
> Whilst all the winds with melody are ringing.
> It seems to float ever, for ever,
> Upon that many-winding river,
> Between mountains, woods, abysses,
> A paradise of wildernesses!
> Till, like one in slumber bound,
> Borne to the ocean, I float down, around,
> Into a sea profound, of ever-spreading sound:
> Meanwhile thy spirit lifts its pinions

In music's most serene dominions;
Catching the winds that fan the happy heaven.
And we sail on, away, afar,
Without a course, without a star,
By the instinct of sweet music driven;
Till through Elysian garden islets
By thee, most beautiful of pilots,
Where never mortal pinnace glided,
The boat of my desire is guided.—p. 94.

The following comparison of a poet to a cameleon has no more meaning than the jingling of the bells of a fool's cap, and far less music.

Poets are on this cold earth,
As camelions might be,
Hidden from their early birth
In a cave beneath the sea;
Where light is camelions change:
Where love is not, poets do:
Fame is love disguised; if few
Find either never think it strange
That poets range.—p. 186.

Sometimes to the charms of nonsense those of doggerel are added. This is the conclusion of a song of certain beings, who are called 'Spirits of the human mind:'

And Earth, Air, and Light,
And the Spirit of Might,
Which drives round the stars in their fiery flight;
And Love, Thought, and Breath,
The powers that quell Death,
Wherever we soar shall assemble beneath.
And our singing shall build
In the void's loose field
A world for the Spirit of Wisdom to wield;
We will take our plan
From the new world of man,
And our work shall be called the Promethean.—p. 130.

Another characteristic trait of Mr. Shelley's poetry is, that in his descriptions he never describes the thing directly, but transfers it to the properties of something which he conceives to resemble it by language which is to be taken partly in a metaphorical meaning, and partly in no meaning at all. The whole of a long poem, in three parts, called 'The Sensitive Plant,' the object of which we cannot discover, is an instance of this. The first part is devoted to the description of the plants. The sensitive plant takes the lead:

> No flower ever trembled and panted with bliss,
> In the garden, the field, or the wilderness,
> Like a doe in the noon-tide with love's sweet want,
> As the companionless sensitive plant.—p. 157.

Next come the snow-drop and the violet:

> And their breath was mixed with fresh odour, sent
> From the turf, *like the voice and the instrument.*

The rose, too,

> ———Unveiled the depth of her glowing breast,
> Till, fold after fold, *to the fainting air*
> *The soul of her beauty and love lay bare.*

The hyacinth is described in terms still more quaint and affected:

> The hyacinth, purple, and white, and blue;
> Which flung from *its bells a sweet peal anew,*
> Of music so delicate, soft, and intense,
> It was felt like an odour within the sense.

It is worth while to observe the train of thought in this stanza. The bells of the flower occur to the poet's mind; but ought not bells to ring a peal? Accordingly, by a metamorphosis of the odour, the bells of the hyacinth are supposed to do so: the fragrance of the flower is first converted into a peal of music, and then the peal of music is in the last line transformed back into an odour. These are the tricks of a mere poetical harlequin, amusing himself with

> The clock-work tintinnabulum of rhyme.

In short, it is not too much to affirm, that in the whole volume there is not one original image of nature, one simple expression of human feeling, or one new association of the appearances of the moral with those of the material world.

As Mr. Shelley disdains to draw his materials from nature, it is not wonderful that his subjects should in general be widely remote from every thing that is level with the comprehension, or interesting to the heart of man. He has been pleased to call *Prometheus Unbound* a lyrical drama, though it has neither action nor dramatic dialogue. The subject of it is the transition of Prometheus from a state of suffering to a state of happiness; together with a corresponding change in the situation of mankind. But no distinct account is given of either of these states, nor of the means by which Prometheus and the world pass from the one to the other. The Prometheus of Mr. Shelley is not the Prometheus of ancient mythology. He is a being who is neither a God nor a man, who has conferred supreme power on Jupiter. Jupiter torments him; and Demogorgon, by annihilating Jupiter's power, restores him to happiness. Asia, Panthea, and Ione, are female beings of a nature similar to that of Prometheus. Apollo, Mercury, the Furies, and a faun, make their appearance; but have not much to do in the piece. To fill up the *personae dramatis*, we have voices of the mountains, voices of the air, voices of the springs, voices of the whirlwinds, together with several echoes. Then come spirits without end: spirits of the moon, spirits of the earth, spirits of the human mind, spirits of the hours; who all attest their super-human nature by singing and saying things which no human being can comprehend. We do not find fault with this poem, because it is built on notions which no longer possess any influence over the mind, but because its basis and its materials are mere dreaming, shadowy, incoherent abstractions. It would have been quite as absurd and extravagant in the time of Æschylus, as it is now.

It may seem strange that such a volume should find readers, and still more strange that it should meet with admirers. We are ourselves surprized by the phenomenon: nothing similar to it occurred to us, till we recollected the numerous congregations which the incoherencies of an itinerant Methodist preacher attract. These preachers, without any connected train of thought, and without attempting to reason, or to attach any definite meaning to the terms which they use, pour out a deluge of sonorous words that relate to sacred objects and devout feelings. These words, connected as they are with all that is most venerable in the eyes of man, excite a multitude of pious associations in the hearer, and produce in him a species of mental intoxication. His feelings are awakened, and his heart touched, while his imagination and understanding are bewildered; and he receives temporary pleasure, sometimes even temporary improvement, at the expense of the essential and even permanent depravation of his character. In the same way, poetry like that of Mr. Shelley presents every where glittering constellations of words, which taken separately have a meaning, and either communicate some activity to the imagination, or dazzle it by their brilliance. Many of them relate to beautiful or interesting objects, and are therefore capable of imparting pleasure to us by the associations attached to them. The reader is conscious that his mind is raised from a state of stagnation, and he is willing to believe, that he is astounded and be-wildered, not by the absurdity, but by the originality and sublimity of the author.

It appears to us much more surprizing, that any man of education should write such poetry as that of *Prometheus Unbound*, than, that when written, it should find admirers. It is easy to read without atten-tion; but it is difficult to conceive how an author, unless his intellectual habits are thoroughly depraved, should not take the trouble to observe whether his imagination has definite forms before it, or is gazing in stupid wonder on assemblages of brilliant words. Mr. Shelley tells us, that he imitates the Greek tragic poets: can he be so blinded by self-love, as not to be aware that his productions have not one feature of likeness to what have been deemed classical works, in any country or in any age? He, no doubt, possesses considerable mental activity; for without industry he could never have attained to so much facility in the art of throwing words into fantastical combinations: is it not strange that he should never have turned his attention from his verses to that which his verses are meant to express? We fear that his notions of poetry are fundamentally erroneous. It seems to be his maxim, that reason and sound thinking are aliens in the dominions of the Muses, and that, should they ever be found wandering about the foot of Parnassus, they ought to be chased away as spies sent to discover the nakedness of the land. We would wish to persuade him, if possible, that the poet is distinguished from the rest of his species, not by wanting what other men have, but by having what other men want. The reason of the poet ought to be cultivated with as much care as that of the philosopher, though the former chooses a peculiar field for its exercise, and associates with it in its labours other faculties that are not called forth in the mere investigation of truth.

But it is often said, that though the poems are bad, they at least show poetical power. Poetical power can be shown only by writing good poetry, and this Mr. Shelley has not yet done. The proofs of Mr. Shel-ley's genius, which his admirers allege, are the very exaggeration, copiousness of verbiage, and incoherence of ideas which we complain of as intolerable. They argue in criticism, as those men do in morals, who think debauchery and dissipation an excellent proof of a good heart. The want of meaning is called sublimity, absurdity becomes venerable under the name of originality, the jumble of metaphor is the richness of imagination, and even the rough, clumsy, confused structure of the style, with not unfrequent violations of the rules of grammar, is, forsooth, the sign and effect of a bold overflowing genius, that disdains to walk in common trammels. If the poet is one who whirls round his reader's brain, till it becomes dizzy and confused; if it is his office to envelop he knows not what in huge folds of a clumsy drapery of splendid words and showy metaphors, then, without doubt, may Mr. Shelley place the Delphic laurel on his head. But take away from him the unintelligible, the confused, the incoherent, the bombastic, the affected, the extravagant, the hideously gorgeous, and *Prometheus*, and the poems which accompany it, will sink at once into nothing.

But great as are Mr. Shelley's sins against sense and taste, would that we had nothing more to complain of! Unfortunately, to his long list of demerits he has added the most flagrant offences against morality and religion. We should abstain from quoting instances, were it not that we think his language too gross and too disgusting to be dangerous to any but those who are corrupted beyond the hope of amendment. After a revolting description of the death of our Saviour, introduced merely for the sake of intimating, that *the religion he preached is the great source of human misery and vice*, he adds,

—Thy name I will not speak,
It hath become a curse.

Will Mr. Shelley, to excuse this blasphemy against the name '*in which all the nations of the earth shall be made blessed*,' pretend, that these are the words of Prometheus, not of the poet? But the poet himself hath told us, that his Prometheus is meant to be 'the type of the highest perfection of moral and intellectual excellence.' There are other passages, in which Mr. Shelley speaks directly in his own person. In what he calls an *Ode to Liberty*, he tells us that she did

—groan, not weep,
When from its sea of death to kill and burn
The Galilean serpent forth did creep
And made thy world an undistinguishable heap.—p. 213.

And after a few stanzas he adds,

O, that the free would stamp the impious name
Of****** into the dust! or write it there,
So that this blot upon the page of fame
Were as a serpent's path, which the light air

Erases, and that the flat sands close behind!
  Ye the oracle have heard:
  Lift the victory-flashing sword,
And cut the snaky knots of this foul Gordian word,
  Which weak itself as stubble, yet can bind
  Into a mass, irrefragably firm,
  The axes and the rods which awe mankind;
  The sound has poison in it, 'tis the sperm
Of what makes life foul, cankerous, and abhorred;
  Disdain not thou, at thine appointed term,
  To set thine armed heel on this reluctant worm.
O, that the wise from their bright minds would kindle
  Such lamps within the dome of this dim world,
That the pale name of PRIEST might shrink and dwindle
  Into the hell from which it first was hurled,
A scoff of impious pride from fiends impure;
  Till human thoughts might kneel alone
  Each before the judgement-throne
Of its own awless soul, or of the power unknown!—p. 218.

At present we say nothing of the harshness of style and incongruity of metaphor, which these verses exhibit. We do not even ask what is or can be meant by *the kneeling of human thought before the judgment-throne of its own awless soul*: for it is a praiseworthy precaution in an author, to temper irreligion and sedition with nonsense, so that he may avail himself, if need be, of the plea of lunacy before the tribunals of his country. All that we now condemn, is the wanton gratuitous impiety thus obtruded on the world. If any one, after a serious investigation of the truth of Christianity, still doubts or disbelieves, he is to be pitied and pardoned; if he is a good man, he will himself lament that he has not come to a different conclusion; for even the enemies of our faith admit, that it is precious for the restraints which it imposes on human vices, and for the consolations which it furnishes under the evils of life. But what is to be said of a man, who, like Mr. Shelley, wantonly and unnecessarily goes out of his way, not to reason against, but to revile Christianity and its author? Let him adduce his arguments against our religion, and we shall tell him where to find them answered: but let him not presume to insult the world, and to profane the language in which he writes, by rhyming invectives against a faith of which he knows nothing but the name.

The real cause of his aversion to Christianity is easily discovered. Christianity is the great prop of the social order of the civilized world;

this social order is the object of Mr. Shelley's hatred; and, therefore, the pillar must be demolished, that the building may tumble down. His views of the nature of men and of society are expressed, we dare not say explained, in some of those '*beautiful idealisms of moral excellence,*' (we use his own words,) in which the *Prometheus* abounds.

The painted veil, by those who were, called life, which mimicked, as with colours idly spread, all men believed and hoped, is torn aside; the loathsome mask has fallen, the man remains sceptreless, free, uncircumscribed, but man equal, unclassed, tribeless, and nationless, exempt from awe, worship, degree, the king over himself; just, gentle, wise: but man passionless; no, yet free from guilt or pain, which were for his will made or suffered them, nor yet exempt, tho' ruling them like slaves, from chance and death, and mutability, the clogs of that which else might oversoar the loftiest star of unascended heaven, pinnacled dim in the intense inane.—p. 120.

Our readers may be puzzled to find out the meaning of this paragraph; we must, therefore, inform them that it is not prose, but the conclusion of the third act of *Prometheus* verbatim et literatim. With this information they will cease to wonder at the absence of sense and grammar; and will probably perceive, that Mr. Shelley's poetry is, in sober sadness, *drivelling prose run mad.*

With the prophetic voice of a misgiving conscience, Mr. Shelley objects to criticism. 'If my attempt be ineffectual, (he says) let the punishment of an unaccomplished purpose have been sufficient; let none trouble themselves to heap the dust of oblivion upon my efforts.' Is there no respect due to common sense, to sound taste, to morality, to religion? Are evil spirits to be allowed to work mischief with impunity, because, forsooth, the instruments with which they work are contemptible? Mr. Shelley says, that his intentions are pure. Pure! They be so in his vocabulary; for, (to say nothing of his having unfortunately mistaken nonsense for poetry, and blasphemy for an imperious duty,) vice and irreligion, and the subversion of society are, according to his system, pure and holy things; Christianity, and moral virtue, and social order, are alone impure. But we care not about his intentions, or by what epithet he may choose to characterize them, so long as his works exhale contagious mischief. On his own principles he must admit, that, in exposing to the public what we believe to be the character and tendency of his writings, we discharge a sacred duty. He professes to write in order to reform the world. The essence of the proposed reformation is the destruction of religion and government. Such a reformation is not to our taste; and he must, therefore, applaud us for scrutinizing the merits of works which are intended to promote so detestable a purpose. Of Mr. Shelley himself we know nothing, and desire to know nothing. Be his private qualities what they may, his poems (and it is only with his poems that we have any concern) are at war with reason, with taste, with virtue, in short, with all that dignifies man, or that man reveres.

55. Henry Crabb Robinson, diary entry

December 28, 1821

From *Henry Crabb Robinson on Books and their Writers*, ed. Morley (1938), i, p. 279.

DEC. 28th. . . . In the evening reading at home. I began Shelley's *Prometheus*, which I could not get on with. I was quickened in my purpose of throwing it aside by the *Quarterly Review*, which exposes the want of meaning in his poems with considerable effect. It is good to be now and then withheld from reading bad books. Shelley's polemical hatred of Christianity is as unpoetical as it is irrational. He says in an address to Liberty:

> What if the tears rained through thy shattered locks
> Were quickly dried? For thou didst groan, not weep,
> When from its sea of death to kill and burn
> The Galilean Serpent forth did creep,
> And made thy world an undistinguishable heap.

This is part of an ode in which he traces the history of the world as regarding Liberty. He afterwards exclaims:

> Oh that the free would stamp the impious name
> Of **** into the dust, etc.
> Disdain not thou, at thy appointed term,
> To set thine armed heel on this reluctant worm.

The *Quarterly Review* unfairly puts six instead of four stars. However, the context shows that Christ was meant. This is miserable rant, and would be so were it as true as it is false. I shall send Shelley back to Godwin unread. Godwin himself is unable to read his works.

56. Henry Crabb Robinson, diary entries

March 2 and 31, 1828

From *Henry Crabb Robinson on Books and their Writers*, ed. Morley, (1938), i, p. 279.

MARCH 2nd. . . . I read the second act of *Prometheus*, which raised my opinion very high of Shelley as a poet and improved it in all respects. No man had ever more natural piety than he who was not a fanatic, and his supposed atheism is a mere metaphysical crotchet in which he was kept by the affected scorn and real malignity of dunces. . . .

MARCH 31st. . . . Finished also to-day Shelley's *Prometheus*—an utterly unintelligible rhapsody, but all the smaller poems of the same volume are delightful. . . .

57. James Russell Lowell, extract from review of *The Life and Letters of James Gates Percival*, *North American Review*

1866

Percival, a mediocre poet, was second only in popularity to Bryant. This edition permitted Lowell to discuss provincialism in America, one of his favorite themes. Printed in *The Literary Criticism of James Russell Lowell*, ed. Herbert Smith (1969), p. 139.

In *Prometheus* it is Shelley who is paramount for the time, and Shelley at his worst period, before his unwieldy abundance of incoherent words and images, that were merely words and images without any meaning of real experience to give them solidity, had been compressed in the stricter moulds of thought and study.

58. Extract from unsigned 'Portraits of the Metropolitan Poets, No. III, Mr. Percy Byshe [*sic*] Shelley,' in *The Honeycomb*

ix, Saturday, August 12, 1820, 65–72

Man is a gregarious animal, else we should have been at a loss to discover for what possible reason Mr. Shelley could have enrolled himself under the banners of Mr. Leigh Hunt. It must surely have been merely for the benefit of company—protection he could not afford him! and the author of *The Revolt of Islam* should not stoop to require it from the hands of the writer of 'Rimini.' Mr. Shelley is far above his compeers, and he seems only to have associated his name with theirs from personal motives, and not from the consciousness of any poetical approximation. Except on account of some of the principles which he professes, we should never have classed Mr. Shelley with Leigh Hunt, or even with Barry Cornwall, as in power and extent of intellect, richness of imagination, and skill in numbers, he is far their superior. It is only as forming one of the phalanx which we have before described that this poet can be accounted a member of the Metropolitan School. If he cannot be said to be a native soldier, he is yet a very redoubted ally, and from the plains of Italy he trumpets forth the praises of his Sovereign. There is a vignette in Bewick's *Beasts*, representing two horses in a field kindly scratching one another, by mutually nibbling with their teeth at each other's main [*sic*]. There cannot be a more faithful picture than this of the friendship which exists between Mr. Shelley and Leigh Hunt,

> . . . Friends, how fast sworn,
> Whose double bosoms seem to wear one heart.

Mr. Shelley dedicates his Tragedy to Mr. Leigh Hunt, assuring the public that he is the most amiable character in the world, and Mr. Leigh Hunt in his *Examiner* compares Mr. Shelley to an Apostle, while the *Quarterly* in a mysterious note would make us believe that the latter person more nearly resembles a fallen Angel. But with the personal characters of these gentlemen we have nothing in the world to do; when the pen becomes the instrument of private scandal, and when such an employment of it meets with encouragement from the public, it bespeaks a vitiated state of the public taste. There are indeed some publications which have stooped to pander to this low passion, and which, by the genius and talents wasted in such evil purposes, have rendered their degradation still more conspicuous. To attacks from adversaries like these a wise man will always be insensible, and it did not shew any very high-minded forbearance in Mr. Leigh Hunt when he noticed the personal attacks which were made upon him, in what is said to be a popular periodical work. The venom of a slanderer's tongue must recoil upon himself; and that infamy which he would heap upon his victim's head will be doubled upon his own.—But we wander—

The public do not look with favour on combinations like these; and we question very much whether they do not come within the purview of the statutes which declare all combinations among journeymen illegal. The only difference is, that the journeymen manufacturers conspire to raise the price of their *work*, and the journeymen poets to raise the price of their *works*. There is always something suspicious in this herding together; an appearance of want of confidence in the integrity of a man's own powers; a sort of attempt to carry public opinion by storm and force of numbers, which raises a prejudice in the public mind. When one poet pours forth praises of another, we can in general judge of the coin in which he expects to be repaid.

But while the bards of the metropolis have been securing sweet words from each other's mouths, they have contrived, but with strangely different success, to extort some laudatory articles from some of the reviews. It is we believe well known to whom Mr. Leigh Hunt is indebted for the favourable notice of 'Rimini' in the *Edinburgh*. On the *Quarterly* none of these authors have yet made any impression. Mr. Gifford and his coadjutors have poured out the vial of wrath with undistinguishing bitterness on the whole company of them. As an advocate of freedom, and a new system of things, Mr. Shelley has merited their severest vengeance; and the 'Endymion' of poor Keats almost withered in their grasp. The mode in which *Blackwood's*

SHELLEY

Magazine deals with our little knot of poets is, however, the most
curious. With Leigh Hunt they are sworn foes, and we conclude must
ever continue, so, while Barry Cornwall has elicited praises from them
that might make him write 'under the ribs of death.' Mr. Shelley too,
and this is odd enough, has been favoured with sundry high commendations, though we do not believe that his real poetical merits
have been the cause of them. The principles which he professes, and the
views of things which he takes, so contrary to the principles, if they
may so be called, which distinguished that magazine, would be fully
sufficient to counter-balance in the minds of the persons who contribute
to that work, the harping of an Angel's Lyre. There is therefore undoubtedly some secret machinery of which we are not aware, some
friend behind the scenes, or some working of personal interest, which
thus induces that magazine for once to throw aside the trammels of
party prejudice, and to do justice to a man who even advocates the
French Revolution. It would be a curious thing if the public could be
made acquainted with the history of every review, and see the hidden
springs of affection or hatred by which the pen of the impartial critic
was moved. The empiricism of patent medicines is nothing to this
quackery.

Now let us proceed to examine Mr. Shelley's merits a little more
particularly. While Mr. Leigh Hunt has met at the hands of the public
about as much encouragement as he deserves, or perhaps too much,
and Barry Cornwall has gained certainly a greater reputation than he
is entitled to, we think Mr. Shelley has never been duly appreciated.
This neglect, for it almost amounts to that, is, however, entirely owing
to himself. He writes in a spirit which people do not comprehend:
there is something too mystical in what he says—something too high or
too deep for common comprehensions. He lives in a very remote
poetical world, and his feelings will scarcely bear to be shadowed out
in earthly light. There are, no doubt, in the mind of a poet, and they
evidently exist in the mind of Mr. Shelley, shades of thought, which it
is impossible to delineate, and feelings which cannot be clearly expressed;when, therefore, he attempts to clothe these ideas with words,
tho' he may himself perceive the force of them, it will very frequently
happen that his readers will not, or that such words at most will only
convey a very imperfect idea of the high meanings which the
writer attached to them. This is no fault peculiar to Mr. Shelley—
the finest geniuses have felt it most, and in reading many passages of
Shakespeare, if we were asked to define the exact meaning of some of

272

the most beautiful parts, we should be unable to do so. Expressions of this kind are very frequent in the works of Mr. Shelley, and his sentiments are sometimes equally obscure. The first poem which he published, *Alastor, or the Spirit of Solitude*, tho' full of fine writing, abounds with these dimly shadowed feelings, and we seem as we read it, as if we were walking through a country where beautiful prospects extend on every side, which are hidden from us by the mists of evening. Mr. Shelley seems to nurse this wildness of imagination, at the expense of clearness and vigour of style. He has extended the same spirit to the whole composition of his longest poem, *The Revolt of Islam*, in which he undertakes to teach every great principle—freedom—patriotism—philanthropy—toleration—under an allegory; or as he expresses it, 'for this purpose I have chosen a story of human passion in its most universal character, diversified with moving and romantic adventures, and appealing, in contempt of all artificial opinions or institutions, to the common sympathies of every human breast.' So well did Mr. Shelley imagine this poem qualified to accomplish the philanthropic object for which it was written, that we have heard, he actually wished that a cheap edition of it should be printed in order that it might be distributed amongst all classes of persons; certainly one of the very wildest of his imaginations. He should have written intelligibly to common understandings if he wished to become popular.

We wished to give such of our readers as have not access to the volume itself, some idea of *The Revolt of Islam*; but this we find it impossible to do, both from the nature of the poem itself and the limits to which we are confined. In versification, we consider this poem to be a very high effort of genius. In fact, Mr. Shelley has new-modelled the Spenserian Stanza, and given it a beauty and power of expression which it did not possess before. He manages his pauses very skillfully, and he has introduced double rhymes with fine effects. Of the truth of these remarks the following stanzas selected from the introductory address will afford a sufficient proof.

TO MARY . . . .
So now my summer-task is ended, Mary,

[quotes stanzas 1–4, 7–9, 14]

It will be instantly perceived that in Mr. Shelley's poetry there are none of the puerilities which disgrace the compositions of the persons with whom he has chosen to confound his name. There is no attempt to attain a simplicity out of nature; no determination like Barry Cornwall's 'to follow the scent of strong-smelling phrases.' He knows that poetry is not composed of the language of common life as Mr. Wordsworth supposes, or its spirit of common feelings,—he knows that the nature of poetry is above the common nature of man, and that in reducing it to that level we are in fact depriving it of all its great characteristics. He knows likewise that one man does not look well in another's clothes, and he refuses, unlike Mr. Barry Cornwall, to wear the cast-off garments of antiquity. In short, Mr. Shelley is essentially, a poet.

There is another feature in the poetical character of Mr. Shelley which favourably distinguishes him from his more imitative and trivial companions—he is an *improving* author. The difference between a superior poet and one of mediocrity consists in the stationary or progressive spirit in which they write. All inferior geniuses and wits display their best efforts at once. They easily find 'the length of their tether,' and like many other ruminating animals we have seen, sport and amble round the prescribed circle with the delighted consciousness of a little freedom and power. It is the case with all secondary poets; and if our readers will turn to Mr. Barry Cornwall's *Dramatic Scenes*, and compare them with his latest production; or to Mr. Leigh Hunt's earliest lucubrations, and his last poetical attempts, they will acknowledge the extraordinary sameness, or even deterioration, which exists between the earliest and most recent writings of these gentlemen. 'Can these dry bones live?' We cannot, however, bring a similar charge against Mr. S.; there is a soul and a fire in his poetical genius which is not so suddenly burnt out. Without that perpetual straining and eagerness to accomplish something great, which characterizes Mr. B. C., in quiet and serene strength of spirit he in truth performs much more. Compared with the dramatic powers of Mr. Shelley, the solitary and mutilated scenes of Mr. B. C. are insignificant indeed. These possess little claim to originality. The subject, the very names and argument, are borrowed. The scene is ready sketched to the hand; a little colour, and a few *most natural* touches, and behold a picture, which Mr. C. may as reasonably claim for his own, as a friseur the head of a poetical coxcomb which he has just dressed. Yet Mr. Shelley ranks as one of this pigmy race. He is not ashamed to pander to the reputation of poets like these. An interchange of fulsome compliments and gross flattery, takes place—their publishers propagate it, and the public is not yet sickened of this 'got up' and ludicrous scene. We will unfold the secret springs of this poetical pantomime, and disclose the managers of the puppet show to view. We promise ourselves no little pleasure, however, in exhibiting it more freely, and exposing it more clearly to the contempt of an injured and insulted public, which we know these authors and publishers ridicule behind the scenes. This system of literary hoaxing was introduced by a convenient and time-serving publication in the North.

59. Lord Byron, from a letter to Richard Belgrave Hoppner

September 10, 1820

George Gordon, Lord Byron (1788–1824): Printed in *Byron: A Self-Portrait*, ed. Peter Quennell (1967), ii, p. 527.

I regret that you have such a bad opinion of Shilah [Shelley]; you used to have a good one. Surely he has talent and honour, but is crazy against religion and morality. His tragedy *The Cenci* is a sad work; but the subject renders it so. His *Islam* has much poetry. You seem lately to have got some notion against him.

60. Unsigned article, 'Critical Remarks on Shelley's Poetry'

The Dublin Magazine or General Repository of Philosophy, Belles Lettres, and Miscellaneous Information, November 1820, i, 393–400

We have been deterred from before noticing Mr. Shelley's poems by the obvious difficulty of the task, and it is not without some feelings of dread that we now approach them. Some credit has, we hope, been given us for the manner in which we have generally spoken of young poets: we have done the little we could to encourage and animate them to exertion. We have ventured to speak of more than one of the number, as if he had already attained that fame, which it is idle to suppose can be won without earnest and continual labour; but if our praises have, at times, been exaggerated, they have always been suggested and justified by circumstances of high promise—by something in the character of the poet or the poem that claimed affectionate sympathy. Young critics, we declined assuming the fastidious tone which characterizes, and renders contemptible, most of the periodical criticism of our day, and which must prevent its becoming valuable even as a register of contemporary opinion. It is, indeed, painful to us to speak otherwise than in the language of encouragement: we know as well as Coleridge the value of literary praise, and agree with him that suppressing one favorable opinion of a work is an act of positive injustice. Now the fact is, we think unfavorably of Mr. Shelley; we think his talents unworthily devoted to evil purposes in his imitations; —and, let him account for the fact as he will, all his poetry is imitative. We see little else than an eloquent use of language, wild and rhapsodical declamation: this very common accomplishment is, no doubt, a valuable one, but while we are listening to this orator, we are often tempted to enquire what is the subject of his discourse. We feel that he has told us nothing, and has nothing to tell us: we would rest the decisions of the question—is Mr. Shelley a poet, on the circumstance that, whatever excitement may be felt during the perusal of his works, not one line of them remains on the ear when we have closed the volume; and of all the gorgeous images with which they are loaded, scarcely one is retained in the memory.

It does not strike us as a task by any means difficult to colour the cold speculations of Godwin with the language of poetry, though we think such subjects would be avoided by a poetical mind. That a state of society may be imagined in which men will be 'kingless, and tribeless, and nationless,' we admit; and even feel that the conception has an imposing and sublime appearance in the same way that the idea of utter desolation is sublime; but we must remember that these notions are put forward by Mr. Shelley, with avowed admiration of the consequences he expects to result from their being applied to the test of experience. Now we must continue to believe that such views are likely to lessen the exercise of the domestic charities; that, when no adequate object is offered to the affections, they will, being left without a support, droop and die in the heart. We believe that man's duty here is something different from comparing phantoms with phantoms: and that whatever his talents, or whatever his professed object may be, no man is justified in giving to the world wild and crude notions, the first effect of which, if reduced to practice, would be the overthrow of all existing institutions, and the substitution of a waste and howling wilderness—the revolutionary Eden, of which the uncontrolled passions of men are to be protecting angels. The facility with which this new philosophy removes the possibility of crime, is one of the most admirable parts of the theory. Murder, as we still call it, is innocent, for it is but diverting a few ounces of blood from their proper channel, and the dead body is soon converted into living beings many times happier than man. Adultery, as Leigh Hunt proved, is founded only on the custom of marriage; and who is there that does not see that we will get rid of it at once by abolishing that odious tyranny. Incest is but a name; we suppose it a crime merely from vulgar prejudices, which, in the new order of things, cannot exist, as when marriage is removed, the degrees of relationship will seldom be strictly ascertained. All those duties, the neglect of which sometimes occasions a little uneasiness to us at present, will no longer be required of a man: prayer is done away with, for we are to live without a God in the world: and repentance is quite idle, for there will be no longer any sin, or if evil is supposed to continue, how can repentance alter the past? and of the future we know nothing. Such is the creed of the enlightened friends of humanity; such are the opinions on man's nature and destiny, which form the groundwork of the *Prometheus Unbound*—the dreams of this enthusiast. . . .

We have spoken of Mr. Shelley's poetry as imitation: this is a severe charge, for it is easily made, idly repeated, and with difficulty repelled: —in writers of the same age a resemblance will, perhaps, necessarily exist; nothing is more common than coincidences of thought and expression between writers in such circumstances as preclude the supposition of imitation: passages of striking similarity are found in Homer and the Hebrew poets; but this is not the kind of resemblance on which we found our accusation, to us Mr. Shelly appears in his poetry, like a man speaking a foreign language, translating his thoughts into a dialect in which he does not think—writing under the inspiration of ambition rather than of genius or feeling. His success, if he finally does succeed, will justify Johnson's definition of poetical genius, which he speaks of as the accidental direction of general talents to that particular pursuit. We write hastily, and are not satisfied that our meaning has been clearly expressed; but in these compositions it seems to us that poetical embellishments are often heavily laid on over conceptions essentially unpoetical, which would not actually have excited them; that in all his poetry he is thinking of some other poet with whom he is mentally comparing himself, that the best passages remind us of better in Wordsworth, or Byron, or Aeschylus, which have, we feel, originated those in Shelly; yet while we write down this opinion, we feel it very probable that his active mind is engaged in compositions that will refute all our decisions—be it so.

[A closing paragraph ends with 'The Cloud' and 'To a Skylark' quoted in full.]

61. Extract from unsigned article, 'On the Philosophy and Poetry of Shelley'

The London Magazine and Theatrical Inquisitor,
February 1821, iii, 122–7

Unhappily the [French] revolution, while it passed, like a mighty inundation of the Nile, from country to country, and gladdened the fair face of nature by its waters, subsided ere the glebe land was yet fattened by the overflow of its healthful springs. It was dammed up by the dykes of bigotry and prejudice, and compelled once again to return to its original channels. But still, though its inundation has ceased, its effect shall be long felt. It has deposited a fruitful spawn upon the earth; which, fostered by the sun of heaven, and invigorated by the cheering breeze of freedom, shall dawn into a glorious maturity. Mirabeau, with the philosophers and patriots of the French school; Byron, Godwin of our own times; and Shelley, the subject of our article, are the spawn of this mighty revolution. The minutiae of their system, perhaps, may be replete with errors, but its abstract abounds in the most beautiful sensibilities of truth and religion. Shelley in particular seems to have a higher notion of the capability of human nature than any poet or philosopher of his day. He has seen, as from a distance, the glorious truths of divinity, but his mind has not yet embraced the whole. 'A bold inquirer,' as he himself terms Milton, 'into morals and religion,' he has come armed 'as a hero of yore' to the contest, and divested himself of the dense clouds of prejudice that overhang the mass of mankind, and thicken the natural obtuseness of their intellect. The ground-work of his system is of the purest that can be possibly conceived, and well worthy of that Deity from whom it originally emanated. 'Love,' says Mr. Shelley in the preface to his *Revolt of Islam*, 'is the sole tie that should govern the moral world'; and though the idea is somewhat too Utopian, the basis on which it rests is divine. It is possible, however, that axioms of this nature may tend to shock the sensitive feelings of nine-tenths of the community, who are accustomed to groan over their mental disquietude, while they dread the application of the axe to the root of their disease. It is possible that they may be appalled at the convenient latitude of the word 'Love'; and not finding it in the weekly sermons of their spiritual pastors and masters, may shrewdly exclaim, 'I cannot find it—'tis not in the bond.' But let such people consider, that the great and infinitely wise Deity who endowed man with intellect, and bade him look up to heaven, gave him that intellect, not as a gift that was to be hid like the talent in the earth, until reclaimed by the donor, but as a largess, that was to be actively and beneficially employed; and can intellect be better employed, than when applied to the purposes of religion; in separating the dross from the gold, and rendering the metal pure and unadulterated? Such are the leading principles of Mr. Shelley. In endeavoring to restore religion to its primitive purity, and to render it the voluntary incense of love and brotherly communion, he is performing an acceptable service to the Deity, and a benefit to society at large. It is not with religion that he bickers, but with the adulterations that have so long disgraced it. He has discovered that 'there's something rotten in the state of Denmark,' and applied his utmost ingenuity to remedy the defect. He has ascertained that religion, in the common acceptance of the term, has been made a stalking-horse for the purposes of Mammon, and has become the most intolerant of all creeds. The 'beautiful idealisms of moral excellence,' that once shed grace and splendour on the annals of sacred history, have been blotted with the tears of martyrs. The vengeance of the bigot has been let loose on society; religion, like the timid hare, has been chased to and fro; and a loud pack of evangelical alarmists have been let loose upon her haunches, and she has been fairly torn in pieces.

In differing from the religious opinions of society, Mr. Shelley is only sustaining a more elevated tone of feeling, and applying himself to the fountain-head of devotion, instead of stopping to slake his thirst at the numerous streamlets that wander by the way-side. He has not bewildered himself in the folio controversies of Warburton and Lowth; or versed his mind in the learned disputes of Travis, Porson, and Co. about the credit of the three witnesses; or puzzled himself with the sage Jesuits of old, as to the startling fact of ten thousand angels dancing on the point of a needle, without jostling each other; but he has consulted his own heart; he has 'held converse' with his own reason; and instead of arriving at the truth by a circumbendibus, has reached it by a straight-forward direction. His principal feeling respecting religion appears to consist in the sentiment of benevolence toward mankind, that strikes home to the heart as an immediate emanation of the Deity. His mind revolts at intolerance and bigotry; and he believes in his devotional creed as one that deserves love as well as admiration. His moral and political principles all spring from the same source, and are founded on the same dignified contempt for bigotry and the 'sway of tyranny.'

> Oh that the free would stamp the impious name
>   Of King into the dust! or write it there,
> So that this blot upon the page of fame
>   Were as a serpent's path, which the light air
> Erases, and the flat sands close behind!
>   Ye the oracle have heard.
>   Lift the victory-flashing sword,
> And cut the snaky knots of this foul gordian word,
>   Which, weak itself as stubble, yet can bind
>   Into a mass, irrefragably firm,
>   The axes and the rods which awe mankind;
>   The sound has poison in it, 'tis the sperm
> Of what makes life foul, cankerous, and abhorred;
>   Disdain not thou, at thine appointed term,
>   To set thine armed heel on this reluctant worm.

If these are opinions carried to an extravagant excess, they are at least the excesses of a devotional mind and a generous disposition. They are the excesses of an enthusiastic spirit, soaring above the trammels of superstition, relying on its own capabilities, and asserting the rights of man as a thinking and independent being.

In his dramatic poem of *Prometheus Unbound* Mr. Shelley has given us, in the portraiture of the noble-minded victim, a most 'beautiful idealism of moral excellence.' He has drawn us Virtue, not as she is, but as she should be,—magnanimous in affliction, and impatient of unauthorized tyranny. Prometheus, the friend and the champion of mankind, may be considered as a type of religion oppressed by the united powers of superstition and tyranny. He is for a time enchained, though not enfeebled, by the pressure of his misfortunes, but is finally triumphant; and by the manful exertions of his own lawful claims frees himself from his ignominious thraldom; and proves the truth of that axiom which is engraved in undying characters on the 'fair front of nature'—that right shall always overcome might. This is the leading principle in Mr. Shelley; in its more trifling bearings it is occasionally inconsistent, but exhibits a noble illustration of the intuitive powers and virtues of the human mind. This is the system that he is anxious to disseminate, and a more sublime one was never yet invented. It appeals at once from nature to God, discards the petty bickerings of different creeds and soars upward to the throne of grace as the lark that sings 'at heaven's gate' her matin song of thanksgiving. There may be different opinions respecting matters of taste, feeling, and metaphysics, but there can be but one respecting the holiness of bene-volence, and universal philanthropy. Before this great, this important truth, all minor creeds sink into their native insignificance. It is the ladder by which man mounts to Heaven,—the faith which enables him to hear the voice of the Deity welcoming him as he ascends. . . .

Having advanced thus much on the philosophical opinions of Shelley, it remains to say a few words respecting his poetical qualifications. He is perhaps the most intensely sublime writer of his day, and, with the exception of Wordsworth, is more highly imaginative, than any other living poet. There is an air of earnestness, a tone of deep sincerity in all his productions, that give them an electrical effect. No one can read his *Prometheus Unbound* or the magnificent 'Ode to Liberty' without a sensation of the deepest astonishment at the stupendous mind of their author. The mental visions of philosophy contained in them are the most gorgeous that can be conceived, and expressed in language well suited to the sentiment. They soar with an eagle's flight to the heaven of heavens, and come back laden with the treasures of humanity. But with all the combined attractions of mind and verse, we feel that Mr. Shelley can never become a popular poet. He does not sufficiently link himself with man; he is too visionary for the intellect of the generality of his readers, and is ever immersed in the clouds of religious and metaphysical speculations. His opinions are but skeletons, and he does not sufficiently embody them to render them intelligible. They are magnificent abstractions of mind,—the outpourings of a spirit 'steeped to the very full' in humanity and religious enthusiasm.

In intensity of description, depth of feeling, and richness of language, Mr. Shelley is infinitely superior to Lord Byron. He has less versatility of talent, but a purer and loftier imagination. His poetry is always adapted to the more kindly and sublime sensibilities of human nature, and enkindles in the breast of the reader a corresponding enthusiasm of benevolence. It gives him an added respect for the literature of his country, and warms his whole soul, as he marks in the writings of his contemporaries the progressive march of the human intellect to the very perfection of divinity.

62. Lord Byron, in conversation to P. B. Shelley

August 26, 1821

Shelley reported this conversation to Leigh Hunt, and it is printed in *His Very Self and Voice*, ed. Ernest Lovell (1954), p. 256.

Byron—I suppose from modesty, on account of his being mentioned in it—did not say a word of *Adonais*, though he was loud in his praise of *Prometheus Unbound*, and censures of *The Cenci*.

63. William Hazlitt, from 'On Paradox and Commonplace' in *Table Talk*

1821–2

Printed in *The Complete Works of William Hazlitt*, ed. P. P. Howe (1931), viii, pp. 148–50.

William Hazlitt, essayist and periodical reviewer, knew and wrote about most of the early and mid-nineteenth-century literary figures. Since his politics did not usually agree with those of *The Edinburgh*, the editor Jeffrey usually assigned literary topics to him. Since Jeffrey exercised his editorial power to an unusual degree, the personal characteristics of Hazlitt's style are often missing from his contributions to *The Edinburgh*.

. . . The author of the *Prometheus Unbound* (to take an individual instance of the last character) has a fire in his eye, a fever in his blood, a maggot in his brain, a hectic flutter in his speech, which mark out the philosophic fanatic. He is sanguine-complexioned, and shrill-voiced. As is often observable in the case of religious enthusiasts, there is a slenderness of constitutional *stamina*, which renders the flesh no match for the spirit. His bending, flexible form appears to take no strong hold of things, does not grapple with the world about him, but slides from it like a river—

> And in its liquid texture mortal wound
> Receives no more than can the fluid air.

The shock of accident, the weight of authority make no impression on his opinions, which retire like a feather, or rise from the encounter unhurt, through their own buoyancy. He is clogged by no dull system of realities, no earth-bound feelings, no rooted prejudices, by nothing that belongs to the mighty trunk and hard husk of nature and habit, but is drawn up by irresistible levity to the regions of mere speculation and fancy, to the sphere of air and fire, where his delighted spirit

THE CRITICAL HERITAGE

floats in 'seas of pearl and clouds of amber.' There is no *caput mortuum*[1] of worn-out, thread-bare experience to serve as ballast to his mind; it is all volatile intellectual salt of tartar, that refuses to combine its evanescent, inflammable essence with any thing solid or any thing lasting. Bubbles are to him the only realities:—touch them, and they vanish. Curiosity is the only proper category of his mind, and though a man in knowledge, he is a child in feeling. Hence he puts every thing into a metaphysical crucible to judge of it himself and exhibit it to others as a subject of interesting experiment, without first making it over to the ordeal of his common sense or trying it on his heart. This faculty of speculating at random on all questions may in its over-grown and uninformed state do much mischief without intending it, like an overgrown child with the power of a man. Mr. Shelley has been accused of vanity—I think he is chargeable with extreme levity; but this levity is so great, that I do not believe he is sensible of its consequences. He strives to overturn all established creeds and systems: but this is in him an effect of constitution. He runs before the most ex-travagant opinions, but this is because he is held back by none of the merely mechanical checks of sympathy and habit. He tampers with all sorts of obnoxious subjects, but it is less because he is gratified with the rankness of the taint, than captivated with the intellectual phos-phoric light they emit. It would seem that he wished not so much to convince or inform as to shock the public by the tenor of his produc-tions, but I suspect he is more intent upon startling himself with his electrical experiments in morals and philosophy; and though they may scorch other people, they are to him harmless amusements, the corus-cations of an Aurora Borealis, that 'play round the head, but do not reach the heart.' Still I could wish that he would put a stop to the in-cessant, alarming whirl of his Voltaic battery. With his zeal, his talent, and his fancy, he would do more good and less harm, if he were to give up his wilder theories, and if he took less pleasure in feeling his heart flutter insunison with the panic-struck apprehensions of his readers. Person of this class, instead of consolidating useful and acknowledged truths, and thus advancing the cause of science and virtue, are never easy but in raising doubtful and disagreeable questions, which bring the former into disgrace and discredit. They are not con-tented to lead the minds of men to an eminence overlooking the prospect of social amelioration, unless, by forcing them up slippery paths and to the utmost verge of possibility, they can dash them down

[1] 'Dead head.'

285

the precipice the instant they reach the promised Pisgah. They think it nothing to hang up a beacon to guide or warn, if they do not at the same time frighten the community like a comet. They do not mind making their principles odious, provided they can make themselves notorious. To win over the public opinion by fair means is to them an insipid, common place mode of popularity: they would either force it by harsh methods, or seduce it by intoxicating potions. Egotism, petulance, licentiousness, levity of principle (whatever be the source) is a bad thing in any one, and most of all, in a philosophical reformer. Their humanity, their wisdom is always 'at the horizon.' Any thing new, any thing remote, any thing questionable, comes to them in a shape that is sure of a cordial welcome—a welcome cordial in proportion as the object is new, as it is apparently impracticable, as it is a doubt whether it is at all desirable. Just after the final failure, the completion of the last act of the French Revolution, when the legitimate wits were crying out, 'The farce is over, now let us go to supper,' these provoking reasoners got up a lively hypothesis about introducing the domestic government of the Nayrs into this country as a feasible set-off against the success of the Boroughmongers. The practical is with them always the antipodes of the ideal; and like other visionaries of a different stamp, they date the Millennium or New Order of Things from the Restoration of the Bourbons. Fine words butter no parsnips, says the proverb. 'While you are talking of marrying, I am thinking of hanging,' says Captain Macheath. Of all people the most tormenting are those who bid you hope in the midst of despair, who, by never caring about any thing but their own sanguine, hair-brained Utopian schemes, have at no time any particular cause for embarrassment and despondency because they have never the least chance of success, and who by including whatever does not hit their idle fancy, kings, priests, religion, government, public abuses or private morals, in the same sweeping clause of ban and anathema, do all they can to combine all parties in a common cause against them, and to prevent every one else from advancing one step farther in the career of practical improvement than they do in that of imaginary and unattainable perfection.

64. Notice signed 'J. W.,' *The Champion*

December 23, 1821, no. 468, 815

It is our opinion, that the poetical merits of Mr. Percy Bysshe Shelley have never been duly appreciated by the public. This neglect (for, in reality, it amounts to that) is chiefly to be attributed to himself. He writes in a spirit which the *million* do not comprehend: there is something too mystical in what he says—something too high or too deep for common comprehensions. He lives in a very remote poetical world, and his feelings will scarcely bear to be shadowed out in earthly light. There are, no doubt, in the mind of a poet, and none will be found to deny their existence in the mind of Mr. Shelley, shades of thought which defy the power of delineation, and feelings which it is impossible to lay before the reader in expressions sufficiently lucid; when, therefore, he attempts to clothe these ideas with words, tho he may *himself* perceive the force of them, it will not unfrequently happen, that his readers cannot; or that such words, at most, will only convey a very imperfect and shadowy idea of the lofty meanings which the writer attached to them. This is no fault peculiar to Mr. Shelley— *the finest geniuses have felt it most*; and in reading many passages of Shakespeare, if we were called upon for a definition of the exact meaning of some of his most beautiful sentences, we should be obliged to declare the utter impossibility of doing so. Expressions of this kind not unfrequently occur in the works of Mr. Shelley, and, in our opinion, his sentiments are sometimes equally obscure. The first poem which he published,[1] tho containing many exquisite passages, abounds with these dimly shadowed feelings, and we seem, while perusing it, as if we were walking thro' a country where beautiful prospects extend on every side, which are nearly hidden from us by the mists of evening. Mr. Shelley seems to nurse this wildness of imagination, at the expense of perspicuity and vigour of style. The same spirit appears strikingly manifest in every page of his longest poem,[2] in which he undertakes to teach every great principle—freedom, patriotism, philanthropy, toleration—under an allegory; or, to make use of his

[1] *Alastor; or, the Spirit of Solitude.* (Reviewer's footnote)
[2] *The Revolt of Islam.* (Reviewer's footnote)

287

own words, 'for this purpose I have chosen a story of human passion in its most universal character, diversified with moving and romantic adventures, and appealing, in contempt of all artificial opinions or institutions, to the common sympathies of every human breast.' So fully convinced was Mr. Shelley, that this poem was qualified to accomplish the philanthropic object for which it was written, that he actually wished that a cheap edition of it should be printed, in order that it might be within the reach of all classes of persons; certainly one of the wildest of his imaginations. If he desired popularity, he should have written in a style intelligible to common understandings.

65. 'Seraphina and Her Sister Clementina's Review of Epipsychidion,' *The Gossip*

July 14, 1821, no. 20, pp. 153–9

SIR,

I and my sister Clementina were sitting on the sofa on which we had often sat in days of 'childhood innocence,' and

> like two artificial gods
> Created with our needles both one flower,
> Both on one sampler, sitting on one cushion;
> Both warbling of one song, both in one key;
> As if our hands, our sides, voices, and minds
> Had been incorporate,—

When a gentleman, who had long been an admirer of Clementina, entered with the Seventeenth Number of the *Gossip*.

We were reading Goldsmith's delightful poem of *The Deserted Village*, and had finished that part of it which describes the fond mother who

> Kiss'd her thoughtless babes with many a tear,
> And clasp'd them close, in sorrow doubly dear,

just as the gentleman made his appearance; and at the same instant the tears which were trembling in Clementina's fine blue eyes, being forced by a gentle sigh to quit their sapphire spheres, fell glistening on her bosom. 'What,' exclaimed the gentleman, 'Clementina in tears!' He might well be surprised, for my lively sister is much more inclined to the laughing than the 'melting mood,' though she has a heart susceptible of the finest emotions. I explained to him the cause, and desired him to say something pretty and poetical on the occasion. He immediately pronounced the following impromptu:

> I've seen the tear in beauty's eye,
>   Await the sob suppress'd,
> There, shaken by a trem'lous sigh,
>   Fall on the heaving breast.
> Oh! how I've wished that I might kiss
>   The pearly drop away,
> And give the heart a sweeter bliss,
>   The eye a brighter ray.

Clementina put her fan to his lips, bid him hold his saucy tongue, and let her hear what the *Gossip* had to say, which she was sure would be more entertaining than his nambypamby poetry. He told her it contained extracts from a poem which he believed would excite emotions very different from those produced by the beautiful lines of Goldsmith.

I seized the number, for I am passionately fond of poetry. It contained a review of 'Epipsychidion.' I read the first extract—but did not understand it. 'It is poetry *intoxicated*,' said Clementina. 'It is poetry in *delirium*,' said I. 'It is a new system of poetry,' said the gentleman, 'which may be taught by a few simple rules, and when it is learned it may be written by the league.' 'But in that case,' said Clementina, 'it would be as well to be provided with a pair of seven-league boots.' 'It is the poetical currency of the day,' said the gentleman.

> A plague on him who did refine it,
> A plague on him who first did coin it,

said Clementina, altering a word in Dryden's couplet. But she is a wild creature, as you well know, from the strange letter which she sent you, and in which she accuses me of making dress my *hobby*. She is a great fibber. Poetry is *my* hobby—yes, poetry, 'sweet poetry, dear charming nymph'! But not such poetry as 'Epipsychidion'. 'Bless me!' said Clementina, what a number of adjectives, and how strangely coupled with nouns! Only hear—'Odours deep, odours warm, warm fragrance, wild odour, arrowy odour; golden prime, golden purity, golden immortality; living morning, living light, living cheeks; wintry forest, wintry wilderness; blue Ionian weather, blue nightshade, blue heavens; (good Heavens!) wonder-level dream, tremulous floor, unentangled intermixture, crimson pulse, fiery dews, delicious pain;

green heart, green immortality, withered hours.' 'I have not repeated a hundredth part of them,' said she, quite out of breath. The gentleman observed, 'It is a species of poetry that excites no emotion but that of wonder—we wonder what it means! It lives without the vitality of life; it has animation but no heart; it worships nature but spurns her laws; it sinks without gravity and rises without levity. Its shadows are substances, and its substances are shadows. Its odours may be felt, and its sounds may be penetrated—its frosts have the melting quality of fire, and its fire may be melted by frost. Its animate beings are inanimate things, and its local habitations have no existence. It is a system of poetry made up of adjectives, broken metaphors, and indiscriminate personifications. In this poetry everything must live, and move, and have a being, and they must live and move with intensity of action and passion, though they have their origin and their end in nothing.'

'It is a poetical phantasmagoria,' said Clementina. 'Whatever is possible to our imaginations, or in our dreams,' said the gentleman, 'is possible, probable, and of common occurrence in this new system of poetry. Things may exchange their nature, they may all have a new nature, or have no nature.' 'Then they must be non-naturals,' said Clementina. 'There is a new omnipotence in this poetry,' said the gentleman, 'things may do impossibilities with, or without impossible powers—this is the *ne plus ultra* of poetical omnipotence.'

I read the extract again, with more attention—but, to use the author's phraseology, it was 'too deep for the brief fathom-line of thought or sense.' It appears that there was a Being whom the spirit oft met on its 'visioned wanderings,' which it seemed were 'far aloft.' It met him on fairy isles, and among a great variety of other strange places, 'in the air-like waves of wonder-level dream, whose tremulous floor paved her light steps.' This is, indeed, metaphor run mad. To pave a person's steps is certainly strange; but for the tremulous floor of wonder-level dream to pave them is wondrous strange indeed. 'Steps for path,' said the gentleman, 'is to me a new metonymy, and the tremulous floor of wonder-level dream is either a new pavior or a new pavement.' 'It is *immaterial* be it which it may,' said Clementina. 'Did the malapert mean to *pun*, think you?' But to proceed—the voice of this Being came to him 'through the whispering woods, and from the fountains, and from the *odours* deep of flowers.' 'How can a voice come from the odour of flowers?' asked Clementina, 'can an odour emit, or convey a sound?' 'That is one of the possible impossibilities of the omnipotence of this new poetry,' said the gentleman. 'I do not understand it,' said Clementina. 'Do you understand metaphysics?' said he. 'No,' replied she, 'but

> I know what's what, and that's as high
> As metaphysicist can fly!'

Did you ever know such a giddy creature? I proceeded—this voice came to him from 'the breezes, whether low or loud, and from the rain of every passing cloud.' 'Bless me,' said Clementina, 'he might have said to this voice what Falstaff says to Prince Henry.' 'What is that?' said the gentleman. 'Something about iteration,'[1] said Clementina. The gentleman laughed. I went on—'the voice came from the singing of the summer birds, and from *all* sounds, and from *all* silence!' 'She was the most extraordinary ventriloquist I ever heard of,' said Clementina. I now came to the second extract, and read as follows:

> And every gentle passion sick to death
> *Feeding* my *course* with expectation's breath,
> Into the wintry forest of our lives.

Here I could not help asking how a course, or track, could be fed, and that too with expectation's breath. 'But allowing the incongruous metaphor of feeding a course, how could it be fed into a forest?' 'A man may be fed into a fever,' said Clementina. 'I am inclined to think,' said the gentleman, 'from the pointing of the passage, the meaning of it is, that while he was diverting his course into the wintry forest, he was feeding it with the breath of expectation.' 'Well,' said Clementina, 'you have helped a lame dog over a stile, but he walks as lamely as he did before. Your elucidation of the passage reminds me of La Bruyère's famous French wit, who made it a rule never to be *posed* upon any occasion! and being asked a little abruptly, what was the difference between dryads and hamadryads, answered very readily, "You have heard of your bishops and your archbishops".' 'Dryden,' said I, (wishing to put a stop to my sister's pertness) 'has been ridiculed for writing the following couplet:

> Yet when that flood in its own depths was drowned,
> It left behind its false and slippery ground.

Here, it has been observed, we have a drowned flood; and what is more extraordinary, a flood so excessively deep that it drowned

---

[1] No doubt Clementina's allusion was to Falstaff's saying to Prince Henry, 'Thou hast damnable iteration.' (Reviewer's footnote)

itself. But in my opinion when a flood, which has overflowed lands, is receding into a greater depth, so as to contract its breadth, and surface, it is not a more extravagant figure of speech to say that it has drowned itself in its own depths, and left its false and slippery ground behind, than it is to talk of feeding a man's course with expectation's breath; the metaphors are equally heterogeneous and extravagant.' 'Before we employ any figure,' said the gentleman, 'we should consider what sort of a picture it would make on canvas. How an artist could paint the feeding of a man's course with the breath of expectation, I cannot conceive!' I went on with my reading, and came to one 'Whose voice was venomed melody.' 'Then the creature must have poured poison into the porches of his ears,' said Clementina. I went on— 'Flame out of her looks into my *vitals* came.' 'Flame out of her looks!' exclaimed Clementina. 'Flame might come out of her mouth, or out of her eyes, or out of her nostrils, as I think it did from that shocking creature's, the Dragon of Wantley; but the looks are a mere modality, and he might as well have said that flame came not from her face, but merely from its length, or its breadth. Flame from her looks! they must have been fiery indeed!' I continued—

> And from her living cheeks and bosom flew
> A killing air, which pierced like honey dew
> Into the core of my green heart, and lay
> Upon its leaves.

Here I stopped to ask what he could mean by a *green* heart with leaves. 'Oh, he means the heart of a cabbage, to be sure,' said Clementina. 'But the heart of a cabbage is generally white,' said the gentleman. 'This green heart with leaves would be a bad figure to paint on canvas.' 'It would look like an *hearty*choke,' said Clementina. I now read without interruption till I came to those lines—

> And music from her respiration spread
> Like light,—all other sounds were penetrated
> By the small still spirit of that sound.

Bless me! can a sound be penetrated? And what can the spirit of a sound be? 'That,' said Clementina, 'must be the ghost that is said to have appeared in the sound of a drum.' I laughed at the oddness of the conceit, and read till I came to the following lines:

> I stood, and felt the dawn of my long night,
> Was penetrating me with living light.

'It is darkness becoming visible,' said Clementina. 'How can that be?' 'Why you know,' continued she, 'the dawn of day is *light* becoming visible, consequently, the dawn of night must be darkness becoming visible.' 'But you must observe that this dawn of night was penetrating him with a *living light*.' 'A living light!—that must have been a *glow-worm* creeping among the leaves of his green heart,' said Clementina. I now proceeded to make my way through a crowd of disjointed figures that darkened the subject they were intended to illumine, till I arrived at

> The glory of her being, issuing thence,
> Stains the dead, blank cold air with a warm shade
> Of unentangled intermixture, made
> By love, of life and motion; one intense
> Diffusion, one serene omnipresence,
> Whose flowing outlines mingle in their flowing
> Around her cheeks. . . .

'How can light and motion be so mixed up as to stain the cold night with a warm shade, I do not know,' said Clementina, 'but the flowing *outlines* of omnipresence must be in the circumference of infinite space.' 'The circumference of infinite space,' said the gentleman, 'is nowhere, though its centre is everywhere.' But what is a flowing outline in a centre? 'An eccentric line,' said Clementina. What an eccentric creature! I continued my reading.

> Warm fragrance seems to fall from her light dress—

'Well,' said my sprightly sister, 'her dress must be much lighter and cooler after the warm fragrance has fallen from it—pray proceed.'

> The sweetness seems to satiate the faint wind;
> And in the soul a wild odour is felt
> Beyond the sense.

Here I could not help asking how an odour could be felt. But, allowing the metaphor, what does he mean by its being felt beyond the sense? Does he mean beyond sense of feeling or sense of smelling? 'He means beyond *all* sense,' said Clementina. I asked what was beyond all sense. 'Nonsense, to be sure,' said she. But he does not mean nonsense. 'I don't pretend to know what he means,' said she, 'I am now only speaking of what he writes.' But he says it is felt in the heart, 'like fiery dews that melt in the bosom of the frozen bud.' Now admitting that there may be fire-dew as well as honey-dew, I cannot conceive

how fire can melt it in frost, though I know from experience that frost
will melt in fire. 'Dryden,' said our visitor, 'has produced a similar line
as example of excellent imagining:

> Cherubs dissolv'd in Hallelujahs lie.'

'Well, I have heard of anchovies dissolved in sauce; but never
angels in hallelujahs,' said Clementina. But, putting on a serious look,
she continued, 'when you read such poetry you may say, as the college
lad expressed himself by a happy blunder, "I read six hours a day and
no one is the wiser!"' I acknowledged the justness of her remark,
threw down the number, and retired to my chamber to write this
letter.

St. James's Square

SERAPHINA

66. Unsigned review, *The Literary Chronicle and Weekly Review*

December 1, 1821, no. 133, 751–4

Through the kindness of a friend, we have been favoured with the
latest production of a gentleman of no ordinary genius, Mr. Bysshe
Shelley. It is an elegy on the death of a youthful poet of considerable
promise, Mr. Keats, and was printed at Pisa. As the copy now before
us is, perhaps, the only one that has reached England, and the subject
is one that will excite much interest, we shall print the whole of it.

It has been often said, and Mr. Shelley repeats the assertion, that
Mr. Keats fell a victim to his too great susceptibility of a severe,
criticism on one of his poems. How far this may have been the case we
know not. Cumberland used to say, that authors should not be thin
skinned, but shelled like the rhinoceros; but poor Keats was of too
gentle a disposition for severity, and to a mind of such exquisite

295

sensibility, we do not wonder that he felt keenly the harsh and un-generous attack that was made upon him. Besides, we are not without instances of the effects of criticism on some minds.—Hawkesworth died of criticism: when he published his account of the voyages in the South Seas, for which he received £6000, an innumerable host of enemies attacked it in the newspapers and magazines; some pointed out blunders in matters of science, and some exercised their wit in poetical translations and epigrams. It was, says Dr. Kippis, 'a fatal undertaking, and which, in its consequences, deprived him of presence of mind and of life itself.'

Tasso was driven mad by criticisms; his susceptibility and tenderness of feeling were so great, that when his sublime work, *Jerusalem Delivered*, met with unexpected opposition, the fortitude of the poet was not proof against the keenness of disappointment. He twice attempted to please his ignorant and malignant critics, by recomposing his poem; and, during the hurry, the anguish, and the irritation attend-ing these efforts, the vigour of a great mind was entirely exhausted, and, in two years after the publication of his work, the unhappy bard became an object of pity and of terror.

Even the mild Newton, with all his philosophy, was so sensible to critical remarks, that Whiston tells us he lost his favour, which he had enjoyed for twenty years, for contradicting Newton in his old age; for, says he, no man was of 'a more fearful temper.' Whiston declares that he would never have thought proper to have published his work against Newton's Chronology during the life of the great philosopher, 'because,' says he, 'I knew his temper so well, that I should have ex-pected it would have killed him.'

We have never been among the very enthusiastic admirers of Mr. Keats's poetry, though we allow that he possessed considerable genius; but we are decidedly averse to that species of literary condemnation, which is often practised by men of wit and arrogance, without feeling and without discrimination.

Mr. Shelley is an ardent admirer of Keats; and though he declares his repugnance to the principles of taste on which several of his earlier compositions were modelled, he says that he considers 'the fragment of "Hyperion" as second to nothing that was ever produced by a writer of the same years.' Mr. Shelley, in the preface, gives some details respect-ing the poet:—

[quotes all but the first paragraph of the Preface]

Of the beauty of Mr. Shelley's elegy we shall not speak; to every poetic mind, its transcendant merits must be apparent.

[quotes all of 'Adonais']

67. Unsigned review, *The Literary Gazette and Journal of Belles Lettres*

December 8, 1821, no. 255, 772–3

We have already given some of our columns to this writer's merits, and we will not now repeat our convictions of his incurable absurdity. On the last occasion of our alluding to him, we were compelled to notice his horrid licentiousness and profaneness, his fearful offences to all the maxims that honorable minds are in the habit of respecting, and his plain defiance of Christianity. On the present occasion we are not met by so continued and regular a determination of insult, though there are atrocities to be found in the poem quite enough to make us caution our readers against its pages. 'Adonais' is an elegy after *the manner of Moschus*, on a foolish young man, who, after writing some volumes of very weak, and, in the greater part, of very indecent poetry, died some time since of a consumption: the breaking down of an infirm constitution having, in all probability, been accelerated by the discarding his neck cloth, a practice of the cockney poets, who look upon it as essential to genius, inasmuch as neither Michael Angelo, Raphael or Tasso are supposed to have worn those antispiritual incumbrances. In short, as the vigour of Sampson lay in his hair, the secret of talent with these persons lies in the neck; and what aspirations can be expected from a mind enveloped in muslin. Keats caught cold in training for a genius, and, after a lingering illness, died, to the great loss of the Independents of South America, whom he had intended to visit with an English epic poem, for the purpose of exciting them to liberty. But death, even the death of the radically presumptuous profligate, is a serious thing; and as we believe that Keats was made presumptuous chiefly by the treacherous puffing of his cockney fellow gossips, and profligate in his poems merely to make them saleable, we regret that he did not live long enough to acquire common sense, and abjure the pestilent and perfidious gang who betrayed his weakness to the grave, and are now panegyrising his memory into contempt. For what is the praise of cockneys but disgrace, or what honourable inscription can be placed over the dead by the hands of notorious libellers, exiled adulterers, and avowed atheists.

'Adonais, an Elegy,' is the form in which Mr. Shelley puts forth his woes. We give a verse at random, premising that there is no story in the elegy, and that it consists of fifty-five stanzas, which are, to our seeming, altogether unconnected, interjectional, and nonsensical. We give one that we think among the more comprehensible. An address to Urania:—

> Most musical of mourners, weep anew!
> Not all to that bright station dared to climb;
> And *happier they their happiness who knew,*
> Whose *tapers yet burn thro' that night of time*
> *In which suns perish'd;* Others more sublime,
> Struck by the *envious* wroth of man or GOD!!
> *Have sunk extinct in their refulgent prime;*
> And some yet live, &c.———

Now what is the meaning of this, or of any sentence of it, except indeed that horrid blasphemy which attributes crime to the Great Author of all virtue! The rest is mere empty absurdity. If it were worth our while to dilate on the folly of the production, we might find examples of every species of the ridiculous within those few pages.

Mr. Shelley summons all kinds of visions round the grave of this young man, who, if he has now any feeling of the earth, must shrink with shame and disgust from the touch of the hand that could have written that impious sentence. These he classifies under names, the greater number as new we believe to poetry as strange to common sense. Those are—

> ———Desires and *Adorations*
> Winged *Persuasions* and veiled Destinies,
> *Splendours,* and *Glooms,* and glimmering *Incarnations*
> Of hopes and fears and twilight Phantasies,
> And Sorrow with her family of *Sighs,*
> And Pleasure, *blind with tears!* led by the *gleam*
> Of her own *dying* SMILE instead of eyes!!

Let our readers try to imagine these weepers, and close with '*blind Pleasure led*,' by what? 'by the *light* of *her own dying smile*—instead of *eyes*!!!'

We give some specimens of Mr. S.'s

Nonsense—pastoral.
Lost Echo sits amid the *voiceless mountains*,[1]
    And feeds her grief with his remember'd lay,
    And will no more reply to winds and fountains.
        Nonsense—physical.
—for whose disdain she (Echo) pin'd away
Into a *shadow of all sounds!*
        Nonsense—vermicular.
Flowers springing from the corpse
————————————————illumine death
And *mock* the *merry* worm that wakes beneath.
        Nonsense—pathetic.
Alas! that all we lov'd of him should be
    But for our grief, as if it had not been,
And *grief itself be mortal!* WOE IS ME!
        Nonsense—nondescript.
    In the death chamber for a moment Death,
Blush'd to annihilation!
        Nonsense—personal.
A pardlike spirit, beautiful and swift—
    A love in *desolation mask'd;* —a Power
Girt *round with weakness;*—it can scarce *uplift*
    The *weight* of the *superincumbent hour!*

We have some idea that this fragment of character is intended for Mr. Shelley himself. It closes with a passage of memorable and ferocious blasphemy:—

————————————He with a sudden hand
Made bare his branded and ensanguin'd brow,
Which was like Cain's or CHRIST's!!!

What can be said to the wretched person capable of this daring profanation. The name of the first murderer—the accurst of God—brought into the same aspect image with that of the Saviour of the World! We are scarcely satisfied that even to quote such passages may not be criminal. The subject is too repulsive for us to proceed even in

[1] Though there is *no Echo* and the mountains are *voiceless*, the woodmen, nevertheless, in the last line of this verse hear 'a drear murmur between their Songs!!' (Reviewer's footnote)

expressing our disgust for the general folly that makes the Poem as miserable in point of authorship, as in point of principle. We know that among a certain class this outrage and this inanity meet with some attempt at palliation, under the idea that frenzy holds the pen. That any man who insults the common order of society, and denies the being of God, is essentially mad we never doubted. But for the madness, that retains enough of rationality to be wilfully mischievous, we can have no more lenity than for the appetites of a wild beast. The poetry of the work is *contemptible*—a mere collection of bloated words heaped on each other without order, harmony, or meaning; the refuse of a schoolboy's common-place book, full of the vulgarisms of pastoral poetry, yellow gems and blue stars, bright Phoebus and rosy-fingered Aurora; and of this stuff is Keats's wretched Elegy compiled.

We might add instances of like incomprehensible folly from every stanza. A heart *keeping*, a mute *sleep*, and death *feeding* on a mute *voice*, occur in one verse (page 8); Spring in despair 'throws down her *kindling* buds as if she Autumn were,' a thing we never knew Autumn do with buds of any sort, the kindling kind being unknown to our botany; a *green lizard* is like an *unimprisoned flame*, *waking* out of its *trance* (page 13). In the same page the *leprous corpse* touched by the tender spirit of Spring, so as to exhale itself in flowers, is compared to '*incarnations of the stars, when splendour is changed to fragrance!!!*' Urania (page 15) *wounds* the 'invisible palms' of her tender feet by treading on human hearts as she journeys to see the corpse. Page 22, somebody is asked to 'clasp with panting soul the pendulous earth,' an image which, we take it, exceeds that of Shakespeare, to 'put a girdle about it in forty minutes.'

It is so far a fortunate thing that this piece of impious and utter absurdity can have little circulation in Britain. The copy in our hands is one of some score sent to the Author's intimates from Pisa, where it has been printed in a quarto form 'with the types of Didot,' and two learned Epigraphs from Plato and Moschus. Solemn as the subject is, (for in truth we must grieve for the early death of any youth of literary ambition,) it is hardly possible to help laughing at the mock solemnity with which Shelley charges the *Quarterly Review* for having murdered his friend with—a critique![1] If criticism killed the disciples of that school, Shelley would not have been alive to write an Elegy on another:—but the whole is most farcical from a pen which on other

[1] This would have done excellently for a coroner's inquest like that on *Honey*, which lasted *thirty* days, and was facetiously called 'Honey-moon.' (Reviewer's footnote)

occasions, has treated of the soul, the body, life and death agreeably to the opinions, the principles, and the practice of Percy Bysshe Shelley.—

68. Unsigned review, 'Remarks on Shelley's *Adonais*,' *Blackwood's Edinburgh Magazine*

December 1821, x, 696–700

In his *A Bibliography of Articles in Blackwood's Magazine* (*1817–1825*) (1959), Alan Strout attributes this review to George Croly.

Between thirty and forty years ago, the *Della Crusca* school was in great force. It poured out monthly, weekly, and daily, the whole fulness of its raptures and sorrows in verse, worthy of any 'person of quality.' It revelled in moonlight, and sighed with evening gales, lamented over plucked roses, and bid melodious farewells to the 'last butterfly of the season.' The taste prevailed for a time; the more rational part of the public, always a minority, laughed, and were silent; the million were in raptures. The reign of 'sympathy' was come again,—poetry, innocent poetry, had at length found out its true language. Milton and Dryden, Pope and the whole ancestry of the English Muse, had strayed far from nature. They were a formal and stiff-skirted generation, and their fame was past and forever. The trumpet of the morning paper, in which those 'inventions rich' were first promulgated, found an echo in the more obscure fabrications of the day, and milliners' maids and city apprentices pined over the mutual melancholies of *Arley* and *Matilda*. At length the obtrusiveness of this tuneful nonsense grew insupportable; a man of a vigorous judgment shook off his indolence, and commenced the long series of his services to British literature, by sweeping away, at a brush of his pen, the whole light-winged, humming, and loving population. But in this world folly is immortal; one generation of absurdity swept away, another succeeds to its glories and its fate. The *Della Crusca* school has visited us again, but with some slight change of localities. Its verses now transpire at one time from the retreats of Cockney dalliance in the London suburbs; sometimes they visit us by fragments from Venice, and sometimes invade us by wainloads from Pisa. In point of subject and execution, there is but slight difference; both schools are 'smitten with nature, and nature's love,' run riot in the intrigues of anemones, daisies, and buttercups, and rave to the 'rivulets *proud*, and the deep *blushing* stars.' Of the individuals in both establishments, we are not quite qualified to speak, from the peculiarity of their private habits; but poor Mrs. Robinson and her correspondents are foully belied, if their moral habits were not to the full as pure as those of the Godwinian colony, that play 'the Bacchanal beside the Tuscan sea.' But we must do the defunct *Della Crusca* the justice to say, that they kept their private irregularities to themselves, and sought for no reprobate popularity, by raising the banner to all the vicious of the community. They talked nonsense without measure, were simple down to the lowest degree of silliness, and 'babbled of green fields' enough to make men sick of summer, but they were not daring enough to boast of impurity; there was no pestilent hatred of everything generous, true, and honourable; no desperate licentiousness in their romance; no daring and fiend-like insult to feeling, moral ties, and Christian principle. They were foolish and profligate, but they did not deliver themselves, with the steady devotedness of an insensate and black ambition, to the ruin of society.

We have now to speak of Mr. P. B. Shelley and his poem. Here we must again advert to the *Della Crusca*. One of the characteristics of those childish persons was, the restless interest which they summoned the public to take in every thing belonging to their own triviality. If Mrs. Robinson's dog had a bad night's repose, it was duly announced to the world; Mr. Merry's accident in paring his nails solicited a similar sympathy; the falling off of Mrs. R.'s patch, at the last ball, or the stains on Mr. M.'s full-dress coat, from the dropping of a chandelier, came before the earth, with praise-worthy promptitude. All within their enchanted ring was perfection; but there the circle of light and darkness was drawn, and all beyond was delivered over to the empire of Dullness and Demogorgon. The New School are here the imitators of those original arbiters of human fame.

The present story is thus:—A Mr. John Keats, a young man who had left a decent calling for the melancholy trade of Cockney-poetry, has lately died of a consumption, after having written two or three little books of verses, much neglected by the public. His vanity was probably wrung not less than his purse; for he had it upon the authority of the Cockney Homers and Virgils, that he might become a light to their region at a future time. But all this is not necessary to help a consumption to the death of a poor sedentary man, with an unhealthy aspect, and a mind harassed by the first troubles of verse-making. The New School, however, will have it that he was slaughtered by a criticism of the *Quarterly Review*.—'O flesh, how art thou fishified!'— There is even an aggravation in this cruelty of the *Review*—for it had taken three or four years to slay its victim, the deadly blow having been inflicted at least as long since. We are not now to defend a publication so well able to defend itself. But the fact is, that the *Quarterly* finding before it a work at once silly and presumptuous, full of the servile *slang* that Cockaigne dictates to its servitors, and the vulgar indecorums which that Grub Street Empire rejoiceth to applaud, told the truth of the volume, and recommended a change of manners and of masters to the scribbler. Keats wrote on; but he wrote *indecently*, probably in the indulgence of his social propensities. He selected from Boccaccio, and, at the feet of the Italian Priapus, supplicated for fame and farthings.

Both halves the winds dispersed in empty air.

Mr. P. B. Shelley having been the person appointed by the *Pisan* triumvirate to canonize the name of this apprentice, 'nipt in the bud,' as he fondly tells us, has accordingly produced an Elegy, in which he weeps 'after the manner of Moschus for Bion.' The canonizer is worthy of the saint.—'*Et tu, Vitula!*'—Locke says, that the most resolute liar cannot lie more than once in every three sentences. Folly is more engrossing; for we could prove, from the present Elegy, that it is possible to write two sentences of pure nonsense out of every three. A more faithful calculation would bring us to ninety-nine out of every hundred, or,—as the present consists of only fifty-five stanzas,— leaving about five readable lines in the entire. It thus commences:—

[quotes 'Adonais,' lines 1–9]

Now, of this unintelligible stuff the whole fifty-five stanzas are composed. Here an hour—a *dead* hour too—is to say that Mr. Keats died *along with it!* yet this hour has the heavy business on its hands of mourning the loss of its *fellow-defunct*, and of rousing all its *obscure compeers* to be taught its *own sorrow*, &c. Mr. Shelley and his tribe have been panegyrized in their turn for power of language; and the man of *Tabletalk* swears by all the gods he owns, that he has a great command of words, to which the most eloquent effusions of the Fives Court are *occasionally* inferior. But any man may have the command of every word in the vocabulary, if he will fling them like pebbles from a sack; and even in the most fortuitous flinging, they will sometimes fall in pleasing though useless forms. The art of the modern *Della Cruscan* is thus to eject every epithet that he can conglomerate in his piracy through the Lexicon, and throw them out to settle as they will. He follows his own rhymes, and shapes his subject to the close of his measure. He is a glutton of all names of colours, and flowers, and smells, and tastes, and crowds his verse with scarlet, and blue, and yellow, and green; extracts tears from every thing, and makes moss and mud hold regular conversations with him. 'A goosepye talks,'— it does more, it thinks, and has its peculiar sensibilities,—it smiles and weeps, raves to the stars, and is a listener to the western wind, as fond as the author himself.

On these principles, a hundred or a hundred thousand verses might be made, equal to the best in Adonais, without taking the pen off the paper. The subject is indifferent to us, let it be the 'Golden age,' or 'Mother Goose,'—'Waterloo,' or the 'Wit of the Watchhouse,'—'Tom Thumb,' or 'Thistlewood.' We will undertake to furnish the requisite supply of blue and crimson daisies and dandelions, not with the toilsome and tardy lutulence of the puling master of verbiage in question, but with a burst and torrent that will sweep away all his weedy trophies. For example—*Wotner*, the city marshal, a very decent person, who campaigns it once a year, from the Mansion-house to Blackfriars bridge, truncheoned and uniformed as becomes a man of his military habits, had the misfortune to fracture his leg on the last Lord Mayor's day. The subject is among the most unpromising. We will undertake it, however, (premising, that we have no idea of turning the accident of this respectable man into any degree of ridicule).

O Weep for Adonais, &c.

> O weep for *Wontner*, for his leg is broke,
> O weep for Wontner, though our pearly tear
> Can never cure him. Dark and dimly broke
> The thunder cloud o'er Paul's enamel sphere,
> When his black barb, with lion-like career,
> Scatter'd the crowd.—Coquetting Mignonet,

Thou Hyacinth fond, thou Myrtle without fear,
Haughty Geranium, in your beaupots set,
Were then your soft and starry eyes unwet?
The pigeons saw it, and on silver wings
Hung in white flutterings, for they could not fly,
Hoar-headed Thames checked all his crystal springs,
Day closed above his pale, imperial eye,
The silken Zephyrs breathed a vermeil sigh.
High Heavens! ye Hours! and thou Ura-ni-a!
Where were ye then! Reclining languidly
Upon some green Isle in the empurpled Sea
Where laurel-wreathen sprites love eternally.

Come to my arms, &c.

We had intended to call attention by *italics* to the *picturesque* of these lines; but we leave their beauties to be ascertained by individual perspicacity; only requesting their marked admiration of the epithets *coquetting*, *fond*, *fearless*, and *haughty*, which all tastes will feel to have so immediate and inimitable an application to mignonet, hyacinths, myrtles, and geraniums. But *Percy Bysshe* has figured as a sentimentalist before, and we can quote largely without putting him to the blush by praise. What follows illustrates his power over the language of passion. In *The Cenci*, Beatrice is condemned to die for parricide,—a situation that, in a true poet, might awaken a noble succession of distressful thought. The mingling of remorse, natural affection, woman's horror at murder, and alternate melancholy and fear at the prospect of the grave, in Percy Bysshe works up only this frigid rant:—

How comes this hair undone?
Its wandering strings must be what blind me so.
And yet I *tied it f-ast!!*

. . . .

The sunshine on the floor is *black!* The air
Is changed to vapours such as the dead breathe
In charnel pits! Poh! I am choak'd! There creeps
A clinging, black, contaminating mist
About me,—'tis substantial, heavy, thick.
I cannot pluck it from me, for it glues
My fingers and my limbs to one another,
And eats into my sinews, and dissolve
My flesh to a pollution.

So much for the history of 'Glue'—and so much easier it is to rake together the vulgar vocabulary of rottenness and reptilism, than to paint the workings of the mind. This raving is such as perhaps no excess of madness ever raved, except in the imagination of a Cockney, determined to be as mad as possible, and opulent in his recollections of the shambles.

In the same play, we have a specimen of his 'art of description.' He tells of a ravine—

> And in its depths there is a mighty Rock,
> Which has, from unimaginable years,
> Sustain'd itself with *terror and with toil!*
> Over a gulph, and with the *agony*
> *With which it clings*, seems slowly coursing down;
> Even as a wretched soul, hour after hour,
> Clings to the mass of life, yet clinging *leans*,
> And leaning, makes *more dark* the dread abyss
> In which it fears to fall. Beneath this crag,
> *Huge as despair*, as if *in weariness*,
> The *melancholy* mountain *yawns* below.

And all this is done by a rock—What is to be thought of the *terror* of this novel sufferer—its *toil*—the *agony* with which so sensitive a personage clings to its paternal support, and from *unimaginable* years? The magnitude of this *melancholy* and injured monster is happily measured by its being the *exact size of despair*! Soul becomes substantial, and *darkens a dread abyss*. Such are Cockney darings before 'the Gods, and columns' that abhor mediocrity. And is it to this dreamy nonsense that is to be attached the name of poetry? Yet on these two passages the whole lauding of his fellow-Cockneys has been lavished. But *Percy Byshe* feels his hopelessness of poetic reputation, and therefore lifts himself on the stilts of blasphemy. He is the only verseman of the day, who has dared, in a Christian country, to work out for himself the character of direct ATHEISM! In his present poem, he talks with impious folly of 'the *envious* wrath of man or God'! Of a

> Branded and ensanguined brow,
> Which was like *Cain's* or CHRIST'S.

Offences like these naturally come before a more effective tribunal than that of criticism. We have heard it mentioned as the only apology for the predominant irreligion and nonsense of this person's works, that his understanding is unsettled. But in his Preface, there is none of the exuberance of insanity; there is a great deal of folly, and a great deal of bitterness, but nothing of the wildness of his poetic fustian. The Bombastes Furioso of these stanzas cools into sneering in the preface; and his language against the *death-dealing Quarterly Review*, which has made such havoc in the Empire of Cockaigne, is merely malignant, mean, and peevishly personal. We give a few stanzas of his performance, taken as they occur.

[quotes lines 19–27]

The seasons and a whole host of personages, ideal and otherwise, come to lament over *Adonais*. They act in the following manner:

> Grief made the young spring *wild*, and she threw down
> Her kindling buds, as if the Autumn were
> Or they dead leaves; since her delight is flown,
> For whom should she have wak'd the sullen year?
> To Phoebus was not Hyacinth so dear,
> Nor to himself Narcissus, as to both,
> Thou, Adonais; wan they stand, and sere,
> Amid the drooping comrades of their youth,
> With dew all turn'd to tears, odour to sighing ruth.

Here is left, to those whom it may concern, the pleasant perplexity, whether the lament for Mr. J. Keats is shared between Phoebus and Narcissus, or Summer and Autumn. It is useless to quote these absurdities any farther *en masse*, but there are flowers of poesy thickly spread through the work, which we rescue for the sake of any future Essayist on the Bathos.

> *Absurdity*
> The green lizard, and the golden snake,
> Like *unimprison'd* flowers out of their
>   trance awake. An hour—

>   Say, with me
> Died Adonais, *till the Future dares*
> *Forget the Past*—his fate and fame shall be
>   An *echo* and a *light* to all eternity.

> Whose tapers yet burn through the night of Time
> In which *Sun perish'd!*

>   Echo,—pined away
> Into a *shadow* of all *sounds!*

That mouth whence it was wont to draw the breath
Which gave it strength to pierce the guarded wit!

       Comfortless!
As *silent* lightning leaves the starless night.

Live thou whose *infamy* is not thy *fame!*

Thou *noteless* blot on a remembered name!

We in mad trance *strike with our spirit's* knife,
Invulnerable nothings!

       Where lofty thought
Lifts a young heart above its mortal lair,
And love, and life, contend in it—for what
Shall be its earthly doom—The dead live there,
And move, like *winds of light*, on dark and stormy air.

Who mourns for Adonais—oh! come forth,
Fond wretch! and know thyself and him aright,
Clasp with thy *panting* soul the *pendulous Earth!*

       Dart thy spirit's light
Beyond all worlds, until its *spacious might*
Satiate the *void circumference!*

       Then sink
Even to a point within our day and night,
And keep thy heart *light*, lest it make *thee sink*,
When *hope has kindled hope*, and *lured thee to the* brink.

A light is past from *the revolving year*;
And man and woman, and what still is dear
Attracts to crush, repels to make thee wither.

That benediction, which th' *eclipsing curse*
Of birth can quench not, that sustaining love,
Which, through *the web of being blindly wove*,
By man, and beast, and earth, and air, and sea!
Burns bright or dim, as each are mirrors of
The *fire* for which all *thirst*.

Death makes, as becomes him, a great figure in this 'Lament,'—but in rather curious operations. He is alternately a person, a thing, nothing, &c.

       He is, 'The coming bulk of Death,'
       Then 'Death feeds on the *mute voice*.'
           A clear sprite

Reigns over Death—
                    Kingly Death
Keeps his pale court.
                    Spreads apace
The *shadow* of *white* Death.
                    The damp Death
Quench'd its caress—
                    Death
Blush'd to annihilation!
                    Her distress
Roused Death. Death rose and smiled—
He lives, he wakes, 'tis Death is *dead!*

As this wild waste of words is altogether beyond our comprehension,
we will proceed to the more gratifying office of giving a whole, unbroken specimen of the Poet's powers, exercised on a subject rather
more within their sphere. The following poem has been sent to us as
written by Percy Bysshe, and we think it contains all the essence of his
odiferous, colorific, and daisy-enamoured style. The motto is from
Adonais.

Elegy on My Tom Cat.

And others came.—Desires and Adorations,
Wing'd Persuasions, and veil'd Destinies,
Splendours, and Glooms, and glimmering Incantations
Of hopes and fears, and twilight Phantasies;
And Sorrow, with her family of Sighs;
And Pleasure, *blind* with tears, led by the *gleam*
Of her own *dying smile instead of eyes!*

ELEGY.

Weep for my Tomcat! all ye Tabbies weep,
    For he is gone at last! Not dead alone,
In flowery beauty sleepeth he no sleep;
    Like that bewitching youth Endymion!
My love is dead, alas, as any stone,
    That by some violet-sided smiling river
Weepeth too fondly! He is dead and gone,
    And fair Aurora, o'er her young believer,
With fingers gloved with roses, doth make moan,
And every bud its petal green doth sever,
    And Phoebus sets in night for ever, and for ever!
And others come! ye Splendours! and ye Beauties!

Ye Raptures! with your robes of pearl and blue;
Ye blushing Wonders! with your scarlet shoe-ties;
  Ye horrors bold! with breasts of lily hue;
Ye Hope's stern flatterers! He would trust to you,
  Whene'er he saw you with your chesnut hair,
Dropping sad daffodils; and rosepinks true!
  Ye Passions proud! with lips of bright despair;
Ye Sympathies! with eyes like evening star,
When on the flowing east she rolls her crimson car.

Oh, bard-like spirit! beautiful and swift!
  Sweet lover of pale night; when Luna's lamp
Shakes sapphire dew-drops through a cloudy rift;
  Purple as woman's mouth, o'er ocean damp;
Thy quivering rose-tipped tongue—thy stealing tramp;
  The dazzling glory of thy gold-tinged tail;
Thy whisker-waving lips, as o'er the swamp
  Rises the meteor, when the year doth fail,
Like beauty in decay, all, all are flat and stale.

This poem strikes us as evidence of the improvement that an appropriate subject makes in a writer's style. It is incomparably less nonsensical, verbose, and inflated, than 'Adonais'; while it retains all its knowledge of nature, vigour of colouring, and felicity of language. 'Adonais' has been published by the author in Italy, the fitting soil for the poem, sent over to his honoured correspondents throughout the realm of Cockaigne, with a delightful mysteriousness worthy of the dignity of the subject and the writer.

69. Leigh Hunt, 'Letters to the Readers of the Examiner, No. 6—On Mr. Shelley's New Poem, Entitled *Adonais*'

The Examiner, July 7, 1822, no. 754, 419–21

Since I left London, Mr. Shelley's 'Adonais, or Elegy on the Death of Mr. Keats,' has, I find, made its appearance. I have not seen the London edition; but I have an Italian one printed at Pisa, with which I must content myself at present. The other was to have had notes. It is not a poem calculated to be popular, any more than the *Prometheus Unbound*; it is of too abstract and subtle a nature for that purpose; but it will delight the few, to whom Mr. Shelley is accustomed to address himself. Spenser would be pleased with it if he were living. A mere town reader and a *Quarterly* Reviewer will find it *caviare*. 'Adonais,' in short, is such an elegy as poet might be expected to write upon poet. The author has had before him his recollections of 'Lycidas,' of Moschus and Bion, and of the doctrines of Plato; and in the stanza of the most poetical of poets, Spenser, has brought his own genius, in all its etherial beauty, to lead a pomp of Loves, Graces, and Intelligences, in honour of the departed.

Nor is the Elegy to be considered less sincere, because it is full of poetical abstractions. Dr. Johnson would have us believe, that 'Lycidas' is not 'the effusion of real passion.'—'Passion, says he, in his usual conclusive tone, (as if the force of critic could no further go) 'plucks no berries from the myrtle and ivy; nor calls upon Arethuse and Mincius, nor tells of rough Satyrs and Fauns with cloven heel. Where there is leisure for fiction, there is little grief.' This is only a more genteel common-place, brought in to put down a vulgar one. Dr. Johnson, like most critics, had no imagination; and because he found nothing natural to his own impulses in the associations of poetry, and saw them so often abused by the practice of versifiers inferior to himself, he was willing to conclude, that on natural occasions they were always improper. But a poet's world is as real to him as the more palpable one to people in general. He spends his time in it as truly as Dr. Johnson did his in Fleet-street or at the club. Milton felt that the happiest hours he had passed with his friend had been passed in the regions of poetry. He had been accustomed to be transported with him 'beyond the visible diurnal sphere' of his fire-side and supper-table, things which he could record nevertheless with a due relish. (See the *Epitaphium Domonis*.) The next step was to fancy himself again among them, missing the dear companion of his walks; and then it is that the rivers murmur complainingly, and the flowers hang their heads,—which to a truly poetical habit of mind, though to no other, they may literally be said to do, because such is the aspect which they present to an afflicted imagination. 'I see nothing in the world but melancholy,' is a common phrase with persons who are suffering under a great loss. With ordinary minds in this condition the phrase implies a vague feeling, but still an actual one. The poet, as in other instances, gives it a life and particularity. The practice has doubtless been abused; so much so, that even some imaginative minds may find it difficult at first to fall in with it, however beautifully managed. But the very abuse shews that it is founded in a principle in nature. And a great deal depends upon the character of the poet. What is mere frigidity and affectation in common magazine rhymers, or men of wit and fashion about town, becomes another thing in minds accustomed to live in the sphere I spoke of. It was as unreasonable in Dr. Johnson to sneer at Milton's grief in 'Lycidas,' as it was reasonable in him to laugh at Prior and Congreve for comparing Chloe to Venus and Diana, and pastoralizing about Queen Mary. Neither the turn of their genius, nor their habits of life, included this sort of ground. We feel that Prior should have stuck to his tuckers and boddices, and Congreve appeared in his proper Court mourning.

Milton perhaps overdid the matter a little when he personified the poetical enjoyments of his friend and himself under the character of actual shepherds. Mr. Shelley is the more natural in this respect, inasmuch as he is entirely abstract and imaginative, and recalls his lamented acquaintance to mind in no other shape than one strictly poetical. I say acquaintance, because such Mr. Keats was; and it happens, singularly enough, that the few hours which he and Mr. Shelley passed together were almost entirely of a poetical character. I recollect one evening in particular, which they spent with the writer of these letters in composing verses on a given subject. But it is not as a mere acquaintance, however poetical, that Mr. Shelley records him. It is as the intimate acquaintance of all lovely and lofty thoughts, as the nursling of the

Muse, the hope of her coming days, the creator of additional Beauties and Intelligences for the adornment and inhabitation of the material world. The poet commences with calling upon Urania to weep for her favourite; and in a most beautiful stanza, the termination of which is in the depths of the human heart, informs us where he is lying. You are aware that Mr. Keats died at Rome:—

> To that high Capital, where kingly Death
> Keeps his pale court in beauty and decay,
> He came;—and bought, with price of purest breath,
> A grave among the eternal—Come away!
> Haste, while the vault of blue Italian day
> Is yet his fitting charnel-roof! while still
> He lies, as if in dewy sleep he lay;
> Awake him not! surely he takes his fill
> Of deep and liquid rest, forgetful of all ill.

'The forms of things unseen,' which Mr. Keats's imagination had turned into shape,—the 'airy nothings' to which it is the high prerogative of the poet to give 'a local habitation and a name,' are then represented, in a most fanciful manner, as crowding about his lips and body, and lamenting him who called them into being:

[quotes lines 109–17]

A phrase in the first line of the following passage would make an admirable motto for that part of the *Literary Pocket Book*, in which the usual lists of kings and other passing dominations are superseded by a list of Eminent Men:

> And he is gathered to *the kings of thought*,
> Who waged contention with their time's decay,
> And of the past are all that cannot pass away.

The spot in which Mr. Keats lies buried is thus finely pointed out. The two similes at the close are among the happiest we recollect, especially the second:

[quotes lines 433–41]

> And gray walls moulder round, on which dull Time
> Feeds, like slow fire upon a hoary brand.

In the course of the poem some living writers are introduced; among whom Lord Byron is designated as

> The Pilgrim of Eternity, whose fame
> Over his living head like Heaven is bent
> An early but enduring monument!

The poet of Ireland is called, with equal brevity and felicity,

> The sweetest lyrist of her saddest wrong:

And among 'others of less note,' is modestly put one, the description of whom is strikingly calculated to excite a mixture of sympathy and admiration. The use of the Pagan mythology is supposed to have been worn out; but in fact, they who say so, or are supposed to have worn it out, never wore it at all. See to what a natural and noble purpose a true scholar can turn it:—

[quotes lines 274–88]

> Ah! te meae si partem animae rapit
> Maturior vis![1]

But the poet is here, I trust, as little of a prophet, as affection and a beautiful climate, and the extraordinary and most vital energy of his spirit, can make him. The singular termination of this description, and the useful reflections it is calculated to excite, I shall reserve for another subject in my next. But how is it, that even that termination could not tempt the malignant common-place of the *Quarterly* Reviewers to become blind to the obvious beauty of this poem, and venture upon laying some of its noble stanzas before their readers? How is it that in their late specimens of Mr. Shelley's powers they said nothing of the style and versification of the majestic tragedy of *The Cenci*, which would have been equally intelligible to the lowest, and instructive to the highest, of their readers? How is it that they have not even hinted at the existence of this 'Elegy on the Death of Mr. Keats,' though immediately after the arrival of copies of it from Italy they thought proper to give a pretended review of a poem which appeared to them the least calculated for their readers' understandings? And finally, how happens it, that Mr. Gifford has never taken any notice of Mr. Keats's *last* publication,—the beautiful volume containing *Lamia*, the Story from Boccaccio, and that magnificent fragment *Hyperion*? Perhaps the following passage of the Elegy will explain:

[quotes lines 316–33]

1 'Ah! If a more timely force snatches you, a part of myself, away.'

This, one would think, would not have been 'unintelligible' to the dullest *Quarterly* peruser, who had read the review of Mr. Keats's *Endymion*. Nor would the following perhaps have been quite obscure:

[quotes lines 334-42]

However, if further explanation had been wanted, the Preface to the Elegy furnishes it in an abundance, which even the meanest admirers of Mr. Gifford could have no excuse for not understanding. Why then did he not quote this? Why could he not venture, once in his life, to try and look a little fair and handsome; and instead of making all sorts of misrepresentations of his opponents, lay before his readers something of what his opponents say of him? He only ventures to allude, in convulsive fits and starts, and then not by name, to the *Feast of the Poets*. He dares not even allude to Mr. Hazlitt's epistolary dissection of him. And now he, or some worthy coadjutor for him, would pretend that he knows nothing of Mr. Shelley's denouncement of him, but criticises his other works out of pure zeal for religion and morality! Oh these modern 'Scribes, Pharisees, and Hypocrites!' How exactly do they resemble their prototypes of old!

'It may well be said,' observes Mr. Shelley's Preface, 'that these wretched men know not what they do. They scatter their insults and their slanders without heed as to whether the poisoned shaft lights on a heart made callous by many blows, or one, like Keats's, composed of more penetrable stuff. One of their associates is, to my knowledge, a most base and unprincipled calumniator. As to "Endymion," was it a poem, whatever might be its defects, to be treated contemptuously by those who had celebrated with various degrees of complacency and panegyric, "Paris," and "Woman," and a "Syrian Tale," and Mrs. Lefanu, and Mr. Barrett, and Mr. Howard Payne, and a long list of the illustrious obscure? Are these men, who in their venal good-nature, presumed to draw a parallel between the Rev. Mr. Milman and Lord Byron? What gnat did they strain at here, after having swallowed all those camels? Against what woman taken in adultery, dares the foremost of these literary prostitutes to cast his opprobrious stone? Miserable man! you, one of the meanest, have wantonly defaced one of the noblest specimens of the workmanship of God. Nor shall it be your excuse, that murderer as you are, you have spoken daggers but used none.'

Let us take the taste of the Gifford out of one's mouth with the

SHELLEY

remainder of the Preface, which is like a sweet nut after one with a worm in it.

[quotes the fifth paragraph of Shelley's Preface to *Adonais*]

Amen! Says one who knew the poet, and who knows the painter.

70. Unsigned review, *The General Weekly Register of News, Literature, Law, Politics, and Commerce*

June 30, 1822, no. 13, 501–3

The increase of periodical works cannot be wondered at, considering the multiplicity of new publications that are almost daily issued from the press; the public are nearly sated with the quantity which has been forced upon their attention, and are now satisfied with viewing the generality of works through the medium of reviews. This attaches a good deal of responsibility to the editors of such works, and imposes not only a strict and candid impartiality, but an opinion unbiased either by party, prejudice, or interest. The pledge which we have given to the public, it has been our object to redeem, and we trust our readers have found, so far, that we have kept our promise. Poetry, like states, has been considerably revolutionized, but we fear it has not received much benefit from the change; taste has become subservient to new laws; and public opinion biassed by new principles:—thus a gradual change has been effected, and poetry has assumed a new character. The modern school of poetasters are not satisfied with following the footsteps of the great masters, but by constantly aiming at novelty and originality they become obscure and unintelligible, and by the misapplication of words, and the misconception of ideas, they lead the imagination into a labyrinth of thought from which it is with difficulty disentangled. Whether the revolution which poetry has undergone be for the better, it is not for us to determine, but as admirers of the old school we cannot but lament the change. If harmony, if beauty of expression, if loftiness

316

of idea, and terseness of thought be the constituents of poetry, where can we find them so brilliantly displayed as in Dryden, Pope, Goldsmith, Milton, and the writers of the last century? In offering these opinions, we do not mean to question the genius of some of our present poets, but we could wish to see poetry flowing in its former channels, and instead of being the enchanting vehicle of sensuality, become again the delightful source of all that is truly beautiful and *sublime*.

Mr. Shelley is one of those writers who seems gifted with a strong imagination, and but little judgment; he is often inharmonious and much too obscure and intricate for the generality of his readers. In the volume before us, which he calls a mere *improvise*, we find much to censure and but little to admire; the ideas are neither original nor poetical, the language obscure and frequently unpolished, and although the poem undoubtedly possesses some beauties, yet its defects as certainly predominate. In the first scene Mahmud is discovered sleeping whilst the captive Greek women are chaunting the following wild chorus:

> We strew these opiate flowers
> On thy restless pillow,—
> They were stript from orient bowers,
> By the Indian billow.
> Be thy sleep
> Calm and deep,
> Like theirs who fell, not ours who weep.

Had Mr. Shelley continued in the manner he commenced, our former observations would have been unnecessary and unjust; but the ear is tired by the monotonous repetition of 'keep', 'deep', and 'sleep', and the senses bewildered in a maze of inexplicable thought: *their panting loud and fast at length awakens Mahmud*, who, starting from his sleep, is strangely moved, and enquires of Hassan concerning an old Jew to whom he wishes to relate a dream which 'has thrice hunted him into the troubled day.' Hassan gives him the following absurd description of the Israelite, which, for its extravagancy, can, perhaps, scarcely be equalled:

> The Jew of whom I spoke is old; so old
> He seems to have outlived a world's decay;
> The hoary mountains and the wrinkled ocean
> Seem younger still than he;—his hair and beard
> Are whiter than the tempest-sifted snow;

His cold pale limbs and pulseless arteries
Are like the fibres of a cloud instinct
With light, and to the soul that quickens them
Are as the atoms of the mountain-drift
To the winter-wind;—but from his eye looks forth
A life of unconsumed thought which pierces
The present, and the past, and the to-come.

The *Pre-Adamite* is described as dwelling *in a sea cavern mid the Demonesi less accessible than the Sultan or God himself*; what is the poet's meaning by this passage we are utterly at a loss to conjecture, and what follows is not less extravagant. After this conversation Mahmud and Hassan retire, meanwhile the chorus of Greek women continues; this is so far from lyric poetry that we hardly consider it worthy the name of poetry at all;—*worlds sinking to decay are compared to bubbles bursting on a river;* PORTAL is brought in rhyme with *immortal; Mahomet* with *shall set; spirits are represented as hurrying to and fro thro' the dark chasm of death; brief dust; and the robes cast upon the bare ribs of Death,* are originalities quite beyond our comprehension. The pages which follow are much better, and were Mr. Shelley to confine himself to the dead syllabic verse, he might be more successful; true sublimity consists not in the mere sound of august words, but in brightness and simplicity of idea, and it is this principle upon which the best writers of every age have built their poems. A long dialogue ensues between Mahmud and Hassan in which the former exclaims,

A miserable dawn after a night
More glorious than the day which it usurpt!
O faith in God! O power on earth! O word
Of the great prophet, whose o'ershadowing wings
Darkened the thrones and idols of the West,
Now bright!—For thy sake cursed be the hour,
Even as a father by an evil child,
When the Orient moon of Islam rolled in triumph
From Caucasus to White Ceraunia!
Ruin above, and anarchy below;
Terror without, and treachery within;
The chalice of destruction full, and all
Thirsting to drink; and who among us dares
To dash it from his lips? and where is Hope?

This is certainly good poetry, nor are some of the following pages less poetical. Hassan endeavours to rally the spirits of Mahmud by portraying the strength, power, and invincibility of the Turkish arms, to which Mahmud replies,—

> Proud words, when deeds come short, are seasonable;
> Look, Hassan, on yon crescent moon, emblazoned
> Upon that shattered flag of fiery cloud
> Which leads the rear of the departing day;
> Wan emblem of an empire fading now!
> See how it trembles in the blood-red air,
> And like a mighty lamp whose oil is spent
> Shrinks on the horizon's edge, while, from above,
> One star with insolent and victorious light
> Hovers above its fall, and with keen beams,
> Like arrows thro' a fainting antelope,
> Strikes its weak form to death.

Hassan then relates in strong and not unpoetical terms, the events at Wallachia, and the defeat of the Turkish fleet. This conversation is interrupted by a messenger, who informs them of the departure of the Muscovite ambassador from the city, and the treaty of peace at Stromboul; he is succeeded by a second, who after relating the assault of Thebes and Corinth, and a truce brought from Ypsilanti, gives place to a third, who like the comforters of Job, gives place to a fourth; at length an attendant informs Mahmud that the Jew waits to attend him. The chorus is again resumed in the following extraordinary stanza:

> Of the free—
> I would flee
> A tempestuous herald of victory!
> My golden rain
> For the Grecian slain
> Should mingle in tears with the bloody main,
> And my solemn thunder-knell
> Should ring to the world the passing-bell
> Of Tyranny!

This is the voice of a *winged cloud*, or spirits who are transformed to clouds; see first stanza. Again

> I hear! I hear!
> The crash as of an empire falling,
> The shrieks as of a people calling
> 'Mercy! mercy!'—How they thrill!
> And then a shout of 'kill! kill! kill!'
> And then a small still voice.

Falling and calling certainly rhyme, as do thrill and kill, which in order to make up the line is repeated like fal, lal, lal, in an old ballad to make up the measure; but surely Mr. Shelley does not call this lyric poetry, whose very essence ought to be harmony and easiness of thought.

We are next introduced to Mahmud, and Ahasuerus the old Jew, whose words *stream like a tempest of drizzling mist within the brain of Mahmud, and convulses with wild and wilder thoughts his spirit.* Mahmud is then summoned to a visionary world, and hears the assault of cities, the clash of arms, the blasts of trumpets and other forebodings of the final overthrow of the Turkish empire; he then stretches his eyes and beholds a kingless diadem glittering in the dust, and one of kingly port casting himself beneath the stream of war; ominous signs! After a further disclosure of the *to come*, Ahasuerus conjures up a phantom, which approaching like the ghost of Hamlet, exclaims—

> I come
> Thence whither thou must go! The grave is fitter
> To take the living than give up the dead;
> Yet has thy faith prevailed, and I am here.

To which Mahmud replies,—

> Spirit, woe to all!
> Woe to the wronged and the avenger! Woe
> To the destroyer, woe to the destroyed!
> Woe to the dupe, and woe to the deceiver!
> Woe to the oppressed, and woe to the oppressor!
> Woe both to those that suffer and inflict;
> Those who are born and those who die! But say,
> Imperial shadow of the thing I am,
> When, how, by whom, Destruction must accomplish
> Her consummation?

The imperial shadow tells him to—

> Ask the cold pale Hour,
> Rich in reversion of impending death,
> When *he* shall fall upon whose ripe gray hairs
> Sit care, and sorrow, and infirmity.

The ghost at the sound of voices vanishes, and Mahmud enquiring whether he lives or wakes, after a little hesitation makes his exit. Meanwhile a voice is heard at intervals exulting in the overthrow of the Greeks, which is answered by a chorus and semi-chorus predicting the revival of the Grecian empire; and the poem concludes with a chorus, which as the author observes in notes, is rather indistinct and obscure. We have given 'Hellas' more attention than it deserves, but the former celebrity of the author occasioned us to dwell so minutely upon the work before us, which upon the whole, though not entirely devoid of merit, is but a bad specimen of Mr. Shelley's powers, and but ill calculated to increase the former fame of its author.

71. Leigh Hunt, *The Examiner*

January 20, 1822, no. 770, 35; June 9, 1822, no. 750, 355–7; June 16, 1822, no. 751, 370–1; June 23, 1822, no. 752, 389–90

WE HAVE no objection to the review of Mr. Shelley, as far as it merely opposes his opinions and criticisms the excess of abstraction and consequent mysticism which form their principal and characteristic defect. In the first particular, they regularly labour in their vocation; and it is the quality rather than the purport of their arguments which can be objected to. The same allowance cannot be made for the literary remarks which are composed precisely in the liberal and agreeable style of those which operated so mercilessly on the too sensitive Keats. It is not, however, the selection of a few cloudy or obscure passages that can always form the requiem of a man of genius, and such is Mr. Shelley even by the specimens produced, and allowing the general justice of much of the objection. The conclusion of this critique is mere rant; the intentions of a writer, it seems, are to be regarded for nothing. Upon certain indications, he must be knocked o'-the-head as a matter of course; and for want of real thunder, the *Quarterly Review* will perform the part of *Salmoneus*, and hurl its bombastic bolts with the most impotent self-importance. All this is folly, even upon its own views; the excursiveness of intellect is not to be bounded

by a few hired and bigotted pedants, rancorous in their enmity, but
only affected in their indignation—Who publishes *Cain?*

The article in the *Quarterly* alluded to in my last letter, is a pretended
review of Mr. Shelley's poem, entitled *Prometheus Unbound.* It does
not enter into any discussion of the doctrines contained in that poem.
It does not pretend to refute them. It knows very well that it does not
dare to enter into the merit of Mr. Shelley's propositions, and answer
them as it would answer a treatise by a theological sectarian. And the
reason is obvious. I do not mean to say that all those propositions are
unanswerable; but I say the *Quarterly* Reviewers, by the very nature
of their office, as civil and religious State-hirelings, are not the men to
answer them fairly; and accordingly their criticism has all the malice
of conscious inability to reply, and eagerness to put down. I am very
sincere when I say that I have no knowledge of the writer of the article
in question; but if I were asked to guess who it was, I should say it was
neither Mr. Gifford with all his bitter common-place, nor Mr. Croker
with all his pettifogging, nor Mr. Southey with all his cant; but some
assistant clergyman, who is accustomed to beg the question in the
pulpit, and who thinks that his undertoned breath of malignity will
be mistaken for Christian decorum. What renders this the more probable (though, to be sure, the ordinary readers of the *Quarterly Review*
are as much prepared to take things on trust as if they were sitting in
pews) is, that the critic thinks it sufficient to quote a passage against
priests, in order to have proved its erroneousness. The amount of his
reasoning is this:—Here is a rascal! He wishes there were no such things
as priests! Upon which all the priests and pluralists shake their well-
fed cheeks in a shudder of reprobation, and the poet is confuted.
Observe too a little genuine *Quarterly* touch lurking by the way. The
Reviewer is collecting passages to prove his author's enmity to the
Christian faith,—an enmity, by the bye, which Mr. Shelley always
takes care to confine to the violent consequences of faith as contrasted
with practice, there being in the latter sense no truer Christian than
himself. The poet exclaims—

> O, that the free would stamp the impious name
>   Of **** into the dust! or write it there,
> So that this blot upon the page of fame
>   Were as a serpent's path, which light the air
> Erases, and the flat sands close behind!

These *four* stars, which in fact imply a civil title, and not a religious
word, as the allusion to 'the page of fame' might evince, are silently
turned by the Reviewer into *six* stars, as if implying the name of
Christ:—

> O, that the free would stamp the impious name
> Of****** into the dust.

I fancy some inexperienced reader doubting whether it be possible
even for a *Quarterly* Reviewer to be guilty of such a meanness, and
suggesting that he might have written the stars at random. Alas, my
old friends, he does not know the nature of these people as you and I
do! Doubtless, when the Reviewer wrote his six stars, he was aware
that decent persons, unacquainted with the merits of him and his
subject, would make the same good-natured suggestion, had they
chanced to observe the difference between the original and the quotation. But when we know the misrepresentations which these Reviewers
are in the habit of making, when we know how often their mean arts
have been exercised and exposed, when we know that they have *put
marks of quotation to sentences which are not to be found in the authors they
criticise*, have left out parts of a context to *render the remainder absurd*,
and have *altered words into words of their own* for the same purpose,
nobody will doubt that the writer of the article in question wilfully
put down his six stars instead of four, and deserves (like some others
who wear as many) to have 'the mean heart bared' that 'lurks' beneath
them. Take another description of similar pettiness. The Reviewer,
speaking of one of the most striking passages of the poem, says,
'After a revolting description of the death of our Saviour, introduced
merely for the sake of intimating that the *religion he preached is the great
source of human misery and vice*, Mr. Shelley adds,

> Thy name I will not speak,
> It hath become a curse.

Will Mr. Shelley,' continues the indignant moralist, 'to excuse this
blasphemy against the name *in which all the nations of the earth shall be
made blessed*, pretend that these are the words of Prometheus, not of
the poet?'—No; Mr. Shelley will pretend nothing. He leaves it to
the *Quarterly* Reviewers to pretend, and cant, and commit 'pious
frauds,' in order to make out their case, and act in an unchristian
manner in order to prove their Christianity. It is the critic who pretends
in this case. He pretends that Mr. Shelley has 'added' nothing further;

that he has not explained *how* the name in question has become a curse;—and that he has not 'intimated,' that the religion he preached has been turned against its very essence by those who pretend to preach it in modern times. Who would suppose, from the Reviewer's quotation, that Mr. Shelley, in this very passage, is instancing Christ as a specimen of the fate of benevolent reformers? Yet nothing is more true. Who would suppose, that in this very passage, which they pretend to have quoted entirely, Mr. Shelley puts the consequences which they make him deduce as the only result of the Christian religion, into the mouth of one of the Furies,—not indeed as untrue to a certain extent, but as the only lasting result which she can perceive, and delights to perceive: for in any other sense the whole tenor of Mr. Shelley's poem and speculation is quite the reverse of any such deduction, with reference to what must always *continue* to be. All that he meant in short is this,—that as Christ's benevolence subjected him to the torments he endured, so the uncharitable dogmas produced by those who make a *sine qua non* of the Christian *faith*, have hitherto done more harm than good to mankind; and all the rest of his poem may be said to be occupied in shewing, that it is benevolence, as opposed to faith, which will survive these horrible consequences of its associate, and make more than amends for them. I will quote the whole of the passage in question, that the reader may see what the Reviewer, cunning in his 'sins of omission,' chose to leave out. Besides, it is very grand and full of matter. Prometheus,—(who is a personification of the Benevolent Principle, subjected for a time to the Phantasm Jupiter, or in other words to that False Idea of the great and beneficient First Cause, which men create out of their own follies and tyrannies)—is lying under the infliction of his torments, patient and inflexible, when two of the Ocean Nymphs, who have come to comfort him, hear a terrible groan, and look out to see what has caused it.

[quotes Act I, lines 578–634]

This is a terrible picture, and doubtless exaggerated, if the latter part is to be taken as a picture of all the good as well as ill which the world contains; but the painter uses his sombre colours to cast a corresponding gravity of reflection on people's minds. I will concede to anybody who requires it, that Mr. Shelley, from the excess of his wishes on this point, is too apt to draw descriptions of the state of mankind without sufficient light on his canvas; but in the lesser extent to which they do apply—(and Heaven knows it is wide enough)—let

the reader judge for himself how applicable they are. I will also concede to the *Quarterly* Reviewer, that Mr. Shelley's poetry is often of
too abstract and metaphysical a cast; that it is apt to be too wilful and
gratuitous in its metaphors; and that it would be better if he did not
write metaphysics and polemics in verse, but kept his poetry for more
fitting subjects. But let the reader judge, by this passage out of one
of his poems least calculated to be popular, whether 'all' his poetry is
the nonsense the Reviewer pretends it to be. The Reviewer says that the
above picture of the death of Christ is 'revolting.' The power of exciting pity and terror may perhaps be revolting to the mind of one
who cannot 'go and do so likewise'; but I will tell him what is a great
deal more revolting to the minds of mankind in general, however
priest-ridden or pension-ridden,—the feelings that induced the Reviewer to omit the passage which I have marked.

So much for the charges of nonsense and want of decency. In my
next, I shall have something edifying to shew you in answer to the
charge of nonsense and obscurity, and more assumptions of honesty
and candour on the part of the *Quarterly* critics. Adieu.

As a conclusive proof of Mr. Shelley's nonsense, the Reviewer selects
one of his passages which most require attention, separates it from its
proper context, and turns it into prose: after which he triumphantly
informs the reader that this prose is not prose, but 'the conclusion of
the third act of *Prometheus verbatim et literatim.*'[1] Now poetry has often
a language as well as music of its own, so distinct from prose, and so
universally allowed a right to the distinction (which none are better
aware of than the versifiers in the *Quarterly Review*), that secretly to
decompose a poetical passage into prose, and then call for a criticism
of a reader upon it, is like depriving a body of its distinguishing properties, or confounding their rights and necessities, and then asking where
they are. Again, to take a passage abruptly from its context, especially
when a context is more than usually necessary to its illustration, is like
cutting out a piece of shade from a picture, and reproaching it for
want of light. And finally, to select an obscure passage or two from
an author, or even to shew that he is often obscure, and then to pretend from these specimens, that he is nothing but obscurity and
nonsense, is mere dishonesty.

For instance, Dante is a great genius who is often obscure; but
suppose a critic were to pick out one of his obscurest passages, and

[1] 'Prometheus word for word and letter for letter.'

assert that Dante was a mere writer of jargon. Suppose he were to select one of the metaphysical odes from his *Amoroso Convivio*; or to take a passage from Mr. Cary's translation of his great poem, and turn it into prose for the better mystification of the reader. Here is a specimen:—

Every orb, corporeal, doth proportion its extent unto the virtue through its parts diffused. The greater blessedness preserves the more. The greater is the body (if all parts share equally) the more is to preserve. Therefore the circle, whose swift course enwheels the universal frame, answers to that, which is supreme in knowledge and in love. Thus by the virtue, not the seeming breadth of substance, measuring, thou shalt see the heavens, each to the intelligence that ruleth it, greater to more, and smaller unto less, suited in strict and wondrous harmony. (*Paradise*, Canto 28.)

The lines in question from Mr. Shelley's poem are as follows. A spirit is describing a mighty change that has just taken place on earth. It is the consummation of a state of things for which all the preceding part of the poem has been yearning:—

> The painted veil, by those who were, called life,
> Which mimicked, as with colours idly spread,
> All men believed and hoped, is torn aside;
> The loathsome mask is fallen, the man remains
> Sceptreless, free, uncircumscribed, but man
> Equal, unclassed, tribeless, and nationless,
> Exempt from awe, worship, degree, the king
> Over himself; just, gentle, wise: but man
> Passionless; no, yet free from guilt or pain,
> Which were, for his will made or suffered them;
> Nor yet exempt, tho' ruling them like slaves,
> From chance, and death, and mutability,
> The clogs of that which else might oversoar
> The loftiest star of unascended heaven,
> Pinnacled dim in the intense inane.

That is to say,—The veil, or superficial state of things, which was called life by those who lived before us, and which had nothing but an idle resemblance to that proper state of things, which we would fain have thought it, is no longer existing. The loathsome mask is fallen; and the being who was compelled to wear it, is now what he ought to be, one of a great family who are their own rulers, just, gentle, wise, and passionless; no, not passionless, though free from guilt or pain, which

were only the consequences of their former wilful mistakes; nor are they exempt, though they turn them to the best and most philosophical account, from chance, and death, and mutability; things, which are the clogs of that lofty spirit of humanity, which else might rise beyond all that we can conceive of the highest and happiest star of heaven, pinnacled, like an almost viewless atom, in the space of the universe:—
The intense inane implies excess of emptiness, and is a phrase of Miltonian construction, like 'the palpable obscure' and 'the vast abrupt.' Where is the unintelligible nonsense of all this? and where is the want of 'grammar,' with which the 'pride' of the Reviewer, as *Mr. Looney M'Twoulter* says, would 'come over' him?

Mr. Shelley has written a great deal of poetry equally unmetaphysical and beautiful. The whole of the tragedy of *The Cenci*, which the Reviewers do not think it to their interest to notice, is written in a style equally plain and noble. But we need not go farther than the volume before us, though, according to the Reviewer, the 'whole' of it does not contain '*one* original image of nature, *one* simple expression of human feeling, or *one* new association of the appearances of the moral with those of the material world.' We really must apologize to all intelligent readers who know anything of Mr. Shelley's genius, for appearing to give more notice to these absurdities than they are worth; but there are good reasons why they ought to be exposed. The *Prometheus* has already spoken for itself. Now take the following 'Ode to a Skylark,' of which I will venture to say, that there is not in the whole circle of lyric poetry a piece more *full* of 'original images of nature, of simple expressions of human feeling, and of the associations of the appearances of the moral with those of the material world.' You shall have it entire, for it is as fitting for the season, as it is true to the musical and etherial beauty of its subject.

TO A SKYLARK

[The poem is quoted entire]

I know of nothing more beautiful than this,—more choice of tones, more natural in words, more abundant in exquisite, cordial, and most poetical associations. One gets the stanzas by heart unawares, and repeats them like 'snatches of old tunes.' To say that nobody who writes in the *Quarterly Review* could produce any thing half as good (unless Mr. Wordsworth writes in it, which I do not believe he does) would be sorry praise. When Mr. Gifford 'sings' as the phrase is, one is reminded of nothing but snarling. Mr. Southey, though the gods have made him more poetical than Mr. Gifford, is always affecting something original, and tiring one to death with common-place. 'Croker,' as Goldsmith says, 'rhymes to joker'; and as to the chorus of priests and virgins,—of scribes and pharisees,—which make up the poetical undersong of the *Review*, it is worthy of the discordant mixture of worldliness and religion, of faith and bad practice, of Christianity and malignity, which finds in it something ordinary enough to merit its approbation.

One passage more from this immoral and anti-christian volume, that contains 'not one simple expression of human feeling,' and I will close my letter. It is part of 'An Ode, written October 1819, before the Spaniards had recovered their liberty:'—

> Glory, glory, glory,
> To those who have greatly suffered and done!
> Never name in story
> Was greater than that which ye shall have won.
> Conquerors have conquered their foes alone,
> Whose revenge, pride, and power they have overthrown:
> *Ride ye, more victorious, over your own.*

Hear that, ye reverend and pugnacious Christian of the *Quarterly*!

> Bind, bind every brow
> With crownals of violet, ivy, and pine:
> Hide the blood-stains now
> With hues which sweet nature has made divine;
> Green strength, azure hope, and eternity;
> But let not the pansy among them be;
> *Ye were injured, and that means memory.*

How well the Spaniards have acted up to this infidel injunction is well known to the whole of wondering Christendom and affords one of the happiest presages to the growth of true freedom and philosophy. Why did not the Reviewer quote such passages as these by way of specimens of the author's powers and moral feeling? Why did his boasted Christianity lead him to conceal these, as well as to omit what was necessary to the one quoted in my last? You pretty well understand why by this time; but I have still further elucidations to give, which are more curious than any we have had yet, and which you shall (soon) see.—I shake your hands.

72. Extract from an anonymous article, 'The Augustan Age in England'

The Album, July, 1822, i, 222–3

Besides this host of poets whose names are in everybody's mouth, there are many others of very great—some of the greatest merit, who are, from various causes, less celebrated. There is Mr. Shelley; who possesses the powers of poetry to a degree, perhaps, superior to any of his distinguished contemporaries. The mixing of his unhappy philosophical tenets in his writings has prevented, and will prevent, their becoming popular. His powers of thought, too, equally subtle and profound, occasionally lead him beyond the capability of expression, and in those passages he, of course, becomes unintelligible. The recurrence of these has led some readers to stigmatize his works generally as incomprehensible, whereas they are only blemishes which disfigure them, and which are far more than repaid by countless and exquisite beauties. Can any one, indeed, read the *Prometheus Unbound* with a candid spirit, and not admit it to be a splendid production? We condemn, most unreservedly—for in these days it is necessary to speak with perfect clearness on these subjects—the introduction of his offensive philosophy. We admit the occasional obscurity, sometimes amounting to unintelligibility, of his expression; but we do say that, in despite of these faults, and we fully admit their magnitude, *Prometheus Unbound* is a production of magnificent poetical power. Did our limits permit us to give extracts, we would place this on indisputable ground. The length, however, to which this paper has already run obliges us to content ourselves with referring our readers to the poem. Nor does Mr. Shelley want sweetness and tenderness when he chooses to display them. 'The Sensitive Plant' is as beautiful a specimen of playful yet melancholy fancy as we remember to have seen. If Mr. Shelley would write a poem in which he would introduce more tenderness and less gloom; never permit his subtlety of thought to run into obscurity; and, above all, totally omit all allusion to his philosophical opinions, we are very sure that it would become universally and deservedly popular. This, to be sure, is asking him to cure himself of all his faults; but where they are those of *com*mission not of *o*mission—where they arise from the misapplication of genius, not from want of it—we always look upon it to be within the power of volition to get rid of them—at least, in a very great degree.

73. Bernard Barton, letter to Robert Southey

1822

Bernard Barton, a popular but ephemeral poet of the early nineteenth century, carried on a correspondence with many literary figures including Southey, Lamb, and Lockhart. This letter to Robert Southey is printed with notes in *The Literary Correspondence of Bernard Barton*, ed. Barcus (1966), pp. 62–3.

My dear Friend
....My health and Spirits are not the better for it;[1] but I did not take up my pen to tell thee this, or

> Give thee, in recitals of disease
> A doctor's trouble, but without the fees—

Just before this most unlucky business I had written and sent to the Publisher a few Verses on the Death of Shelley, of which I directed a Copy to be left at Longman's for thee. It would give me pleasure to know they had reached thee, and obtain'd, in good degree thy approval — I think they came out a fortnight since— but I hardly know how time goes, or one day from another—

We differ I expect very considerably in our view of Shelley's Genius; I think it had some traits of uncommon power; but his

---

[1] A robbery at Dyke and Samuel Alexander's Bank forced the bank to call in all its circulating paper money.

principles, or rather opinions I regard as having been pernicious in the extreme— I know it has been said his practice was no better, but I have heard this as flatly contradicted: be the latter, or let it have been what it may, my object has been only to controvert the tendency of his opinions; I expect the *manner* in which I have attempted this will be thought by many too tame &feeble, it may, possibly, be consider'd by thee, too lenient— but I have acted according to the best of my judgment— I have not written in the hope of converting the club at Pisa nor of convincing their admirers here, but with a view of arresting the progress of skepticism in a few young and inexperienced minds, which may possibly have been seduced into admiration of the more delusive features of the Satanic School, but in which a lingering regard to better feelings, and purer hopes may still exist. These are not to be *won* by conferring opprobious epithets on those in whom they think they see much to admire Those who have deceived, and warped such minds, I have neither abilities nor inclination to contend with, but if I can recal one wavering mind, or reclaim a single heart not wholly harden'd in unbelief, I shall not have written in vain—

Talking of the Pisa Club thou hast of course seen the <annonce> of their new Periodical[1]— and art aware that its first object is an attack on thyself— I congratulate thee on it— Farewell— my eyes— my head— my hand forbid me to write more, and I fear what I have written is hardly legible but my heart as candidly as ever bids me subscribe myself sincerely thine

[1] Shelley and Byron, along with Leigh Hunt, formerly of *The Examiner*, planned the new journal, *The Liberal*, which survived only four issues (1822–3).

74. Bernard Barton, letter to William Pearson

August 29, 1822

This letter was written to William Pearson, a close personal friend of Barton, who lived in the nearby town of Ipswich. Printed in *The Literary Correspondence of Bernard Barton*, ed. Barcus (1966), pp. 60-1.

My excellent & valued Friend

I should be ashamed to send thee these few Pages,[1] as a memorial of our Friendship were it not for the belief I entertain that the Cause they are design'd (however feebly) to promote, is one as dear to thee as to those whom the assumption of a *sacred* Profession may have constituted its legitimate and proper Guardians. But believing this to be the case, and that the defence of Revelation, even by the humblest of its Believers, is in thy view deserving encouragement; I venture to request thy acceptance of this trifle— By many I am prepared to expect that it will be consider'd tame and insipid, because I have not hurled anathemas on the head of an infidel, and because I have not attempted to heap on Shelley's memory the obloquy wch if report speak true, his private character might justify— But I *know* nothing, positively, of that private character; and even if I did, I do not consider that I should have felt justified in making a question of *principle*, a *personal* one. It is with Shelley's principles, as an *avowed* Infidel that I am at issue, his practice if ever so virtuous, would not have made these less exceptionable, and if it were bad, it makes them no worse— Incalculable evil is done to the cause of Truth by confounding principles with persons: and every malignant feeling is gratified by prying into the private character of those from whom we differ in opinion— But on these topics I need not enlarge: thy generous & liberal views are fully sufficient to ensure thy accordance with me, and to justify my manner

---

[1] Barton published 'Verses on the Death of Shelley,' a lament for misdirected genius, in 1822.

however defective the matter may prove— My object has been simply to appeal to feelings which early associations may have render'd in degree sacred to those whose principles are unconfirm'd, and whose faith may be wavering.

Farewell most affectionately
thine ever

[Postscript omitted] BB

75. Robert Southey, letter to Bernard Barton

March 6, 1823

Printed with notes in *New Letters of Robert Southey*, ed. Curry, (1965), ii, p. 241.

TO BERNARD BARTON[1]

Keswick. 6 March 1823.

My dear Sir

I can at last thank you for your Verses on the death of the miserable Shelley, which did not reach me till yesterday evening, whereby you will perceive that my communication with the booksellers is not very frequent. But this parcel has been a fortnight longer than it should have been, on the way, owing I suppose to the accumulation of packages in the warehouses during the continuance of the snow. The panegyrical Elegy[2] which called forth your wiser verses was sent me also by its author, whom I know not, but who probably writes under a *nom de guerre*. Whether the sending it was intended as a compliment, or as an insult, is to me a matter of perfect indifference. Shelleys is a flagitious history, and by far the worst tragedy in real life which has

---

[1] MS.: Boult Mss.
[2] This elegy is presumably Arthur Brooke's (John Chalk Claris) *Elegy on the Death of Percy Bysshe Shelley* (1822). See N. I. White, *The Unextinguished Hearth: Shelley and His Contemporary Critics* (Durham, N.C., 1938), pp. 343, 348–52.

ever fallen within my knowledge. As I told him myself in the last communication I had with him, it is truly the Atheist's Tragedy.

It is indeed a strange piece of ill-fortune that an act of robbery should have drawn upon you so heavy a burthen of unprofitable and ungrateful employment: and but a poor satisfaction that when this unusual imposition is over the regular task work will appear almost like a holyday. Meantime however your name is making its way, and I think I might venture to predict, that if you were to try a volume of tales in verse, you would find a lucrative adventure.

Peradventure I may see you in the course of spring, as I have the intention of passing a day with Thomas Clarkson on the way between Norwich and London. Farewell, and believe me Yours truly

Robert Southey.

76. William Hazlitt, extract from 'Preface and Critical List of Authors' in *Select British Poets*

1824

Printed in *The Complete Works of William Hazlitt*, ed. P. P. Howe, (1931), ix, p. 244.

The late Mr. Shelley . . . was chiefly distinguished by a fervour of philosophic speculation, which he clad in the garb of fancy, and in words of Tyrian die. He had spirit and genius, but his eagerness to give effect and produce conviction often defeated his object, and bewildered himself and his readers.

ENGLISH AND AMERICAN CRITICISM
FROM 1824 TO 1840

77. William Hazlitt, review of Shelley's
Posthumous Poems

Edinburgh Review, July 1824, xi, 494–514

Mr Shelley's style is to poetry what astrology is to natural science—a passionate dream, a straining after impossibilities, a record of fond conjectures, a confused embodying of vague abstractions,—a fever of the soul, thirsting and craving after what it cannot have, indulging its love of power and novelty at the expense of truth and nature, associating ideas by contraries, and wasting great powers by their application to unattainable objects.

Poetry, we grant, creates a world of its own; but it creates it out of existing materials. Mr Shelley is the maker of his own poetry—out of nothing. Not that he is deficient in the true sources of strength and beauty, if he had given himself fair play (the volume before us, as well as his other productions, contains many proofs to the contrary): But, in him, fancy, will, caprice, predominated over and absorbed the natural influences of things; and he had no respect for any poetry that did not strain the intellect as well as fire the imagination—and was not sublimed into a high spirit of metaphysical philosophy. Instead of giving a language to thought, or lending the heart a tongue, he utters dark sayings, and deals in allegories and riddles. His Muse offers her services to clothe shadowy doubts and inscrutable difficulties in a robe of glittering words, and to turn nature into a brilliant paradox. We thank him—but we must be excused. Where we see the dazzling beacon-lights streaming over the darkness of the abyss, we dread the quicksands and the rocks below. Mr Shelley's mind was of 'too fiery a quality' to repose (for any continuance) on the probable or the true— it soared 'beyond the visible diurnal sphere,' to the strange, the improbable, and the impossible. He mistook the nature of the poet's calling, which should be guided by involuntary, not by voluntary impulses. He shook off, as an heroic and praise-worthy act, the trammels of sense, custom, and sympathy, and became the creature of his own will. He was 'all air,' disdaining the bars and ties of mortal mould. He ransacked his brain for incongruities, and believed in whatever was incredible. Almost all is effort, almost all is extravagant, almost all is quaint, incomprehensible, and abortive, from aiming to be more than it is. Epithets are applied, because they do not fit: subjects are chosen, because they are repulsive: the colours of his style, for their gaudy, changeful, startling effect, resemble the display of fire-works in the dark, and, like them, have neither durability, nor keeping, nor discriminate form. Yet Mr Shelley, with all his faults, was a man of genius; and we lament that uncontrollable violence of temperament which gave it a forced and false direction. He has single thoughts of great depth and force, single images of rare beauty, detached passages of extreme tenderness; and, in his smaller pieces, where he has attempted little, he has done most. If some casual and interesting idea touched his feelings or struck his fancy, he expressed it in pleasing and unaffected verse: but give him a larger subject, and time to reflect, and he was sure to get entangled in a system. The fumes of vanity rolled volumes of smoke, mixed with sparkles of fire, from the cloudy tabernacle of his thought. The success of his writings is therefore in general in the inverse ratio of the extent of his undertakings; inasmuch as his desire to teach, his ambition to excel, as soon as it was brought into play, encroached upon, and outstripped his powers of execution.

Mr Shelley was a remarkable man. His person was a type and shadow of his genius. His complexion, fair, golden, freckled, seemed transparent with an inward light, and his spirit within him

> ——so divinely wrought,
> That you might almost say his body thought.

He reminded those who saw him of some of Ovid's fables. His form, graceful and slender, drooped like a flower in the breeze. But he was crushed beneath the weight of thought which he aspired to bear, and was withered in the lightning-glare of a ruthless philosophy! He mistook the nature of his own faculties and feelings—the lowly children of the valley, by which the skylark makes its bed, and the bee murmurs, for the proud cedar or the mountain-pine, in which the eagle builds its eyry, 'and dallies with the wind, and scorns the sun.'—He wished to make of idle verse and idler prose the frame-work of the universe, and to bind all possible existence in the visionary chain of intellectual beauty—

> More subtle web Arachne cannot spin,
> Nor the fine nets, which oft we woven see
> Of scorched dew, do not in th' air more lightly flee.

Perhaps some lurking sense of his own deficiencies in the lofty walk which he attempted, irritated his impatience and his desires; and urged him on, with winged hopes, to atone for past failures, by more arduous efforts, and more unavailing struggles.

With all his faults, Mr Shelley was an honest man. His unbelief and his presumption were parts of a disease, which was not combined in him either with indifference to human happiness, or contempt for human infirmities. There was neither selfishness nor malice at the bottom of his illusions. He was sincere in all his professions; and he practised what he preached—to his own sufficient cost. He followed up the letter and the spirit of his theoretical principles in his own person, and was ready to share both the benefit and the penalty with others. He thought and acted logically, and was what he professed to be, a sincere lover of truth, of nature, and of human kind. To all the rage of paradox, he united an unaccountable candour and severity of reasoning: in spite of an aristocratic education, he retained in his manners the simplicity of a primitive apostle. An Epicurean in his sentiments, he lived with the frugality and abstemiousness of an ascetick. His fault was, that he had no deference for the opinions of others, too little sympathy with their feelings (which he thought he had a right to sacrifice, as well as his own, to a grand ethical experiment)—and trusted too implicitly to the light of his own mind, and to the warmth of his own impulses. He was indeed the most striking example we remember of the two extremes described by Lord Bacon as the great impediments to human improvement, the love of Novelty, and the love of Antiquity. 'The first of these (impediments) is an extreme affection of two extremities, the one Antiquity, the other Novelty; wherein it seemeth the children of time do take after the nature and malice of the father. For as he devoureth his children, so one of them seeketh to devour and suppress the other; while Antiquity envieth there should be new additions, and Novelty cannot be content to add, but it may deface. Surely the advice of the Prophet is the true direction in this matter: *Stand upon the old ways, and see which is the right and good way, and walk therein.* Antiquity deserveth that reverence, that men should make a stand thereupon, and discover what is the best way; but when the discovery is well taken, then to take progression. And to speak truly, *Antiquitas seculi Juventas mundi.*[1] These times are the ancient times, when the world is ancient, and not those which we count ancient, *ordine retrogrado,* by a computation backwards from ourselves.' (ADVANCE-MENT OF LEARNING, Book I. p. 46.)—Such is the text: and Mr Shelley's writings are a splendid commentary on one half of it. Considered in this point of view, his career may not be uninstructive even to those whom it most offended; and might be held up as a beacon and warning no less to the bigot than the sciolist. We wish to speak of the errors of a man of genius with tenderness. His nature was kind, and his sentiments noble; but in him the rage of free inquiry and private judgment amounted to a species of madness. Whatever was new, untried, unheard of, unauthorized, exerted a kind of fascination over his mind. The examples of the world, the opinion of others, instead of acting as a check upon him, served but to impel him forward with double velocity in his wild and hazardous career. Spurning the world of realities, he rushed into the world of nonentities and contingencies, like air into a *vacuum.* If a thing was old and established, this was with him a certain proof of its having no solid foundation to rest upon: if it was new, it was good and right. Every paradox was to him a self-evident truth; every prejudice an undoubted absurdity. The weight of authority, the sanction of ages, the common consent of mankind, were vouchers only for ignorance, error, and imposture. Whatever shocked the feelings of others, conciliated his regard; whatever was light, extravagant, and vain, was to him a proportionable relief from the dulness and stupidity of established opinions. The worst of it however was, that he thus gave great encouragement to those who believe in all received absurdities, and are wedded to all existing abuses: his extravagance seeming to sanction their grossness and selfishness, as theirs were a full justification of his folly and eccentricity. The two extremes in this way often meet, jostle,—and confirm one another. The infirmities of age are a foil to the presumption of youth; and 'there the antics sit,' mocking one another—the ape Sophistry pointing with reckless scorn at 'palsied eld,' and the bed-rid hag, Legitimacy, rattling her chains,

[1] 'The antiquity of the age (is) the youth of the world.'

338

counting her beads, dipping her hands in blood, and blessing herself from all change and from every appeal to common sense and reason! Opinion thus alternates in a round of contradictions: the impatience or obstinacy of the human mind takes part with, and flies off to one or other of the two extremes 'of affection' and leaves a horrid gap, a blank sense and feeling in the middle, which seems never likely to be filled up, without a total change in our mode of proceeding. The martello-towers with which we are to repress, if we cannot destroy, the systems of fraud and oppression should not be castles in the air, or clouds in the verge of the horizon, but the enormous and accumulated pile of abuses which have arisen out of their own continuance. The principles of sound morality, liberty and humanity, are not to be found only in a few recent writers, who have discovered the secret of the greatest happiness to the greatest numbers, but are truths as old as the creation. To be convinced of the existence of wrong, we should read history rather than poetry: the levers with which we must work out our regeneration are not the cobwebs of the brain, but the warm, palpitating fibres of the human heart. It is the collision of passions and interests, the petulance of party-spirit, and the perversities of self-will and self-opinion that have been the great obstacles to social improvement—not stupidity or ignorance; and the caricaturing one side of the question and shocking the most pardonable prejudices on the other, is not the way to allay heats or produce unanimity. By flying to the extremes of scepticism, we make others shrink back and shut themselves up in the strongholds of bigotry and superstition—by mixing up doubtful or offensive matters with salutary and demonstrable truths, we bring the whole into question, fly-blow the cause, risk the principle, and give a handle and a pretext to the enemy to treat all philosophy and all reform as a compost of crude, chaotic, and monstrous absurdities. We thus arm the virtues as well as the vices of the community against us; we trifle with their understandings, and exasperate their self-love; we give to superstition and injustice all their old security and sanctity, as if they were the only alternatives of impiety and profligacy, and league the natural with the selfish prejudices of mankind in hostile array against us. To this consummation, it must be confessed that too many of Mr Shelley's productions pointedly tend. He makes no account of the opinions of others, or the consequences of any of his own; but proceeds—tasking his reason to the utmost to account for every thing, and discarding every thing as mystery and error for which he cannot account by an effort of mere intelligence—

measuring man, providence, nature, and even his own heart, by the limits of the understanding—now hallowing high mysteries, now desecrating pure sentiments, according as they fall in with or exceeded those limits; and exalting and purifying, with Promethean heat, whatever he does not confound and debase.

Mr Shelley died, it seems, with a volume of Mr Keats's poetry grasped with one hand in his bosom! These are two out of four poets, patriots and friends, who have visited Italy within a few years, both of whom have been soon hurried to a more distant shore. Keats died young; and 'yet his infelicity had years too many.' A canker had blighted the tender bloom that o'erspread a face in which youth and genius strove with beauty. The shaft was sped—venal, vulgar, venomous, that drove him from his country, with sickness and penury for companions, and followed him to his grave. And yet there are those who could trample on the faded flower—men to whom breaking hearts are a subject of merriment—who laugh loud over the silent urn of Genius, and play out their game of venality and infamy with the crumbling bones of their victims! To this band of immortals a third has since been added!—a mightier genius, a haughtier spirit, whose stubborn impatience and Achilles-like pride only Death could quell. Greece, Italy, the world, have lost their poet-hero; and his death has spread a wider gloom, and been recorded with a deeper awe, than has waited on the obsequies of any of the many great who have died in our remembrance. Even detraction has been silent at his tomb; and the more generous of his enemies have fallen into the rank of his mourners. But he set like the sun in his glory; and his orb was greatest and brightest at the last; for his memory is now consecrated no less by freedom than genius. He probably fell a martyr to his zeal against tyrants. He attached himself to the cause of Greece, and dying, clung to it with a convulsive grasp, and has thus gained a niche in her history; for whatever *she* claims as hers is immortal, even in decay, as the marble sculptures on the columns of her fallen temples!

The volume before us is introduced by an imperfect but touching Preface by Mrs Shelley, and consists almost wholly of original pieces, with the exception of *Alastor, or the Spirit of Solitude*, which was out of print; and the admirable Translation of the *May-day Night*, from Goethe's Faustus.

Julian and Maddalo (the first Poem in the collection) is a Conversation or Tale, full of that thoughtful and romantic humanity, but rendered perplexing and unattractive by that veil of shadowy or of glittering obscurity, which distinguished Mr Shelley's writings. The depth and tenderness of his feelings seems often to have interfered with the expression of them, as the sight becomes blind with tears. A dull, waterish vapour, clouds the aspect of his philosophical poetry, like that mysterious gloom which he has himself described as hanging over the Medusa's Head of Leonardo da Vinci. The metre of this poem, too, will not be pleasing to every body. It is in the antique taste of the rhyming parts of Beaumont and Fletcher and Ben Jonson—blank verse in its freedom and unbroken flow, falling into rhymes that appear altogether accidental—very colloquial in the diction—and sometimes sufficiently prosaic. But it is easier showing than describing it. We give the introductory passage.

[quotes lines 1–33, 53–111, and 132–40]

The march of these lines is, it must be confessed, slow, solemn, sad: there is a sluggishness of feeling, a dearth of imagery, an unpleasant glare of lurid light. It appears to us, that in some poets, as well as in some painters, the organ of colour (to speak in the language of the adepts) predominates over that of form; and Mr Shelley is of the number. We have every where a profusion of dazzling hues, of glancing splendours, of floating shadows, but the objects on which they fall are bare, indistinct, and wild. There is something in the preceding extract that reminds us of the arid style and matter of Crabbe's versification, or that apes the labour and throes of parturition of Wordsworth's blank-verse. It is the preface to a story of Love and Madness—of mental anguish and philosophic remedies—not very intelligibly told, and left with most of its mysteries unexplained, in the true spirit of the modern metaphysical style—in which we suspect there is a due mixture of affectation and meagreness of invention.

This poem is, however, in Mr Shelley's best and *least mannered* manner. If it has less brilliancy, it has less extravagance and confusion. It is in his stanza-poetry, that his Muse chiefly runs riot, and baffles all pursuit of common comprehension or critical acumen. 'The Witch of Atlas,' the 'Triumph of Life,' and 'Marianne's Dream,' are rhapsodies or allegories of this description; full of fancy and of fire, with glowing allusions and wild machinery, but which it is difficult to read through, from the disjointedness of the materials, the incongruous metaphors and violent transitions, and of which, after reading them through, it is impossible, in most instances, to guess the drift or the moral. They abound in horrible imaginings, like records of a ghastly dream;—life, death, genius, beauty, victory, earth, air, ocean, the trophies of the past, the shadows of the world to come, are huddled together in a strange and hurried dance of words, and all that appears clear, is the passion and paroxysm of thought of the poet's spirit. The poem entitled 'The Triumph of Life,' is in fact a new and terrific 'Dance of Death'; but it is thus Mr Shelley transposes the appellations of the commonest things, and subsists only in the violence of contrast. How little this poem is deserving of its title, how worthy it is of its author, what an example of the waste of power, and of genius 'made as flax,' and devoured by its own elementary ardours, let the reader judge from the concluding stanzas.

[quotes lines 480–514 and 523–34]

Any thing more filmy, enigmatical, discontinuous, unsubstantial than this, we have not seen; nor yet more full of morbid genius and vivifying soul. We cannot help preferring 'The Witch of Atlas' to *Alastor, or the Spirit of Solitude*; for, though the purport of each is equally perplexing and undefined, (both being a sort of mental voyage through the unexplored regions of space and time), the execution of the one is much less dreary and lamentable than that of the other. In the 'Witch,' he has indulged his fancy more than his melancholy, and wantoned in the felicity of embryo and crude conceits even to excess.

[quotes lines 161–4 and 169–76]

We give the description of the progress of the 'Witch's' boat as a slight specimen of what we have said of Mr Shelley's involved style and imagery.

> And down the streams which clove those mountains vast,
> Around their inland islets, and amid
> The panther-peopled forests, whose shade cast
> Darkness and odours, and a pleasure hid
> In melancholy gloom, the pinnace past:
> By many a star-surrounded pyramid
> Of icy crag cleaving the purple sky,
> And caverns yawning round unfathomably.
>
> And down the earth-quaking cataracts which shiver
> Their snow-like waters into golden air,
> Or under chasms, unfathomable ever
> Sepulchre them, till in their rage they tear

A subterranean portal for the river,
  It fled—the circling *sunbows* did upbear
Its fall down the hoar precipice of spray,
Lighting it far upon its lampless way.

This we conceive to be the very height of wilful extravagance and mysticism. Indeed it is curious to remark every where the proneness to the marvellous and supernatural, in one who so resolutely set his face against every received mystery, and all traditional faith. Mr Shelley must have possessed, in spite of all his obnoxious and indiscreet scepticism, a large share of credulity and wondering curiosity in his composition, which he reserved from common use, and bestowed upon his own inventions and picturesque caricatures. To every other species of imposture or disguise he was inexorable; and indeed it is his only antipathy to established creeds and legitimate crowns that ever tears the veil from his *ideal* idolatries, and renders him clear and explicit. Indignation makes him pointed and intelligible enough, and breathes into his verse a spirit very different from his own boasted spirit of Love.

The 'Letter to a Friend in London' shows the author in a pleasing and familiar, but somewhat prosaic light; and his 'Prince Athanase, a Fragment,' is, we suspect, intended as a portrait of the writer. It is amiable, thoughtful, and not much over-charged. We had designed to give an extract, but from the apparently personal and doubtful interest attached to it, perhaps it had better be read altogether, or not at all. We rather choose to quote a part of the 'Ode to Naples,' during her brief revolution—in which immediate and strong local feelings have at once raised and pointed Mr Shelley's style, and 'made of light-winged toys of feathered cupid,' the flaming ministers of Wrath and Justice.

[quotes lines 52–8, 77–90, and 102–76]

This Ode for Liberty, though somewhat turbid and overloaded in the diction, we regard as a fair specimen of Mr Shelley's highest powers —whose eager animation wanted only a greater sternness and solidity to be sublime. The poem is dated *September* 1820. Such were then the author's aspirations. He lived to see the result,—and yet Earth does not roll its billows over the heads of its oppressors! The reader may like to contrast with this the milder strain of the following stanzas, addressed to the same city in a softer and more desponding mood.

[quotes lines 1–18 and 28–45 of 'Stanzas Written in Dejection, near Naples']

We pass on to some of Mr Shelley's smaller pieces and translations, which we think are in general excellent and highly interesting. His 'Hymn of Pan' we do not consider equal to Mr Keats's sounding lines in the 'Endymion.' His 'Mont Blanc' is full of beauties and of defects; but it is akin to its subject, and presents a wild and gloomy desolation. GINEVRA, a fragment founded on a story in the first volume of the *Florentine Observer*, is like a troublous dream, disjointed, painful, oppressive, or like a leaden cloud, from which the big tears fall, and the spirit of the poet mutters deep-toned thunder. We are too much subject to these voluntary inflictions, these 'moods of mind,' these effusions of 'weakness and melancholy,' in the perusal of modern poetry. It has shuffled off, no doubt, its old pedantry and formality; but has at the same time lost all shape or purpose, except that of giving vent to some morbid feeling of the moment. The writer thus discharges a fit of the spleen or a paradox, and expects the world to admire and be satisfied. We are no longer annoyed at seeing the luxuriant growth of nature and fancy clipped into arm-chairs and peacocks' tails; but there is danger of having its stately products choked with unchecked underwood, or weighed down with gloomy nightshade, or eaten up with personality, like ivy clinging round and eating into the sturdy oak! The 'Dirge,' at the conclusion of this fragment, is an example of the manner in which this craving after novelty, this desire 'to elevate and surprise,' leads us to 'overstep the modesty of nature,' and the bounds of decorum.

> Ere the sun through heaven once more has roll'd,
> *The rats in her heart*
> *Will have made their nest,*
> And the worms be alive in her golden hair,
> While the spirit that guides the sun,
> Sits throned in his flaming chair,
>   She shall sleep.

The 'worms' in this stanza are the old and traditional appendages of the grave;—the 'rats' are new and unwelcome intruders; but a modern artist would rather shock, and be disgusting and extravagant, than produce no effect at all, or be charged with a want of genius and originality. In the unfinished scenes of *Charles I.*, (a drama on which Mr Shelley was employed at his death) the *radical* humour of the author breaks forth, but 'in good set terms' and specious oratory. We regret that his premature fate has intercepted this addition to our historical drama.

From the fragments before us, we are not sure that it would be fair to give any specimen.

The TRANSLATIONS from Euripedes, Calderon, and Goethe in this Volume, will give great pleasure to the scholar and to the general reader. They are executed with equal fidelity and spirit. If the present publication contained only the two last pieces in it, the 'Prologue in Heaven,' and the 'May-day Night' of the Faust (the first of which Lord Leveson Gower has omitted, and the last abridged, in his very meritorious translation of that Poem), the intellectual world would receive it with an *All Hail*! We shall enrich our pages with a part of the 'May-day Night,' which the Noble Poet has deemed untranslateable.

[quotes Scene ii, lines 146–89, 211–22, and 244–70]

The preternatural imagery in all this medley is, we confess, (comparatively speaking) meagre and monotonous; but there is a squalid nudity, and a fiendish irony and scorn thrown over the whole, that is truly edifying. The scene presently after proceeds thus.

[quotes lines 371–403]

The latter part of the foregoing scene is to be found in both translations; but we prefer Mr Shelley's, if not for its elegance, for its simplicity and force. Lord Leveson Gower has given, at the end of his volume, a translation of Lessing's Faust, as having perhaps furnished the hint for the larger production. There is an old tragedy of our own, founded on the same tradition, by Marlowe, in which the author has treated the subject according to the spirit of poetry, and the learning of his age. He has not evaded the main incidents of the fable (it was not the fashion of the dramatists of his day), nor sunk the chief character in glosses and episodes (however subtle or alluring), but has described Faustus's love of learning, his philosophic dreams and raptures, his religious horrors and melancholy fate, with appropriate gloom or gorgeousness of colouring. The character of the old enthusiastic inquirer after the philosopher's stone, and dealer with the Devil, is nearly lost sight of in the German play: its bold development forms the chief beauty and strength of the old English one. We shall not, we hope, be accused of wandering too far from the subject, if we conclude with some account of it in the words of a contemporary writer.

[Hazlitt quotes a page from his own *The Dramatic Literature of the Age of Elizabeth* (*The Complete Works of William Hazlitt*, ed. P. P. Howe, London, 1931, vi, pp. 202–3).]

345

78. Charles Lamb, letter to Bernard Barton

August 17, 1824

Charles Lamb (1775–1834), essayist, poet and letter writer.
Printed in *The Letters of Charles and Mary Lamb*, ed. E. V. Lucas (1935), II, pp. 436–7.

Dear B. B.,

. . . I can no more understand Shelley than you can. His poetry is 'thin sewn with profit or delight.' Yet I must point to your notice a sonnet conceivd and expressed with a witty delicacy. It is that addressed to one who hated him, but who could not persuade him to hate *him* again. His coyness to the other's passion (for hate demands a return as much as Love, and starves without it) is most arch and pleasant. Pray, like it very much.

For his theories and nostrums they are oracular enough, but I either comprehend 'em not, or there is miching malice and mischief in 'em. But for the most part ringing with their own emptiness. Hazlitt said well of 'em—Many are wiser and better for reading Shakspeare, but nobody was ever wiser or better for reading Sh—y.

C. Lamb.

79. Henry Crabb Robinson, diary entry

December 20, 1824

From *Henry Crabb Robinson on Books and their Writers*, ed. Morley, (1938), i, p. 351.

DEC. 20th. . . . Began this evening to look into Shelley's poems. His 'Lines written among the Euganean Hills' and his 'Sensitive Plant' are very pleasing poems. Fancy seems to be his best quality; he is rich and exuberant. When he endeavours to turn the abstractions of metaphysics into poetry he probably fails—as who does not? But even in his worst works, I have no doubt there is the enthusiasm of virtue and benevolence. I think him worth studying and understanding if possible. I recollect Wordsworth places him above Lord Byron. . . .

DEC. 20th. I extract from a note about Shelley's poems which I then began to read. I at once enjoyed his smaller poems and have not yet mastered his larger works. Wordsworth had then, I mention, placed him higher in [his] estimation than Lord Byron. I recognized in him then as I believe every one does now, a misdirected benevolence and zeal for humanity. 'The Euganean Hills,' 'Sensitive Plant,' and ['Skylark']¹ were my favourites.

¹ He writes 'Nightingale,' but this is obviously a slip. 'The Woodman and the Nightingale,' a much inferior poem, was not published at that date. (Morley's footnote)

80. Unsigned notice, 'Criticism: Percy Bysshe Shelley,' *New York Literary Gazette and Phi Beta Kappa Repository*

September 1825—March 1826, i, 53–4

Although other periodicals carried notices of publications of Shelley's poetry, this review is the first serious American periodical criticism completely devoted to Shelley.

MR. SHELLEY was one of those unfortunate beings in whom the imagination had been exalted and developed at the expense of the reasoning faculty; and with the confidence, or presumption, of talent, he was perpetually obtruding upon that public whose applause he still courted, the startling principles of his religious and political creed. He naturally encountered the fate which even the highest talent cannot avert, when it sets itself systematically in array against opinions which men have been taught to believe and to venerate, and principles with which the majority of mankind are persuaded the safety of society is connected. He was denounced as a poetical *enfant perdu* by the *Quarterly*, and passed over in silence by other periodical works, which, while they were loth to censure, felt that they could not dare to praise. Whether abuse of this nature may not engender, or, at all events, increase the evil it professes to cure; and whether in the case of Shelley, as in that of another great spirit of the age, his contemporary and his friend, this contempt for received opinions, at first affected, may not have been rooted and made real by the virulence with which it was assailed, is a question which it is difficult to answer. But even when death, the great calmer of men's minds, has removed from the scene of critical warfare its unfortunate subject,—when we can turn to the passages of pure and exquisite beauty, which brightens even the darkest and wildest of his poetical wanderings, with that impartiality which it was vain to expect while the author lived, and wrote, and raved, and reviled,—what mind of genius of poetical feeling would not wish that

348

his errors should be buried with him in the bosom of the Mediterranean, and lament that a mind so fruitful of good as well as of evil, should have been taken from us, before its fire had been tempered by experience, and its troubled but majestic elements had subsided into calmness?

We doubt not that Mr. Shelley, like many other speculative reformers and species, ventured in theory to hazard opinions which in his life he contradicted. His domestic habits seem to have been as different as possible from those which, in the dreams of a distempered fancy, he has sometimes dwelt upon with an alarming frequency and freedom; as if the force of nature and early associations had asserted their paramount sway, in the midst of his acquired feelings, and compelled him, while surrounded by those scenes, and in the presence of these beings among whom their pure impulses are most strongly felt, to pay homage to their power.

His perfection of poetical expression will always give to Shelley an original and distinct character among the poets of the age; and in this, we have little hesitation in saying, that we consider him decidedly superior to them all. Every word he uses, even though the idea he labours to express be vague, or exaggerated, or unnatural, is intensely poetical. In no writer of the age is the distinction between poetry and prose so strongly marked: deprive his verses of the rhymes, and still the exquisite beauty of the language, the harmony of the pauses, the arrangement of the sentences, is perceptible. This is in itself a talent of no ordinary kind, perfectly separate in its nature, though generally found united with that vigour of imagination which is essential to a great poet, and in Mr. Shelley it overshadows even his powers of conception, which are unquestionably very great. It is by no means improbable, however, that this extreme anxiety to embody his ideas in language of a lofty and uncommon cast, may have contributed to that which is undoubtedly the besetting sin of his poetry, its extreme vagueness and obscurity, and its tendency to allegory and personification.

Hence it is in the vague, unearthly, and mysterious, that the peculiar power of his mind is displayed. Like the Goute in the Arabian Tales, he leaves the ordinary food of men, to banquet among the dead, and revels with a melancholy delight in the gloom of a churchyard and the cemetery. He is in poetry what Sir Thomas Browne is in prose, perpetually hovering on the confines of the grave, prying with a terrible curiosity into the secrets of mortality, and speculating with painful earnestness on every thing that disgusts or appals mankind.

But when abandoning these darker themes, he yields himself to the description of the softer emotions of the heart, and the more smiling scenes of Nature, we know no poet who has felt more intensely, or described with more glowing colours the enthusiasm of love and liberty, or the varied aspects of Nature. His descriptions have a force and clearness of painting which are quite admirable; and his imagery, which he accumulates and pours forth with the prodigality of genius, is, in general, equally appropriate and original.

81. Article signed 'P. P.,'
Philadelphia Monthly Magazine

July 15, 1828, 245–7

The Philadelphia Monthly Magazine (October 1827–September 1829) was the project of Dr Isaac Clarkson Snowdon. A. H. Smith praised the magazine for its series of fine articles on the history of literature in Pennsylvania written by Richard Penn Smith (*Philadelphia Magazines and their Contributors*, 1892). The magazine emphasized the fine arts, sciences, and literature, and contained frequent articles on American literature. This essay probably represents a popular review of Shelley among those vaguely familiar with him.

THERE are few men of genius who have so misused their powers as Shelley. There are few whose character is so little understood on this side of the Atlantic, as is that of this extraordinary poet. He is here considered as a dark, selfish unbeliever; who defiled every subject he touched upon; under whose hands the marble assumed only hideous forms; who delighted to degrade, and blight, and destroy the loveliest works of nature. He is thought a man without principle, and a poet without merit.

There are few men who have received so much ill treatment and hard accusation as Shelley, without in good measure deserving them. There are very few men, with intentions really pure and honest and honourable, who have done so much that is to be regretted, and suffered so much that might have been avoided. Though a great deal that he did was exceedingly wrong, yet he seems always to have been acting under so strong an impression that he is doing what is right; sacrifices so much in order to arrive at those very ends for which we chiefly blame him, that no one can rise from the consideration of his character with the conviction that he was a bad man. We pity him for the blind fatality by which he seems to have been led, and mourn for that waywardness of fancy and disposition which lost to the world powers of so high an order as Shelley unquestionably possessed.

Shelley was an amiable man. The testimony of all who knew him tends to establish this point. His wife loved him with an affection which nothing but great kindness and tenderness could have awakened, and lamented him with a degree of sorrow that indicates alike his worth, and her sensibility. Whatever may have been his actions, his motives appear to have been always pure.

As to the poems he has left behind him, it is impossible in a short notice properly to consider them. The school to which he belonged, or rather which he established, can never become popular. His poems will probably be read for some time by scholars, but even they will eventually neglect them.

It requires too great a stretch of mind to follow all the windings of his thought. There is too much obscurity and intricacy in his writings. In passages where he condescends to be intelligible, he is often splendid, and sometimes sublime. But most frequently his volumes are closed in despair. We cannot grope our way unaided through gloom and darkness, where even Mr. Shelley himself, we fear, could scarcely have guided us. Writing that we cannot help understanding is always more agreeable than that which we can never be sure we do not mistake.

In many of his shorter pieces, Shelley was eminently successful, and a number of his translations are excellent. Of his larger poems, *Alastor* is the best. It is in these that he chiefly failed. He aimed at too much. He aspired after that which he was not only incapable of attaining, but which few ever approached. He was ambitious of awing and startling his readers, and his ambition leads him where his genius was unable to follow. The visions he imperfectly conceived are rendered still more obscure by a necessarily imperfect expression of them. We sometimes, for pages, cannot get a glimpse at the author's meaning. Occasional passages of great strength and beauty can never compensate for general obscurity; and therefore Shelley will be for many years wondered at, but not long read.

There are few men in the whole course of literary history in whom our feelings and sympathies are more interested than they are in Shelley. He is a striking example of the mischief that misdirected genius can cause to its possessor. In his heart every thing was pure and gentle and generous. In his mind, every thing was wild, extravagant, and diseased. We cannot help respecting the man, though we disapprove of many of his actions. We cannot help admiring the poet, though we are wearied by many of his writings.

82. William Hazlitt, extract from 'Poetry' in *The Atlas*

March 8, 1829

Printed in *The Complete Works of William Hazlitt*, ed. P. P. Howe, (1931) XX, p. 211.

Mr. Shelley, who felt the want of originality without the power to supply it, distorted everything from what it was, and his pen produced only abortions. The one [Byron] would say that the sun was a 'ball of dazzling fire'; the other, not knowing what to say, but determined to elevate and surprize, would swear that it was *black*. This latter class of poetry may be denominated the Apocalyptical.

83. Thomas Moore, from a letter to Mary Shelley

September 3, 1829

Thomas Moore (1779–1852), song-writer and poet.

Printed with notes in *The Letters of Thomas Moore*, ed. Wilfred S. Dowden (1964), II, p. 653.

I find Shelly [*sic*] not so easily dealt with as I expected—such men are not to be dispatched in a sentence. But you must leave me to manage it my own way—I must do with him, as with Byron—blink nothing (that is, nothing but what is ineffable)—bring what I think *shadows* fairly forward, but in such close juxtaposition with the *lights*, that the latter will carry the day. This is the way to do such men real service. I have been reading a good deal of Shelley's poetry, but it is, I confess (always excepting some of the minor gems) *beyond* me, in every sense of the word. As Dante says (and, by the bye, the quotation [might] not be a bad one to apply to him) 'Con suo lume medesimo cela'.[1]

---

[1] '[He hides by his own light.]' Moore did not quote the passage correctly. It should read, 'E col suo lume se medesmo cela', *Purgatorio*, canto xvii, l. 57.

84. Coleridge, letter to John E. Reade

December 1830

Samuel Taylor Coleridge (1772–1834), poet, critic and friend of Wordsworth, wrote this letter to John Reade, a poetaster and minor novelist who imitated and borrowed from Byron and Scott among others.

Printed with notes in *The Collected Letters of Samuel Taylor Coleridge*, ed. Griggs (1971), vi, pp. 849–50.

I think as highly of Shelley's Genius—yea, and of his *Heart*—as you can do. Soon after he left Oxford, he went to the Lakes, poor fellow! and with some wish, I have understood, to see me; but I was absent, and Southey received him instead.[1] Now, the very reverse of what would have been the case in ninety-nine instances of a hundred, I *might* have been of use to him, and Southey could not; for I should have sympathised with his poetico-metaphysical Reveries, (and the very word metaphysics is an abomination to Southey), and Shelley would have felt that I understood him. His Atheism would not have scared *me*—for *me*, it would have been a semi-transparent Larva, soon to be *sloughed*, and, through which, I should have seen the true *Image*; the final metamorphosis. Besides, I have ever thought *that* sort of Atheism the next best religion to Christianity—nor does the better faith, I have learned from Paul and John, interfere with the cordial reverence I feel for Benedict Spinoza. As far as Robert Southey was concerned with him, I am quite certain that his harshness arose entirely from the frightful reports that had been made to him respecting Shelley's moral character and conduct—reports essentially false, but, for a man of Southey's strict regularity and habitual self-government, rendered plausible by Shelley's own wild words and horror of hypocrisy.[2]

1 Shelley resided at Keswick in 1811–12.

2 Allsop reports Coleridge as saying of Shelley: I was told by one who was with Shelley shortly before his death, that he had in those moments, when his spirit was left to prey inwards, expressed a wish, amounting to anxiety, to commune with me, as the one only being who could resolve or allay the doubts and anxieties that pressed upon his mind. (*Letters, Conversations and Rec.*, 139.)

85. Samuel Taylor Coleridge, conversation with John Frere

December, 1830

John Frere, a friend of Tennyson and Hallam, held a B.A. and M.A. from Cambridge where he was one of the 'Apostles.' He prepared this abstract immediately after his conversation with Coleridge. It was first printed in the *Cornhill Magazine* in 1917 and reprinted in *Coleridge the Talker*, ed. Armour and Howes (1940), p. 220.

F. Did you ever see Shelley's translation of the Chorus in 'Faust' you were just mentioning?

C. I have, and admire it very much. Shelley was a man of great power as a poet, and could he only have had some notion of order, could you only have given him some plane whereon to stand, and look down upon his own mind, he would have succeeded. There are flashes of the true spirit to be met with in his works. Poor Shelley, it is a pity I often think that I never met with him. I could have done him good. He went to Keswick on purpose to see me and unfortunately fell in with Southey instead. There could have been nothing so unfortunate. Southey had no understanding for a toleration of such principles as Shelley's.

I should have laughed at his Atheism. I could have sympathised with him and shown him that I did so, and he would have felt that I did so. I could have shown him that I had once been in the same state myself, and I could have guided him through it. I have often bitterly regretted in my heart of hearts that I did never meet with Shelley.

86. Review signed 'Egeria,' 'Character and Writings of Shelley'

The Literary Journal and Weekly Register of Science and the Arts, January 18, 1834

This ephemeral Providence, Rhode Island, periodical carried several notices of Shelley, of which this is the most important and most original.

The poetry of Shelley has been but little read in this country, and is, indeed, of a nature too abstract and spiritual to become popular with the majority of readers in any country. Yet, Bulwer, in his late work on England, has attributed to it, a higher and more powerful influence than to that of any other poet of the present age, Wordsworth alone excepted. Those who have read the poems of Shelley with attention, will not be greatly surprised at this assertion.—They are formed to produce an impression on minds of a certain class, that may not soon be obliterated. His phraseology is remarkably rich, varied, and beautiful; and his imagination luxuriant and inventive: but the principal charm of his writings consists in that liberality of thought and of feeling, and in that enlarged philanthropy which inspires every line, and makes us the more deeply regret that with so much that is excellent and true, much also is blended that is pernicious and false. Bulwer has drawn the following very just distinction between the writings of Shelley and of Wordsworth. 'Wordsworth,' he observes, 'is the apostle and spiritualizer of things that are—Religion and her houses—Loyalty and her monuments—The tokens of the sanctity that overshadows the past. Shelley, on the other hand, in his more impetuous but equally intellectual and unearthly mind, is the spiritualizer of all who forsake the past and the present, and with lofty aim and a bold philanthropy, press forward to the future.'

From his earliest youth, Shelley appears to have discovered that ardor in the investigation of moral and metaphysical truth, that contempt for prejudice under all its modifications, that indifference to the opinion of the world, when opposed to the convictions of his own reason, and that independence of thought and of action, which characterised him through life; drew upon him so much censure; and involved him in so many embarrassments. His acute and penetrating mind soon perceived with indignation and astonishment, the injustice and the wrongs that were perpetrated under the sacred names of Religion and of Law: and untaught by experience to distinguish between the real and the apparent, the essential and the accidental, his hatred of oppression and hypocrisy led him into the opposite extremes of infidel and revolutionary principles.

How appropriately has Luther compared the human mind to a drunken peasant on horseback; who, when you prop him up on the one side, falls down on the other. Though expelled from the University of Oxford, for the publication of his sceptical opinions, and suffering under the deep resentment of his father, incurred by his apostacy, Shelley still continued his pursuit of truth, with undiminished ardor; questioning religion and philosophy, the christian and the pagan, the bigot and the infidel, for that concealed treasure which ever eluded his researches. The Bible was studied by him with deep interest and attention, and the character and precepts of the Saviour were held by him in high veneration. Generous and benevolent, as well by nature as from principle, he is said to have conformed his practice to the golden rule, in its most literal interpretation. It appears, however, that the Scriptures, considered as a divine revelation, presented obstacles to his subtle and speculative reason, which his faith was unhappily incapable of surmounting. It is to be regretted that Shelley's early errors of opinion had not been met by charitable forbearance and mild expostulation; the most effective weapons Christianity can employ in her holy warfare against scepticism and unbelief.

Perhaps it ought not to excite surprise, that a mind so peculiarly constituted as was that of Shelley, should in its first eager but unenlightened survey of life, have been betrayed into inconsequent reasoning, and have arrived at false deductions,—that it should have been darkened by doubts, and perplexed by apparent inconsistencies.

It appears from the tenor of his writings, that his mind was often exercised in speculations on the origin and existence of Evil—that difficult problem—that dark enigma! over which, every reflecting being has at some period of his existence, mused, until thought grew dizzy, and the mind was lost in a labyrinth of contradictory and perplexing speculations. This, with the apparently partial distribution of happiness and of misery, appear to have been the principal obstacles to Shelley's faith. Yet he had a mind open to conviction; and had it not been confirmed in error by severity and intolerance;—had not his pride been interested in the support of those opinions for which he had incurred so much obloquy, he might, and doubtless *would*, have renounced them.

Reason and observation would have taught him the secrets of that divine alchymy by which apparent ills are transmuted into real blessings; and by which partial evil tends to the promotion of universal good. More enlightened views of the economy of nature would have prepared his mind for the reception of the divine truths of Revelation; and in every arrangement of Providence, he would have recognized unbounded benevolence and infinite wisdom.

Shelley was considered a profound metaphysician and an admirable classical scholar. He has clothed some of the beautiful speculations of the Grecian philosophers, in most exquisite verse; and has woven from their fine-drawn theories, a woof so brilliant and so beautiful, that its dazzling splendour almost blinds us to its fragility. His glowing fancies were richly nourished by the pure naptha of true poetic inspiration: and his keen relish for the charms of nature, enabled him to discover many remote analogies and latent sources of beauty, in objects that would have been passed unnoticed by common observers. His description of a poet, in *Alastor, or the Spirit of Solitude*, may well be applied to himself.

> By solemn visions, and bright, silver dreams,
> His infancy was nurtured—Every sight
> And sound, from the vast earth and ambient air,
> Lent to his heart its choicest impulses.
> The fountains of divine philosophy
> Fled not his thirsting lips—and all of great
> Or good, or lovely, which the sacred past
> In truth or fable consecrates, he felt
> And knew.

Almost all his poems appear to have had for their object the illustration of some philosophical or moral truth. His philanthropy led him earnestly to desire the reformation of all those errors which custom and authority alone have sanctioned, in religion, laws, governments and social conventions. And his firm belief in the perfectibility of human nature, and in the final prevalence on earth of virtue and of happiness over vice and misery, served faintly to cheer those moments of dejection, when the pressure of existing and present evil, and fearful doubts of the soul's immortality, weighed upon his mind.

He is said to have practised great self-denial in his mode of living; and to have been liberal, almost to a fault, in his charities. Emulation and ambition he appears to have considered as false principles of action. Revenge, and malice, and envy, found no place in his candid and gentle nature.—He condemned them as passions unfit to be harbored in the breast of a reflecting being. He constantly inculcated universal love and unbounded charity; and his writings are replete with passages like the following:

> ——Justice is the light
> Of love, and not revenge, and terror, and despite.

> ——We should
> Own all sympathies, and outrage none;
> And live as if to love and live, were one.

In his preface to the tragedy of *The Cenci*, observing on the mistaken idea entertained by Beatrice, in supposing that the crime of any individual could reflect dishonor on the innocent victim of that crime; he says; 'No person can be truly dishonored by the guilt of another; and the fit return to make to the most enormous injuries, is kindness and forbearance, and an endeavor to convert the injurer from his dark passions, to truth and love.' Who can contemplate such sentiments, without regretting that a heart so gentle, a soul so generous, should pass through life's weary pilgrimage, without the consolations of religion, the hope of immortality? Dangerous, indeed, is the gift of intellect, when it tempts its possessor to daring speculations and unhallowed researches: and too often does the unchastened desire of knowledge lead to errors more fatal than could have been encountered in the repose of unquestioning ignorance.

Montaigne has well expressed this truth, in one of his essays; though we might in vain seek to transfuse the peculiar force and expressiveness of his quaint and nervous diction, into an English translation. 'Genius,' he observes, 'is a hazardous possession. It is seldom found united with circumspection and order. In my own time, I have observed all who were possessed of any rare excellence or extraordinary vivacity of intellect, indulge in some licence of opinion or of morals. Intellect is a piercing sword; dangerous even to its possessor, unless he knows how to arm himself with it discreetly and soberly. It is curious and eager: we may in vain seek to bridle and restrain it: we shall still find it escaping by its volatility, from the restraints of customs and of laws, of religions and of precepts, of penalties and of rewards.' Shelley's intellectual history is a striking exemplification that 'the tree of knowledge is not that of life:' of that first great truth taught in the garden of Eden,—that truth which had it been received on the word of God without a reference to stern experience, might have saved the human race from its inheritance of sorrow.

[The reviewer closes with a summary of Shelley's marital difficulties and a quotation from Mary Shelley's Preface to *Posthumous Poems* beginning with the sentence 'In the wild but beautiful Bay of Spezia . . .' and closing with '. . . and the world's sole monument is enriched by his remains.']

87. Unsigned review, extracts from 'The Shelley Papers'

American Quarterly Review, June 1836, xix, 257–87

The three greatest poets of this century are, we think, Shelley, Words-worth and Byron. We place them in what seems to us the order of their merit, though this of course will be a matter of dispute—and it will be a very difficult thing to reconcile opinions where the question concerns minds of such various and different powers. Between the first and last, there can hardly be a doubt as to which deserves pre-eminence—the difficulty lies only between the first two. We are conscious that in thus putting Byron beneath any one, whether of the present time or the past, it will appear to many as a depreciation, arising from ignorance of his works, or an incapacity to estimate them. To this we must submit. We only give private opinion, and oppose prevailing notions; neither from eccentricity or an absurd wish to claim originality, but from conviction. It is but a short time since we so far escaped from the fascination of Byron's muse as to be able to judge of his poetry, or to yield any thing but an unhesitating and impetuous admiration. The feelings were too deeply interested to admit an appeal to the judgment. He stood in relief, beyond all contemporary genius, the personification of human perfections, and the only poet of his age. The voices of all the rest sounded from a distance. They could gain no audience, find no response, in the preoccupied bosom of his admirer. But time has checked all this: our intensity has died away. And we are now able to compare and class, where before we saw nothing but unqualified perfection. . . .

The influence of this poet's writings went to this end. The times were filled with action, and passion, and convulsion. He felt the movement, took the tide, and was borne like a bubble on its surface. He aided and gave impulse to the heady current of revolution. His extraordinary popularity as a writer mingled him with the affections of the public. It wrought into their souls the doubt of the existence of virtue as a principle of action, and all the ribald jests and sneers with which he assaulted the motives of men and their institutions; it gave a vicious bias to the principles and the characters of the young; and it will only be with time, the decay of his name and works as a fashion, and an admiration for a higher standard of morals and purer sources of poetry, that an entire change in these effects may be expected. These fountains of better poetry and morals we open in the works of Wordsworth and Shelley. During the ascendency of Byron, and the confusion he created, these two poets were for the time nearly overwhelmed; but they were forming a strong though tranquil under current, deeper, though less observed—more powerful, though never swelling with the turbid fury and impetuosity that belong to those who are the idols of the mass. But they were gradually making their way, and if they are not now, will be in a few years, more read than any poets of the time. We are inclined to think that in all the higher matters of taste, popularity is suspicious. There is something low and debasing in catering for the majority at all. It shows a desire for the worst part of fame—its notoriety—that in itself betrays a vulgar and feeble mind. No one would ask the judgment of the mob alone, and no one would feel exalted by its praise; yet to gain it he must bring his intellect to their level, he must reduce the fineness of his sentiments, the energy and elevation of his feelings, all that he feels within himself separating and distinguishing him from those around, to the meagre standard of general opinion. Is there a single great work, of whatever nature, on whose merits the mass of men are able to decide? Would Raphael have hung his picture in the streets of Rome; Dante have thrown his poem as a peace offering to those who drove him from the walls of Florence; or Milton offered the result of his toils, whose every line, like the rays of light, is wrought with a beauty, brilliancy, and power, that show the deep effulgence, the magnificence, and the vastness of the orb whence they spring, to the crop-eared fanatics or profligate cavaliers, that formed the rude and fierce factions of his country, undoubtedly not; and whoever is conscious of an inward power, a genius that he is well aware the world will not appreciate, let him not strive to subdue its struggles for expression—check its impulse and compel it to a career that from being uncongenial must wither every effort. From the great variety of human character, comes equal variety of tastes, and there is nothing in nature or intellect but will find a congenial alliance. But all minds when exerted in a sphere to which they are ill disposed, lose half their power. The will is backed by no zeal, there is straining for effect without the ability to produce it. There is no ease, no grace, no repose, in these extorted labours. The strongest minds will not yield to the whim of fashion of the moment. They seem borne up by a strength of conviction and energy of will, that resembles inspiration. They mark their course and adhere to it, through opposition and persecution, with a pertinacity that becomes obstinate in proportion to the violence with which it is assaulted. Heretofore literature was only meant for the few. The great men of the past looked to immortality, but not to popularity; they could not imagine the enormous multiplication of readers, but gave their souls to the world, with no hope that time would enlarge the sphere of their intellectual influence, or make their thoughts flow onwards in an incessant pilgrimage to the shrine of mind. They made no offerings to the passions of the hour, but like legislators seemed to be ever looking to the future. They gazed into the abyss of time, and saw moving in its depths, not the countless multitude of the gleaners of thought that multiply with the improvement of old empires, and the creation of new, but the limited few; the small brotherhood of congenial spirits, who, stood divided from the world and its interests—who loved study for itself, not for the fame it gave—and gathered around learning as the altar where all their affections were warmed—all their feelings purified—all their hopes elevated or sacrificed. This state of things has not yet passed away—and whoever has the courage to forego the intoxicating gratification of an immediate and premature reputation, and to permit his genius to take its course, will find, or make an audience. There are two things belonging to every work, that seem to require distinct faculties; the conception, and the execution; with the first, the majority of men have nothing to do, the last, is their only ground for admiration, criticism, or calumny; yet it is the first only that shows the mind—the last is matter of detail, of industry and habit. The first proves the power of imagination, the strength and extent of the intellect; the second, dexterity in managing the materials. . . .

We are aware that in speaking of him we shall stir very strong prejudices. His early conduct, and his more mature opinions on subjects that the wisest consider as involving man's deepest interests, have given to his name an unfortunate celebrity, and a reputation that the most liberal must regret, the more moral portion of society regard with suspicion. Yet if there are any who should know how to forgive, it is those who have the best right to condemn. But in this instance there is every excuse, every motive for pardon, that youth and inexperience, a deep love of truth; a strong spirit of enquiry, and an openness to conviction, can create. There was no expression of doubt, no scepticism for the mere love of argument, or for the sake of singularity. But he could not yield to the reasonings and the faith of others, because he saw sources of hesitation which others, perhaps, could not reach, or which they declined trying to open with the keen edge of reason, feeling satisfied that their powers were insufficient. There is a great difference between one who struggles with his whole soul, to develope the deep mysteries that encompass his being, that lie around and beyond him, that belong to the visible and the invisible, are partly matter, partly spirit, and one who falls supinely on the faith that is given him, without seeking farther than those barren limits the human intellect has formed—without roaming on those high quests that lose us in their vastness, and make us droop with their difficulties. We do not say that it is wise, thus to question of things that give no response, to send the soul among the dark confusion of unintelligible existences, the wild chaos of dim uncertainties, and try to grasp the very foundations of creation and the worlds that lie beyond. It may not be wise thus to ascend among the realms of light, where it was never intended the human mind should move, while it holds its present relations, and where all it gathers is still farther doubt as to its nature and powers, a still stronger confirmation of its ignorance and incapacity. But there are spirits that appear to have no home upon the earth, who cannot so control themselves as never to burst the bonds of mere reason, and float with glad wings in the far spheres of speculation. They love the mysterious—all that is without the scope of thought—where they may hazard the wildest fancies, and follow all their strange suggestions, engage among those transcendental wonders, where imagination, like the eagle, seems to rise towards the sun's eye and enter the depths of its blaze and glory.

Of this cast was Shelley. And no poet ever seems so completely to have lost himself in the wild abstractions of his brain—to have removed himself so far from the sphere in which he lived, or to have held counsel with creations so totally different from those about him, as to make the world and life but matters of inferior consideration. His thoughts were seldom of, or on the earth; they were gathered in regions where others were strangers—they were expressed in a way that showed their dreamy and distant origin; and altogether his mind seemed to be as far removed from this orb, as is consistent with the possession of sanity. He was indeed a visioned poet in his dreams, with no grossness, no sensuality, but with every mental operation bearing the blush of that beauty and refinement that were parts of his nature. He was truly the poet of intellect and feeling, but not of passion, in its common sense. Poets seem generally acted on from without. From the acuteness of their sensibilities all external things have a deep influence, and they are moved as the harp by the wind. But it was not so with Shelley. He was purely a creature of imagination—a being so spiritual that he and the world had nothing in common; their only bond was in the higher powers of mind—the purity of moral excellence—of sentiment, and all that was great or exalted; but through nothing that partook of earth or its energies. Thence he was cut off from the common lines of communication with his fellow creatures; and save the communion of a few who could understand the order of his character, his soul lived in solitude, without sympathy or its solace.

By all those who have the presumption or the courage to mock at this species of intellect, it should be remembered, that they are not, themselves, persons of genius; that they are united by no common bond with such; that they hold no power by which they can unravel the workings of a great soul, or enter the recesses whence all that is marvellous in its passions and its energies is made to flow. Genius is in itself a mystery; a wonderful endowment, and first of all created things. Whatever may be its real nature, which it is not given to man to know, it forms the sole link between him and the spirit of the universe. This is enough to show its importance in the scale of things, though it does not declare its destiny. There should be, then, great caution, in ridiculing its peculiarities, for these are not acts of volition, but parts of its very nature. Because it dares to rise beyond the realities of ordinary existence, to question of the great intent of all it sees, and search out their origin, however wild it may seem to those who are content with the humble offices of their inferior intellects, there need still be nothing absurd in the endeavour,—it may be, as indeed nearly all the movements of genius are, an impulse it cannot resist, coming with the strength and heat of inspiration; something ordained to en-large the bounds of mind, and add, as has been done, by the discovery of new bodies in the farthest parts of the heavens, to the knowledge of man, to the light that now gleams but dimly over the wishes of his spirit, and the prospects of his being. All should judge of the eccen-tricities, the perversities, the apparent inconsistencies of a great soul, with benevolence, and decide on them with mercy. There is, un-doubtedly, a feeling of humiliation, even of despair, in viewing those errors, and dangerous aberrations that often mark the course of the greatest intellects, and which overshadow the hopes that inferior minds are disposed to affix to their high powers, and cloud the destinies that sometimes break upon us, in following the track of the highest order of intellectual greatness. But it is, perhaps, only when the devia-tions are from the path of morals that they should be judged with severity. Then all can be their censors; but in things relating exclusively to the movements of mind, censure should be cast on them in the spirit of kindness and pardon. It is given to few to conceive, to still fewer to feel, the influences that act on such beings from within and from without; the keen susceptibility the dark and even fierce aspira-tions, the wild wanderings of a tortured spirit, when in its moody moments it mediates on the inefficiency of all its efforts to discover, by thought, more than fancy has already suggested, or to shape from the records of its knowledge a more certain and less obscure evidence, as to all relating to its position and its prospects. It was in some of these moments of deep despondency, that Shelley expressed himself an atheist. His mind was ever directed, even at the earliest age, towards the most abstruse and the loftiest speculations. There was no love of trifling, nothing humorous in his character; but all his faculties were intensely bent on matters that concerned the welfare of his species,—on subjects that humble reason can grasp, though they may be made to blend with the wildest metaphysical absurdity; and where that which belongs to the common affairs of life becomes irradiated by imagination, and the real, obscured by intermingling with the fanciful. At Oxford he involved himself in the doctrines of Plato; and, like most imaginative persons, was impelled, in the heat of enthusiasm, to yield an implicit faith and give an actual existence to the visions of his brain. He believed, with that philosopher, that all knowledge is reminiscence; that our immortal part has belonged to some predecessor; and that our minds, instead of gleaning for themselves, the desire of sympathy coming forth from the depth and sternness of his high resolve, with some one who would appreciate him, and on whom he might bestow the tenderness of his sensibility, and its intensity. In the 'Hymn to Intellectual Beauty,' we trace the same imaginative being, borne on by the great faculty of his nature, and pursuing all the fancies it created and nurtured.

[quotes 'Hymn to Intellectual Beauty,' lines 49–52; 54–62; 68–72; 78–84]

In these extracts we can discover the character of the man and his mind; the germ both of his conduct and his writings; and that love of the ideal rather than the actual, that forms the beauty and vice of his poetry. Of this, the pervading fault is an indistinctness; a remoteness from the usual association of ideas, from that continuous chain, connecting the minds of men,—a something wild, and singular, and unnatural, in the thoughts, and mode of expressing them,—a peculiarity so extraordinary that but few are or can be interested, and still fewer are roused to the degree of sympathy with the author, which produces pleasure, or even awakens attention; for most persons read poetry as a pastime, and a luxury, but seldom as a study. They are, therefore, repelled, by difficulty, by all that is harsh, all that does not flow and melt into their minds without exertion. Yet there are some who are willing to meditate and not lounge over the poet's thoughts; who have too high a respect for poetry as an art, to enjoy it merely as a temporary and idle gratification. And such are the best judges of its merits, since they disentangle all obscurites, and unfold the remote allusions the poet's imagination brings within the range of his subject, and scale the heights where beauty gradually bursts upon them, as they rise, and the scene becomes more full of splendour and power, as the view takes in all its parts. It is to such adventures in the realms of poetry that

Shelley will be an idol; to that choice few whose taste can find congeniality, or whose faculty of admiration can extend beyond the
bounds of a particular species of composition; and, fortunately for
literature, it is this select few who confer fame and immortality; but
to the mass of readers he will ever remain unknown, or be as little
read as Milton.

All his best works are idealisms of virtue, expressive of conditions
of the human being that he is not yet fitted for; poetical abstractions,
beautiful visions that are first conceived in the purity of the heart,
and then encircled with the magic influence of imagination, and all the
gravity and grandeur of deep thought. *The Revolt of Islam* is one of
these high-wrought fancies. There we have the vain conflict between
wisdom and power, an emblem of things as they were; the desolation
that tyranny and its capricious will brings over empires and ages; the
degrading effects of custom, from the servility with which men obey
it; the blight with which ignorance withers and oppression crushes the
human soul; at length the terrible reaction, when the over-tortured
spirit of man bounds from its chains at the call of liberty—and then,
mild and beautiful images of perfect love and perfect happiness; the
advancement of knowledge, the elevation of human hopes in the
change of man's destinies, and the gradual preparation and steady
approach towards perfection. These form the poet's vision, and there
needs no other testimony to the nature of the object for which he
lived. It fails in interest with common readers from metaphysical
obscurity, an overlaboured refinement of thought perhaps from too
excessive a brilliancy in the ideas, and the sea of metaphor over which
the reader is obliged to move in the roll of the poet's mind; yet there is
a vigour and a richness both of imagination and intellect, that remind
one, though they exceed him, of Spenser. But perhaps the best of
Shelley's works are *The Cenci* and the *Prometheus*. The first, revolting
as the subject may be, is the best drama of the time. It is the only entire
production of his, in which he has allowed himself to descend to earth,
and mingle with the common passions of his nature. But here he comes
down from the lofty, dazzling, and over-elevated spheres, where his
conceptions seemed to float with an easy strength that showed they
were in their element, to the actual existences and realities that were too
gross for his affections or his thoughts, to that common life from which
he recoiled with an instinctive sensitiveness. It was written with more
labour than any other of his works, so little accustomed was he to
make man, in his more degrading points of view, the subject of his

contemplations; but the result is in proportion to the difficulties with which he contended. The fearful ferocity of the father, the hideously unnatural mockery with which he scoffs at the feelings of a parent, the cold-blooded determination to commit the crime, that men's lips can hardly utter; the noble spirit and daring resolution of the daughter, that triumphs over fear, and all the mildness of her sex and love of a child; her hesitation, between doubt that her nature calls up, and the determination that self-defence, and the claims of virtue, and even duty demand—together with the necessity of perpetrating a horrid purpose, and the shrinking from its execution—are delineated with great force and consummate art. But the effect is heightened, by knowing that the tragedy is the relation of a fact: that it is not one of the dark and terrible delineations that are sometimes framed by an overwrought and heated brain, a morbid and distorted caricature of human passion, but a plain matter of real life and actual occurrence, which history has recorded among its scenes of pain, disgust, and horror.

The *Prometheus* forms a medium between his disposition to metaphysical analysis and refinement, and that which is more appreciable and intelligible to minds in general. It displays the greatest command of language, when we consider the extraordinary nature of his ideas, and on an occasion the most difficult. He gives an interest to the agony of the Titan, by making us feel that in his sufferings he expresses his own detestation of tyranny and oppression. But the imagery is drawn from obscure sources, and though highly intellectual, is too far removed from any association with ordinary incidents and the ordinary feelings of men, to give it the hue of action and passion that produces popularity; yet the whole is wrought with a Titanic energy that declares how near he could approach to the models he professed to imitate. Both these works were written at Rome, whose name, whose climate, whose dying grandeur and forsaken ruins, sink deep into the minds of the most humble, and forbid that there should be any thing mean or common-place even in their thoughts. But to genius it is the shrine before which it falls in ecstacy and admiration; the soul there drinks deep of all beauty; the walls and arches and columns, all the gigantic fragments of men's minds, though but dust, and though its greatness is now a dream, yet all are sources of power: and the spirit, in breathing the atmosphere of inspiration, seems to be elevated and to partake of the immortal life that dwells among the monuments which surround it. The shades of the dead, the ruins of empires, the majesty and glory of the past, with the mysterious influence with which genius hallows all that memory there rests upon, rouse an emulation, deeper, purer, and more powerful and noble in its ends and energies, than the coarse ambition excited by throwing our hopes on the rough struggles and fierce passions of everyday life; and though Shelley had no ambition, in the general meaning of this word, he could not escape from the charm and enchantment that breathed over his intellect. It is impossible to say all we would wish, as to his poetry, but we cannot close our remarks without noticing the 'Adonais,' or Elegy on the Death of Keats. Our only extracts will be a few lines from the stanzas, where he brings round the grave of Adonais, those of the poets whom he knew best. First is Byron:

> The Pilgrim of Eternity, whose fame
> Over his living head, like heaven is bent.

The second, Moore:

> From her wilds Ierne sent
> The sweetest lyrist of her saddest wrong,
> And love taught grief to fall like music from his tongue.

The third is himself.

> Midst others of less note, came one frail form,
> A phantom among men; companionless
> As the last cloud of an expiring storm
> Whose thunder is its knell;
> A pard-like spirit, beautiful and swift,
> A love in desolation masked: a power
> Girt round with weakness.

The fourth is Leigh Hunt. The denunciations he calls down on the Reviewer of Keats's 'Endymion' are powerfully expressed:

> Live thou, whose infamy is not thy fame;
> Live! fear no heavier chastisement from me,
> Thou noteless blot on a remembered name;
> But be thyself, and know thyself to be.

Among his minor pieces there are many very beautiful, but we have done enough to declare our own admiration both of the man and his writings. Our sole wish has been to draw from the imperfect towards the more perfect, to raise on this side of the water our voice in favour of one, who is perhaps but little known, and this knowledge acquired from those who were his persecutors—whose task and duty it was to make him infamous. But time and truth ever move together, and both of these are now working in men's minds, and both ere long will establish the fame and hallow the genius of the gentle and desolate Shelley.

88. Margaret Fuller Ossoli, extract from memoir, entry under 'Literature'

c. 1836

Printed in *Memoirs of Margaret Fuller Ossoli*, ed. R. W. Emerson, W. W. H. Channing, and J. F. Clarke (1884), pp. 165–6. Margaret Fuller Ossoli, one of the few members of the Transcendental Club to recognize and appreciate Shelley's poetry, praised Shelley several years before his reputation was established in America.

As to what you say of Shelley, it is true that the unhappy influences of early education prevented his ever attaining clear views of God, life, and the soul. At thirty, he was still a seeker,—an experimentalist. But then his should not be compared with such a mind as ——'s, which, having no such exuberant fancy to tame, nor various faculties to develop, naturally comes to maturity sooner. Had Shelley lived twenty years longer, I have no doubt he would have become a fervent Christian, and thus have attained that mental harmony which was necessary to him. It is true, too, as you say, that we always feel a melancholy imperfection in what he writes. But I love to think of those other spheres in which so pure and rich a being shall be perfected; and I cannot allow his faults of opinion and sentiment to mar my enjoyment of the vast capabilities, and exquisite perception of beauty, displayed everywhere in his poems.

89. Robert Southey, extract from letter to John E. Reade

June 12, 1838

Printed with notes in *New Letters of Robert Southey*, ed. Curry (1965), ii, pp. 474–5.

Coleridge was entirely mistaken in what he says of my manner towards Shelley. So far from there having been any thing harsh or intolerant in it, I took a great liking to him, believed (most erroneously as it proved) that he would outgrow all his extravagances, that his heart would bring him right, and that the difference between us was that at that time he was just nineteen and I was eight and thirty. The observation appeared not to please him, for he would not allow that that could make any difference.

Coleridge was equally mistaken in saying that the reports of Shelley's moral character and conduct were essentially false. I *know them to be true*, and the story is the most frightful tragedy that I have ever known in real life. His metaphysics would never have shocked me. I told him that he was wrong in calling himself an Atheist which he delighted in doing, for that as far as he might be called any thing, he was a Pantheist. He had never heard the word before, and seemed much pleased at discovering what he really was. When he left this place where he resided some months we parted in mutual good will. He had not then entered upon his career of guilt.

The late Duke of Norfolk who knew Shelleys father, requested a neighbour[1] of mine to notice him, and be of any use to him that he could. That neighbour introduced him to me, and as long as he remained here he was upon the most familiar terms in this house, coming to it whenever he pleased and always finding a cordial reception. His only complaint of me was that I would not talk Metaphysicks with

[1] William Calvert of Windybrow near Keswick.

him. And now Sir farewell. I wish your present poem all the success that it so well deserves, and that you may long continue to write poetry without any abatement either of the power or inclination which are both required for it. Believe me to be Yours with sincere respect and good will

Robert Southey.

90. Ralph Waldo Emerson, from a letter to Margaret Fuller Ossoli

May 27 or 29, 1840

Ralph Waldo Emerson (1803–82) American philosopher, essayist and poet, was one of the leaders of the Transcendental Movement.

Printed in *The Letters of Ralph Waldo Emerson*, ed. Rusk (1939), ii, p. 299.

I have looked into the Shelley book not yet with much satisfaction. It has been detained too long. All that was in his mind is long already the property of the whole forum and this *Defence of Poetry* looks stiff and academical.

91. Ralph Waldo Emerson, from a letter to Margaret Fuller Ossoli

June 7 or 8, 1840

Printed in *The Letters of Ralph Waldo Emerson*, ed. Rusk (1939), ii, p. 305.

I have read Shelley a little more with more love.

92. Henry T. Tuckerman, extracts from 'Shelley,' *Southern Literary Messenger*

June 1840, vi, 393–6

Henry T. Tuckerman, critic, essayist, and poet, had ample independent finances to lead a quiet literary and social life. He followed Hazlitt's critical manner, but wrote travel accounts as well as literary and artistic essays.

The publication of the posthumous prose[1] of Shelley, is chiefly interesting from the fact that it perfectly confirms our best impressions of the man. We here trace in his confidential letters, the love and philanthropy to which his muse was devoted. All his literary opinions evidenced the same sincerity. His refined admiration of nature—his habits of intense

[1] *Essays, Letters from Abroad, Translations and Fragments.* By Percy Bysshe Shelley. Edited by Mrs. Shelley: London, 1840.

study and moral independence, have not been exaggerated. The noble actions ascribed to him by partial friends, are proved to be the natural results of his native feelings. The peculiar sufferings of body and mind, of experience and imagination, to which his temperament and destiny subjected him, have in no degree been overstated. His generosity and high ideal of intellectual greatness and human excellence, are more than indicated in the unstudied outpourings of his familiar correspondence.

Love, according to Shelley, is the sum and essence of goodness. While listening to the organ in the Cathedral of Pisa, he sighed that charity instead of faith was not regarded as the substance of universal religion. Self he considered as the poisonous 'burr' which especially deformed modern society; and to overthrow this 'dark idolatry,' he embarked on a lonely but most honorable crusade. The impetuosity of youth doubtless gave to the style of his enterprize an aspect startling to some of his well-meaning fellow-creatures. All social reformers must expect to be misinterpreted and reviled. In the case of Shelley, the great cause for regret is that so few should have paid homage to his pure and sincere intentions; that so many should have credited the countless slanders heaped on his name; and that a nature so gifted and sensitive, should have been selected as the object of such wilful persecution. The young poet saw men reposing supinely upon dogmas, and hiding cold hearts behind technical creeds, instead of acting out the sublime idea of human brotherhood. His moral sense was shocked at the injustice of society in heaping contumely upon an erring woman, while it recognizes and honors the author of her disgrace. He saddened at the spectacle so often presented, of artifical union in married life—the enforced constancy of unsympathizing beings—hearts dying out in the long struggle of an uncongenial bond. Above all, his benevolent spirit bled for the slavery of the mass—the superstitious enthralment of the ignorant many. He looked upon the long procession of his fellow-creatures plodding gloomily on to their graves, conscious of social bondage yet making no effort for freedom, groaning under self-imposed burdens yet afraid to cast them off, conceiving better things yet executing nothing. Many have felt and still feel thus. Shelley aspired to embody in life action, and to illustrate in life and literature the reform which his whole nature demanded. . . .

As a poet Shelley was strikingly original. He maintained the identity of poetry and philosophy; and the bent of his genius seems to have been to present philosophical speculations, and 'beautiful idealisms of moral excellence,' in poetical forms. He was too fond of looking beyond the obvious and tangible to form a merely descriptive poet, and too meta-physical in his taste to be a purely sentimental one. He has neither the intense egotism of Byron, nor the simple fervor of Burns. In general, the scope of his poems is abstract, abounding in wonderful displays of fancy and allegorical invention. Of these qualities, *The Revolt of Islam* is a striking example. This lack of personality and directness, prevents the poetry of Shelley from impressing the memory like that of Mrs. Hemans or Moore. His images pass before the mind frost-work at moonlight, strangely beautiful, glittering and rare, but of transient duration, and dream-like interest. Hence, the great body of his poetry can never be popular. Of this he seemed perfectly aware. *Prometheus Unbound*, according to his own statement, was composed with a view to a very limited audience; and *The Cenci*, which was written according to more popular canons of taste, cost him great labor. The other dramas of Shelley are cast in classical moulds, not only as to form but in tone and spirit; and scattered through them are some of the most splendid gems of expression and metaphor to be found in the whole range of English poetry. Although these classical dramas seem to have been most congenial to the poet's taste, there is abundant evidence of his superior capacity in more popular schools of his art. For touching beauty, his 'Lines written in Dejection near Naples,' is not surpassed by any similar lyric; and his 'Sky-Lark' is perfectly buoyant with the very music it commemorates. *Julian and Maddalo* was written according to Leigh Hunt's theory of poetical diction, and is a graceful specimen of that style. But *The Cenci* is the greatest evidence we have of the poet's power over his own genius. Horrible and difficult of refined treatment as is the subject, with what power and tact is it developed! When I beheld the pensive loveliness of Beatrice's portrait at the Barbarini palace, it seemed as if the painter had exhausted the ideal of her story. Shelley's tragedy should be read with that exquisite painting before the imagination. The poet has surrounded it with an interest surpassing the limner's art. For impressive effect upon the reader's mind, exciting the emotions of 'terror and pity' which tragedy aims to produce, how few modern dramas can compare with *The Cenci*! Perhaps 'Adonais' is the most characteristic of Shelley's poems. It was written under the excitement of sympathy; and while the style and images are peculiar to the poet, an uncommon degree of natural sentiment vivifies this elegy. In dwelling upon its pathetic numbers, we seem to trace in the fate of

Keats, thus poetically described, Shelley's own destiny depicted by the instinct of his genius.

[quotes 'Adonais,' stanzas ix, xxvii, xxxviii, xl in full and lines 397–9; 410; 430–2; 462–4; 488–90]

Time—the great healer of wounded hearts—the mighty vindicator of injured worth—is rapidly dispersing the mists which have hitherto shrouded the fame of Shelley. Sympathy for his sufferings, and a clearer insight into his motives, are fast redeeming his name and influence. Whatever views his countrymen may entertain, there is a kind of living posterity in this young republic, who judge of genius by a calm study of its fruits, wholly uninfluenced by the distant murmur of local prejudice and party rage. To such, the thought of Shelley is hallowed by the aspirations and spirit of love with which his verse overflows; and, in their pilgrimage to the old world, they turn aside from the more august ruins of Rome to muse reverently upon the poet, where

[quotes 'Adonais,' lines 444–50]

93. Henry Crabb Robinson, diary entries

December 29 and 30, 1840

From *Henry Crabb Robinson on Books and their Writers*, ed. Morley, (1938), ii, p. 587.

DEC. 29th. . . . Came home early and read Shelley's prose from half-past nine to half-past eleven.

DEC. 30th. . . . I have been delighted with Shelley's *Letters*[1] from Italy in the second volume of his Prose Writings. His taste is most delicate and altogether there is a captivating moral sentiment throughout.

[1] *Essays, Letters from Abroad, Translations and Fragments*, 1840. (Morley's footnote)

His contempt for Christianity is strongly expressed and is a stain on the book, but even that I believe was a very honest mistake; I am glad however to find that he was fully sensible of the deformities of Lord Byron's mind and character. One does not, however, see why he should, with his own habits and life, express himself with such abhorrence of *Childe Harold*. His politics violently Radical; *anno* 1819 he seriously advised his friends to sell out of the English Funds; he looked forward to a revolution as inevitable and believed the strangest fables, the news of the day, such as the Inquisition in Spain murdering seven thousand people before they succeeded in effecting a revolution; marvellous ignorance occasionally, thinking Godwin's answer to Malthus trimphant.

94. Orestes Brownson, extracts from 'Shelley's Poetical Works,' *Boston Quarterly Review*

October 1841, iv, 393–436

Orestes Brownson (1803–76), a prolific essayist and commentator, published several periodicals besides this one, mostly written by himself. A friend of Emerson and others in the Transcendental Club, he gradually found himself growing less democratic and more authoritarian, eventually converting to Roman Catholicism.

Much of the clamor which has been raised against him relates to his private character and course through life. One desirous simply of defending him might evade this subject, by taking refuge behind the recognised and important distinction between the man and the author. Our object, however, is to consider the genius of the man, not alone his literary productions. The acts and writings of one like Shelley equally bear the impress of his real character, and must alike be regarded as his authentic *works*. The enthusiasm which dictates his poems was never an excitement got up for the occasion, bastard in its nature and false in its results, but was always present with him as an actuating principle. Its influence may be perceived in every portion of his history, whence this and his writings are each of commentary on the other.

The charges preferred against him are, for the most part, general and indefinite. We rarely find the offences of which he is declared guilty distinctly specified. They are all so intimately connected with his speculative opinions, and these again with his eventful history, that it becomes necessary to regard them at one view. Descended from a noble family, with wealth enough to purchase every advantage of education, he was brought up in the country, in almost entire seclusion, or enjoying the society only of his sisters. He was extremely affectionate and sensitive, as a child, and at the same time, active, intelligent and studious. He was also ardent and visionary, and appears to have been early and deeply impressed by those natural beauties among which he dwelt and dreamed. Like his own Alastor,

> By solemn vision and bright silver dream
> His infancy was nurtured. Every sight
> And sound, from the vast Earth and ambient Air,
> Sent to his heart its choicest impulses.

His education, if we mean by the word the instruction of the schools, was received at Eton and Oxford; but that training which gave its complexion to his life, and made him what he was, was the result of the circumstances of the time, of his own unassisted reflections, and his multifarious and ill-assorted reading. He was indebted to his teachers for little beside his intimate knowledge of the classical writers, for whom (especially the Greek Tragedians) he had an unfailing love.

The age in which he was born was a peculiar one. The high hopes for, and glowing confidence in mankind, awakened by the American and increased by the French revolution, had not yet begun to fade. A new principle had been introduced alike into politics and philosophy,— that of the inalienable rights of man. The writings of Godwin and others of the same school were exerting a powerful influence over the mind of the English people, and circumstances appeared to give much coloring to their high prophecies. In the unparalleled events which had just transpired, a new light had beamed upon men, and they were dazzled by its brightness. A blow had just been struck which shivered the time-honored idols of Europe to pieces. *The People* had arisen in their majesty, and throne and altar, crown and tiara, the mitre of the hierarch and the noble's coronet were about to be swept away forever, before the might of long-oppressed, but now awakened Humanity. Republican notions, even the most extreme, spread widely. Such opinions are naturally captivating to young, ardent, and unsophisticated minds, not yet hardened by the world's wear. It may indeed be predicted of them, that they are especially attractive to those having the greatest goodness and loveliness of character. . . .

The writings of Shelley have been, and still are, seldom spoken of and much more seldom read. His want of popularity may be ascribed in part to certain peculiarities of style and subject, but principally to the bold avowal of religious opinions which are generally considered unsound and unsafe. The prevalent notions upon this subject are much exaggerated, and as they have caused the exclusion of his works from many of our houses and libraries, it is impossible to pass them by in silence. He has been branded as an atheist, and this epithet, once applied to a man, clings to him as closely and as fatally as did the poisoned shirt of Nessus to the back of Hercules. Yet the charge is untrue, and a just consideration of his mental structure would alone be sufficient to forbid such a supposition. His mind was essentially affirmative, not able to rest in doubt or negation, but requiring a positive faith on all subjects presented to it. Atheism, on the other hand, is a mere negative system. Its essence is denial. It is an universal *No*, shrouding the soul in darkness, and blotting out the sun and stars from the moral firmament, without substituting the feeblest rush-light for their genial rays. It destroys and never rebuilds, takes away and gives nothing back. Whether it displays itself in the cold sneers of the mocker, or in that dead spiritless logic, which asks syllogistic proof for truths which are written upon every human heart, and endeavors to measure Infinity and Eternity by mathematical rules; in either case, it is the same demon of blight and desolation, before whose pestilential breath every high hope and holy aspiration perishes. When it takes possession of the mind, it is as if the sand-clouds of Zahara were sweeping over cultivated fields;—before them the land smiles in plenteous fertility, behind lies the parched and dreary desert. It is the entire absence of religious belief and sentiment, and could never, therefore, have been acceptable to one constituted like our poet. Compare him for an instant with the man who, of all others, best deserves the name of Atheist, Voltaire;—the fire-eyed enthusiast, ready to take his life in his hand and rush into the thickest of the fight in search of a higher truth or greater good for his race, with the light *persifleur*[1] ensconced securely behind his bulwark of specious formulas, and sapping the foundations of a nation's belief with his keen irony and bitter sarcasm. The Frenchman could cry incessantly '*ecrasez l'infame;*'[2] but that done, he had nothing to offer in its place. But Shelley was no mere Iconoclast, and respectable as that calling may sometimes be, in clearing the way for reform, it never could have sufficed for him, for he had the spirit of the Reformer himself. He would let the old idols stand, if he could not, by their destruction, open a path to the temple of a purer worship. If he would have torn down the bricks, it was only that he might rebuild with marble. One would have been content to sound his ram's-horn around each Jericho of superstition, and laugh with derision over its crumbling walls, while the other aspired to strike a lyre, 'holier than was Amphion's,' and before whose magic sound should arise a newer, nobler creation than even the seven-gated city. Is there no contrast here?

We are not led to this conclusion by these considerations alone. It has been remarked that 'man is a religious animal,' and it is certain that the principle of veneration is a constituent of every human mind, and stands high among the evidences of the existence of a Deity. This quality Shelley possessed in a preëminent degree. He was compelled to worship as by an irresistible necessity, and his spirit must ever have had an altar at which to bow down in mingled reverence and love. Under these circumstances, it is impossible that he ever could have been satisfied with the void blank of Atheism, for such convictions would have been to him the blackness of darkness. It is not to be denied that he was inclined to this system for a time. When he first became dissatisfied with the dogmas of his teachers, and anxious and distressed, looked about for light, he naturally enough fell upon the writings of their adversaries, the infidels of the French revolutionary school. With these, and especially with the 'Système de la Nature' of d'Holbach, (frequently ascribed to Mirabeau,) he was for the moment enraptured. The novelty and boldness of their views delighted him, and it is not improbable that, like most young men who adopt similar opinions, he felt his vanity flattered by the reflection, that he had the courage to throw off all the shackles of spiritual despotism, and walk forth freely

[1] 'Jeerer.'
[2] 'Crush the infamous thing.' An allusion to Voltaire's famous anticlerical slogan.

into their broad fields of speculation. It was under these influences that he wrote *Queen Mab*; and yet even here we can see his better mind struggling through this, his deepest darkness; for while laboring to disprove the existence of a creative Deity, he enters the special proviso that nothing there said, shall be construed to militate against the hypothesis of an all-pervading and sustaining Spirit, coeternal with the universe, and serving as the soul to this great body of Nature. In the course of time, had he been spared, the native vigor of his intellect would have freed it from much of these heaps of acquired rubbish, and he would gradually have seen with clearer and clearer vision. . . .

But Shelley was no politician, in the ordinary sense of the term. He was a poet, and it was enough for him to embody cardinal principles in his poetry, to arouse the torpid mass from their lethargy, and to urge them on to the assertion of their rights in the burning words of song. While contemplating grand results, he could not distinctly perceive the means by which they might be reached. He could awaken an enslaved people to a sense of their Egyptian bondage, and point them to the promised land, but he could not lead them, step by step, through the wilderness that intervenes. When considering the particular measures to be adopted for the amelioration of the existing condition of Society, he went sometimes wofully astray. Thus, his remarks upon dietetics and the institution of marriage, in the Notes to *Queen Mab*, present a farrago of nonsense which, but for intrinsic evidences of genius, might appear to be the joint production of Frances Wright and Sylvester Graham. With regard to certain measures of political reform, on the contrary, he was unnecessarily timid and hesitating. He even doubted the propriety of introducing the system of universal suffrage into Great Britain, until the further progress of social improvement had rendered the populace better able to exercise a privilege so important. But all this detracts nothing from his general merits. He was true to his principles throughout, and however much he may have doubted their immediate applicability, he died as he had lived, the champion of liberty and the friend of man.

The writings of Shelley have never enjoyed any very great degree of popularity. This is not ascribable solely to the fact, that his heretical opinions caused him to be little read. That he is not always admired when read might be proved, were it not notorious, by the contradictory opinions expressed of him by critics. Many have thrown by his poems, after looking over a page or two, and wondered that any could be found taking delight in what appears to them unmeaning allusions and distorted images. It is not difficult to account for this. Shelley is not easy reading. The impression first made upon one who takes him up is that of obscurity, and he rises from the task, tired by the constant stretch of his attention, or filled only with a sensation of vague delight. On a second reading, however, all is changed; the thought becomes more prominent, the illustrations appear more apt and graceful, and one alights constantly on passages which he is astonished that he could have passed unnoticed. But when read, he has not always been read aright. This is an important consideration. Poetry, in its true sense, is not a thing to be printed on paper or bound in books. Its seat is not in cramped manuscripts or gilded volumes, but in the deep heart of man. The most glowing numbers, which the poet may use to convey to others a sense of what he feels, will not find a response in every breast. Words that burn will not always kindle thoughts that breathe. The deaf serpent will not regard the voice of the charmer, charm he never so wisely. The dim eye may be turned toward a scene instinct with beauty, yet there is the same dull blank as everywhere. So, poetry is a sealed book to that reader who feels no sympathy with the writer. The string when touched may make the sweetest music, but can waken a responsive note in none but those that chord with it. Let a man approach any production with a mind bustling with prejudices on all sides, and he will surely be blind to its merits. Let him even be indifferent, but unable to appreciate the views of the author or partake of his feelings, and there is little likelihood that he will do him justice. Where, however, a sympathy exists, the case is far different, and every line comes home to the reader with power. The rude peasant will feel his breast expand and his pulse quicken at the sound of the most artless ballad of his native land, when all the splendor of Byron and the organ-tones of Milton would fall powerless on his ear.

Here then appears to be the main cause of Shelley's want of popularity. His readers, disapproving his opinions, have found it impossible to comprehend, much less sympathize with his feelings, and consequently could consider his poems only in the colder aspect of works of art. The ethereal spirit was absent, they found little to love in the lifeless form, and turned away in weariness or disappointment. Had they coincided with his sentiments, or been able to assume them for the moment, by projecting, as it were, their minds into his situation, they would have experienced very different results. The majority, however, cannot or will not do this, and hence he remains unknown or unappreciated. That he was aware of this fact and felt its injustice, there can be no doubt. He beautifully alludes to it in the lines prefixed to his 'Epipsychidion.'

> My Song, I fear that thou wilt find but few
> Who fitly shall conceive thy reasoning,
> Of such hard matter thou dost entertain;
> Whence, if by misadventure, chance should bring
> Thee to base company, (as chance may do,)
> Quite unaware of what thou dost contain,
> I prithee, comfort thy sweet self again,
> My last delight! tell them that they are dull,
> And bid them own that thou art beautiful.

Such language is not arrogance in one conscious of his own greatness, but if it were, he had abundant precedent for it. The lines quoted are imitated from a sonnet of Dante; and Ovid, and Horace have prophesied their own immortality in no measured terms.

It is not to be denied, however, that these poems are justly chargeable with a considerable degree of obscurity. This arises, in a measure, from the fact, that they have little claim on the ordinary, every-day feelings of our nature. They do not come home at once to every man's business and bosom. You hear a song of Burns and are held in charmed attention to the end, for it is a stream of melodious affection gushing from the depths of one human heart, and finding its counterpart in every other. You open a volume of Mrs. Hemans, your eye is arrested, and your mind follows that of the poetess, bound to it by the sympathy of a common joy or sorrow. You can read Scott with ease, for his poetry is but a rhymed narrative of thrilling incidents, or a description of external beauties, natural or artificial. Shelley's, however, is the poetry of intellect, rather than of sentiment. It appeals to reason, more than to passion. To be properly understood or felt, it must be read with careful attention. This, in our newspaper age, when most men seem like students in a law-office, to measure their proficiency by the number of pages they have skimmed over in a given time, is an insurmountable obstacle to extended popularity. Few can be found who will sit down with patient diligence, and peruse and ponder over an author till they feel his soul transfused into their own, see his visions, kindle with his aspirations, and glow with his enthusiasm. Yet until this can be generally done, Shelley cannot be generally known. Whoever does it will be amply repaid for all his trouble; for, when he has caught the spirit of the author, he will be like one who, toiling in rude mountain passes, comes suddenly upon a valley with crystal streamlets, redolent of all sweet flowers and vocal with the song of birds.

The distinguishing feature in Shelley's mental constitution was the imaginative power in its highest and purest degree. This was the dominant faculty of his mind, and all the rest were, more or less, subjected to it. It has been well remarked, that the man of genius always continues to resemble the child in this;—that ideality is the very life of life, the most trifling object or incident taking part in some imaginary train of romantic action or feeling. This was curiously exemplified by our poet's abiding fondness for certain amusements considered appropriate only to childhood. He had always a passion for the water, and when at college, and even after, would linger for hours near a pool or stream, twisting pieces of paper into the likeness of boats, and regarding them with intense delight as they floated over its surface. Ridiculous as this may appear to some, it gives us a clue at once to the character of the poet, and some peculiarities of his poems. A large portion of his most striking and beautiful imagery is derived from the water in its various states of repose or agitation, from the majesty of ocean to the rippling brook, or even the putrid marsh. It is probable that many if not most of these struck his fancy, as he watched his tiny fleet, each of which might seem to his excited imagination

> A boat of rare device, which had no sail
> But its own curved prow of thin moonstone,
> Wrought like a web, of texture fine and frail;

or that pink and veined shell, in which bending gracefully, while its delicate colors glowed in reflected light on her joyous face and heaving bosom, Aphrodite was borne over the dancing billows, and first touched the golden sands of Cyprus. His imagination revelled among the most brilliant conceptions. He could invest every object in nature with beauty and interest, and 'cast the shadow of his own greatness' over all that surrounded him. The words prefixed to his 'Epipsychidion,' and there ascribed to the lady to whom the poem is addressed, are emphatically applicable to himself:—'L'anima amante si slancia fuori del Creato, e si crea nel infinito un Mondo tutto per essa, diverso assai da questo oscuro e pauroso l'aratro.'[1] Activity and fertility of imagination, combined with delicacy of apprehension and the ability to

[1] The *Review* article contains a misprint, for Shelley's original read *baratro* rather than *l'aratro*. The quotation says, 'The soul that loves is hurled forth from the created world and creates in the infinite a world for itself and for itself alone, most different from this present dark and dismal pit.'

observe minute resemblances and discrepancies, have caused his writings to abound with varied imagery. This is, for the most part, just and beautiful, but not unfrequently too abundant. Metaphor is sometimes piled upon metaphor and simile upon simile, until the mind is confused, bewildered, lost amidst the shining throng. In a few instances, the thought seems to lie crushed and buried beneath the superabundance of illustration. Whole passages seem more like store-houses of imagery laid by for future use, than portions of a finished poem. It appears as if the thick-coming fancies had crowded upon him with a power he could not resist. Numerous examples of this may be seen in that singular production already referred to, 'Epipsychidion.'

But he is remarkable for the character of his imagery as well as its quantity. Very frequently his meanings are too remote, his allusions not readily followed and his illustrations are to be satisfactorily comprehended only by those who, in the language of a contemporary poet, 'can put on wings of the subtlest conception, and remain in the uttermost parts of idealism.' He delights in the personification of abstract ideas, and uses it more boldly than perhaps any other writer in our language, except Young. Certain often-quoted and discussed passages of the latter, as, for instance, that in the first Book of the *Night Thoughts*,

> Punctual as lovers to the moment sworn,
> I keep an assignation with my Wo,

always have been, and perhaps always will be, a bone for critics to gnaw at. The same thing will obtain with regard to numerous expressions of Shelley, especially in 'Adonais,' which colder spirits will deem overfanciful and extravagant, while those who can follow his excited train of thought will consider them exquisitely apt and true. He had also a disposition to use external objects, not as similes, but impersonations, whence arises one of his chief peculiarities as a descriptive poet. Many of these ideas are seized with difficulty by those who have less vivid conceptions than the author, but when seen as he doubtless saw them, they strike us with their wonderful sublimity, as in the following daring attempt to embody the sensation of elevating awfulness experienced in a stormy night among mountains, when our souls seem to hold communion with the elements, and the giant shapes of the outward world.

> The Appenine by the light of day
> Is a mighty mountain, dim and gray,
> Which betwixt the sea and sky doth lay;

> But when night comes, a chaos dread
> On the dim starlight then is spread,
> *And the Appenine walks abroad with the storm!*

If this be, as it has been denominated, night-mare poetry, it would be
well if the effusions of others of our bards contained more of this 'stuff
that dreams are made of.' Another passage, showing the same tendency,
is the following,

> The pale stars are gone!
> For the Sun, their swift shepherd
> To their fold them compelling
> In the depths of the dawn,
> Hastes in meteor-eclipsing array, and they flee
> Beyond the blue dwelling,
> As fawns flee the leopard.

This disposition is perceived yet more distinctly in those pieces, where
the incidents are of a supernatural character, as the 'Triumph of Life'
and especially the translation of the *Walpurgisnacht*[1] scene from Goethe's
Faust, which some have pronounced untranslatable, but to which he
has done ample justice, and even rendered more wild and weird than
the original.

Analogous to this is another peculiarity to which he himself alludes
in the preface to *Prometheus Unbound*. 'The imagery which I have
employed,' says he, 'will be found in many instances to have been
drawn from the operations of the human mind, or from those external
actions whereby they are expressed.' Poets ordinarily employ material
objects to represent or illustrate the phenomena of life and mental
action, while Shelley does the reverse. He either makes these phenomena attributes of the material object, or uses them to typify those
things which were originally their types. Thus, the autumn leaves have
been used, from the time of Virgil, to symbolize the fleeting-by of
ghosts. With Shelley, it is the leaves which 'like troops of ghosts on the
dry winds pass.' The same figure is repeated in a modified form in the
'Ode to the West Wind,' for it is not uncommon to meet a favorite
simile repeated in several portions of his works.

> Thou wild west wind! thou breath of autumn's being,
> Thou from whose unseen presence the leaves dead
> Are driven like ghosts from an enchanter fleeing,
> Yellow and black and pale and hectic red,
> Pestilence-stricken multitudes!

[1] The evening before May 1. In Germanic folklore, the witches' sabbath.

The half-detached rock, tottering to its fall, and impending over the head of one fastened to the spot has been often employed to represent the horrors of a guilty conscience and anticipated punishment. Shelley makes the terror and the agony reside in the rock itself and illustrates them by a comparison of the kind just alluded to.

> There is a mighty rock,
> Which has from unimaginable years,
> Sustained itself, with terror and with toil,
> Over a gulf and with the agony
> With which it clings, seems slowly coming down;
> Even as a wretched soul, from hour to hour,
> Clings to the mass of life.

Another example of the same kind is as follows:

> Our boat is asleep on the Serchio's stream,
> Its sails are folded, *like thought in a dream.*

But the most striking and powerful passage of the kind is the following sublime description of an avalanche.

> Hark, the rushing snow!
> The sun-awakened avalanche, whose mass,
> Thrice rifted by the storm, had gathered there,
> Flake after flake, in Heaven-defying minds
> As thought by thought is piled, till some great truth
> Is loosened, and the nations echo round,
> Shaken to their base, as do the mountains now!

Passages like these are not comprehended with the same facility as those where the imagery is drawn from objects under the immediate inspection of the senses, and where the connexion with the antitype is plain at first sight. Men are unaccustomed to look to their internal consciousness for illustrations of external existences, and those who are not habituated to reflection do it with pain. Easy reading marks easy writing. That production which requires but little thought in its perusal, cost but little in its composition. Shelley appears to have written with great labor, the rich fulness of conception struggling with the poverty of expression. A number of pieces remain in a fragmentary condition, where the poet appears to have sought in vain to fix the fancies that crowded upon his mind, the key-word to the whole, being sometimes absent. This difficulty might have been overcome in a measure, as experience made him more familiar with the details of his art. For herein lies the true secret of art and use of practice;—that the artist shall acquire such readiness in giving a palpable form to his conceptions, as to keep them vividly before his mind, instead of losing them in attention to the vexatious minutiæ of the process. An uninstructed painter may have present to his mind the idea of a picture, as perfect in its distinctness, softness, and harmonious beauty, as ever grew beneath the pencil of Raphael, yet he cannot transfer it to the canvass, because it fades from his view while his attention is distracted by the labor and embarrassment consequent upon an imperfect knowledge of the art. So it appears to have been with Shelley. In reading many of the fragments mentioned you have an apprehension of some huge indistinct, but sublime conception, which the writer has in vain sought to express, and abandoned in despair. So in many of his poems, which are marked by ruggedness and want of polish, the question appears to have been, which should be sacrificed, thought or expression. Neither would he impair the energy and strength of a first reading by strict reviewing and alteration. 'I appeal,' says he, 'to the greatest poet of the present day, whether it is not an error to assert that the finest passages of poetry are produced by labor and study.' (*Essays*, I. 56.) Still, the finest passages evidently will be written by him who, with equal faculties, has the greatest facility in writing, and can clothe a noble sentiment at once in a dress that will require no revision. The strength of Shelley's poetry, however, lies much more in the thoughts it embodies, than in the form of their expression. Even the finest portions are remembered with difficulty, the words lending very little assistance to the memory.

His versification is not always the smoothest. In some parts, as, for instance, the choruses in *Prometheus Unbound* and 'Hellas' and some of the minor poems, it flows in a stream of continuous melody. To read them is like listening to a strain of soft, sweet music, so unbroken is the harmony of the metre, and so well does it correspond with the sentiments expressed. Too frequently, however, his style is rude, and his verses, although accurately measured according to rule, rather harsh. In framing many of them he appears to have attended only to the division of his lines into the requisite number of feet, without regard to their musical intonation, thereby bringing several consonants together in such a manner as to render the pronunciation rough and difficult, concluding a line in the middle of a sentence in an unusual manner, and in some instances requiring an accent on syllables other than those ordinarily accentuated. He has written in almost every measure or which our language is capable, and with varied degrees of success. His blank verse is generally marked by a noble Doric simplicity and chasteness of finish. The lofty sounding lines correspond admirably with the full stream of exalted sentiment, intense feeling, and sublime imagery which they convey. In the Spenserian stanza he was less happy, and has not often been able to produce those strains of mingled sweetness and grandeur into which it has been wrought by Byron. In some of his minor poems, as the 'Triumph of Life,' 'Prince Athanase,' and others, he has employed the 'terza rima' of the Italians, which Byron has used in his 'Prophecy of Dante,' and which he seems to have considered himself the first to introduce into English poetry. In this measure the thought and imagery are almost necessarily carried on from line to line in accumulative succession, and it is, therefore, well adapted to Shelley's peculiar powers. One idea or illustration succeeds another in close connexion and intertexture, leaving the mind no pause until it arrives at one of the strophic divisions which occasionally occur. His 'Witch of Atlas' runs smoothly in the verse of Pulci, which Byron has made immortal in 'Beppo' and '*Don Juan.*' The lyrics, scattered throughout his dramas and among his fugitive poems, show how complete a master of his art he was, when leisure or the humor of the moment led him to exert his powers. There can be no doubt that most of his poems would have displayed a higher degree of polish, had he been spared to give them a more careful and thoughtful revision in later years.

That one of Shelley's poems, which is most read, and which has done most to place him in the estimation in which he is generally held, is *Queen Mab.* It abounds, as before remarked, in the most heretical opinions, and was written to display the great social and political evils, which the author believed to exist, and to prophesy the coming of a better time. It is a highly finished production, the writer throughout alternating the most captivating lyrical sweetness with the loftiest didactics. On contemplating it we cannot but smile to see the boy-philosopher handling these weighty matters with such ineffable coolness and confidence, especially when he quotes, and in a manner, appropriates to himself, those magnificent lines of Lucretius;[1]

> Suave, mari magno turbantibus æquora ventis,
> E terra magnum alterius spectare laborem, &c.

The machinery of the poem is well adapted to introduce the reflections which it is his object to impress upon his readers. It is more easily read than his other productions, the meaning being more distinct, the senti-

[1] 'Sweet it is, when on a great sea the winds are disturbing the waters, to watch from the land the great distress of another' (Lucretius, *De Rerum Natura*, 2.1-2).

ments more directly and explicitly inculcated, and the illustrations simpler and less abundant. In consequence of these very qualities, however, it is deficient in the beauties that fill the others, and, although of sufficient poetic merit to establish the fame of any man upon a sure foundation, it wants the distinguishing marks of Shelley's genius.

His principal work, in point of size and pretension, is *The Revolt of Islam*, which was originally published under the title of *Laon and Cythna, or the Revolution of the Golden City*. It is a narrative poem, in twelve cantos, and is deeply tinged with the author's speculative opinions. The dedication is one of the very finest short pieces extant. The first Canto is one of those visions of more than earthly beauty and grandeur, with which he delights to introduce his poems to the reader. The remainder is a history in the first person of the aspirations of a pure young heart, yearning for light and liberty,—of the awakening of a great people from the darkness and degradation of slavery by the power of a single voice, inspired by truth and love,—of the dethronement of their tyrants,—of the happiness of a free people,—of the banding together of despots for the extinction of freedom,—of the struggle of the patriots and the ultimate triumph of despotism. The incidents are varied and romantic, and the characters of the principal actors, although drawing too little on our more ordinary sympathies, are generally lovely, and excite a strong interest in their behalf. Beside the occasional impressions intended to be made, the great moral of the whole is apparently this;—that every such revolt, every contest for human rights against arbitrary power, every resistance to creeds and institutions imposed by force, is productive of benefit, and hastens the hour when these rights shall be universally acknowledged and established, even though it results in defeat. This poem is written in the stanza of Spenser, and abounds in elegant and impressive passages. It is comparatively little read, probably because of its length and intricacy, and the general prevalence of those characteristics of his style already adverted to. His tragedy of *The Cenci* has been by many pronounced his master-piece. Leigh Hunt admires it so much, that he contends warmly that its author should have written nothing but dramas. It is founded upon a story of unspeakable guilt and misery, which eventuated in the destruction of the noble Roman house of that name, near the close of the sixteenth century. It is singular that so gentle a spirit should have chosen such a subject; and the only reason, and indeed, excuse for it, is the intense interest in it, which he found among all classes at Rome. Although nearly two centuries and a half have elapsed since these scenes transpired, the rude peasants will kindle at the name of the principal actress in them, and defend her cause with enthusiasm. Shelley's servant instantly recognised a portrait in his possession as that of *La Cenci*, and we frequently see copies of these, with their gentle, pensive face, and golden hair escaping from beneath white drapery, adorning the windows of our transatlantic picture-shops. The whole tale is one from which the mind recoils with instinctive repugnance, and should never have been made the groundwork of a play. Yet it must be admitted that our author has managed it with inimitable skill, bringing forward all its prominent points with vivid distinctness, and avoiding the most repugnant ones with consummate delicacy. The persons are involved throughout in one cloud of unmitigated horror, and the excited reader feels as though he were bewildered among the frightful figures of a feverish dream. The character of Beatrice, nobly as it is conceived, is scarcely a redeeming feature. Innocent, unsuspecting, good as far as any negatively can be, displaying a mixture of unfaltering courage with maiden tenderness, she yet evinces no strength of moral principle, endeavors to expiate one crime by the commission of another, and dies in firm adherence to a resolute lie. The actors are borne on blindly by the strange, wild current of evil; and error follows error, and crime, crime, until the curtain falls and the reader feels relieved that it is done. It is to be regretted that Shelley should have expended his powers upon a subject so ill-calculated to display them, and so generally repulsive. This tragedy will, nevertheless, always stand prominent as a monument of his genius. That one mingling so little with men in the active walks of life, from youth a solitary dreamer or a philosophic recluse, should ever become so intimately acquainted with the varied play of human passions as he here appears to be, is little short of miraculous, and indicates, if anything does, a true poetic inspiration.

Let us turn from this to a more attractive subject, a drama of a different order,—the *Prometheus Unbound*,—which appears to us, both in its conception and execution, superior to all Shelley's other productions. Although it is an attempt to replace the lost tragedy of Æschylus, it yet differs from it considerably. According to the Greek Tragedian, the sufferings of the Titan are terminated by his reconciliation with Jupiter. Shelley makes him ultimately triumphant, and thus obviates the necessity of a compromise between the powers of good and evil. Of the moral of the drama we have already spoken. As regards its high poetic merit there can be but one opinion. It is instinct with beauty from beginning to end. The characters are sustained throughout with wonderful power, and the hero, in particular, presents a combination of all lovely and noble qualities, such as the unaided mind of man never before conceived. The diction is chaste and exquisitely polished, and the imagery is alternately gentle and grand, touching and sublime. The English language has never been wrought into more varied harmony than in the lyrics which occur in the course of the play. The whole scene in Heaven is incomparably sublime. The play of passions on the part of Jupiter, the alternations from the insolence of triumph to the most abject supplication for mercy, and from fierce defiance to the blackest despair, are drawn as the hand of a master alone could draw them.

Similar remarks may be made with regard to his other poems, and his fugitive pieces. Some of the latter are prized more highly by critics than his greater efforts; as, for example, the 'Ode to the West Wind' and 'Lines written in dejection near Naples.' His translations are also of a superior character, especially those from Goethe, which leave us to regret that he did not complete the undertaking, and give us a translation of the great work of the giant-minded German worthy of the original. The present edition contains several poems hitherto suppressed, the principal of which are 'Swellfoot the Tyrant,' 'Peter Bell the Third,' and the 'Masque of Anarchy.' The two first do not please us. Shelley was not made to write humorous poetry, much less travestie. His imagination was too rich and copious, and his spirit too earnest. His fun has always a serious air about it, and the reader is rapt by some burning thought, when he ought to be laughing at a jest. Such writing appears to us no more agreeable than would be the playing of a jig on a cathedral-organ, amid the dim, religious light of the sacred aisles. The 'Masque of Anarchy' is a production of a very different order. Never did the fiery genius of Greece, in its happiest moments, invent a more sublime mythus than that which introduces the poem; and the address to the men of England will rouse any man, who has a man's heart in his bosom, like the sound of a trumpet calling to battle.

Shelley has never been known as a prose writer; but the two volumes of essays and letters now published show a graceful, easy, and perspicuous style. The *Defence of Poetry* is an elegant and triumphant vindication of his glorious art and at the same time, an example showing how poetry may be written without rhyme, and melody of intention, as well as thought observed without a regular division into verses. Pope would have written the *Defence* in heroics and even then it would have been cold in comparison. But Shelley had, as he informs us, 'a horror of didactic poetry,' and agreed with the proposition since laid down by Carlyle, that nothing need be sung which can be as well said, that no thought should be rhymed, unless there is an internal necessity for its being rhymed. His metaphysical fragments display a profundity of thought for which he has never received credit; but are too imperfect to give us any clear view of his opinions.

And now, we have endeavored to introduce to the favorable notice of the readers of this Journal the works of one of the greatest minds of the present century. In life, he was the object of almost universal distrust and contumely, and it is only now, when his heart has ceased to beat with quickened pulsation or the sound of applause, and his bosom to yearn for the approving sympathy of his fellow-men, that his works begin to meet a merited regard. What estimate posterity will ultimately put upon them, it is impossible for us to know. That it will be higher than ours, there can be no doubt. It is the fate of most great men to be unknown or unadmired by their own age and country. Homer wandered, a blind minstrel and beggar, from city to city, and no one was found to record his birthplace for the gratification of the countless thousands whom he has since instructed and entertained. The gallants of Queen Elizabeth's court could crowd the theatre to witness the plays of 'that clever varlet, Will Shakespeare,' but they never dreamed that the nations, in after ages, would bow down to this humble player, as one of the mightiest spirits ever vouchsafed to this undeserving earth. The gay cavaliers of Charles the Second's time knew nothing of the author of *Paradise Lost*, but that there was 'one John Milton, a blind man,' who was sometime Latin Secretary to the usurping Roundhead, Cromwell, and wrote verses. Yet his clear fame shall live through all time, in enduring brilliancy, while their names have long ago rotted with their mortal bodies. That such will be the fate of Shelley we do not pretend to prophesy. This much, however, we may predict, that he will stand in the foremost rank of English poets, when some of the literary idols to whom we have bowed ourselves down shall be forgotten, or remembered, like the monkey-gods of Egypt, only as objects of wonder and contemptuous pity.

95. Ralph Waldo Emerson, journal entry

October 30, 1841

Printed in *The Journals of Ralph Waldo Emerson*, ed. Gilman and Parsons (1970), viii, p. 61.

The ↑Shelley↓ Age is wholly unaffecting to me. I was born a little too soon; but his power is so manifest over a large class of persons, that he is not to be overlooked.

96. Parke Godwin, 'Percy Bysshe Shelley,' *United States Magazine and Democratic Review*

December 1843, xiii, 603–23

This essay reveals Parke Godwin to be a perceptive literary critic. To his credit he does not stress Shelley's marital problems, and he emphasizes Shelley as poet and thinker. His sympathy for Shelley's opposition to fagging and for Shelley's politics probably reflects an enlightened American perspective not uncommon in 1843.

MR. MADISON observed to Harriet Martineau, that it had been the destiny of America to prove many things which were before thought impossible. It may be said, with equal truth, that it is the destiny of the same country to teach the world what men have been among its brightest ornaments and worthiest benefactors. We have an instance of what is to be done in this respect, in the unfortunate but extraordinary man whose name graces the head of this paper. It is reserved for America to rescue his fame from the cold neglect which it is the interest of older nations to gather round it, and to show mankind, by her warm appreciation of his genius and character, how much virtue and excellence were lost when he perished. In his own country, and in his own day and generation, he lived an outcast. . . .

We design to remark upon Shelley as a poet and a man. We think that justice has never yet been done him. His countrymen are not in a mood either to apprehend or to confess his legitimate value. The tincture of the bitter gall of prejudice has not yet passed from their eyes; their judgments are warped by old remembrances, and it is left to their late posterity and other lands to form a proper estimate of all that he was. No time or place more fitting for the formation of such an estimate, than this age of progress and this land of freedom! . . .

Queen Mab, we regard as the most extraordinary production of youthful intellect. The author was but seventeen when he wrote it, yet in boldness and depth of thought, vigor of imagination, and intensity of language, it displays prodigious power. In its metre and general form, it resembles Southey's *Thalaba*, but is even superior to that poem, we think, in wild grandeur and pathos. The versification, though sometimes strained and elaborate, is, for the most part, melodious. Its narrative portions are well sustained, while the descriptions, if we may so express it, are hideously faithful. It is easy to perceive, however, that the writer's ungovernable sensibilities ran away with nearly all his other faculties. In the fragmentary state in which it is given to us in the later editions, it is confused in sentiment and rhapsodical. Yet it has one broad, deep, pervading object. It is a shout of defiance and battle sent up by an unaided stripling, against the powers and principalities of a world reeking in its errors. Every page of it is a fiery protest against the frauds and despotism of priests and kings. It is like the outburst of a mass of flame from a covered and pent up furnace. It is the fierce wail of nature struggling to escape from the accumulated oppressions of ages. Its irregular, convulsive movements, its lurid and dreadful pictures alternating with passages of mild beauty and soft splendor, seem like the protracted battle of Life with Death, of Giant Hope with Giant Despair. The blasphemy and atheism which are so flippantly charged upon it, are the tempestuous writhings of a pure and noble spirit, torn and tossed between the contending winds and waves of a heart full of

Love and a head full of Doubt. It is, throughout, the intense utterance of one shocked into madness by the miseries of the present, and at the same time drunk with intoxicating anticipations of the glories of the future.

It was never the intention of Shelley to have published this indiscreet and immature effort of his genius. But the unfortunate notoriety which certain events in his domestic life had procured him, induced a piratical bookseller to give it to the world. When it did appear, he wrote a note to the London *Examiner*, disclaiming much of what it contained. . . .

Shelley's first acknowledged poem, *Alastor, or, the Spirit of Solitude*, written in 1815, exhibits his mind in a more subdued state than that in which he must have composed *Queen Mab*. He was then residing at Bishopgate Heath, near Windsor Forest, made immortal in the early lays of Pope. There, in the enjoyment of the companionship of cultivated friends, reading the poets of the day, and visiting the magnificent woodland and forest scenery to be met with in a voyage to the source of the Thames, several months of health and tranquil happiness glided away. The more boisterous excitability of earlier years gave place to habits of calm meditation and self-communion, while the vicissitudes and disappointments which had already chequered his young life, tempered, no doubt, his exalted hopes and restrained the impetuosity of his zeal. In *Alastor*, accordingly, we find the traces of more mature and deeper inward reflection. It contains none of those intense and irrepressible bursts of mingled rage and love, which are at once the merit and defect of *Queen Mab*; but is a quiet and beautiful picture of the progressive condition of the mind of a poet. It represents, to borrow the language of his preface, a youth of uncorrupted feelings and adventurous genius, led forth by an imagination inflamed and purified through familiarity with all that is excellent and majestic, to the contemplation of the universe. He drinks deep of the fountains of knowledge, and is still insatiate. The magnificence and beauty of the eternal world sink profoundly into the frame of his conceptions, and afford to their modifications a variety not to be exhausted. So long as it is possible for his desires to point towards objects thus infinite and unmeasured, he is joyous and self-possessed. But the period arises when those objects cease to suffice. His mind is at length suddenly awakened, and thirsts for an intercourse with an intelligence similar to itself; he images to himself the being he loves, and the vision unites all of wonderful, wise, and beautiful, which the poet, the philosopher, or the lover could depicture.[1] He, however, wanders in vain over the populous and desolated portions of the earth, in search for the prototype of his conceptions. Neither earth, nor air, nor yet the pale realms of dreams can accord him the being of his ideal love. Weary at last of the present, and blasted by disappointment, he seeks the retreat of a solitary recess and yields his spirit to death.

Such is the story of a poem, which, Mrs. Shelley says, is rather didactic than narrative, being the outpouring of the poet's own emotions, embodied in the purest form he could conceive, and painted in ideal hues. As much, if not more than any of his works, *Alastor* is characteristic of the author. It is tranquil, thoughtful, and solemn, mingling the exultation animated by the sunny and beautiful aspect of Nature, with the deep, religious feeling that arises from the contemplation of her more stern and majestic mood, and with the brooding thoughts and sad or stormful passion of a heart seeking through the earth for objects to satisfy the restlessness of infinite desires. The impression which it leaves is that of a soft and chastened melancholy. It is full of a touching and mournful eloquence. There is one of these passages we cannot read without tears. It is when the wanderer, in the loneliness and desolation of his heart, after his weary march over the waste, unfriendly earth—

[quotes *Alastor*, lines 271–90]

The Revolt of Islam, though by no means Shelley's greatest work, if his largest, is the one which will endear him most strongly to the lovers of their race. It is written in twelve cantos of the Spenserian stanza, and in his first design was to be entitled *Laon and Cythna, or the Revolution of the Golden City*, thereby implying that it was intended to be a story of passion, and not a picture of more mighty and broadly interesting events. As he advanced in his work, however; as the heavy woes of mankind pressed and absorbed his heart, the mere individual figures around whom the narrative gathers, dwindled in importance, and he poured out the strength of his soul in the description of scenes and incidents involving the fates of multitudes and races. The poem may have lost in interest as a narrative by the change, but Oh, how much it has gained as a poem! It is now a gallery of noble, glowing, and spirit-stirring pictures. It paints, in a series of the finest and boldest sketches—sometimes in dim and silvery outline, and sometimes in a broad mass of black and white—the most interesting conditions of a pure mind in its

[1] Preface of 1815. (Reviewer's footnote)

progress towards light and excellence, and of a great people in the passage from slavery to freedom. It is the great choral hymn of struggling nations. The dedication is a melting prelude addressed to his wife. The first canto, like the introduction to some great overture, runs over in brief but graceful and airy strains, the grand and unearthly harmonies which are to compose the burden of the music. After illustrating in passages of great beauty, the growth of a young mind in its aspirations after liberty, and how the impulses of a single spirit may spread the impatience of oppression until it takes captive and influences every soul, the poet proceeds at once to its great topic,—the awakening of a whole nation from degradation to dignity; the dethronement of its tyrants; the exposure of the religious frauds and political quackeries, by which kings and hirelings delude the multitude into quiet subjection; the tranquil happiness, moral elevation, and mutual love of a people made free by their own patriotic endeavors; the treachery and barbarism of hired soldiers; the banding together of despots without to sustain the cause of tyrants at home; the desperate onset of the armies of the allied dynasties; the cruel murder and expulsion of the patriots, and the instauration of despotism, with its train of pestilence, famine and war. But the poem closes with prophecies for the sure and final reign of freedom and virtue.

In this *argument*, to use the phrase of the older poets, Shelley had a high moral aim. We refer not merely to what he himself describes as an attempt 'to enlist the harmony of metrical language, etherial combinations of fancy, and refined and sudden transitions of passion in the cause of liberality, or to kindle in the bosom of his readers a virtuous enthusiasm for those doctrines of liberty and justice, that faith and hope in something good, which neither violence, nor misrepresentation, nor prejudice can ever totally extinguish;' but to that fixed purpose with which he has avoided the obvious conclusion that an ordinary mind would have given to the poem, and adhered to the loftier moral. It ends, as we said, with the triumphs of despotism. What Shelley wished to teach by this, was the lesson, so necessary in that age, when hopes of mankind had been crushed by the disastrous events of the French Revolution, that every revolt against the oppression of tyranny, that every struggle for the rights of man, though for the time it might be unsuccessful, though it might fail in its resistance of arbitrary power, was, in the end, worth the effort. It destroyed the sanctity that surrounded and shielded the dogmas of the past; it broke the leaden weight of authority; it kindled fear in the breast of the oppressors, by awakening among the people a knowledge of their rights; and it strengthened the confidence of men in each other, while it filled them with visions and hopes of the speedy prevalence of a more universal justice and love. No lesson could then have been more needed by the world. . . .

Yet in this poem, as in most of Shelley's others,—indeed, as in nearly all the poems that have sprung from our past and present state of society, we regret that so much use is made of Violence—that the higher Philosophy, which teaches us how mankind may escape from the darkness and perils of the abyss in which it is everywhere plunged, had not dawned upon the world—and that the best efforts of our best and greatest bards are stained with the taints of destructive and re-volutionary principles.

In 1818, Shelley left England, never to return. That divine region, 'the paradise of exiles,' Italy, became his chosen residence. Under the influence of its beautiful climate, and the inspiration of its scenery, his poetical life seems to receive a new impulse. Three subjects presented themselves to his mind as the ground-work of lyrical dramas; the first, the touching story of Tasso; the second, the woes and endurance of Job; and the third, the *Prometheus Unbound*. With the instinct of genius, and led, no doubt, by his growing delight in the Greek dramatists, he selected the last of the three, as the one best suited to his purposes. In the very choice of the subject, he betrays the tendencies of his nature. There is not in the whole round of the universe, any real or imaginary personage so well fitted to dramatic or epic representation as Prometheus. The mythology of his existence is the grandest fable that the human mind ever conceived. In the Lear of Shakespeare, we behold a grand conception;—we have a man—a noble, towering man,—but only a man—battling, heedless of the war of the elements around him, with the storm of raging emotion in his own breast. Again; in the Satan of Milton, we see the demigod, fierce, defiant, unconquerable, wage proud strife with the Omnipotent; but, while we pity his wrongs and sympathize with his daring, the nature of the combat forbids us to applaud his courage, and the exhibition of envy, falsehood, and revenge, destroys our admiration. But in the Prometheus of the Ancient fabulist, we behold an Innocent One, exposed to the oppressions of Evil, for the good which he had conferred upon others; bearing for ages without complaint, the tortures of Tyranny; a spirit full of godlike fortitude and hope, warring with the gods: a Calm Sufferer, exempt from bitter-ness or hatred, though sustaining the foulest wrongs that Infinite Power can inflict: an Immortal Nature triumphing over mortal pangs; a Moral Will rising superior to the agonies of physical torment; embodied Goodness and Beauty, recovering from the struggle of centuries of Darkness into the clear light of Heaven, and diffusing universal joy through the realms of space.

In the treatment of the ancient fable Shelley has seen fit to alter it so as to adapt it to his more exalted conceptions of the character of its hero. Prometheus, as we gather his story from the ancient writers, was chained to the rock by Jupiter, for having bequeathed to mankind the gift of knowledge. But there was in the possession of the Titan, the secret of a prophecy which it much concerned the perpetuity of Jupiter's kingdom that he should know. On condition that this should be revealed to him, he offered the Sufferer a full pardon for his primitive crime. The Titan resists, and in the sternness and stubborn power of this resistance, the moral sublimity of the myth consists. The story runs, however, that after enduring the inflictions of the god for ages, the Titan purchased freedom from torture by communicating the secret. The latter part of the fable, Shelley rejects. His Prometheus is true to himself to the last, since, to have made him 'unsay his high language, and quail before his successful and perfidious adversary,' would have been reconciling the champion of mankind with its opposer. He had a nobler aim. . . .

It was the lost drama of Æschylus which suggested to Shelley this poem, of which we have given only the meagerest outline. In the earlier portions of it, where he describes the trials of the Titan, he has imitated the lofty grandeur and solemn majesty of the Grecian Master. But to avoid the charge of mere imitation, he has varied the story, and enlarged the groundwork of plot and incident. It would be an exaggeration to say that he had rivalled the sublimity of the Father of the Dramatists; but it is no exaggeration to dwell upon the moral superiority of his conceptions. He has not the force, the strength, and the awful and imposing sternness of his robust and rugged model—but he has, we think, more delicacy, softness, and elegance. Indeed, the lyrical parts of the drama are only surpassed in graceful ease and harmony by Sophocles. They rise upon the ear like strains of sweet melody, ravishing it with delight, and leaving, after they have passed away, the sense of a keen but dreamy ecstacy. For delicacy and beauty, nothing in the range of poetry is finer than the description of the flight of the Hours—not even the imagery in which Ione and Panthea discourse to each other while listening to the music of the rolling worlds. The whole impresses one like a noble oratorio, expressive of the Life of Humanity in its passage from early darkness through pain and strife, through weariness and anguish, to the overflowing joy and sunshine of its mature development.

During the following year, the tragedy of *The Cenci* appeared. It has since attained so wide a popularity, and has so often been criticised, both in England and among the Germans, that we shall have little to say of it in this place. It has more of direct human interest in it than any other of the author's poems—but, like all the rest, it serves to display his character. His keen insight into the workings of the human heart—his dread of evil—his hatred of oppression—and above all, his quick sympathy with the delicate and graceful emotions of the female nature, are exhibited in language of unsurpassed elegance and force. Through all the developments of the terrible story, there appears a lofty, moral aim, not taught as is the case with Euripides, in formal declamations, but as Shakespeare does it—by the unfolding, as it were, of an actual life—as if a curtain were lifted suddenly from before an actual scene, revealing all the actors in their living and breathing reality. While in the *Prometheus* he had shown what Will could accomplish under the dominion of Love, so in *The Cenci* he showed what that same Will could do when under the adverse guidance of subversive passions. The elder Cenci is the personification of unbridled Will. Rich enough to indulge every desire, and to purchase impunity for every crime, the white-haired and passion-torn father, opposing his own will, in a single burst of tremendous and fearful rage, to the will of the Almighty Father, becomes thereby the incarnation of all that is bad. It is a dreadful contrast which is formed between his demoniacal spirit and that of his angelic daughter. Beatrice, the lovely, sincere, high-minded woman, formed to adorn and grace the most exalted position, but bearing about a load of remediless griefs, of heart-wearing sorrows, is the bright light on a back-ground of awful tribulation and darkness. She is purity enveloped in a cloud of falsehood and strange vice. Herself sportive and sincere, she is yet the victim of unnatural crimes and endless woes, 'around her are the curtains of dread fate—no lark-resounding Heaven is above her—no sunny fields before her—no passion throbs in her breast'—but

> The beautiful blue Heaven is flecked with blood.
> The sunshine on the floor is black! The air
> Is changed to vapors such as the dead breathe
> In charnel houses;

and the wronged though beautiful maid is cut off from life and light in youth's sweet prime. Only Shakespeare could have created such another woman.

We must here close our remarks upon Shelley's separate poems, and proceed to give our opinion of his general character as a poet. Let it suffice on the former head, that in what he has written at a date subsequent to that of the poems to which we have referred, he exhibits the same general powers, enriched by experience and use. We could have wished to have spoken in detail of the 'Rosalind and Helen,' that touching tale of the sufferings of woman; of the 'Hellas,' in which he celebrates the revival of the ancient spirit of Grecian freedom, with much of the spirit of the old Greek lyrical poets; of the 'Adonais,' so full of pensive beauty; of the spiritual 'Prince Athanase;' of the wild 'Triumph of Life;' of the 'Ode written in dejection at Naples,' the noblest of the lyrics of melancholy; of the 'Hymn to Intellectual Beauty,' so high and grand in its invocations; of the 'Skylark,' in the profusion and melody of which the author rivals the bird he sings; and, more than all, of those translations from the Greek, German, and Spanish, which are among the best specimens of that kind of composition in the English language. Our space will not suffer us to engage in this agreeable task. We must commend the reader to the poems themselves, in the full conviction that they will impress upon his mind a deeper sense of their surpassing merits than any observations we might make.

What, then, are the claims of Shelley as a poet? This were a hard question to answer in the case of any person, and particularly hard in that of Shelley. His poetry, like his life, is set round by so many prejudices, that it is with difficulty the critic preserves his mind from the influence of common opinion on one side, or the exaggeration of reacting sympathy on the other. Shelley's faults, too, are so nearly allied to his excellences, springing as they do, for the most part, from the very excess of his intellectual energy, that the task of discrimination is felt to be an embarrassing one. Aside from these considerations, however, there were some defects in the structure of his mind. These were shown partly in his use of a peculiar language and diction, and partly existed in the very texture of his thoughts. He was apt to be vague in his phraseology: words were often used not in their common or obvious meaning, but in a sense derived from remote and complicated relations. Thus, referring to the influence of the moon upon the tides, he speaks of the ocean which rises at the *enchantment* of the moon. Thus, too, he indulges in such phrases as the 'wingless-boat,' meaning thereby, not a boat without wings, which would be common-place enough, but a boat propelled by some mysterious power beyond the speed of flight. We might mention many other instances of the same kind. Again; his descriptions are not always recognized as real. They seem to be enveloped in a hazy and wavering atmosphere, as if they were not actual scenes, but the combinations of a remembered dream. One does not look upon them, as he looks upon living nature, when he stands face to face with her beauty. They are seen through a gauzy medium of memory, like places which may have impressed the mind in the earliest period of its consciousness. They strike us, in the same way as those views which come suddenly upon us, when travelling in strange lands, as something which we have seen before, but of which we know neither the time nor place. It may be objected further, that his descriptions possess too much of dazzling glare and splendor. Neither his language nor his imagery is always sufficiently subdued for the nature of the subject. This fault is the common fault of young artists. Their pictures are either all in light or in warm colors. Sir Thomas Lawrence was accustomed, when asked his opinion of the productions of painters, to tell them to put out the lights. Some such monitor should have stood over the writing-desk of Shelley. His many-colored fancy threw its glaring flames over all objects. Arrayed in gold and fire, they stood out, like the forest which lies between our eyes and the horizon, when its trunks and leaves are lit up by the evening sun.

But the greater fault of Shelley's poetry is the frequent obscurity of which so many readers complain. His more enthusiastic admirers, we are aware, answer, that as much of this obscurity may lie in the minds of the readers as in the mind of the poet; and they answer with no little truth. Yet we think that Shelley is chargeable on this score, and chargeable, because the fault springs from a misuse of some of his highest powers. It takes its origin from two peculiarities—from the exceeding subjectivity of his mind, and the exquisite delicacy of his imagination. What we mean by subjectivity is the disposition to dwell upon the forms and processes of inward thought and emotion, rather than upon those of the external world. Shelley was by no means deficient in sensibility: he loved the external world; was ever living in the broad, open air, under the wide skies; and was keenly alive to the picturesque and harmonious in Nature. But his power of reflection predominated over the power of his senses. He was more at home in the microcosm of his own thoughts, than in the larger world of Nature. He was ever proceeding from the centre, that is, his own mind, outward to the visible universe. He was ever transferring the operations of his mind to the operations of Nature. Of this tendency, he was not himself unaware. 'The imagery which I have employed,' he says in the preface to *Prometheus*, 'will be found, in many instances, to have been drawn from the operations of the human mind, or those external actions by which they are expressed.' An appropriate instance of this, we have in the same poem, where he speaks of the avalanche:

> ——whose mass,
> Thrice sifted by the storm, had gathered there,
> Flake after flake—in heaven-defying minds,
> As thought by thought is piled, till some great truth
> Is loosened, and the nations echo round,
> Shaken to their roots, as are the mountains now.

Here the avalanche is compared to the thought, not the thought to the avalanche, which reverses the usual process of comparison. There is a class to whom this kind of imagery may appear natural, but to the larger number of men, and those even intellectual men, it is, to use a common adage, putting the cart before the horse; it is illustrating the known by the less known; it is an attempt to make an object clear and intelligible, by comparing it with that which is not clear and intelligible in itself—a *lucus a non lucendo*.[1] This is one cause of Shelley's obscurity; but a more frequent cause of it, we are persuaded, is the surpassing delicacy and refinement of his imagination. So keen was his intellectual vision that he saw thoughts where others saw none, and shades and distinctions of shade appeared to him where, to others, it was blank vacuity or darkness. He possessed, in a more eminent degree than any man of the day, that faculty from which proceeded Shakespeare's *Midsummer Night's Dream*, which peoples the universe with tenuous and gossamer existences, which sees a world in drops of liquid dew, which sports with the creatures of the elements, and is of finer insight and more spiritual texture than the brains of ordinary mortals. If Shelley has erred in the excessive use of this faculty, we are also indebted to it for some of the most beautiful conceptions that ever adorned the pages of poetry.

While, therefore, admitting his liability to the charge of being obscure, we must be allowed to observe that he is not so obscure as his detractors, many of them, are wont to represent. The dimness, we fear,

[1] 'Light by not giving light.'

is, in too many cases, in their own sight. They are of gross and earthly composition, while the themes which they essay to understand are elevated to the third-heaven of spiritual elevation. The plump and well-fed alderman, whose life has passed amid the coal-dust and fogs of the city, sees not so far into the keen atmosphere of space, as the hardy children of the mountain. 'These things ye cannot behold,' says the Apostle, 'because they are spiritually discerned.' Your eyes are yet filled with the mists of earth,—the reeking vapors of sensualism are still steaming before your hot brains,—the clear spirits have been ruffled by the storms of passion, or darkened by the muddy discolorations of pre-judice,—many-colored life, with its entanglements and delusions, has drawn you down from the higher regions of thought, and having eyes, ye see not, and ears, yet hear nothing! Not to the poet, oh, critical friends! not to the poet, but to your own dark and debased natures must ye look for the solution of many a mystery you may find re-corded! There is a life of the spirit in which Shelley particularly lived; there is a world of experience to which worldlings, and many who are not so, never attain: there are secrets in this wonderful existence of ours, which, to some, are more palpable than the stars, but which, to others, must forever—in this state of being at least—remain hidden and im-perceptible. Look to it, then, that you are yourselves right!

But we pass from the faults of Shelley to a rapid consideration of his excellences. One of the first things that strikes us, in entering upon the topic, is the elevated conception which he had formed, and always strove to carry with him, of the true function and destiny of a Poet. The vocation of the bard impressed him as the highest of all vocations. 'Poetry,' says he, in a glowing passage of a most exquisite prose com-position, 'poetry is, indeed, something divine. It is at once the centre and circumference of knowledge: it is that which comprehends all science, and that to which all science must be referred. It is at the same time the root and blossom of all other systems of thought; it is that from which all spring and that which adorns all; and that which, if blighted, denies the fruit and the seed, and withholds from the barren world the nourishment and the succession of the scions of the tree of life. It is the perfect and consummate surface and bloom of all things; it is as the odor and color of the rose to the texture of the elements which compose it, as the form and splendor of unfaded beauty to the secrets of anatomy and corruption.' Again he says: 'Poetry is the record of the best and happiest moments of the happiest and best minds'—'Poetry turns all things to loveliness. It exalts the beauty of that which is most beautiful, and it adds beauty to that which is most deformed; it marries exultation and horror, grief and pleasure, eternity and change; it subdues to union, under its light yoke, all irreconcilable things. It transmutes all that it touches, and every form moving within the radiance of its presence is changed by wondrous sympathy to an incarnation of the spirit which it breathes: its secret alchemy turns to potable gold the poisonous waters which flow from death through life; it strips the veil of familiarity from the world and lays bare the naked and sleeping beauty, which is the spirit of its forms.'

In this spirit, Shelley composed his own poems. It would be absurd to rank him among the highest of the great English poets as an artist, although it would not be absurd to put him among the highest in other respects. We do not mean that he was altogether deficient as an artist, since he certainly had a singular command of language and rhythm. But we do mean, that the qualities of the artist were not those which predominated in his composition. The opening chorus of 'Hellas' alone, not to refer to other instances, would prove that he possessed most extraordinary artistic capabilities. But the same poem again, not to mention others, would also prove that these capabilities were smothered beneath the exuberance of thought and imagery. The skilfulness with which he has used, in 'Prince Athanase,' the *terza rima* of the Italians, and the stanza of Pulci, in the 'Witch of Atlas,' shows how far he could have been successful in the region of mere art, could he have submitted his chainless impulses to the laborious discipline of Art. When the leisure and humor for such discipline allowed, his minor lyrics betray no want of the most dexterous and versatile power to perfect. In general, however, he impetuously tramples upon the finer laws of creative effort. Like the improvisatore, he gives the rein to his fancy, and dashes wildly onward wherever the bewildering trains of thick-coming associations may lead. It is to be regretted that it was so: it is not a sign of the highest genius.

Not to dwell upon these points, however, let us say, that Shelley's poetry is chiefly distinguished by two characteristics—the first, its imaginative power, and the second, its glowing spirit of freedom and love. Mr. Macaulay, in his beautiful essay on John Bunyan, has anticipated all that we need to say on the first head. 'The strong imagination of Shelley,' says he, 'made him an idolater in his own despite. Out of the most indefinite terms of a hard, dark, cold, metaphysical system, he made a gorgeous Pantheon, full of beautiful, majestic and life-like forms. He turned atheism itself into a mythology, rich with visions as

glorious as the gods that live in the marble of Phidias, or the virgin
saints that smile on us from the canvass of Murillo. The Spirit of
Beauty, the Principle of Good, the Principle of Evil, when he treated of
them, ceased to be abstractions. They took shape and color. They were
no longer mere words; but "intelligible forms," "fair humanities,"
objects of love, of adoration or of fear. Some of the metaphysical and
ethical theories of Shelley were certainly absurd and pernicious. But we
doubt whether any modern poet has possessed in an equal degree the
highest qualities of the great ancient masters. The words bard and inspiration, which seem so cold and affected when applied to other
modern writers, have a perfect propriety when applied to him. He was
not an author, but a bard. His poetry seems not to have been an art, but
an inspiration.'

It was chiefly in the glow and intensity of his sentiments that the vast
fusing powers of his imagination were manifest. His heart, burning
with the purest fires of love, seemed to melt all nature into a liquid mass
of goodness. Over the wildest and darkest wastes of human experience,
he cast the refulgence of his own benignant and glorious nature, as the
many-colored rainbow expands over the dark bosom of the summer
thunder-cloud. Out of the rankest poisons, he extracted the most re-
freshing of sweets.

> ——Medea's wondrous alchemy;
> Which, wherever it fell, made the earth gleam
> With bright flowers, and the wintry boughs exhale
> From vernal blooms fresh fragrance,

was his; and from the exceeding fulness of himself, he poured out into
the mighty heart of the world, a perpetual stream of life. No poet that
has come after him, and few that were gone before him, had equal
power of stirring within the soul of humanity, such noble aspirations—
such fervent love of freedom—such high resolves in the cause of virtue
and intelligence—and such strong prophetic yearnings for the Better
Future. He was the constructive English poet of his century. In the
earlier part of his career, he had been touched with the spirit of scepticism and despair, which was the malady of those times. He sent up to
Heaven, from a heart full of anguish, a keen and infinite wail—as the
wail of a vast inarticulate multitude without God and without Hope in
the world. But through the rifted clouds of the tempestuous night he
soon saw, more clearly than any contemporary, the dawnings of the
day. He became the precursor of that day—its bright and morning star.

With jubilating voice, he prophesied of its glories. While the capacious genius of Scott was exhausting its energies in rummaging the magazines of a worthless and forgotten antiquity, to amuse the fancy, or beguile the languor of children, both great and small; while Byron, with despicable selfishness, like a lubberly boy, was whining and scolding over his self-inflicted and petty miseries—Shelley, with dauntless heart and kindling eye, wrestled in the wild frightful conflict of incoherence and discord, struggling upward, till he stood upon the mountain tops of the century in which he lived, watching the dying agonies of the decrepit Old Order, and hailing with exuberant and frantic joy, the swift approaches of the New. . . .

[The remainder of the review is a defense of Shelley *as* a man who was 'worthy of the highest admiration and love.']

97. T. H. Chivers, 'Shelley,' *Southern Literary Messenger*

February 1844, x, 104–6

T. H. Chivers (1809–58), poet and medical doctor, was a native of Georgia, but travelled widely practicing medicine and writing poetry. He was influenced by Poe who said he wrote some of the best and some of the worst poetry in America.

'How rose in melody that child of Love!'—*Young*.

Shelley was a poet of the highest order. He was the heavenly nightingale of Albion, whose golden eloquence rent the heart of the rose bud of Love. There is an unstudied, natural elegance of expression about his poems which makes them truly enchanting. There is a subtle delicacy of expression, an indication of the wisdom-loving divinity within—which enervates while it captivates the admiring soul. He was the swiftest-winged bee that ever gathered the golden honey of poetry from the Hybla of this world. He was, among the Poets, in delineating natural objects, what Claude was among the painters in delineating the landscape. All his minor poems, and more particularly 'The Question,' 'The Zucca,' and 'The Woodman and the Nightingale,' with a few others, are, as poems, what the works of Titian were among the painters—the execution far surpasses the design. They appear to have been written just for the delight which they gave him. The richness of his genius flowed unconfined, and, like a mighty, crystaline river, gathered volume as it onward flowed. Human language never expressed a more sublime, poetical truth than may be found in his Ode to Liberty, where he calls

The Dædal Earth
THAT ISLAND IN THE OCEAN OF THE WORLD.

A more perfect truth was never uttered than the following, which may be found in his Revolt of Islam—'TO THE PURE ALL THINGS ARE PURE.'[1] What, but a generous nature, could have given birth to such a divine sentiment as this? 'LET SCORN BE NOT REPAID WITH SCORN.'

He was the most purely *ideal* being that ever existed. He possessed the intellectuality of Plato, with the ideality of Æschylus, and the pathos of Sophocles. His divine conceptions are all embalmed in the sacred tenderness of melting pathos. He possessed the artistical skill of Moore, without his *mannerism*. One of his peculiar characteristics is the giving to inanimate objects the attributes of animation. His description of the manner in which the rock overhangs the gulf in *The Cenci*, is an instance of it, where he says it has,

From unimmaginable years,
Sustained itself with terror and with toil
Over a gulf, and WITH THE AGONY
WITH WHICH IT CLINGS SEEMS SLOWLY COMING DOWN,—

No lines ever conveyed to me more meaning than the following, wherein you can see the agony of Beatrice setting itself into a resolve:

All mortal things must hasten thus
To their dark end. LET US GO DOWN.

[1] Shelley was probably indebted for this beautiful sentiment to the Bible, in which the following passage occurs, '*Unto the pure all things are pure*; but unto them that are defiled and unbelieving nothing is pure; but even their mind and conscience is defiled.' Epis. to Tit. I., 15. Though he denied its truth, his mind could not but have appreciated the poetical and moral beauties of the Bible.

Ed. Mess.

The Cenci is far superior to any thing written in modern times. The following lines are not to be surpassed by any thing that Shakespeare ever wrote:

> *They say that sleep,* THAT HEALING DEW OF HEAVEN,
> STEEPS NOT IN BALM THE FOLDINGS OF THE BRAIN, &c.

His delineation of the character of Beatrice is true to the original. It is the most affectingly beautiful that can be conceived. From the divine fountains of her infinite affections the warm tide of her *female nature* gushes forth in unfathomable fullness. There are no leprous stains of *selfishness* spotting the saintly purity of that divine form which stands before us in all its naked majesty. Her unflinching determination is dignified by its sincerity. I *firmly* believe that any being who could thus be induced to vindicate and revenge her injured honor, contains, in her very nature, the *essence* of all that is noble and good. It is the wretchedness by which we are surrounded, which makes us what we are. There is a dignified composure in her resignation to death, which nothing but an inward goodness could impart. Her passions were inspired by a lively respect for the sacredness of her honor, although they were the inaudible prophets of her own destiny. Her love, rising into devotion, is consecrated by her sorrows. There is a mournful sweetness in her death, and we embalm her virtues in our memory, while we weep over her misfortunes!

Shelley has invested the most ideal thoughts in the most beautiful language. His poems are the most perfect idealisms of the subtelty of his divine genius. His spirit was like a Sybil, who saw from the 'heaven-kissing hill' of truth the vision of the coming centuries. The seeds of divine liberty, which he has sown in the hearts of England's slaves, will spring up, like immortal Amaranths, in the glorious Summer of To-come. Soon will the Spring of Liberty, which he so much desired, burst forth, in all its splendor, on the enraptured souls of men. Then will her barren nakedness be covered with the green verdure of perpetual happiness. Then will the winter of her slavery be clad in the rich garments of the Summer of Liberty. Then will she appear like a BLESSED ISLAND rising out of an ocean of divine tranquility, greened with the freshness of an immortal SPRING.

His poems are the elms of the soul, where there are many palm trees, and much running water. Hope was the Evening and Morning Star of his life. The mother of his Hope was FAITH; her daughter, PATIENCE; and her husband, LOVE. Life was to him precisely what Jean Paul

Richter said of it, '*Man has but two minutes and a half to live—one to smile—one to sigh—and a half to love—for in the middle of this minute he dies!*' He was annointed by the hands of Liberty as the Prophet of humanity. Some of his Elysian scenes are as sadly pleasing as the first sight of the green pastures of our native land, from which we have been absent a long time. We are, while perusing his poems, like a Pilgrim in the LAND OF OLIVES, who sees the mournful aspect of the country around, while tasting of its delicious fruit. He treated the most of his enemies like the King of Aragon did his. When some one railed out against him, he sent him a purse of gold. Being asked the reason for so doing, he replied, '*When dogs bark, their mouths must be stopped by some morsel.*' He was that divine harmonist whose seraphic breathings were the requiem-carols of his soul panting after perfection. There was in his patient spirit something of the tender sorrow which dictated the BOOK OF JOB, mixed with the spirit-stirring felicities which filled the heart of Solomon. He embalmed his most tender expressions in the fountain of his heart's best tears, which were the outgushings of the joy of his sorrow. By the astonishing alchemy of his divine genius, he could transmute the most earthly things into the most heavenly idealities. In his own beautiful language on the Death of Keats,

> *He is made one with Nature; there is heard*
> *His voice in all her music, from the moan*
> *Of thunder, to the song of Night's sweet bird.*

He is the Prince Athanase of his own beautiful creation.

> *He had a gentle, yet aspiring mind;*
> *Just, innocent, with various learning fed;*
> *His soul had wedded wisdom, and her dower*
> *Is love and justice, clothed in which he sate*
> *Apart from men, as in a lonely tower,*
> *Pitying the tumult of their dark estate,*
> *For none than he a purer heart could have,*
> *Or that loved good more for itself alone;*
> *Of nought in heaven or earth was he the slave.*

The difference between Byron's poetry and Shelley's consists in this, that the breathings of the former are the melancholy outbreaks of a spirit at war, from disappointment, with the world; those of the latter are the pathetic expressions of a soul which panted after an *ideal of intellectual perfection*. Shelley carolled for the listening ears of an enraptured world, while Byron sang its requiem. Byron was like the sun in eclipse. Shelley was like 'Hesperus, the leader of the starry host of heaven.'

Moore is as different from both as they are from each other. His poetry is the heart-sustaining expression of the phases of his own uninterrupted pleasures. Though widely different from Byron's in many respects, yet it has the same object in view in regard to the perfection of man. They were no reformers—they appealed immediately to the affections and the passions of men. They wrote for the Present and the Future, when it should become Present, without any determinate object in view, save that of conferring on mankind, in general, the same kind of delight which they experienced themselves in their own compositions. Shelley was a *reformer*—he had a more lofty object in view. His poetry is the liquid expression of that undying self-sacrificing desire within, to *perfect* the nature of MAN—to establish some principle, through the deathless yearnings of the divinity within him, for his regeneration. The poetry of Byron and Moore will satisfy the intellectual wants of a Nation, far inferior to what Shelley conceived as his *ideal* of human greatness. The poetry of Byron and Moore is the studied expression of the inspiration of the divinity within. Shelley's poetry is the *artless* expression of the *perfection* of Art. It proceeded from the burning fountains of his soul, in the unpremeditated exercise of his prolific genius, with as much unstudied sweetness, for the gratification of the intellectual wants of perfectly mature man, as did the crystalline waters from the ROCK OF HOREB, when stricken by the rod of Moses, to quench the parching thirst of the Israelites in the valley of Rephidim.

It was the Venus Urania—the intellectual love—which is the handmaid of the heavenly Uranian Muse—which inspired the poetry of Shelley. She was the virgin which kept the fires of love upon the altar of his heart forever bright. It was the Venus Pandemos which inspired the poetry of Byron and Moore—as it appeals more directly to the *passions* of man. The poetry of Shelley was presided over by the elder Venus, the daughter of Uranus, who had no mother, but was co-eternal with the divine *Berazhith*. The poetry of Byron and Moore, and all the poets of passion, is the inspiration of the younger Venus, the daughter of Jupiter and Dione, who is called the *Pandemian*. Those who gaze upon the divine countenance of the Venus Pandemos are inspired with the passion to adore the form—*not the soul*. The former is the companion of the spiritual—the latter of the corporeal. The Venus Urania lives in the poetry of Shelley as the perfume does in the flower—she is the soul of the body of his verse. The intellectual love is the divine redolence of the rosebuds of thought, which adorn the enchanting garden of his soul. He has arrayed the spotless body of his divine love in the snow-white linen garments of the purest poetry. He stands in the TEMPLE OF FAME like a BAS RELIEF cut in the solid wall—you can never move him without pulling it down.

98. Margaret Fuller Ossoli, 'Shelley's Poems'

Life Without and Life Within, ed. Arthur Fuller (1859), 149–52

Margaret Fuller, friend of R. W. Emerson and other Transcenda-lists, praised Shelley when other Transcendentalists did not. She wrote this essay to draw attention to Foster's *The Poetical Works of Percy Bysshe Shelley*, the first complete American edition of Shelley published in 1845.

We are very glad to see this handsome copy of Shelley ready for those who have long been vainly inquiring at all the bookstores for such a one.

In Europe the fame of Shelley has risen superior to the clouds that darkened its earlier days, hiding his true image from his fellow-men, and from his own sad eyes oftentimes the common light of day. As a thinker, men have learned to pardon what they consider errors in opinion for the sake of singular nobleness, purity, and love in his main tendency or spirit. As a poet, the many faults of his works having been acknowledged, there are room and place to admire his far more numerous and exquisite beauties.

The heart of the man, few, who have hearts of their own, refuse to reverence, and many, even of devoutest Christians, would not refuse the book which contains *Queen Mab* as a Christmas gift. For it has been recognized that the founder of the Christian church would have suffered one to come unto him, who was in faith and love so truly what he sought in a disciple, without regard to the form his doctrine assumed.

The qualities of his poetry have often been analyzed, and the severer critics, impatient of his exuberance, or unable to use their accustomed spectacles in the golden mist that broods over all he has done, deny him high honors; but the soul of aspiring youth, untrammelled by the canons of taste, and untamed by scholarly discipline, swells into rapture at his lyric sweetness, finds ambrosial refreshment from his plenteous fancies, catches fire at his daring thought, and melts into boundless weeping at his tender sadness—the sadness of a soul betrothed to an ideal unattainable in this present sphere.

For ourselves, we dispute not with the *doctrinaires* or the critics. We cannot speak dispassionately of an influence that has been so dear to us. Nearer than the nearest companions of life actual has Shelley been to us. Many other great ones have shone upon us, and all who ever did so shine are still resplendent in our firmament, for our mental life has not been broken and contradictory, but thus far we 'see what we foresaw.' But Shelley seemed to us an incarnation of what was sought in the sympathies and desires of instinctive life, a light of dawn, and a foreshowing of the weather of this day.

When still in childish years, the 'Hymn to Intellectual Beauty' fell in our way. In a green meadow, skirted by a rich wood, watered by a lovely rivulet, made picturesque by a mill a little farther down, sat a party of young persons gayer than, and almost as inventive, as those that told the tales recorded by Boccaccio. They were passing a few days in a scene of deep seclusion, there uncared for by tutor or duenna, and with no bar of routine to check the pranks of their gay, childish fancies. Every day they assumed parts which through the waking hours must be acted out. One day it was the characters in one of Richardson's novels; and most solemnly we 'my deared' each other with richest brocade of affability, and interchanged in long, stiff phrase our sentimental secrets and prim opinions. But to-day we sought relief in personating birds or insects; and now it was the Libellula who, tired of wild flitting and darting, rested on the grassy bank and read aloud the 'Hymn to Intellectual Beauty,' torn by chance from the leaf of a foreign magazine.

It was one of those chances which we ever remember as the interposition of some good angel in our fate. Solemn tears marked the change of mood in our little party, and with the words

'Have I not kept my vow?'

began a chain of thoughts whose golden links still bind the years together.

Two or three years passed. The frosty Christmas season came; the trees cracked with their splendid burden of ice, the old wooden country house was banked up with high drifts of the beautiful snow, and the Libellula became the owner of Shelley's *Poems*. It was her Christmas gift, and for three days and three nights she ceased not to extract its sweets; and how familiar still in memory every object seen from the chair in which she sat enchanted during those three days, memorable to her as those of July to the French nation! The fire, the position of the lamp, the variegated shadows of that alcoved room, the bright stars up to which she looked with such a feeling of congeniality from the contemplation of this starry soul,—O, could but a De Quincey describe those days in which the bridge between the real and ideal rose unbroken! He would not do it, though, as *Suspiria de Profundis*, but as sighs of joy upon the mountain height.

The poems we read then are what every one still reads, the *Julian and Maddalo*, with its profound revelations of the inward life; *Alastor*, the soul sweeping like a breeze through nature; and some of the minor poems. *Queen Mab*, the *Prometheus*, and other more formal works we have not been able to read much. It was not when he tried to express opinions which the wrongs of the world had put into his head, but when he abandoned himself to the feelings which nature had implanted in his own breast, that Shelley seemed to us so full of inspiration, and it is so still.

In reply to all that can be urged against him by people of whom we do not wish to speak ill,—for surely 'they know not what they do,'— we are wont simply to refer to the fact that he was the only man who redeemed the human race from suspicion to the embittered soul of Byron. 'Why,' said Byron, 'he is a man who would willingly die for others. *I am sure of it.*'

Yes! balance that against all the ill you can think of him, that he was a man able to live wretched for the sake of speaking sincerely what he supposed to be truth, willing to die for the good of his fellows!

Mr. Foster has spoken well of him as a man: 'Of Shelley's personal character it is enough to say that it was wholly pervaded by the same unbounded and unquestioning love for his fellow-men—the same holy and fervid hope in their ultimate virtue and happiness—the same scorn of baseness and hatred of oppression—which beam forth in all his writings with a pure and constant light. The theory which he wrote was the practice which his whole life exemplified. Noble, kind, generous, passionate, tender, with a courage greater than the courage of the chief of warriors, for it could *endure*—these were the qualities in which his life was embalmed.'

99. Nathaniel Hawthorne, from 'Earth's Holocaust,' *Mosses from an Old Manse*

1846

Nathaniel Hawthorne (1804–64), novelist and short-story writer.

In 'Earth's Holocaust' reformers from around the world gather around a huge bonfire to rid the world of an 'accumulation of worn-out trumpery,' including engines and machinery of war, newspapers and pamphlets, and books. Printed in *The Writings of Nethaniel Hawthorne* (1900), v, pp. 217–18.

It amazed me much to observe how indefinite was the proportion between the physical mass of any given author and the property of brilliant and long-continued combustion. For instance, there was not a quarto volume of the last century—nor, indeed, of the present—that could compete in that particular with a child's little gilt-covered book, containing 'Mother Goose's Melodies.' The 'Life and Death of Tom Thumb' outlasted the biography of Marlborough. An epic, indeed a dozen of them, was converted to white ashes before the single sheet of an old ballad was half consumed. In more than one case, too, when volumes of applauded verse proved incapable of anything better than a stifling smoke, an unregarded ditty of some nameless bard—perchance in the corner of a newspaper—soared up among the stars with a flame as brilliant as their own. Speaking of the properties of flame, methought Shelley's poetry emitted a purer light than almost any other productions of his day, contrasting beautifully with the fitful and lurid gleams and gushes of black vapor that flashed and eddied from the volumes of

Lord Byron. As for Tom Moore, some of his songs diffused an odor like a burning pastil.

100. Nathaniel Hawthorne, from 'P's Correspondence,' *Mosses from an Old Manse*

1846

In this delightful and humorous imaginary correspondence dated London 1845, 'P.' recounts visits to Byron, now grown fat and conservative; Scott, reclining in paralytic unconsciousness at Abbotsford, and Shelley among others. Printed in *The Writings of Nathaniel Hawthorne* (1900), v, pp. 181–4.

You will be anxious to hear of Shelley. I need not say, what is known to all the world, that this celebrated poet has for many years past been reconciled to the Church of England. In his more recent works he has applied his fine powers to the vindication of the Christian faith, with an especial view to that particular development. Latterly, as you may not have heard, he has taken orders, and been inducted to a small country living in the gift of the lord chancellor. Just now, luckily for me, he has come to the metropolis to superintend the publication of a volume of discourses treating of the poetico-philosophical proofs of Christianity on the basis of the Thirty-Nine Articles. On my first introduction I felt no little embarrassment as to the manner of combining what I had to say to the author of *Queen Mab*, *The Revolt of Islam*, and *Prometheus Unbound* with such acknowledgments as might be acceptable to a Christian minister and zealous upholder of the established church. But Shelley soon placed me at my ease. Standing where he now does, and reviewing all his successive productions from a higher point, he assures me that there is a harmony, an order, a regular procession, which enables him to lay his hand upon any one of the earlier poems and say, 'This is my work,' with precisely the same complacency of conscience wherewithal he contemplates the volume of discourses above mentioned. They are like the successive steps of a staircase, the lowest of which, in the depth of chaos, is as essential to the support of the whole as the highest and final one resting upon the threshold of the heavens. I felt half inclined to ask him what would have been his fate had he perished on the lower steps of his staircase instead of building his way aloft into the celestial brightness.

How all this may be I neither pretend to understand nor greatly care, so long as Shelley has really climbed, as it seems he has, from a lower region to a loftier one. Without touching upon their religious merits, I consider the productions of his maturity superior, as poems, to those of his youth. They are warmer with human love, which has served as an interpreter between his mind and the multitude. The author has learned to dip his pen oftener into his heart, and has thereby avoided the faults into which a too exclusive use of fancy and intellect are wont to betray him. Formerly his page was often little other than a concrete arrangement of crystallizations, or even of icicles, as cold as they were brilliant. Now you take it to your heart, and are conscious of a heart warmth responsive to your own. In his private character Shelley can hardly have grown more gentle, kind, and affectionate, than his friends always represented him to be up to that disastrous night when he was drowned in the Mediterranean. Nonsense, again—sheer nonsense! What am I babbling about? I was thinking of that old figment of his being lost in the Bay of Spezzia, and washed ashore near Via Reggio, and burned to ashes on a funeral pyre, with wine, and spices, and frankincense; while Byron stood on the beach and beheld a flame of marvellous beauty rise heavenward from the dead poet's heart, and that his fire-purified relics were finally buried near his child in Roman earth. If all this happened three and twenty years ago, how could I have met the drowned, and burned, and buried man here in London only yesterday?

Before quitting the subject, I may mention that Dr. Reginald Heber, heretofore Bishop of Calcutta, but recently translated to a see in England, called on Shelley while I was with him. They appeared to be on terms of very cordial intimacy, and are said to have a joint poem in contemplation. What a strange incongruous dream is the life of man!

101. Margaret Fuller Ossoli, extract from 'Modern British Poets,' *Papers on Literature and Art*

1846

The author includes this comparison of the merits of Shelley and Wordsworth in an essay which evaluates the 'nine muses' of nineteenth-century British literature. In addition to these poets, she includes Campbell, Moore, Scott, Crabbe, Byron, Southey, and Coleridge. The essay is reprinted in *The Writings of Margaret Fuller*, ed. Mason Wade (1941), pp. 312–46.

I turn to one whom I love still more than I admire; the gentle, the gifted the ill-fated Shelley. . . .

Although the struggles of Shelley's mind destroyed that serenity of tone which is essential to the finest poetry, and his tenderness has not always that elevation of hope which should hallow it; although in no one of his productions is there sufficient unity of purpose and regulation of parts to entitle it to unlimited admiration, yet they all abound with passages of infinite beauty, and in two particulars he surpasses any poet of the day.

First in fertility of fancy. Here his riches, from want of arrangement, sometimes fail to give pleasure, yet we cannot but perceive that they are priceless riches. In this respect parts of his 'Adonais,' 'Marianne's Dream,' and 'Medusa' are not to be excelled except in Shakespeare.

Second in sympathy with Nature. To her lightest tones his being gave an echo; truly she *spoke* to him, and it is this which gives unequaled melody to his versification; I say 'unequaled,' for I do not think either Moore or Coleridge can here vie with him, though each is in his way a master of the lyre. The rush, the flow, the delicacy of vibration in Shelley's verse can only be paralleled by the waterfall, the rivulet, the notes of the bird and of the insect world. This is a sort of excellence not frequently to be expected now, when men listen less zealously than of old to the mystic whispers of Nature; when little is understood that is not told in set phrases, and when even poets write more frequently in curtained and carpeted rooms than 'among thickets of odoriferous blossoming trees and flowery glades,' as Shelley did.

It were a 'curious piece of work enough' to run a parallel between the skylark of Shelley and that of Wordsworth, and thus illustrate mental processes so similar in dissimilitude. The mood of mind, the ideas, are not unlike in the two. Hear Wordsworth:

[quotes Wordsworth's 'To a Skylark,' lines 1, 6–13, 16–25 and Shelley's 'To a Skylark,' lines 1–80]

I do not like to omit a word of it; but it is taking too much room. Should we not say from the samples before us that Shelley, in melody and exuberance of fancy, was incalculably superior to Wordsworth? But mark their *inferences*.

Shelley:

> Teach me half the gladness
> That thy brain must know,
> Such harmonious madness
> From my lips would flow
> The world should listen, then, as I am listening now.

Wordsworth:

> What though my course be rugged and uneven,
> To prickly moors and dusty ways confined,
> Yet, hearing thee and others of thy kind
> As full of gladness and as free of heaven,
> I o'er the earth will go plodding on
> By myself, cheerfully, till the day is done.

If Wordsworth have superiority, then it consists in greater maturity and dignity of sentiment.

102. Henry Crabb Robinson, diary entry

September 12, 1850

From *Henry Crabb Robinson on Books and their Writers*, ed. Morley (1938), ii, p. 704.

SEPT. 12th. . . . I had an agreeable evening reading . . . passages from the *In Memoriam*, which I am more and more pleased with, and from Shelley. . . . His small poems [I] recognised as very beautiful, especially the *Skylark*; but I could not relish the *Adonais* as I do the *In Memoriam*. By the bye, the *Prospective Review* does ample justice to Tennyson, but with an admixture of blame.

103. Ralph Waldo Emerson, from a letter to James Hutchison Stirling

June 1, 1868

When Emerson published a volume entitled *Parnassus* which contained a selection of his favorite poems, Stirling objected to the omission of Shelley.

Printed in *The Letters of Ralph Waldo Emerson*, ed. Rusk (1939), vi, p. 19.

But Shelley,—was he the poet? He was a man in whom the spirit of the Age was poured,—man of inspiration, heroic character; but poet? Excepting a few well-known lines about a cloud and a skylark, I could never read one of his hundreds of pages, and, though surprized by your estimate, despair of a re-attempt.

Select Bibliography

The following articles and books shed light on various aspects of the growth of Shelley's reputation. For a more complete listing, consult the bibliography in Hayden's *The Romantic Reviewers 1802–1824* and Jordan's *The English Romantic Poets: A Review of Research and Criticism.*

BEACH, J. W., 'Latter-day Critics of Shelley,' *Yale Review*, XI (1922), 718–31.

BERNBAUM, ERNEST, *Guide Through the Romantic Movement*, New York, 1949.

BLUNDEN, EDMUND, *Shelley and Keats as They Struck Their Contemporaries*, London, 1925.

CAMERON, KENNETH NEILL, 'Shelley Scholarship: 1940–1953,' *Keats-Shelley Journal*, III (1954), 89–109.

HAYDEN, JOHN O., *The Romantic Reviewers 1802–1824*, Routledge & Kegan Paul, 1969.

HAYDEN, JOHN O., *Romantic Bards and British Reviewers*, Lincoln, Routledge & Kegan Paul, 1971.

INGPEN, ROGER, *Shelley in England*, London, 1917.

JACK, IAN, *English Literature: 1815–1832*, Oxford, 1963.

JONES, FREDERICK L., *The Letters of Percy Bysshe Shelley*. 2 vols, Oxford, 1964.

JORDON, FRANK, ed., *The English Romantic Poets: A Review of Research and Criticism*, New York, 1972.

LIPTZIN, SOLOMON, *Shelley in Germany*, New York, 1924.

MARSH, G. L., 'The Early Reviews of Shelley,' *Modern Philology*, XXVII (1929), 73–95.

MASON, F. C., *A Study in Shelley Criticism in England from 1818 to 1860*, Mercersburg, Pa., 1937.

NELSON, SOPHIA PHILLIPS, 'Shelleyana: 1935–1949,' unpublished dissertation, Pittsburgh, 1950.

NORMAN, SYLVA, *Flight of the Skylark: the Development of Shelley's Reputation*, Norman, Oklahoma, 1954.

NORMAN, SYLVA, 'Twentieth Century Theories on Shelley,' *Texas Studies in Language and Literature*, IX (1967), 223–37.

PEYRE, HENRI, *Shelley et la France*, Paris, 1935.

POWERS, JULIA, *Shelley in America in the Nineteenth Century*, Lincoln, Nebraska, 1940.

PRATT, WILLIS W., *Shelley Criticism in England: 1810–1890*, New York, 1935.

WARD, WILLIAM S., *Literary Reviews in British Periodicals, 1798–1820*, 2 vols, New York, 1972.

WARD, WILLIAM S., 'Shelley and the Reviewers Once More,' *Modern Language Notes*, LIX (1944), 539–42.

WARD, WILLIAM S., 'Some Aspects of the Conservative Attitude Toward Poetry in English Criticism, 1798–1820,' *Publications of the Modern Language Association*, LX (1945), 386–98.

WHITE, NEWMAN I., *Shelley*, 2 vols, New York, 1940; London, 1947.

WHITE, NEWMAN I., ed., *The Unextinguished Hearth*, Durham, N. C., 1938; New York, 1966.

WHITE, WILLIAM, 'Fifteen Years of Shelley Scholarship: 1923–1938,' *English Studies*, XXI (1939), 8–11; 120.

WOODRING, CARL, 'Dip of the Skylark,' *Keats-Shelley Journal*, IX (1960), 10–13.

Index

II SHELLEY: TOPICS AND CHARACTERISTICS

III GENERAL

THE CRITICAL HERITAGE SERIES

GENERAL EDITOR: B. C. SOUTHAM

Volumes published and forthcoming